FRAY™

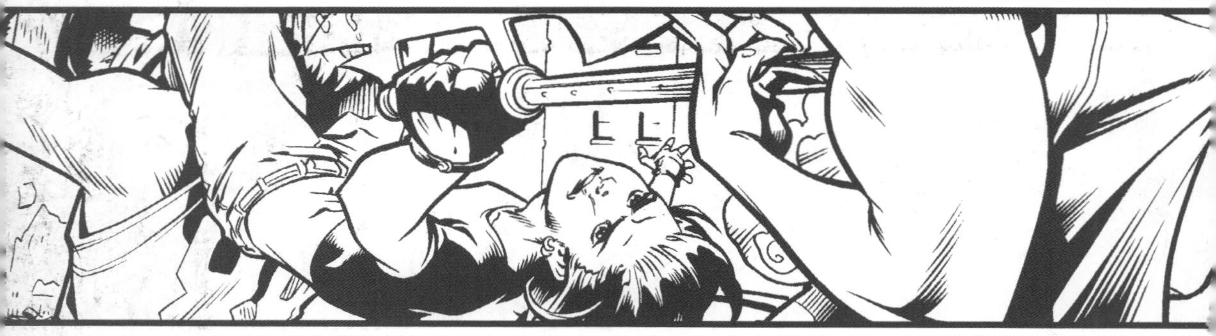

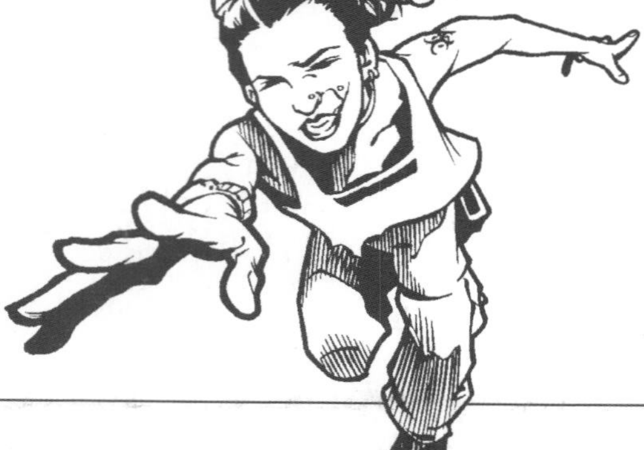

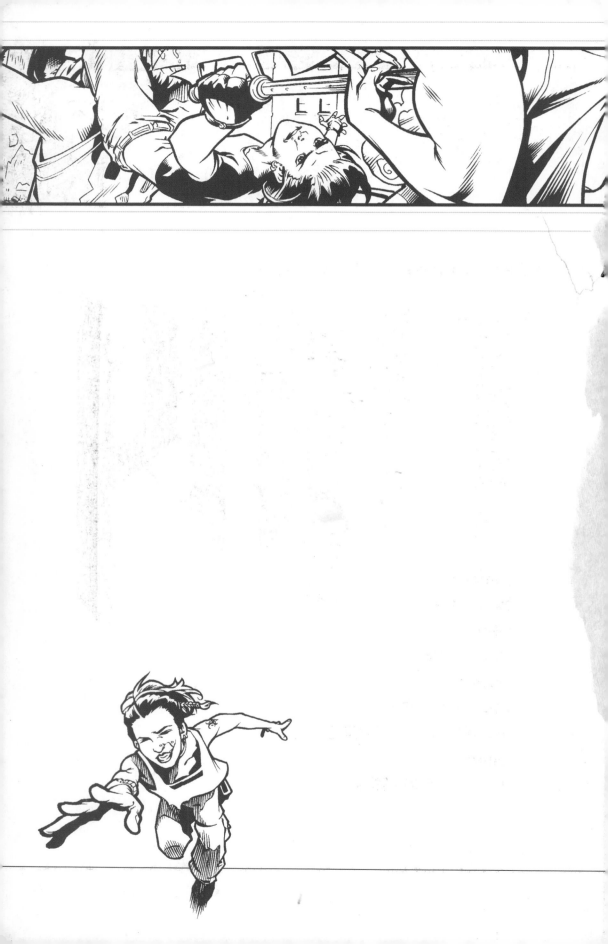

created and written by **JOSS WHEDON**

FRAY ™

penciller
KARL MOLINE

inker
ANDY OWENS

colorists
DAVE STEWART
and **MICHELLE MADSEN**

letterer
MICHELLE MADSEN

logo designer **CHRIS GARDNER**   book designers **LANI SCHREIBSTEIN** and **LIA RIBACCHI**
assistant editors **MATT DRYER, MICHAEL CARRIGLITTO**, and **ADAM GALLARDO**
editor **SCOTT ALLIE**   publisher **MIKE RICHARDSON**

special thanks to **MICHAEL BORETZ, KERN ECCLES, BRETT MATTHEWS, GEORGE SNYDER,
DIEGO GUTIERREZ**, and **HERB APON**

This volume collects issues one through eight of the Dark Horse
comic-book miniseries *Fray*.

Published by
Dark Horse Comics, Inc.
10956 SE Main Street
Milwaukie, OR 97222

www.darkhorse.com

To find a comics shop in your area, call the Comic Shop
Locator Service toll-free at 1-888-266-4226

First edition: November 2003
ISBN: 1-56971-751-6

3 5 7 9 10 8 6 4

Printed in China

Citizen Joss

by Jeph Loeb

There's an old adage in Hollywood that goes something like this: "It's not enough that you are successful; your friends and colleagues have to fail." Now, please, don't act so shocked. You don't really think all those All About Eve-ish stories are merely the fantasies torn out of Jackie Collins's imagination. I mean, she's good, but she ain't recreating reality here.

So, it's with all the love and respect in the world that I can tell you, I hate Joss Whedon. This won't come as any great shock to the man. I've told him myself and often. Confused? Welcome to Hollywood.

Now would probably be a good time for a flashback. About two or three years ago, I got a call from my agent asking if I would meet with the Joss Whedon. It wasn't for anything specific, or so I was led to believe—Joss just wanted to sit and talk. I couldn't imagine why, but I was a fan, and fairly certain I didn't owe him any money. I agreed to go to the meeting.

I like to prep for these sorts of things. There wasn't much to do. I already watched *Buffy* and *Angel* every week. I'd seen *Toy Story* enough times I could quote from it. I'd even downloaded the Joss Whedon draft of *The X-Men* movie off the Internet. But, you never can tell what's going to come up during a conversation and it couldn't hurt to be creative.

I contacted some friends who were *Buffy* fans and asked some simple questions. "What makes it tick? Why does it sing?" (And I wasn't referring to the musical episode.) Now, because I'm lucky enough to work in the comic-book industry, my friends turned out to be the likes of J. Scott Campbell, Joe Madureira, and Jeff Matsuda. For those of you who are not familiar with the comic-book industry and prefer your name dropping to be more of the Hollywood variety, I called the All-In-Color-For-A-Dime equivalent of Tom Hanks, Tom Cruise, and Steven Spielberg.

While all three pretty much pointed to Joss's uncanny ability to create characters whose power stems from their Clever, it was Campbell who summed it up best. "Pretty girls and monsters. You can never go wrong." I had to agree. Turned out so did Joss, and a friendship I treasure blossomed over a project that will someday see the light of day called *Buffy, The Animated Series*.

During that tenure, Joss and I talked about a lot of things. He is an unabashed comic-book fan, and, more to the point, an unabashed fan of comic books that I happen to write. I've already told you I'm a fan of his, and, in Hollywood terms, being Members of the Mutual Admiration Society is good DNA for being pals.

We were merrily rolling along with our mutual mutuals, when one day Joss grabbed the wheel. He told me he was going to write a comic book for Dark Horse called *Fray*. "Write a comic book," I thought I heard him say. Here was a man who had not one, not two, not three, but four television series in some form of production and was about to have his first child. (Actually his beautiful wife was doing the actual having... When you're talking about Joss, it's important to clarify the possible from the impossible.)

Innocently, I asked him, "Why?" As with most things Joss takes on, he responded, "I think it would be fun."

Suddenly, I found myself trapped in the third reel of *Citizen Kane*, where I'm playing the fiscally prudish Guardian and Joss is playing the title role, and he's just told me he thinks "it would be fun to run a newspaper."

He thinks it would be "fun" to write a comic book, I muttered to myself all the way home. Feh.

Oh, I knew where this was headed. He was going to write it, and it would look so effortless how he transitioned from the moving picture to the static panel frame with dialogue that came in a balloon. It would be funny and yet somehow poignant. The characters would live in a fantastical world and still seem real.

Joss would be the new darling of *Wizard Magazine*, appearing on the "Top Ten Hot Writers" even before his first issue hit the stands. And when it did hit the stands, his first issue would be on the "Top Ten Hot Books."

Oh, yes, Eve Harrington, I knew where this was headed.

I encouraged Joss, as Hollywood companions often do, and told him I looked forward to reading it. He demurred, speculating that it would only be a trifle compared to my work. I think I bought a dagger later that day.

Fray #1 appeared at the comic-book store and the *Buffy* office around the same time. I took my copy back to my office and closed the door. I used my dagger to slit open the Mylar bag and began to read.

And then, as they say, the Grinch's heart grew three times that day. As Joss pulled me into the world of *Fray*, I began to smile.

Joss had created something wonderful and unique in comics. He had used the basic foundations of the *Buffy* mythos, sped it up a couple of hundred years, and made it shiny. Pretty girls and monsters, all right, but also flying cars. You can never go wrong with flying cars. Best of all, if you've never seen *Buffy* or *Angel* (yes, we know there are a few of you who've spent the last 900 years inside a Hellmouth), *Fray* opens the door wide enough that no previous Slayer experience is necessary. You just glide with the ride.

Here is the tale of a quick-witted thief named Melaka whose destiny is so much greater than she can imagine. Her unlikely mentor is a beastie named Urkonn, a far cry from the unflappable Giles of the Buffyverse, but nonetheless lovable. Her supporting cast includes her by-the-book, couldn't-be-anymore-different-than-Mel sister Erin and the rest of her family is best left for you to discover inside.

But ... the real treasure and the reason why I don't really hate Joss is ... Loo. That's all I'll say on the subject.

Comic books can be spectacularly written, but if the artwork can't reflect the tale in scope and expression, you are doomed. One of the hallmarks of Joss's talent is his dialogue; it's one thing to see and hear an actress read it aloud, it's another to have it drawn on the page.

None of us "comic-book types" had really heard of Karl Moline before *Fray* first came out. But Karl stepped onto *Fray* with such authority we all stood up and took notice. His women are sexy, strong, and commanding. His layout, his sense of design, and, best of all, his ability to capture the subtle nuances of the faces bring to life Joss's words and descriptions as expertly as it can be done.

Three other equally talented folks join Karl. His inker, Andy Owens's deft black line polishes Karl's delicious pencils. Michelle Madsen has excelled in the extraordinarily challenging job of lettering the book by making the fonts and balloons perfectly match Joss's words in texture and tone. Then it's all made candy and pretty by my pal Dave Stewart, who is one of the finest colorists in the business, and clearly had a ball doing *Fray*.

Lastly, it's important to mention Scott Allie, the editor of the series who stood like a lighthouse on the coast of Oregon, a beacon in the night, patiently waiting for his pages to come in. *Fray* took some time to reach port, but, as Scott will attest, it was so worth it.

I can't wait until you read this collection. It's always nice to meet someone who hates Joss as much as I do.

Hrrm. I wonder what I can get for my dagger on eBay...?

Jeph Loeb
Los Angeles
June 2003

Foreword

by Joss Whedon

Comic books and girls.

Don't get me wrong, there were certainly other things on my mind in my young adolescence. But almost certainly topping the list were girls and comics. And more specifically, girls *in* comics. Because, frustratingly, there weren't that many. At least in the Marvel universe, where I made my nest, there were very few interesting girls young enough for a twelve year old to crush on. My best buddy and I used to fight, in our pathetic—I meant to say "rich"—fantasy lives over the affections of any girl who showed the slightest spirit. But it was deeply slim pickin's. Until Kitty Pryde. She was such a figure of both affection and identification, I even forgave her inability to think of a decent name for herself. If she could be in the *X-Men*, then there was no reason a short, skinny, not-overly-hygienic New Yorker whose mutant power seemed to be the ability to whine amusingly couldn't join up too. (And possibly win her over, since Colossus—not that bright.)

Cut to me grown up—yet somehow not remotely matured. The idea for *Buffy the Vampire Slayer* came from that same lack I had felt as a child. Where are the girls? Girls who can fight, who can stand up for themselves, who have opinions and fears and cute outfits? Buffy was designed to fill that void in movies—and then, ultimately, TV. And the whole Slayer thing kinda took off. The public responded, the show continued, the mythology of the Slayer became more complex, and most importantly, there were comics. Since I was near death from too much creating, I decided I needed to fulfill my kidhood dream of writing a book on top of everything else. I didn't think anybody would be interested in a book from me unless it was somehow *Buffy* related, and I was too busy writing *Buffy* to think about writing about *Buffy*. (That sentence came out interestingly.) I toyed with Faith—but then she was back on *Angel*, and continuity would have been upset. How to avoid that? By telling a story far enough in the future that it wouldn't—couldn't—interfere. By creating a new Slayer, and a new world for her to live in.

My ambitions were slight. I wasn't out to re-imagine, or predict, the future. I wasn't out to challenge the reigning Gods—Moore, Ellis, Ennis, and the gang—in terms of storytelling. (My visions of the future are always pretty much the standard issue: The rich get richer, the poor get poorer, and there are flying cars.) I was keeping it simple. Slayer. Family. Strength. A simple story about a really cool girl. A girl who might share some personal issues with both Buffy and Faith, but who was very much her own person. A mythology I was already comfortable with, with a few twists thrown in. Including, but not limited to, the aforementioned flying cars. I paced around for a few weeks and Melaka Fray was born.

Or conceived. She wasn't actually born until I met Karl Moline. The first conceptual sketch Karl ever did (which should be among the goodies at

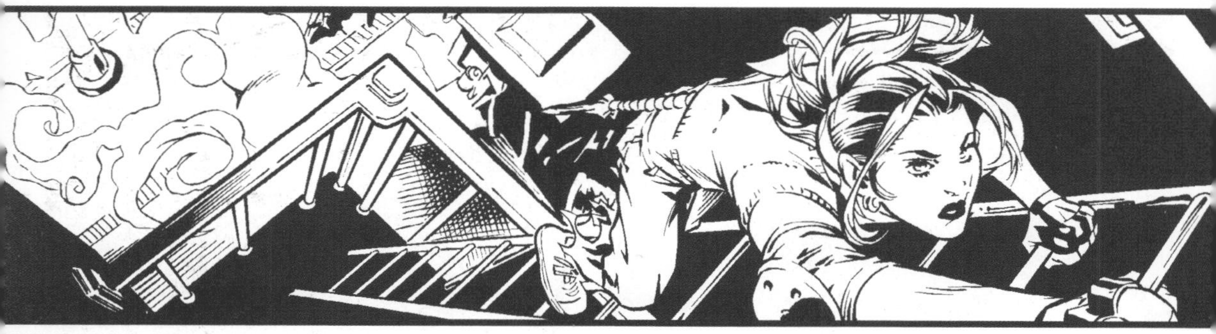

the back of this book) convinced me he was the guy to flesh out my hero. I had come to Dark Horse with pretty much one stipulation: No cheesecake. No giant silicone hooters, no standing with her butt out in that bizarrely uncomfortable soft-core pose so many artists favor. None of those outfits that casually—and constantly—reveal portions of thong. I wanted a real girl, with real posture, a slight figure (that's my classy way of saying "little boobs"), and most of all, a distinctive face. A person. If you've seen *Fray* at all you know how wonderfully Karl succeeded. Not just with her, but with the whole world. He was exactly the kind of artist I hoped to work with: the splashy, over-the-top immediacy of the great old comics mixed with a naturalism and subtlety of expression that is very much of the new. Melaka's every pose is real, lived-in. She is hard, defensive, vulnerable, goofy, and yes, wicked sexy. Look closely, you can actually see her maturing from issue to issue. Thanks largely to Karl (and Andy, whose inks always brought out the most depth in every frame, and, yup, Dave, who is the color-master of mixing the real with the surreal), I got to put a cool girl hero on the stands who may not have been blindingly original in terms of today's graphic arena, but who was someone I had waited a good portion of my life to meet.

So here's me, grateful. To Dark Horse, and Scott Allie in particular, for his encouragement, patience (can I possibly stress that enough?), and insight on this, my maiden voyage. To Kai, for reading it with me, and making me feel like I know what I'm doing. To Karl, for ... well look. To everyone involved in this book. That includes you, if you care to join in. And finally, to Chris Boal, that best buddy I misspent so much of youth with, living in comics. Finally made one of my own. Damn, was it fun.

This book is dedicated to my son, Arden, who is even more wondrous than the work, and embarrassingly, took less time to produce. It's yours to read one day, Arden. Try not to spill anything on it.

Joss Whedon
Los Angeles
May 2003

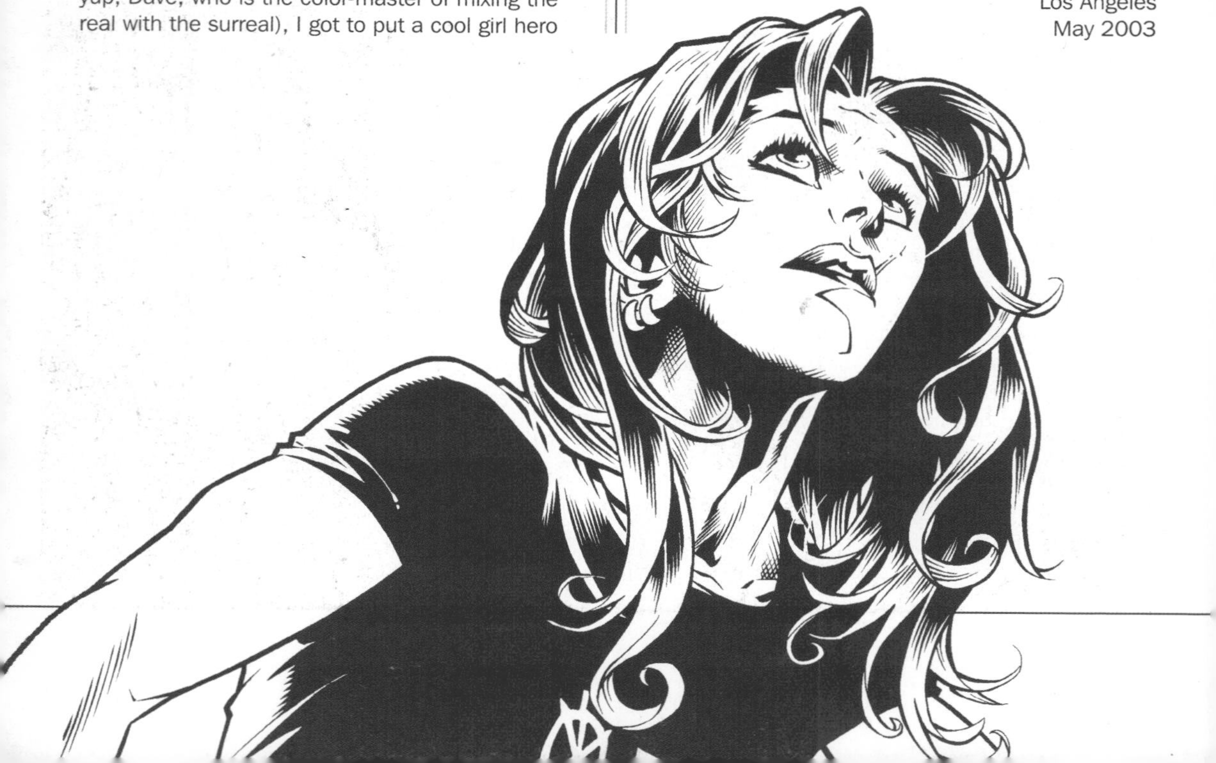

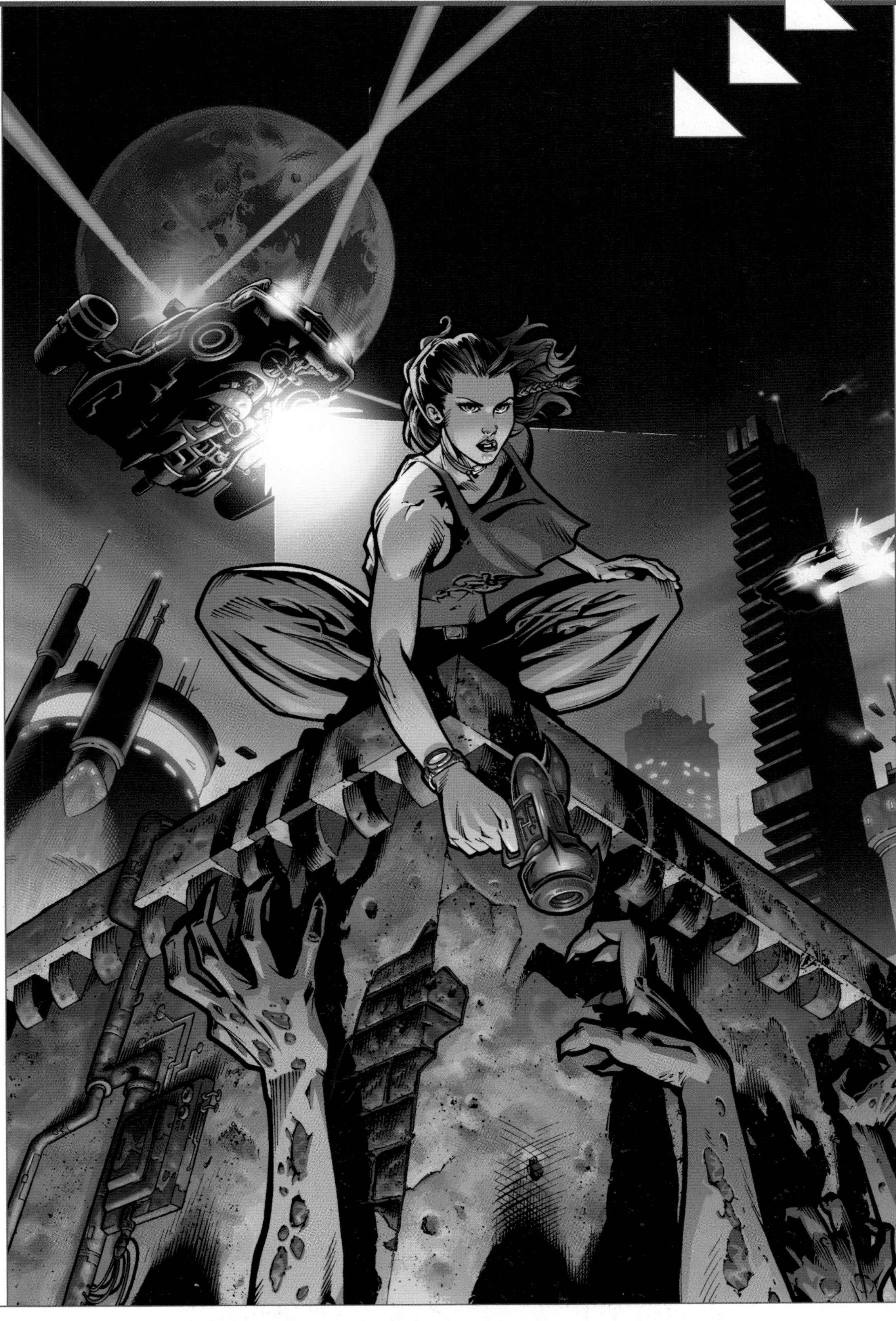

"Bad day."

"Started bad,
stayed that way."

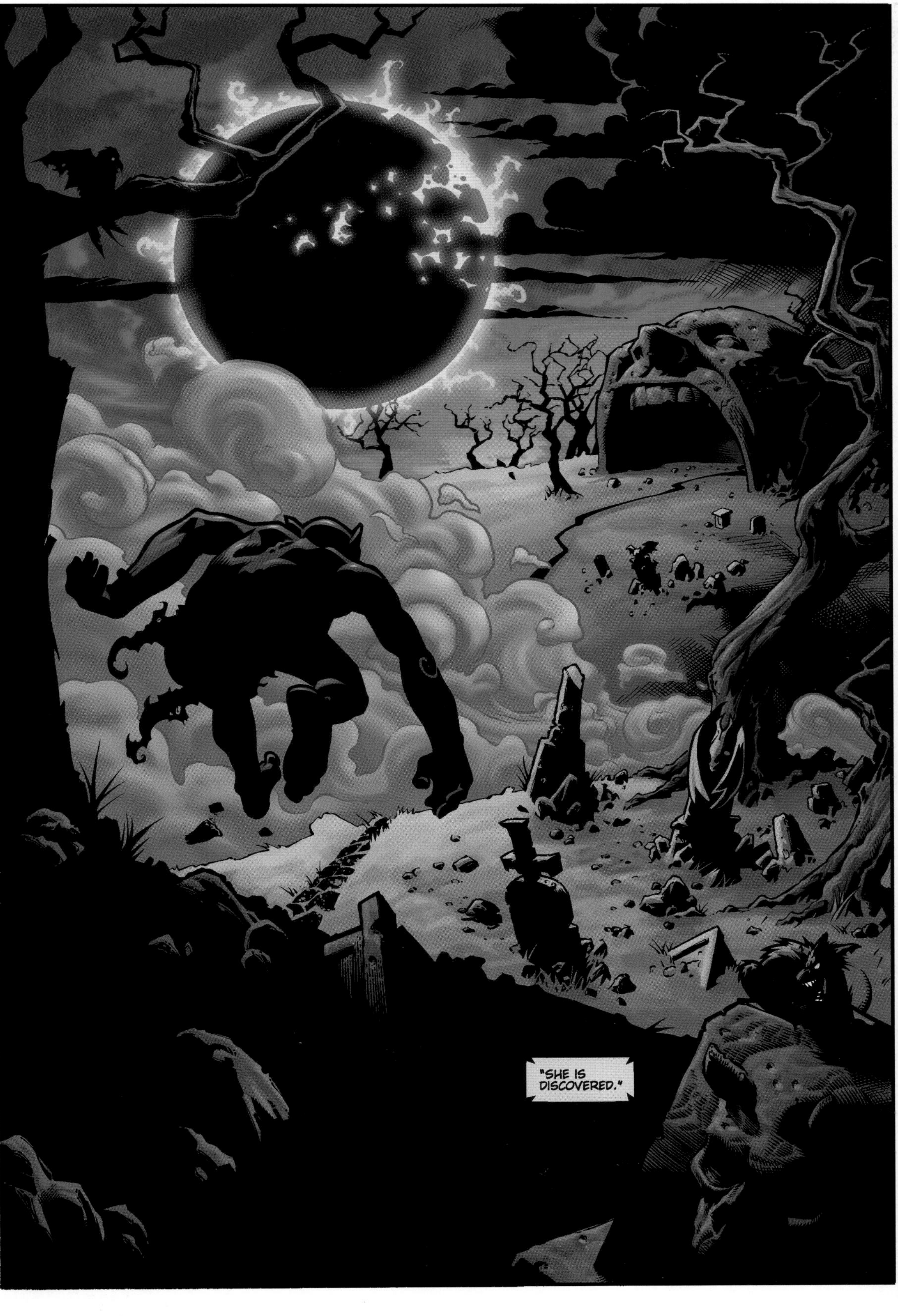
"SHE IS DISCOVERED."

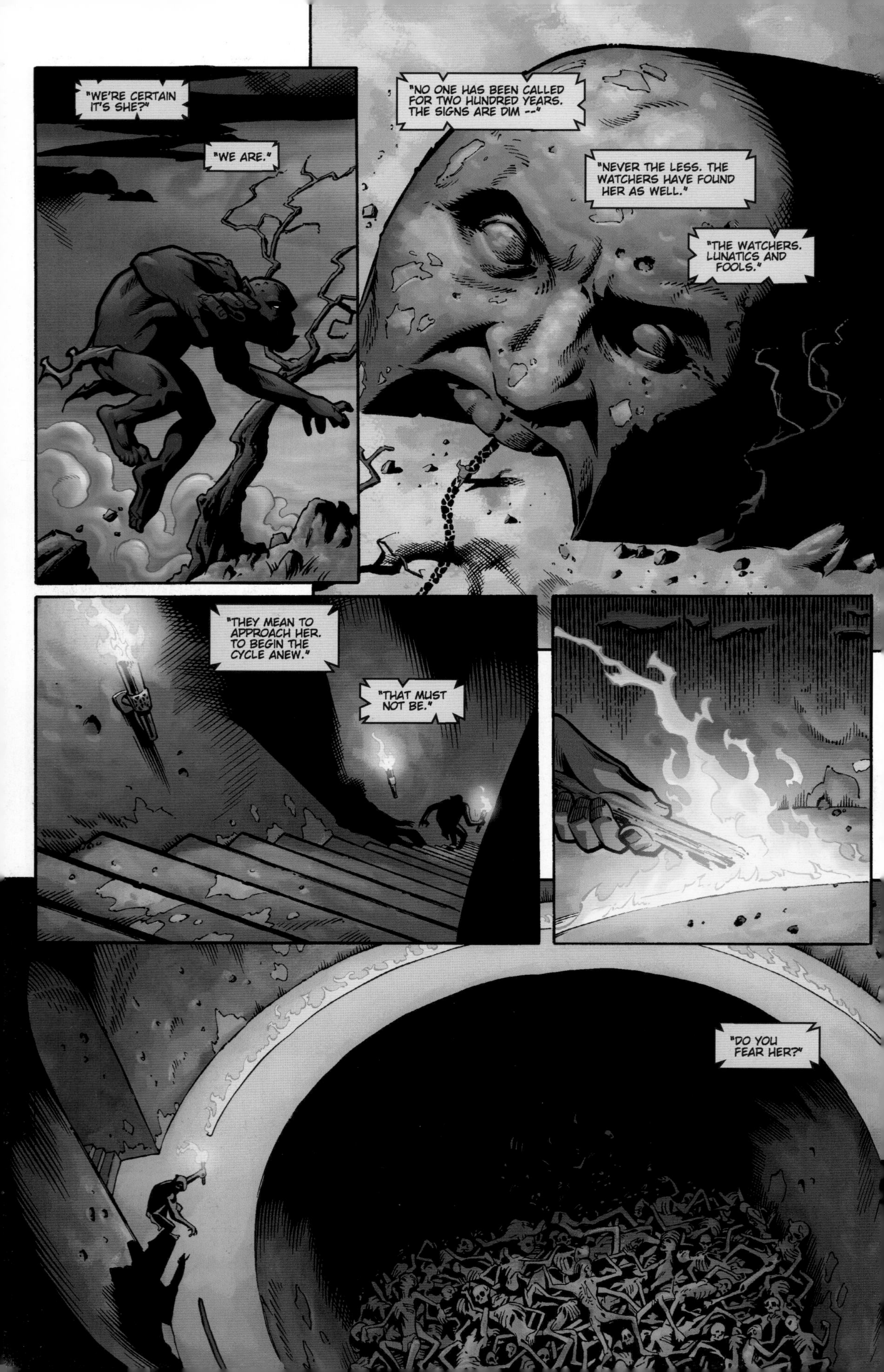
"WE'RE CERTAIN IT'S SHE?"
"WE ARE."
"NO ONE HAS BEEN CALLED FOR TWO HUNDRED YEARS. THE SIGNS ARE DIM --"
"NEVER THE LESS. THE WATCHERS HAVE FOUND HER AS WELL."
"THE WATCHERS. LUNATICS AND FOOLS."
"THEY MEAN TO APPROACH HER. TO BEGIN THE CYCLE ANEW."
"THAT MUST NOT BE."
"DO YOU FEAR HER?"

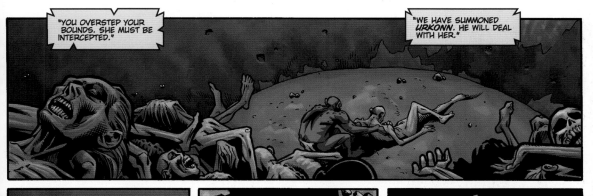

"YOU OVERSTEP YOUR BOUNDS. SHE MUST BE INTERCEPTED."

"WE HAVE SUMMONED *URKONN*. HE WILL DEAL WITH HER."

"HE HAD BEST, FOR HIS OWN SAKE."

"HE'LL NOT FAIL. SHE'S BUT A MORTAL."

"WHAT IS SHE CALLED?"

"FRAY.

"MELAKA FRAY."

"AND SHE HAS NO IDEA WHAT IS TO COME."

"JUST A HUMAN, AMONG TEN BILLION OTHERS. LIVING OUT THE SAME DULL, POINTLESS EXISTENCE.

"NOT THE SLIGHTEST CLUE THAT COME DAY'S END ...

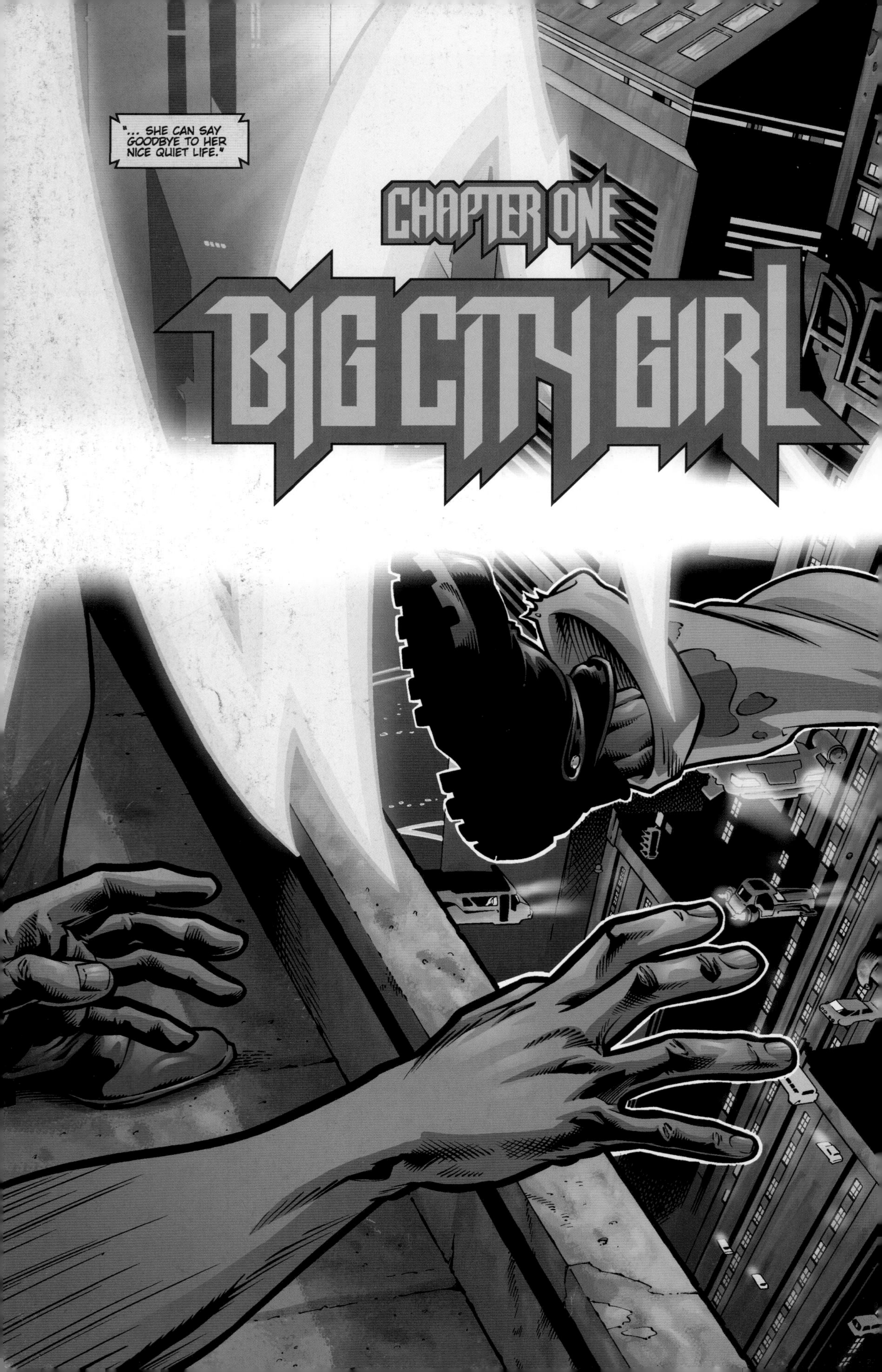
"... SHE CAN SAY GOODBYE TO HER NICE QUIET LIFE."
CHAPTER ONE
BIG CITY GIRL

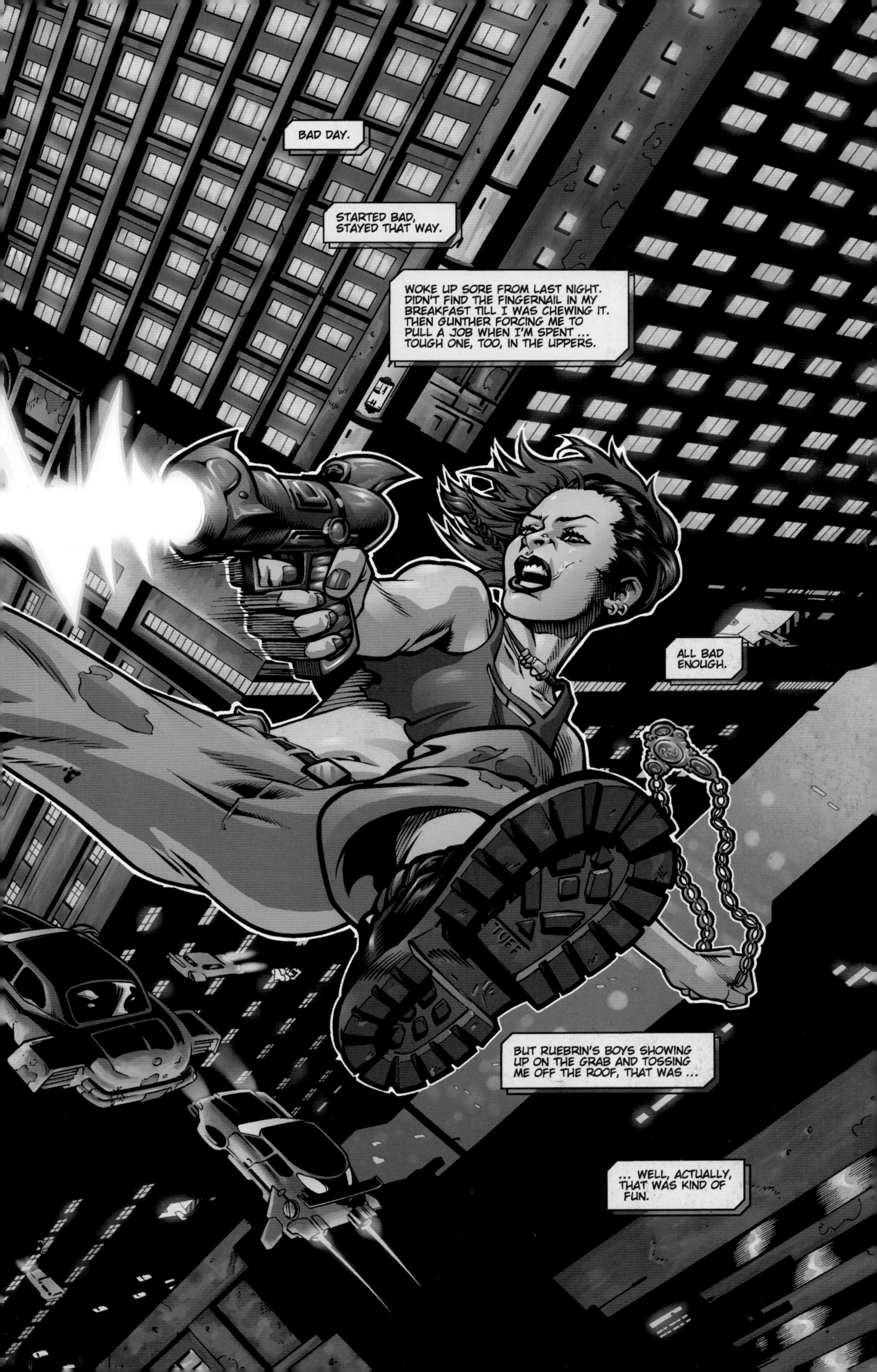
BAD DAY.
STARTED BAD, STAYED THAT WAY.
WOKE UP SORE FROM LAST NIGHT. DIDN'T FIND THE FINGERNAIL IN MY BREAKFAST TILL I WAS CHEWING IT. THEN GUNTHER FORCING ME TO PULL A JOB WHEN I'M SPENT ... TOUGH ONE, TOO, IN THE UPPERS.
ALL BAD ENOUGH.
BUT RUEBRIN'S BOYS SHOWING UP ON THE GRAB AND TOSSING ME OFF THE ROOF, THAT WAS ...
... WELL, ACTUALLY, THAT WAS KIND OF FUN.

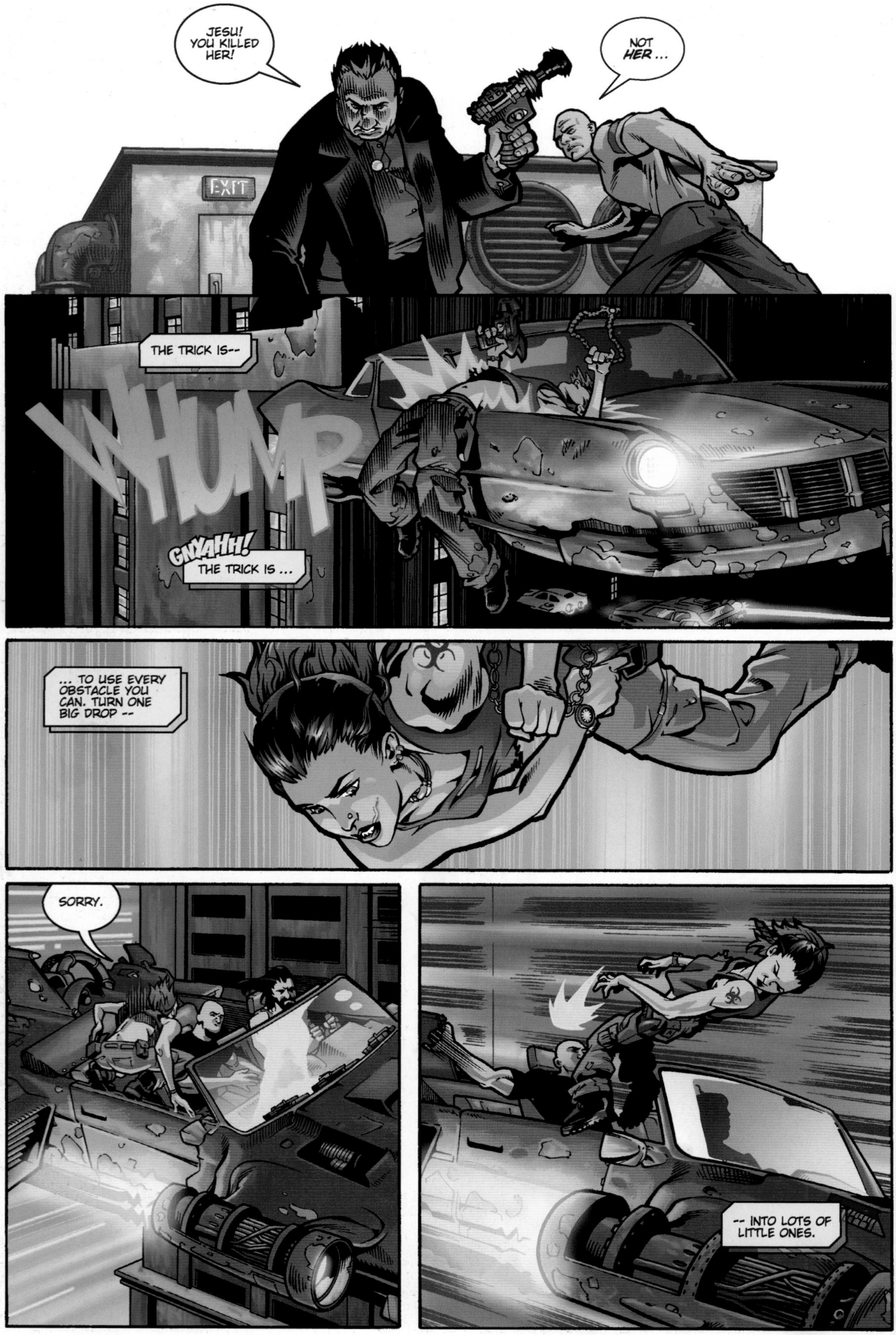
JESU! YOU KILLED HER!
NOT *HER*...
THE TRICK IS--
WHUMP
GNYAHH!
THE TRICK IS ...
... TO USE EVERY OBSTACLE YOU CAN. TURN ONE BIG DROP --
SORRY.
-- INTO LOTS OF LITTLE ONES.

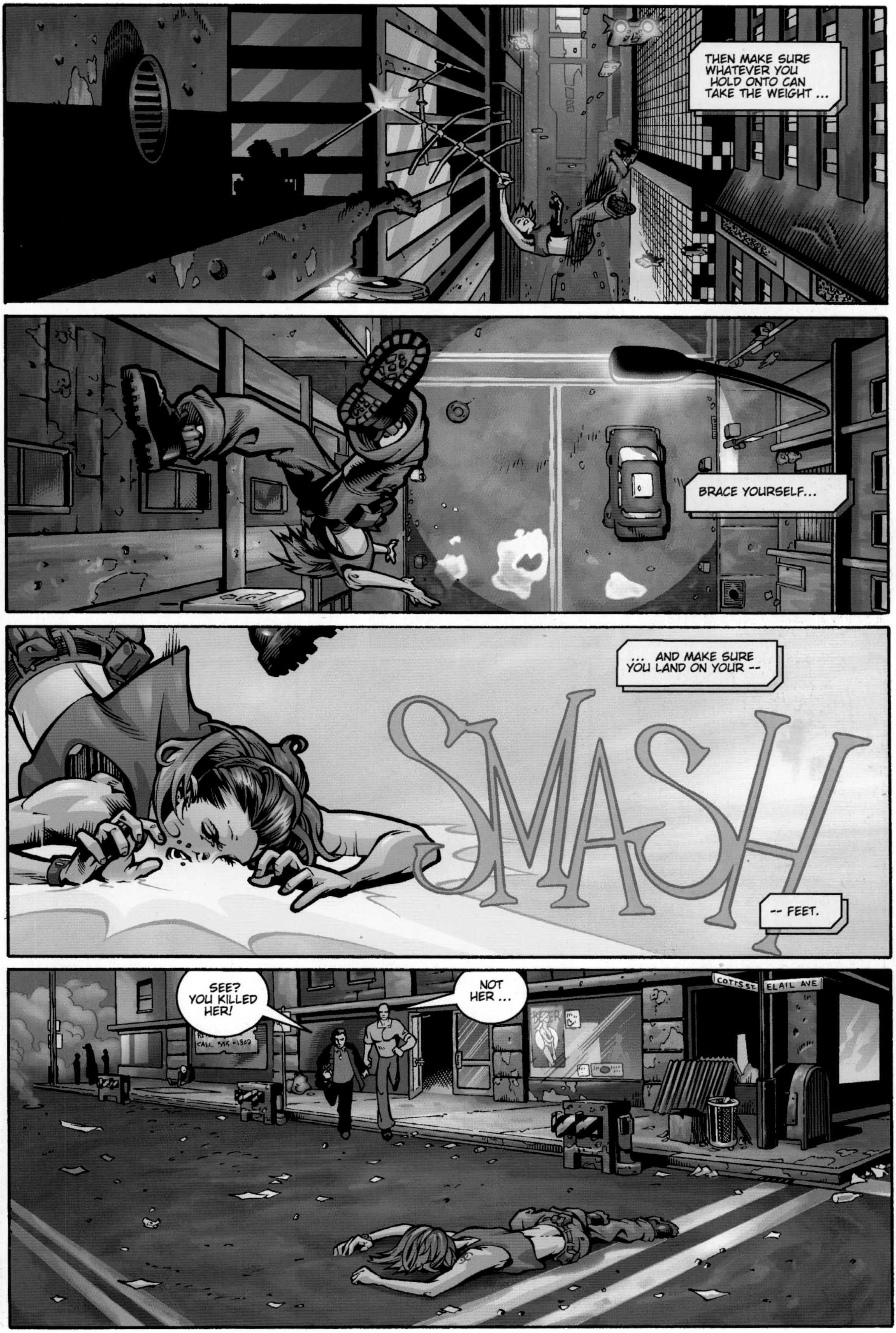
THEN MAKE SURE WHATEVER YOU HOLD ONTO CAN TAKE THE WEIGHT ...
BRACE YOURSELF...
... AND MAKE SURE YOU LAND ON YOUR --
SMASH
-- FEET.
SEE? YOU KILLED HER!
NOT HER ...
COTTS ST.
ELAIL AVE

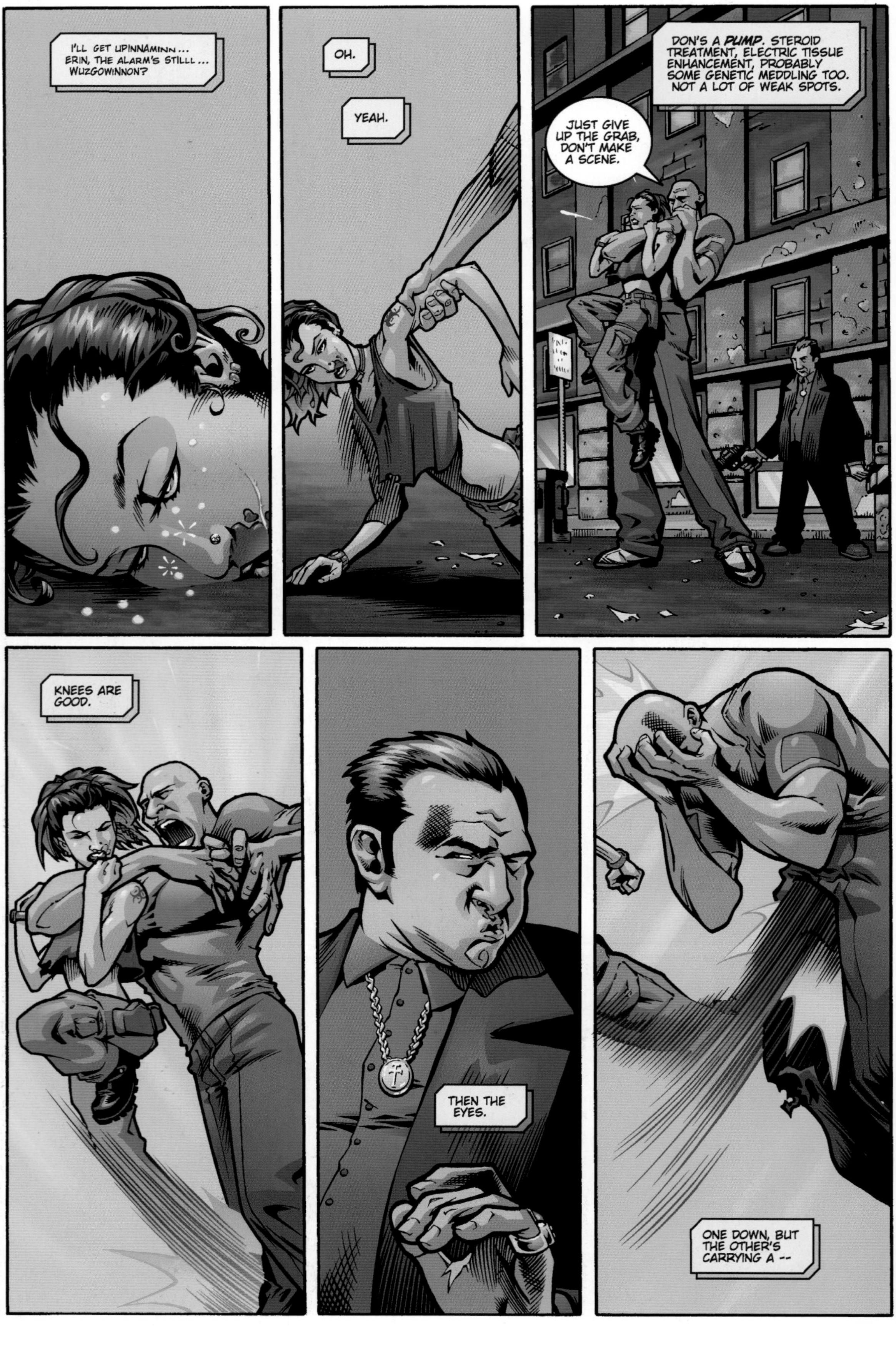
I'LL GET UPINNAMINN... ERIN, THE ALARM'S STILLL... WUZGOWINNON?
OH.
YEAH.
DON'S A PUMP. STEROID TREATMENT, ELECTRIC TISSUE ENHANCEMENT, PROBABLY SOME GENETIC MEDDLING TOO. NOT A LOT OF WEAK SPOTS.
JUST GIVE UP THE GRAB, DON'T MAKE A SCENE.
KNEES ARE GOOD.
THEN THE EYES.
ONE DOWN, BUT THE OTHER'S CARRYING A --

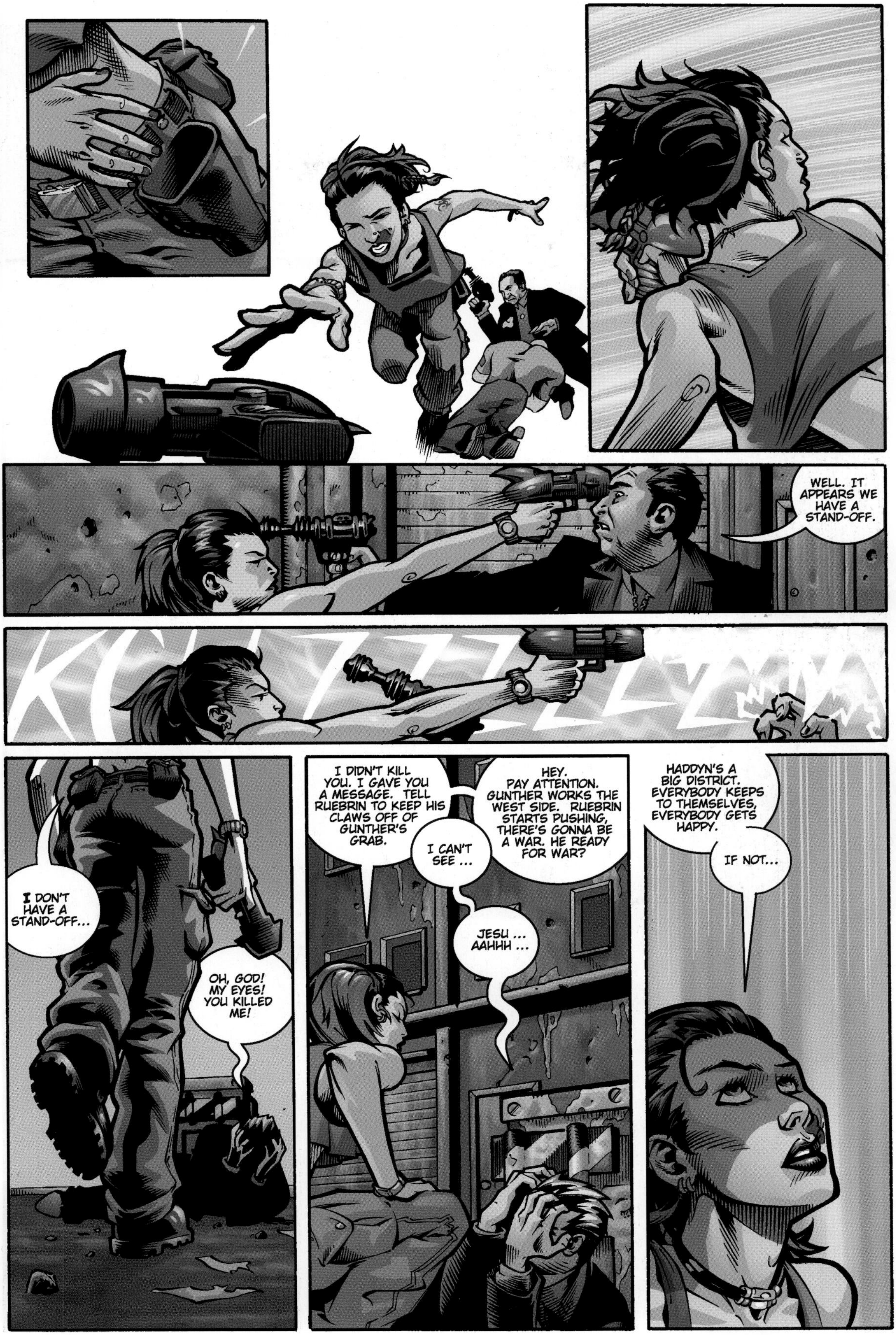
WELL. IT APPEARS WE HAVE A STAND-OFF.
I DON'T HAVE A STAND-OFF...
OH, GOD! MY EYES! YOU KILLED ME!
I DIDN'T KILL YOU. I GAVE YOU A MESSAGE. TELL RUEBRIN TO KEEP HIS CLAWS OFF OF GUNTHER'S GRAB.
I CAN'T SEE ...
HEY. PAY ATTENTION. GUNTHER WORKS THE WEST SIDE. RUEBRIN STARTS PUSHING, THERE'S GONNA BE A WAR. HE READY FOR WAR?
JESU ... AAHHH ...
HADDYN'S A BIG DISTRICT. EVERYBODY KEEPS TO THEMSELVES, EVERYBODY GETS HAPPY.
IF NOT...

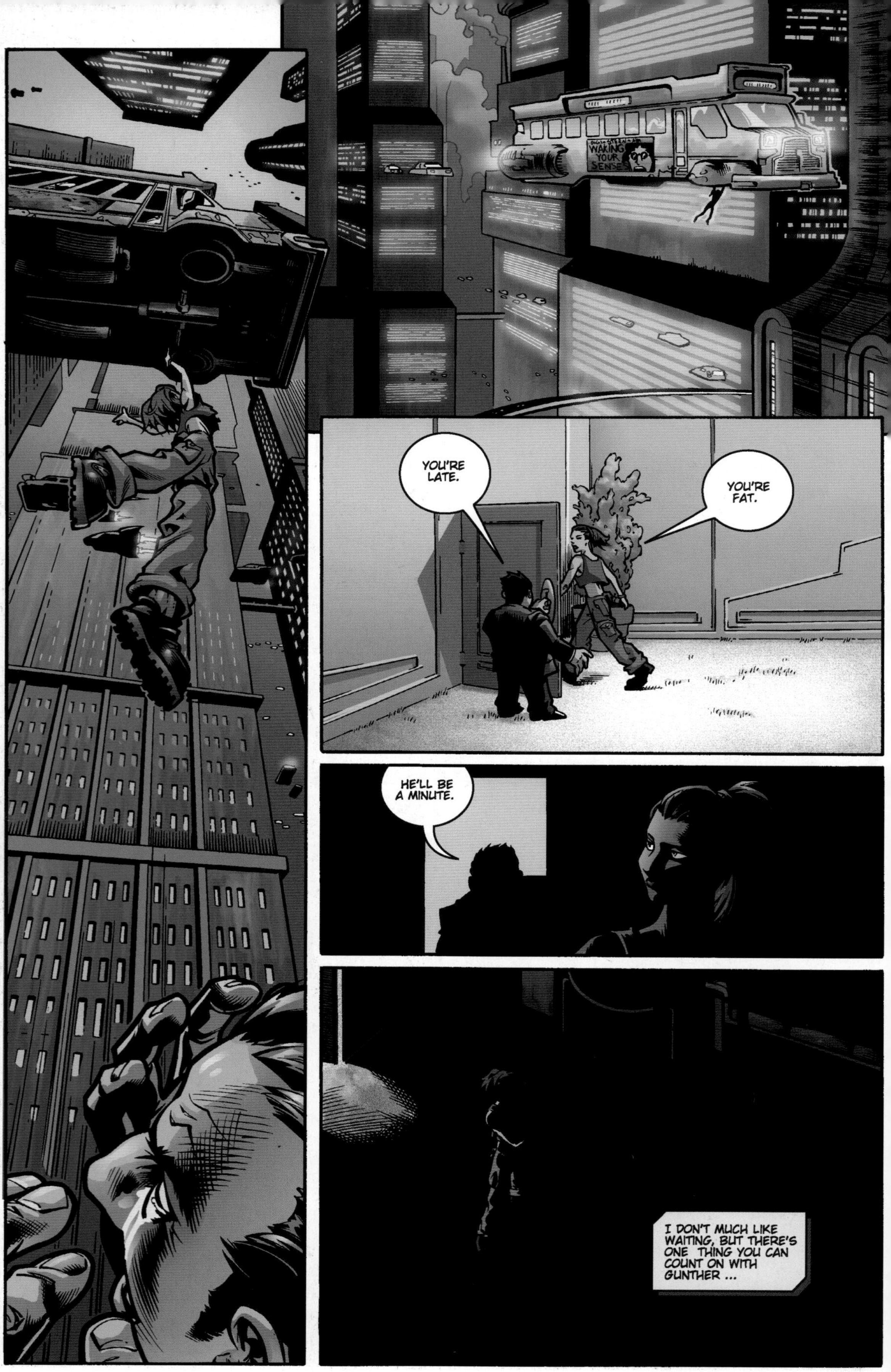
WAKING YOUR SENSES
YOU'RE LATE.
YOU'RE FAT.
HE'LL BE A MINUTE.
I DON'T MUCH LIKE WAITING, BUT THERE'S ONE THING YOU CAN COUNT ON WITH GUNTHER ...

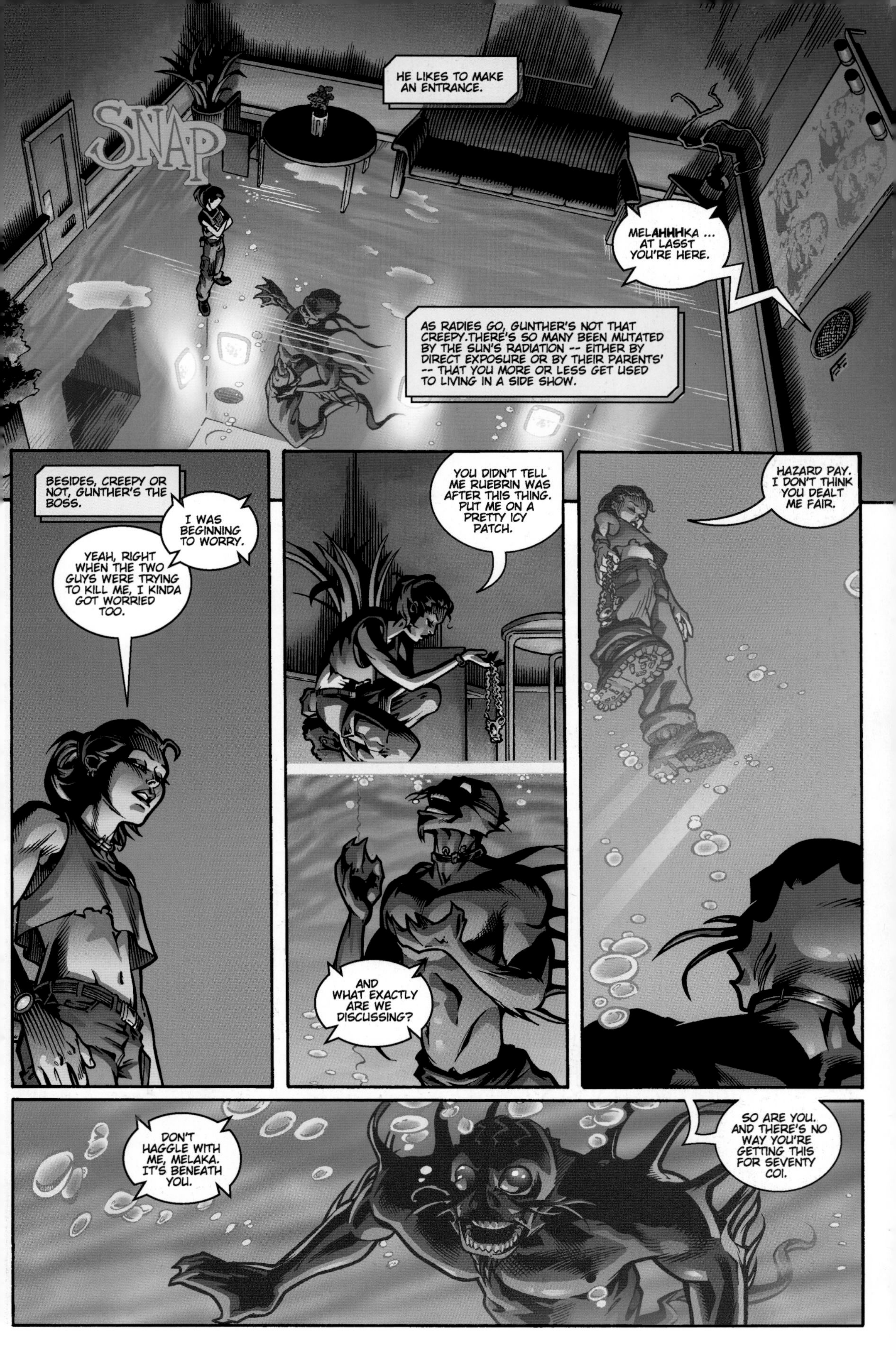
HE LIKES TO MAKE AN ENTRANCE.
SNAP
MELAHHHKA ... AT LASST YOU'RE HERE.
AS RADIES GO, GUNTHER'S NOT THAT CREEPY. THERE'S SO MANY BEEN MUTATED BY THE SUN'S RADIATION -- EITHER BY DIRECT EXPOSURE OR BY THEIR PARENTS' -- THAT YOU MORE OR LESS GET USED TO LIVING IN A SIDE SHOW.
BESIDES, CREEPY OR NOT, GUNTHER'S THE BOSS.
I WAS BEGINNING TO WORRY.
YEAH, RIGHT WHEN THE TWO GUYS WERE TRYING TO KILL ME, I KINDA GOT WORRIED TOO.
YOU DIDN'T TELL ME RUEBRIN WAS AFTER THIS THING. PUT ME ON A PRETTY ICY PATCH.
AND WHAT EXACTLY ARE WE DISCUSSING?
HAZARD PAY. I DON'T THINK YOU DEALT ME FAIR.
DON'T HAGGLE WITH ME, MELAKA. IT'S BENEATH YOU.
SO ARE YOU. AND THERE'S NO WAY YOU'RE GETTING THIS FOR SEVENTY COI.

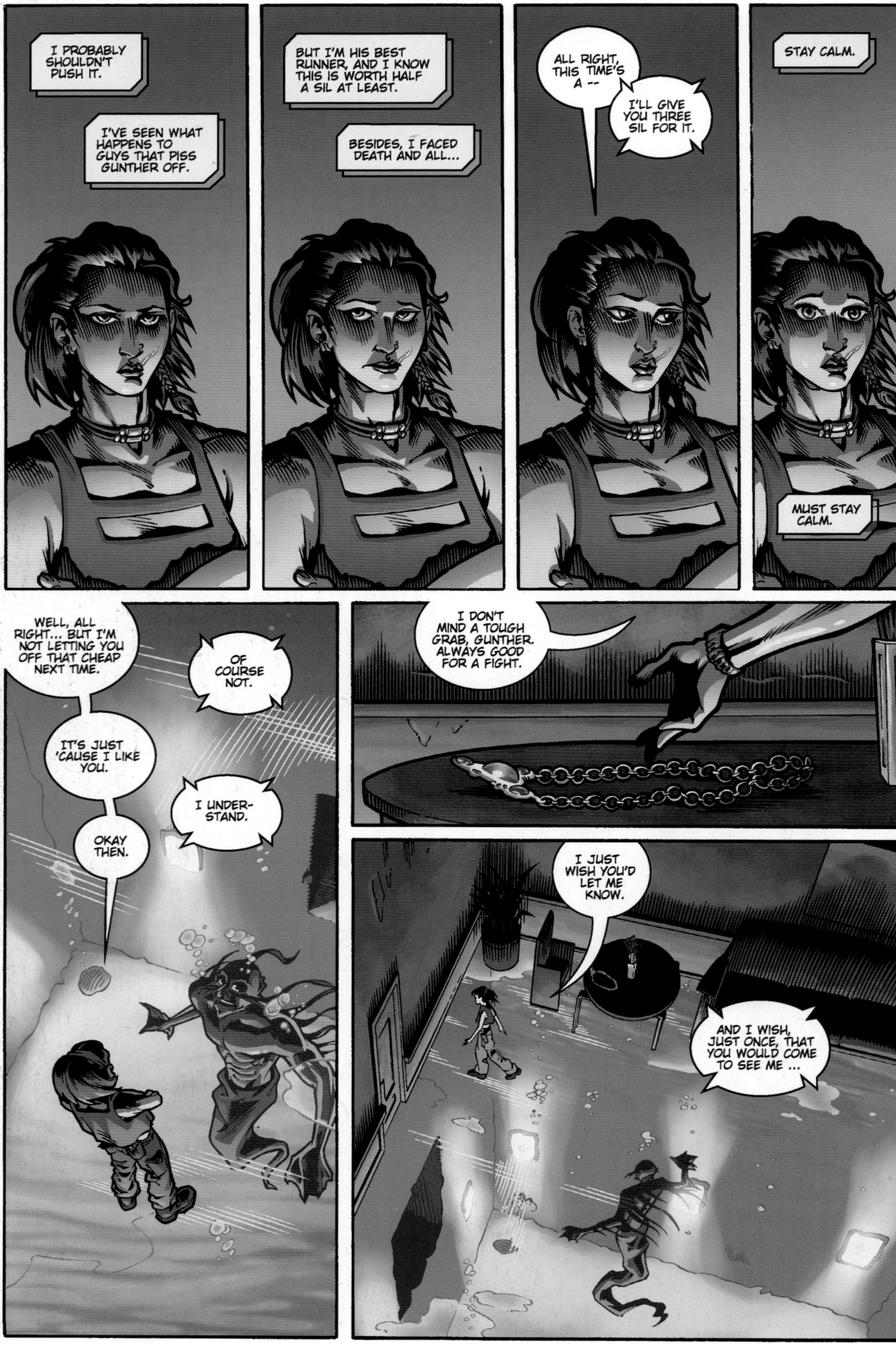
I PROBABLY SHOULDN'T PUSH IT.
I'VE SEEN WHAT HAPPENS TO GUYS THAT PISS GUNTHER OFF.
BUT I'M HIS BEST RUNNER, AND I KNOW THIS IS WORTH HALF A SIL AT LEAST.
BESIDES, I FACED DEATH AND ALL...
ALL RIGHT, THIS TIME'S A --
I'LL GIVE YOU THREE SIL FOR IT.
STAY CALM.
MUST STAY CALM.
WELL, ALL RIGHT... BUT I'M NOT LETTING YOU OFF THAT CHEAP NEXT TIME.
OF COURSE NOT.
IT'S JUST 'CAUSE I LIKE YOU.
I UNDER-STAND.
OKAY THEN.
I DON'T MIND A TOUGH GRAB, GUNTHER. ALWAYS GOOD FOR A FIGHT.
I JUST WISH YOU'D LET ME KNOW.
AND I WISH, JUST ONCE, THAT YOU WOULD COME TO SEE ME ...

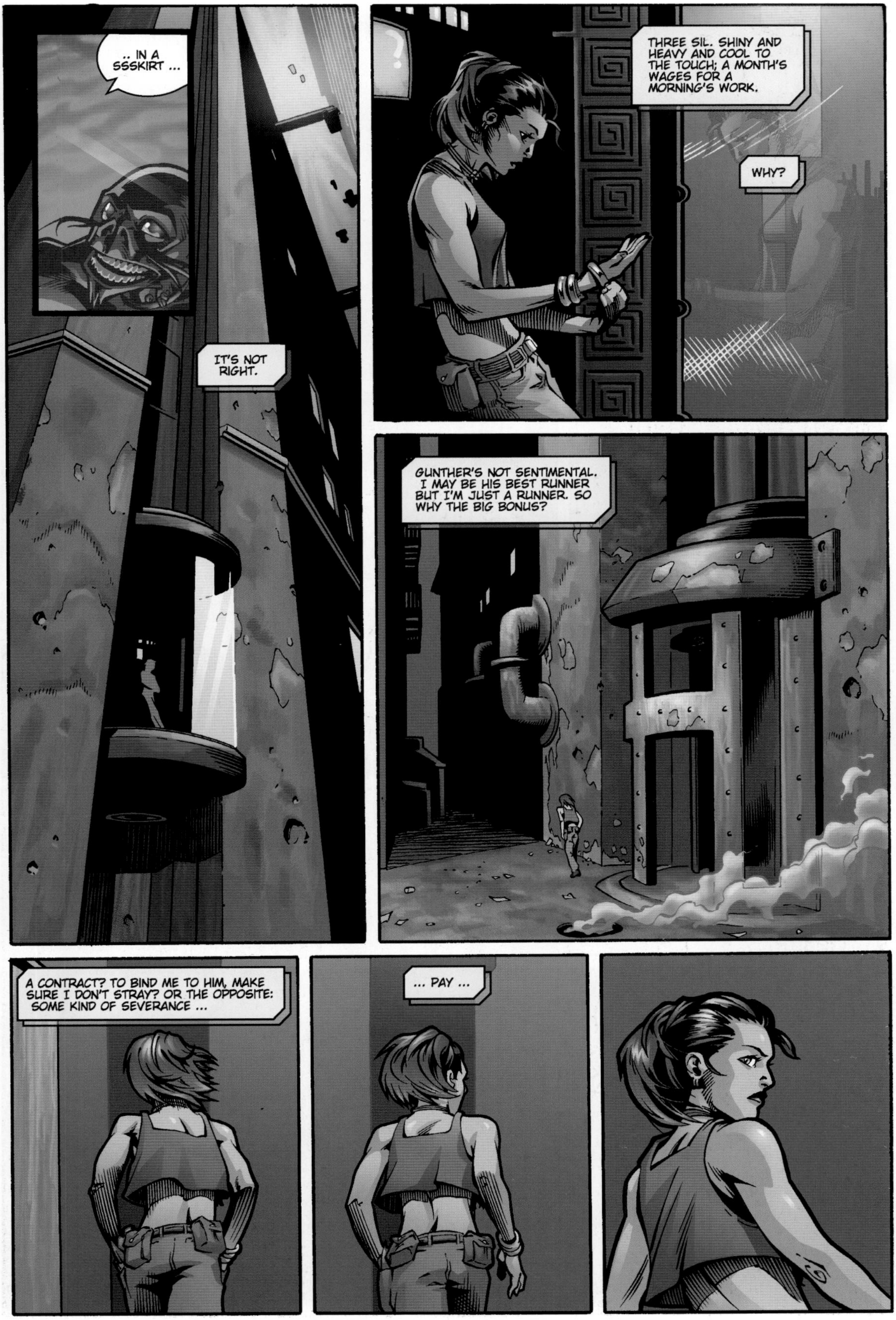
.. IN A SSSKIRT ...
IT'S NOT RIGHT.
THREE SIL. SHINY AND HEAVY AND COOL TO THE TOUCH; A MONTH'S WAGES FOR A MORNING'S WORK.
WHY?
GUNTHER'S NOT SENTIMENTAL. I MAY BE HIS BEST RUNNER BUT I'M JUST A RUNNER. SO WHY THE BIG BONUS?
A CONTRACT? TO BIND ME TO HIM, MAKE SURE I DON'T STRAY? OR THE OPPOSITE: SOME KIND OF SEVERANCE ...
... PAY ...

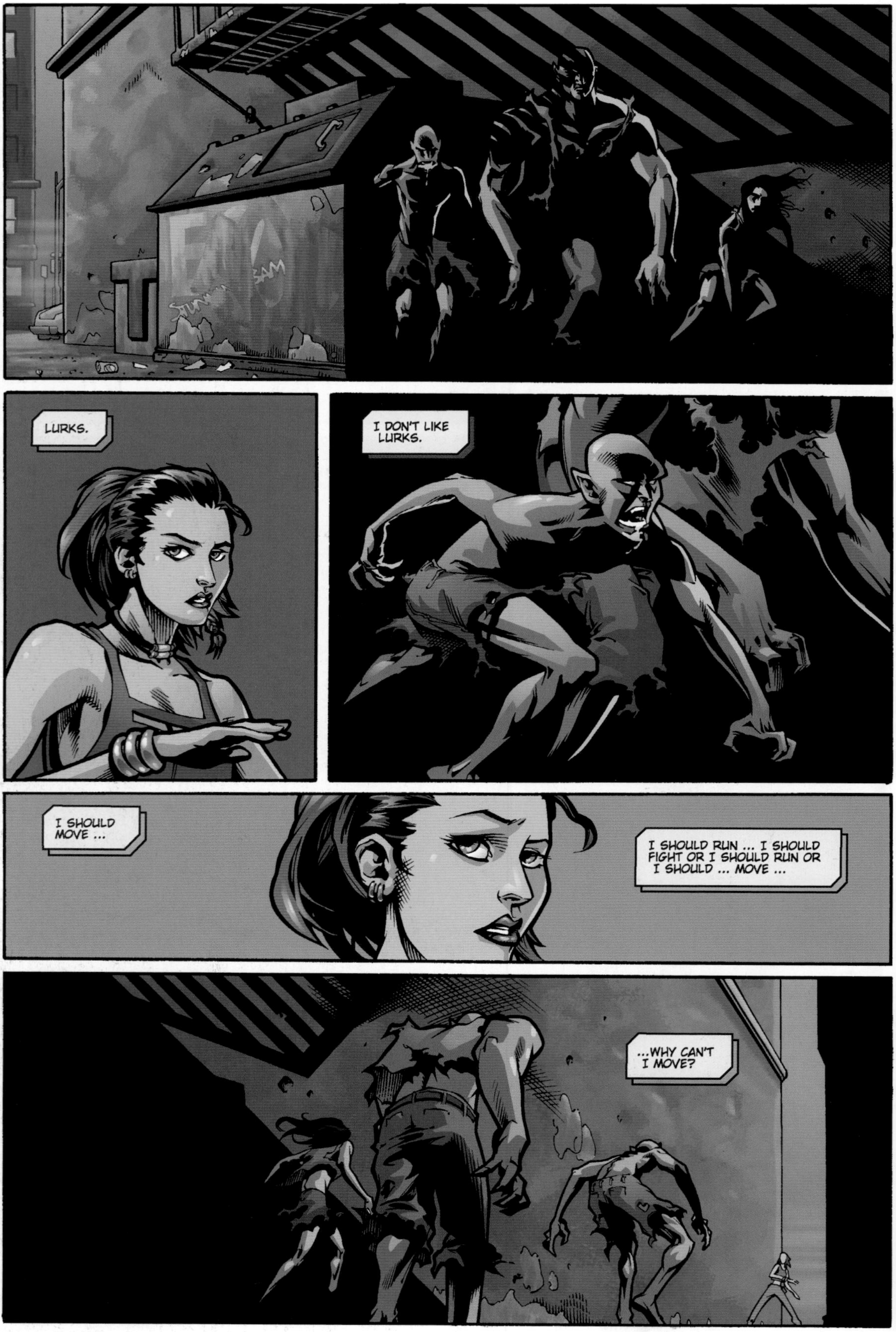
LURKS.
I DON'T LIKE LURKS.
I SHOULD MOVE ...
I SHOULD RUN ... I SHOULD FIGHT OR I SHOULD RUN OR I SHOULD ... MOVE ...
...WHY CAN'T I MOVE?

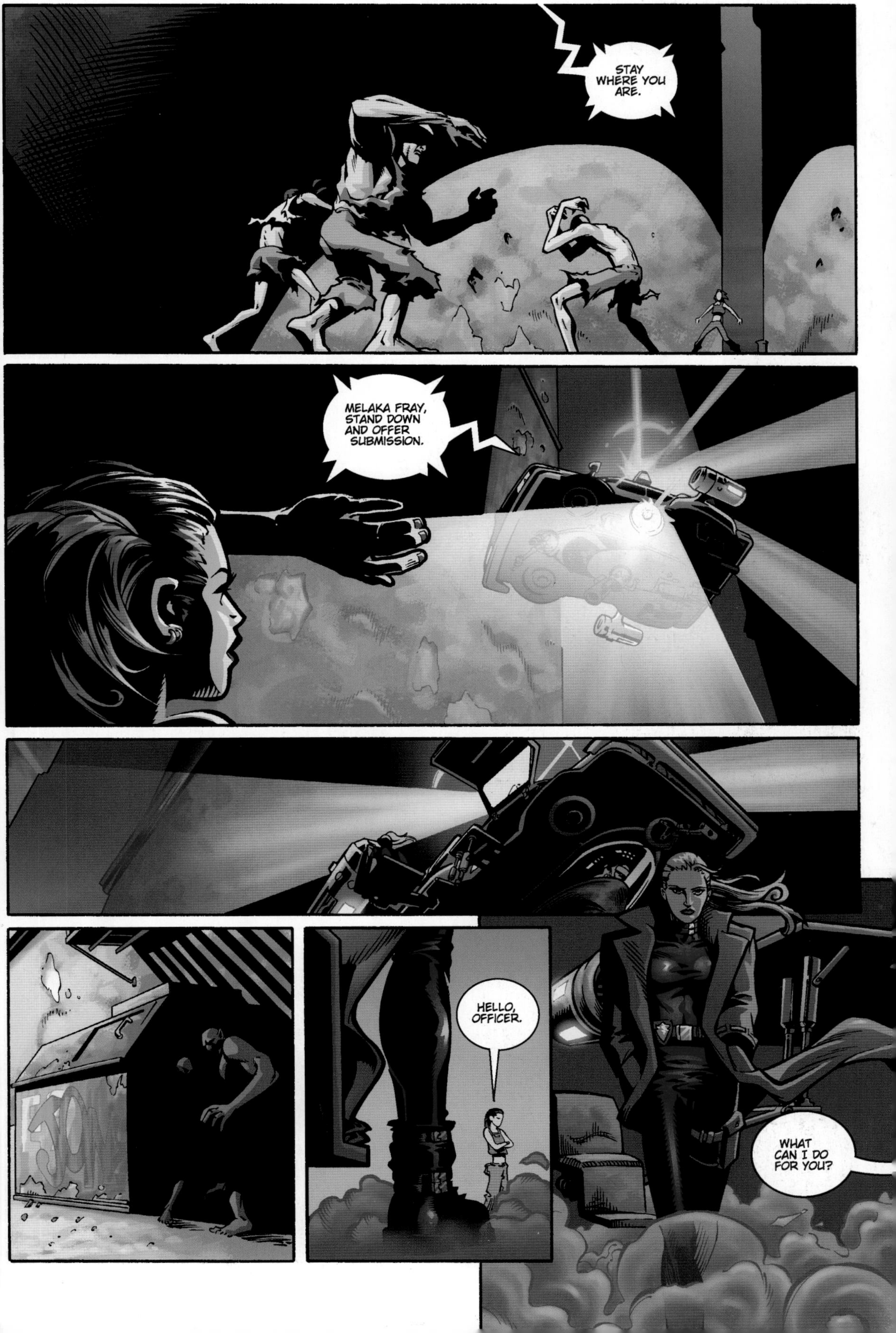
STAY WHERE YOU ARE.
MELAKA FRAY, STAND DOWN AND OFFER SUBMISSION.
HELLO, OFFICER.
WHAT CAN I DO FOR YOU?

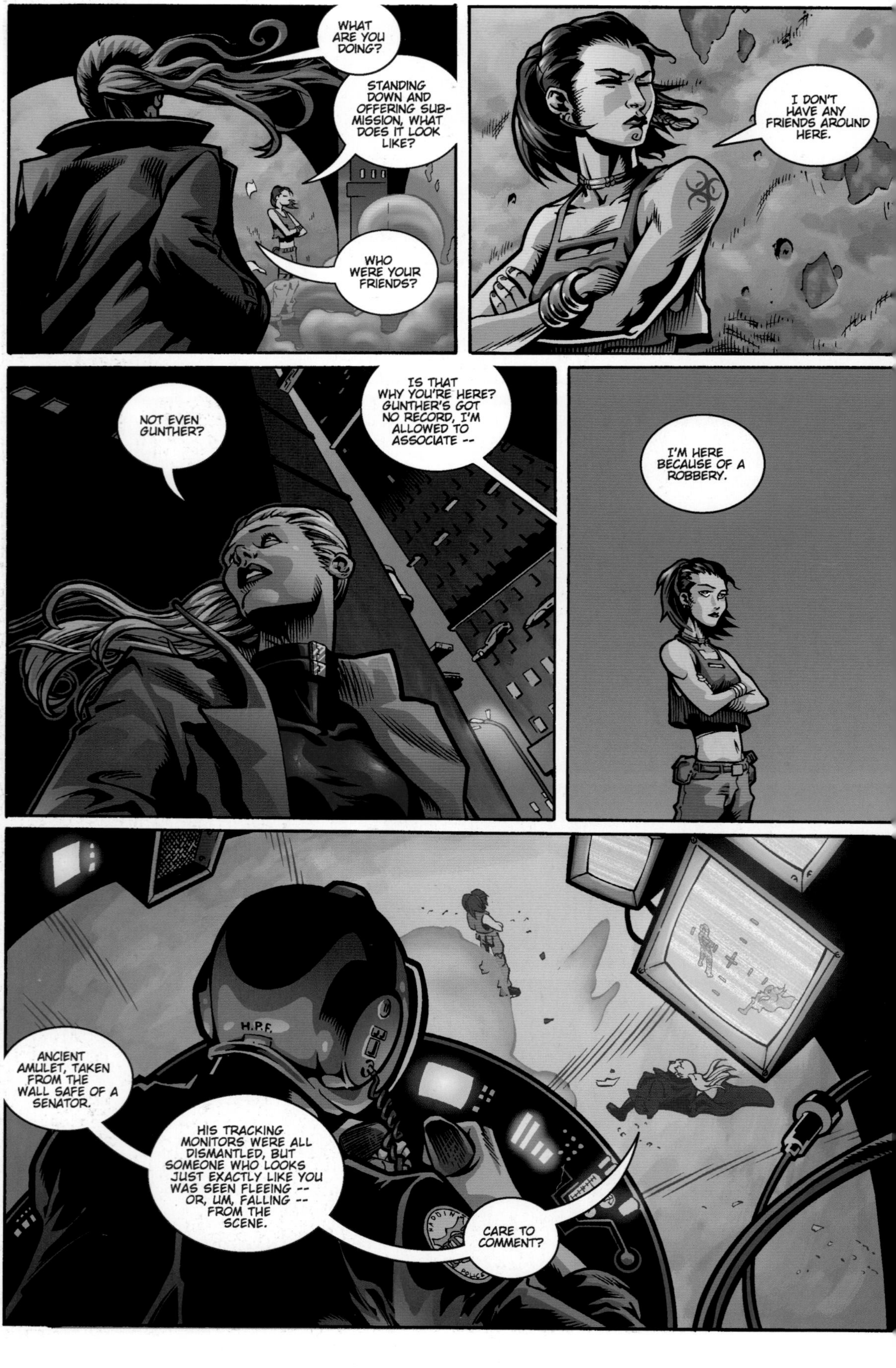
WHAT ARE YOU DOING?
STANDING DOWN AND OFFERING SUB-MISSION, WHAT DOES IT LOOK LIKE?
WHO WERE YOUR FRIENDS?
I DON'T HAVE ANY FRIENDS AROUND HERE.
NOT EVEN GUNTHER?
IS THAT WHY YOU'RE HERE? GUNTHER'S GOT NO RECORD, I'M ALLOWED TO ASSOCIATE --
I'M HERE BECAUSE OF A ROBBERY.
H.P.F.
ANCIENT AMULET, TAKEN FROM THE WALL SAFE OF A SENATOR.
HIS TRACKING MONITORS WERE ALL DISMANTLED, BUT SOMEONE WHO LOOKS JUST EXACTLY LIKE YOU WAS SEEN FLEEING -- OR, UM, FALLING -- FROM THE SCENE.
CARE TO COMMENT?

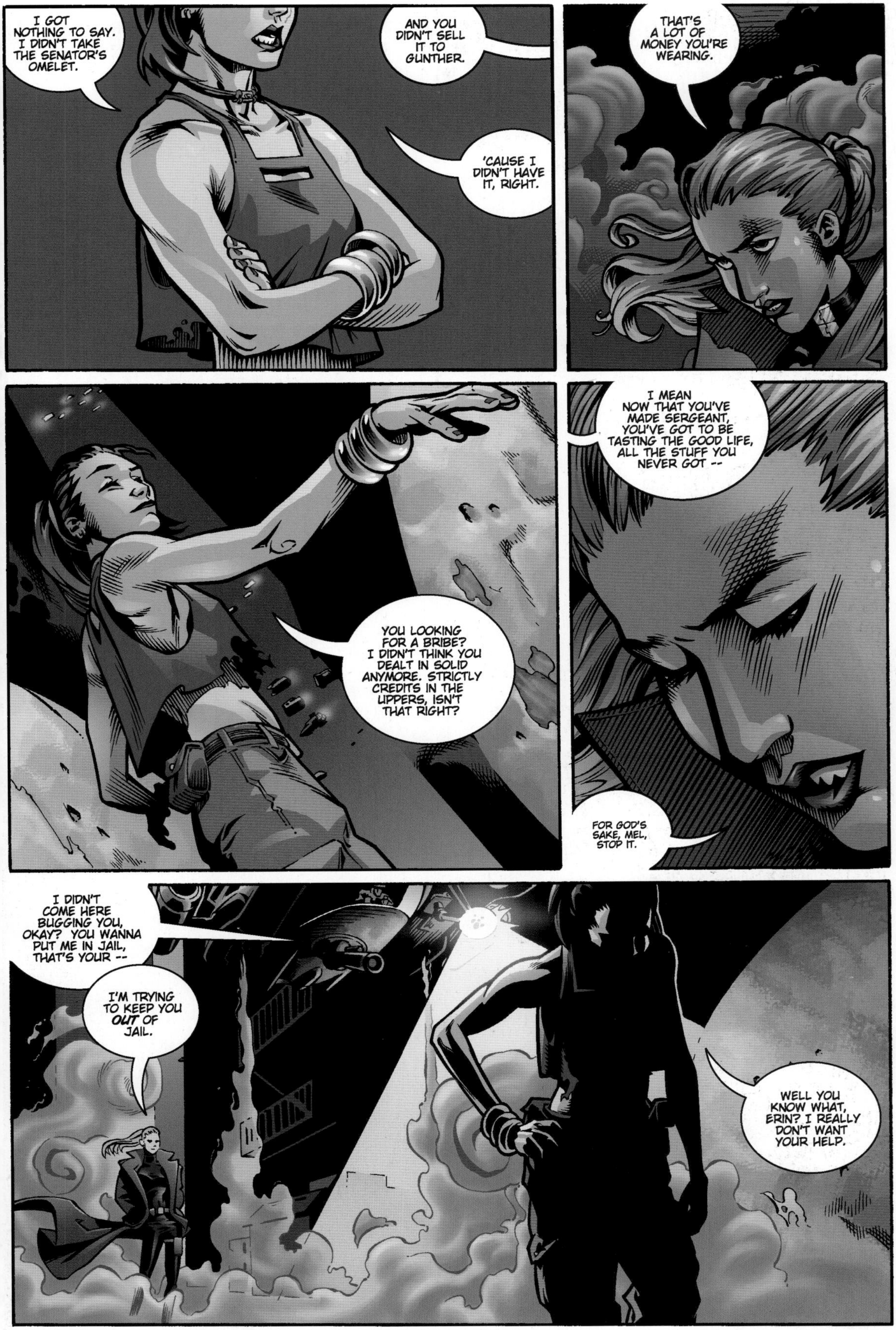
I GOT NOTHING TO SAY. I DIDN'T TAKE THE SENATOR'S OMELET.
AND YOU DIDN'T SELL IT TO GUNTHER.
'CAUSE I DIDN'T HAVE IT, RIGHT.
THAT'S A LOT OF MONEY YOU'RE WEARING.
YOU LOOKING FOR A BRIBE? I DIDN'T THINK YOU DEALT IN SOLID ANYMORE. STRICTLY CREDITS IN THE UPPERS, ISN'T THAT RIGHT?
I MEAN NOW THAT YOU'VE MADE SERGEANT, YOU'VE GOT TO BE TASTING THE GOOD LIFE, ALL THE STUFF YOU NEVER GOT --
FOR GOD'S SAKE, MEL, STOP IT.
I DIDN'T COME HERE BUGGING YOU, OKAY? YOU WANNA PUT ME IN JAIL, THAT'S YOUR --
I'M TRYING TO KEEP YOU *OUT* OF JAIL.
WELL YOU KNOW WHAT, ERIN? I REALLY DON'T WANT YOUR HELP.

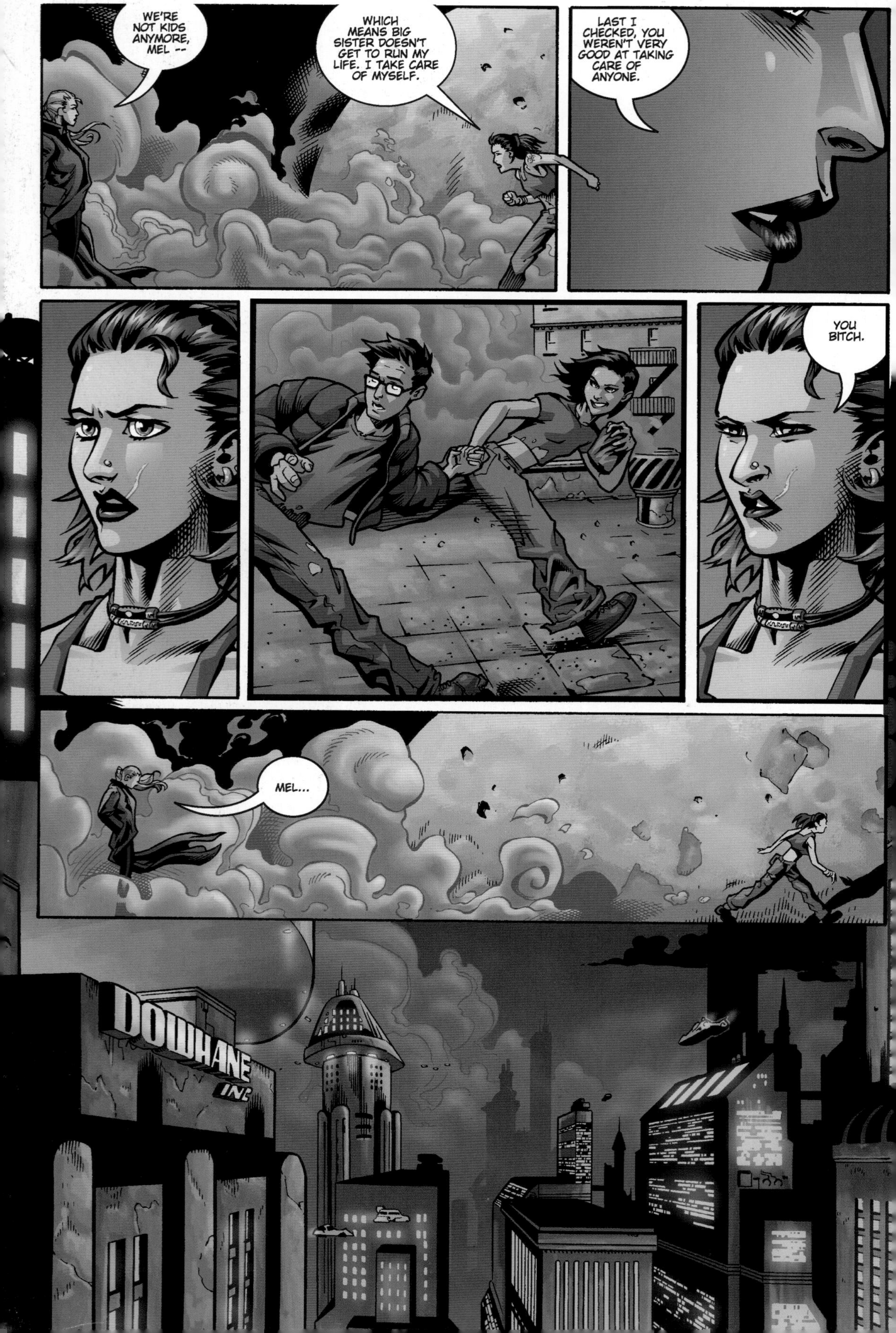
WE'RE NOT KIDS ANYMORE, MEL --
WHICH MEANS BIG SISTER DOESN'T GET TO RUN MY LIFE. I TAKE CARE OF MYSELF.
LAST I CHECKED, YOU WEREN'T VERY GOOD AT TAKING CARE OF ANYONE.
YOU BITCH.
MEL...
DOWHANE INC

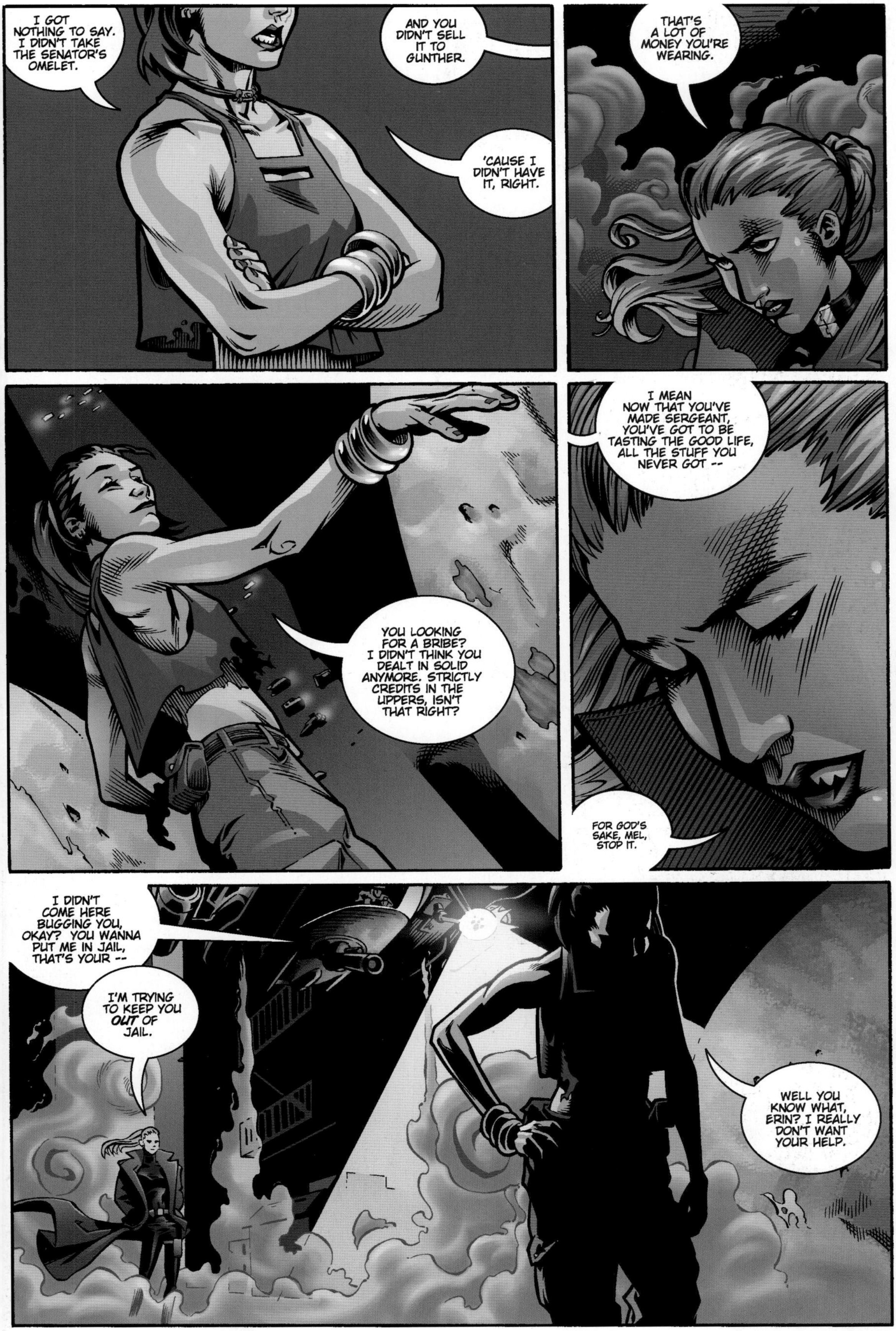
I GOT NOTHING TO SAY. I DIDN'T TAKE THE SENATOR'S OMELET.
AND YOU DIDN'T SELL IT TO GUNTHER.
'CAUSE I DIDN'T HAVE IT, RIGHT.
THAT'S A LOT OF MONEY YOU'RE WEARING.
YOU LOOKING FOR A BRIBE? I DIDN'T THINK YOU DEALT IN SOLID ANYMORE. STRICTLY CREDITS IN THE UPPERS, ISN'T THAT RIGHT?
I MEAN NOW THAT YOU'VE MADE SERGEANT, YOU'VE GOT TO BE TASTING THE GOOD LIFE, ALL THE STUFF YOU NEVER GOT --
FOR GOD'S SAKE, MEL, STOP IT.
I DIDN'T COME HERE BUGGING YOU, OKAY? YOU WANNA PUT ME IN JAIL, THAT'S YOUR --
I'M TRYING TO KEEP YOU *OUT* OF JAIL.
WELL YOU KNOW WHAT, ERIN? I REALLY DON'T WANT YOUR HELP.

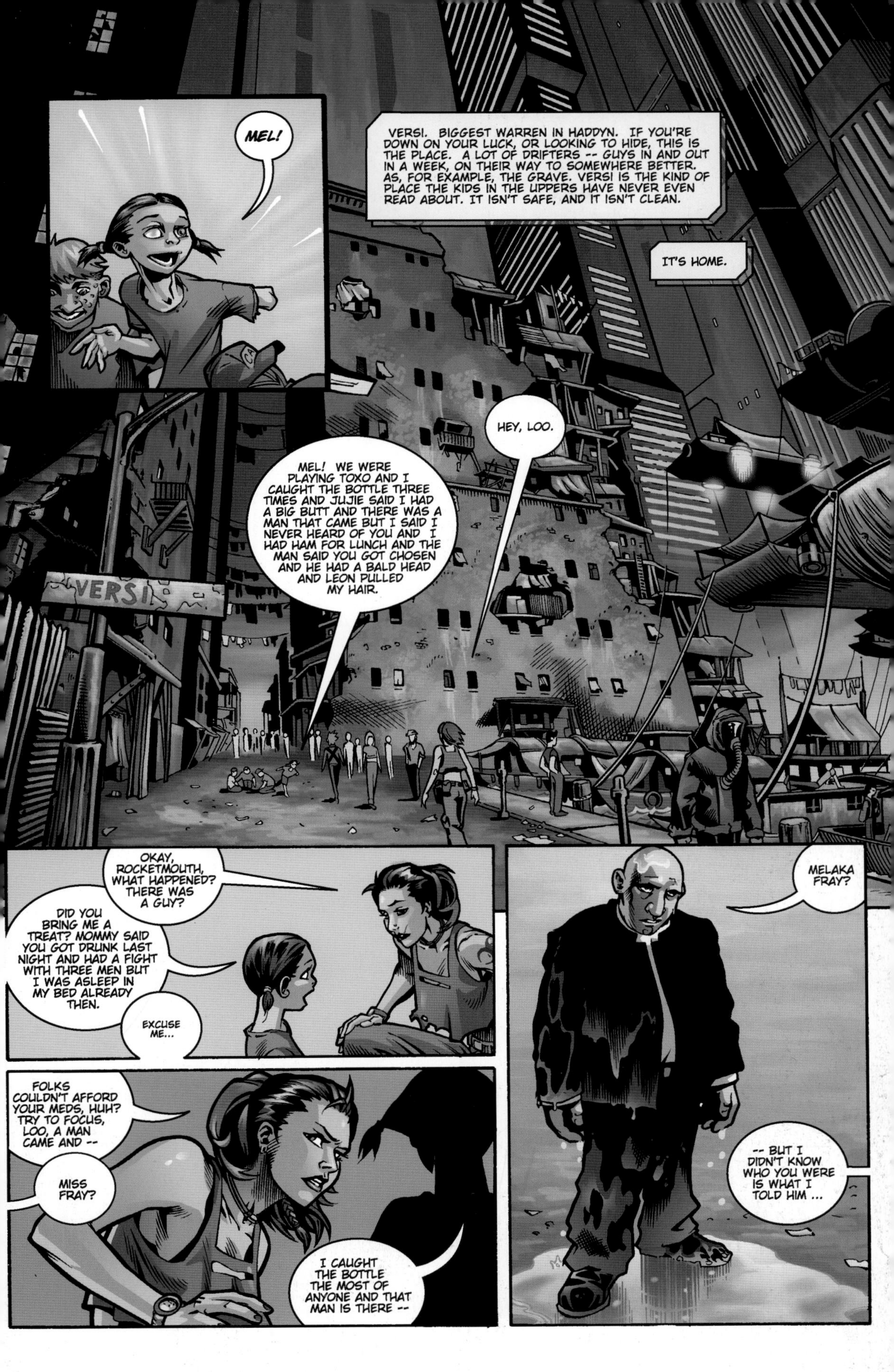
MEL!
VERSI. BIGGEST WARREN IN HADDYN. IF YOU'RE DOWN ON YOUR LUCK, OR LOOKING TO HIDE, THIS IS THE PLACE. A LOT OF DRIFTERS -- GUYS IN AND OUT IN A WEEK, ON THEIR WAY TO SOMEWHERE BETTER. AS, FOR EXAMPLE, THE GRAVE. VERSI IS THE KIND OF PLACE THE KIDS IN THE UPPERS HAVE NEVER EVEN READ ABOUT. IT ISN'T SAFE, AND IT ISN'T CLEAN.
IT'S HOME.
HEY, LOO.
MEL! WE WERE PLAYING TOXO AND I CAUGHT THE BOTTLE THREE TIMES AND JUJIE SAID I HAD A BIG BUTT AND THERE WAS A MAN THAT CAME BUT I SAID I NEVER HEARD OF YOU AND I HAD HAM FOR LUNCH AND THE MAN SAID YOU GOT CHOSEN AND HE HAD A BALD HEAD AND LEON PULLED MY HAIR.
VERSI
OKAY, ROCKETMOUTH, WHAT HAPPENED? THERE WAS A GUY?
DID YOU BRING ME A TREAT? MOMMY SAID YOU GOT DRUNK LAST NIGHT AND HAD A FIGHT WITH THREE MEN BUT I WAS ASLEEP IN MY BED ALREADY THEN.
EXCUSE ME...
MELAKA FRAY?
FOLKS COULDN'T AFFORD YOUR MEDS, HUH? TRY TO FOCUS, LOO, A MAN CAME AND --
MISS FRAY?
I CAUGHT THE BOTTLE THE MOST OF ANYONE AND THAT MAN IS THERE --
-- BUT I DIDN'T KNOW WHO YOU WERE IS WHAT I TOLD HIM ...

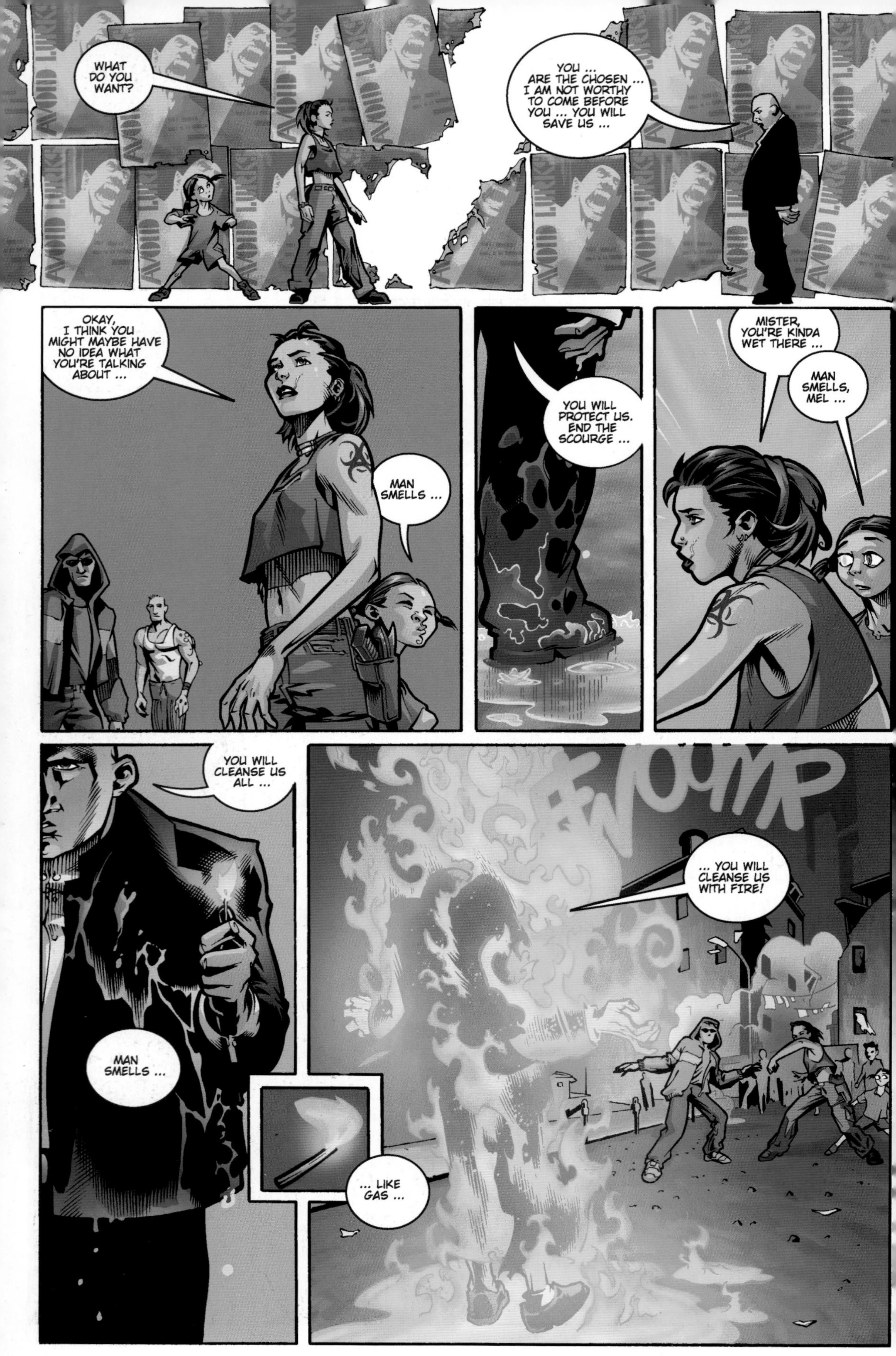

WHAT DO YOU WANT?
YOU ... ARE THE CHOSEN ... I AM NOT WORTHY TO COME BEFORE YOU ... YOU WILL SAVE US ...
OKAY, I THINK YOU MIGHT MAYBE HAVE NO IDEA WHAT YOU'RE TALKING ABOUT ...
MAN SMELLS ...
YOU WILL PROTECT US. END THE SCOURGE ...
MISTER, YOU'RE KINDA WET THERE ...
MAN SMELLS, MEL ...
YOU WILL CLEANSE US ALL ...
MAN SMELLS ...
... LIKE GAS ...
FWOOMP
... YOU WILL CLEANSE US WITH FIRE!

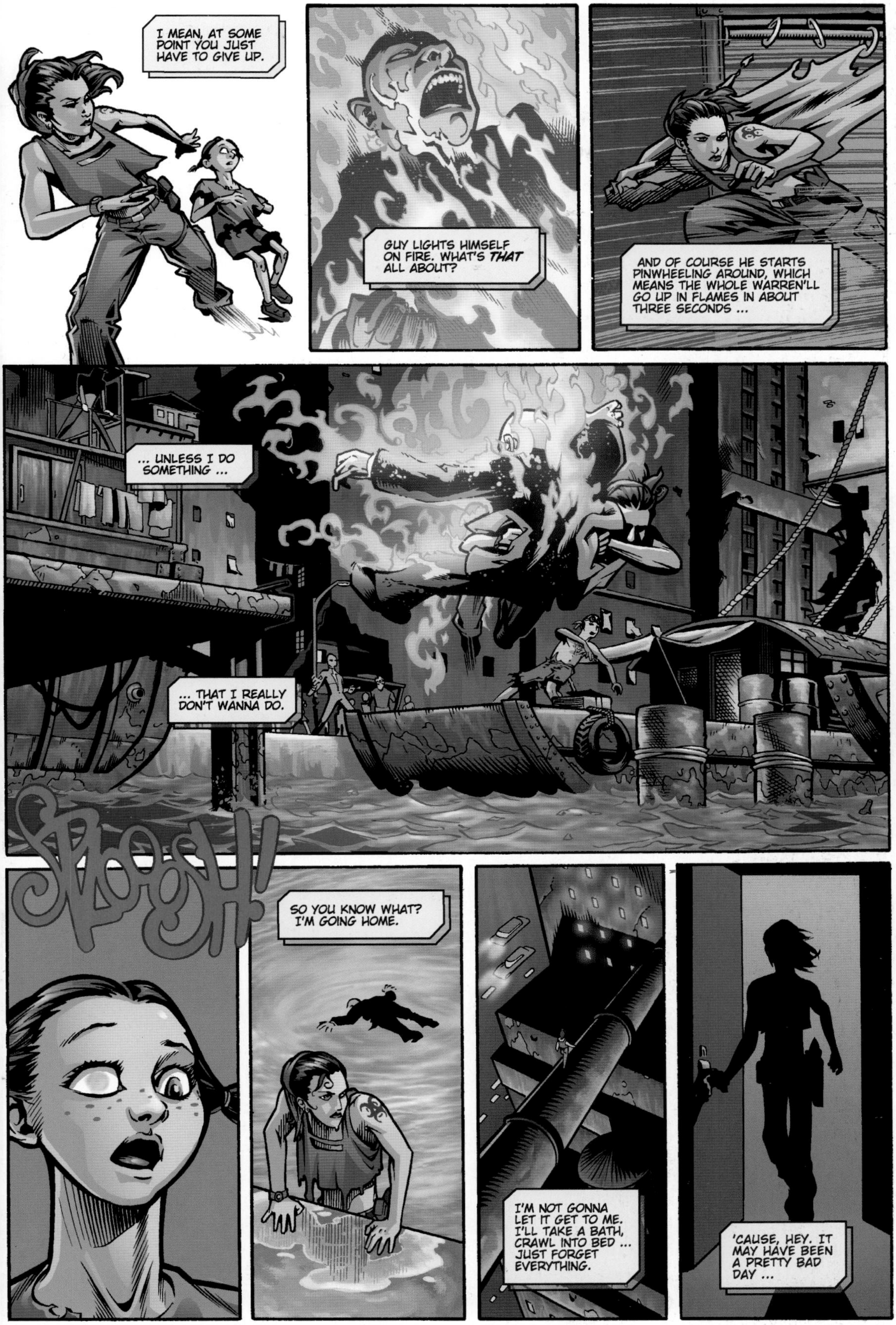
I MEAN, AT SOME POINT YOU JUST HAVE TO GIVE UP.
GUY LIGHTS HIMSELF ON FIRE. WHAT'S *THAT* ALL ABOUT?
AND OF COURSE HE STARTS PINWHEELING AROUND, WHICH MEANS THE WHOLE WARREN'LL GO UP IN FLAMES IN ABOUT THREE SECONDS ...
... UNLESS I DO SOMETHING ...
... THAT I REALLY DON'T WANNA DO.
SPLOOSH!
SO YOU KNOW WHAT? I'M GOING HOME.
I'M NOT GONNA LET IT GET TO ME. I'LL TAKE A BATH, CRAWL INTO BED ... JUST FORGET EVERYTHING.
'CAUSE, HEY. IT MAY HAVE BEEN A PRETTY BAD DAY ...

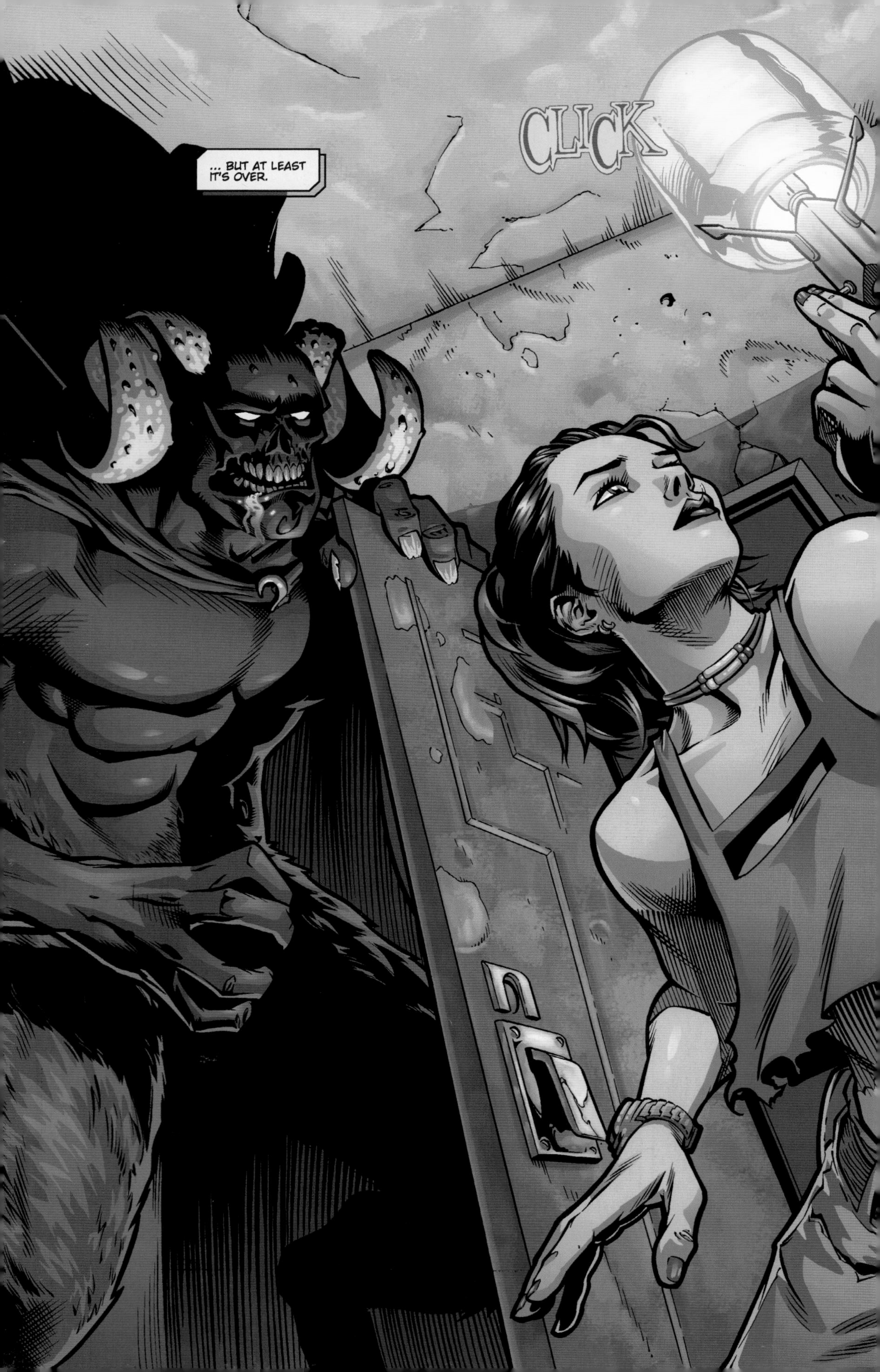
... BUT AT LEAST IT'S OVER.
CLICK

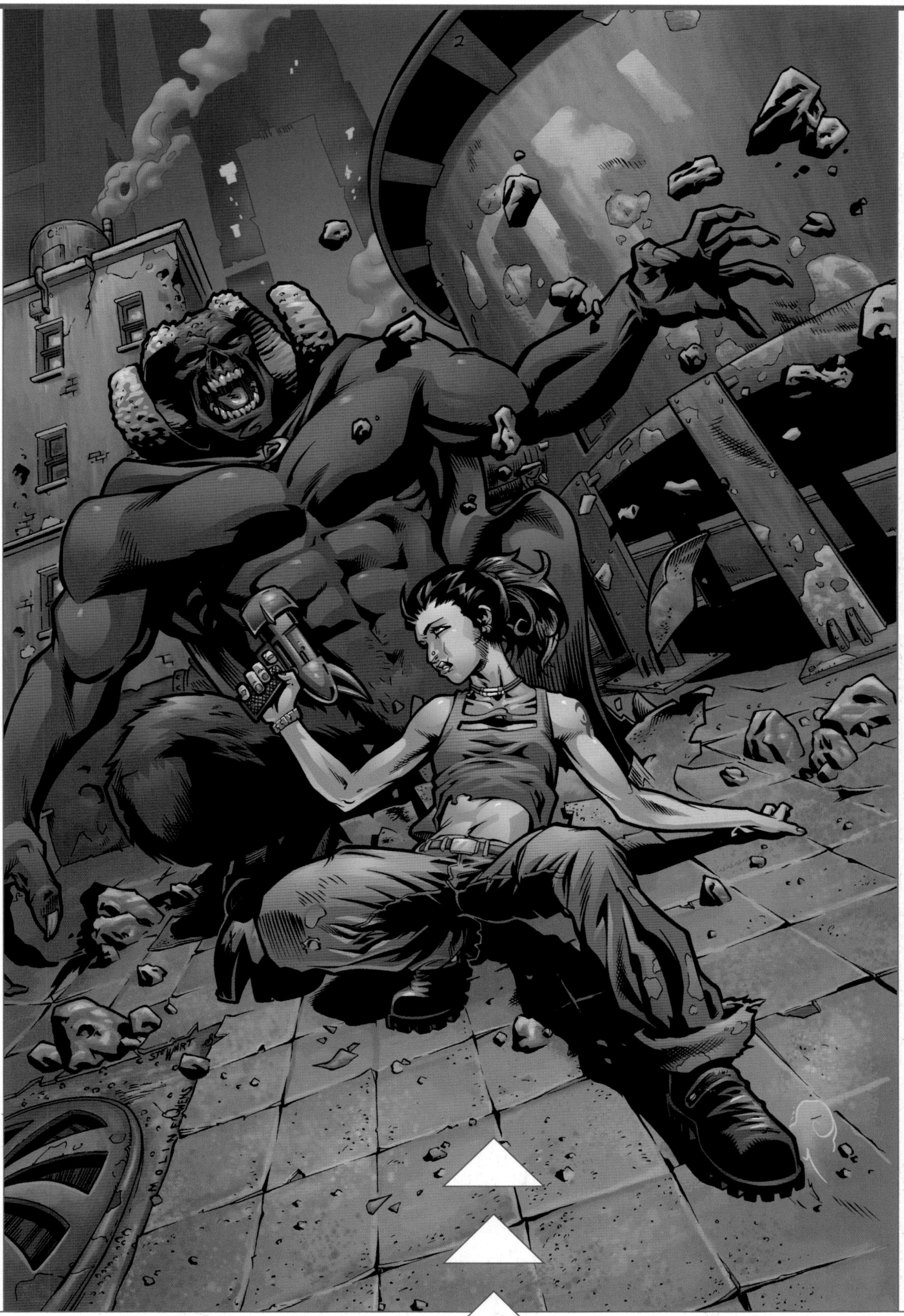

"In your dreams, you're someone else.
A slave. A princess. A girl
in school in a sunlit city."

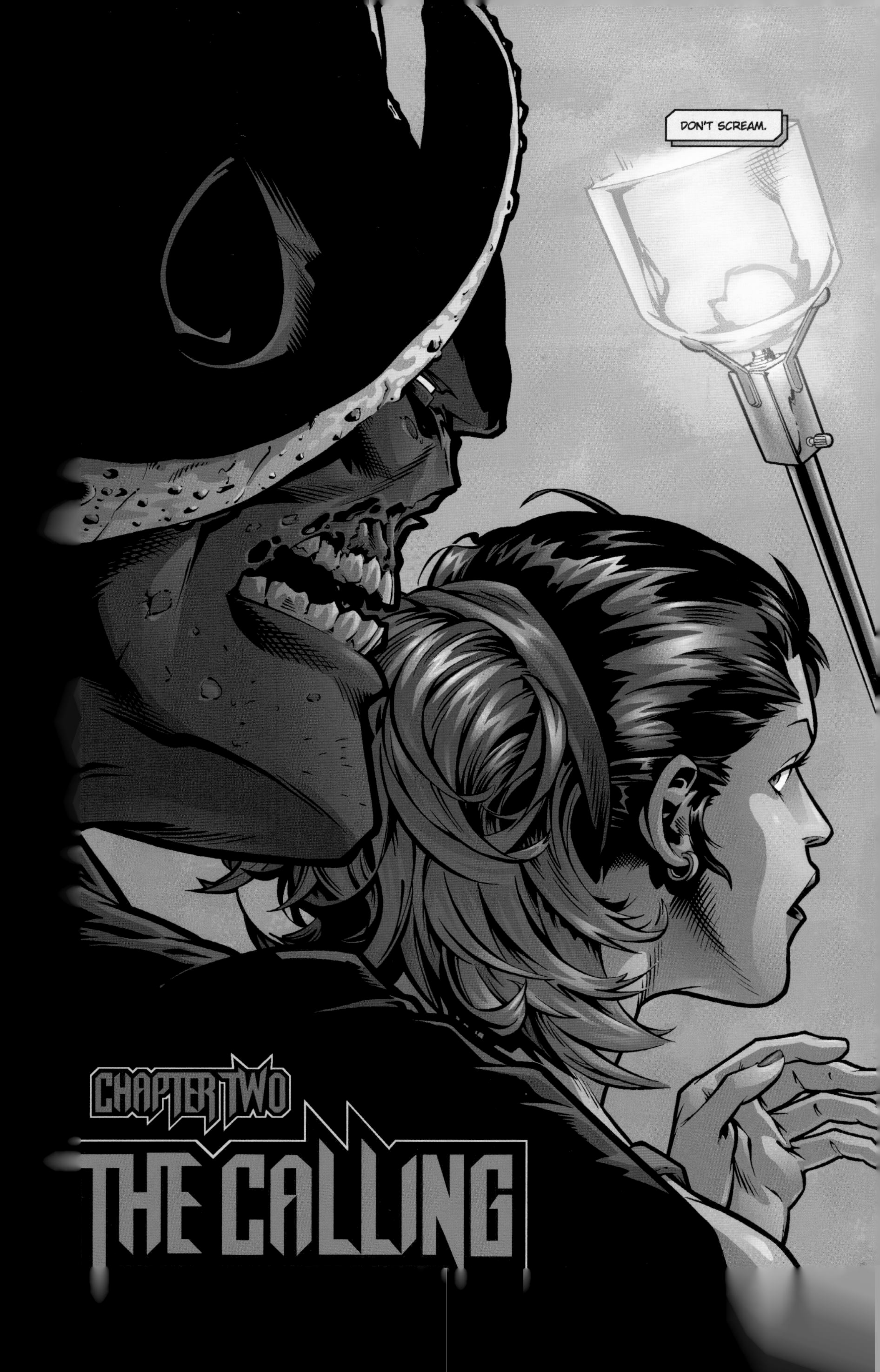
DON'T SCREAM.
CHAPTER TWO
THE CALLING

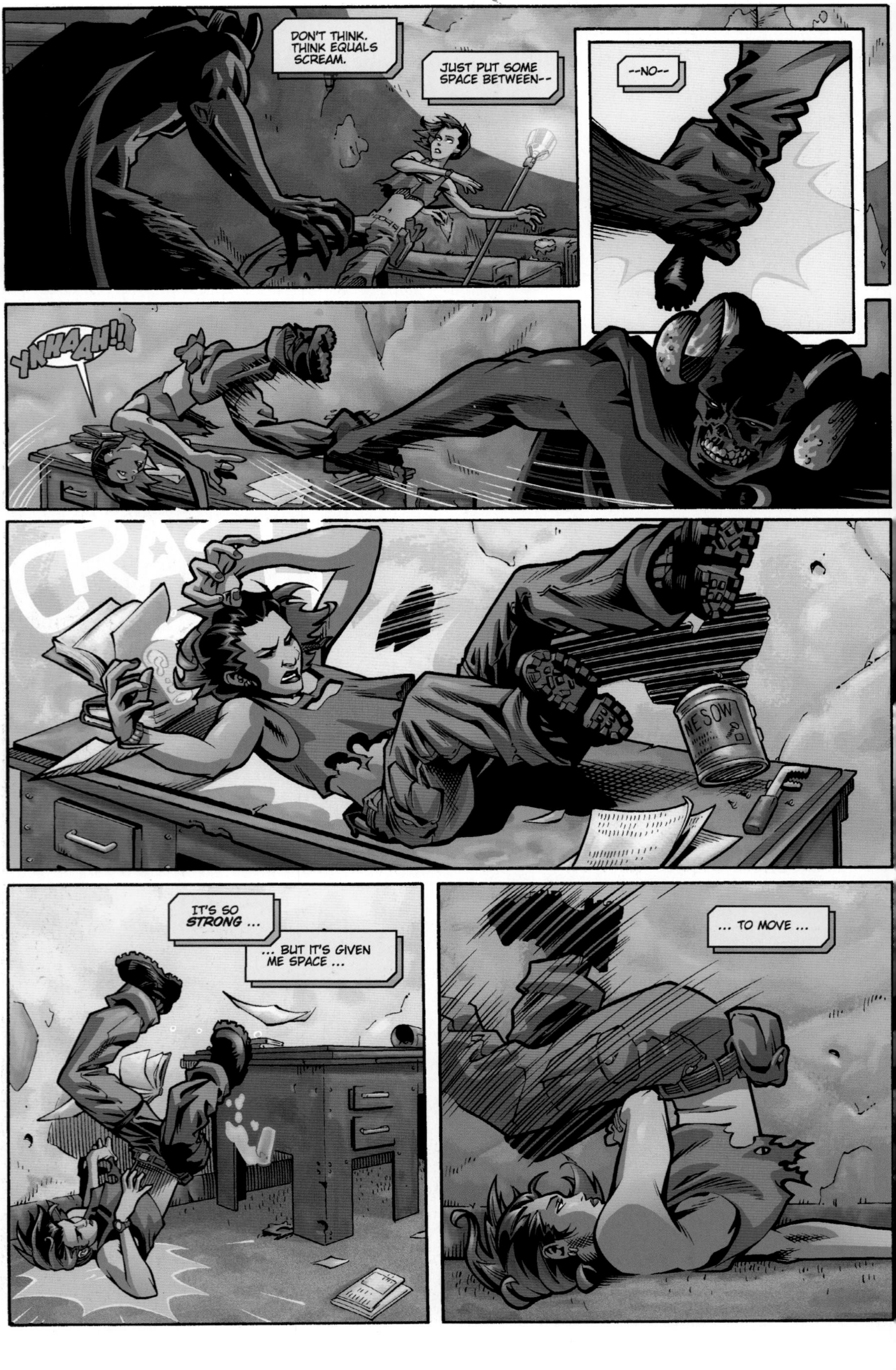
DON'T THINK. THINK EQUALS SCREAM.
JUST PUT SOME SPACE BETWEEN--
--NO--
YNHAAH!!
CRASH
NESOW
IT'S SO STRONG ...
... BUT IT'S GIVEN ME SPACE ...
... TO MOVE ...

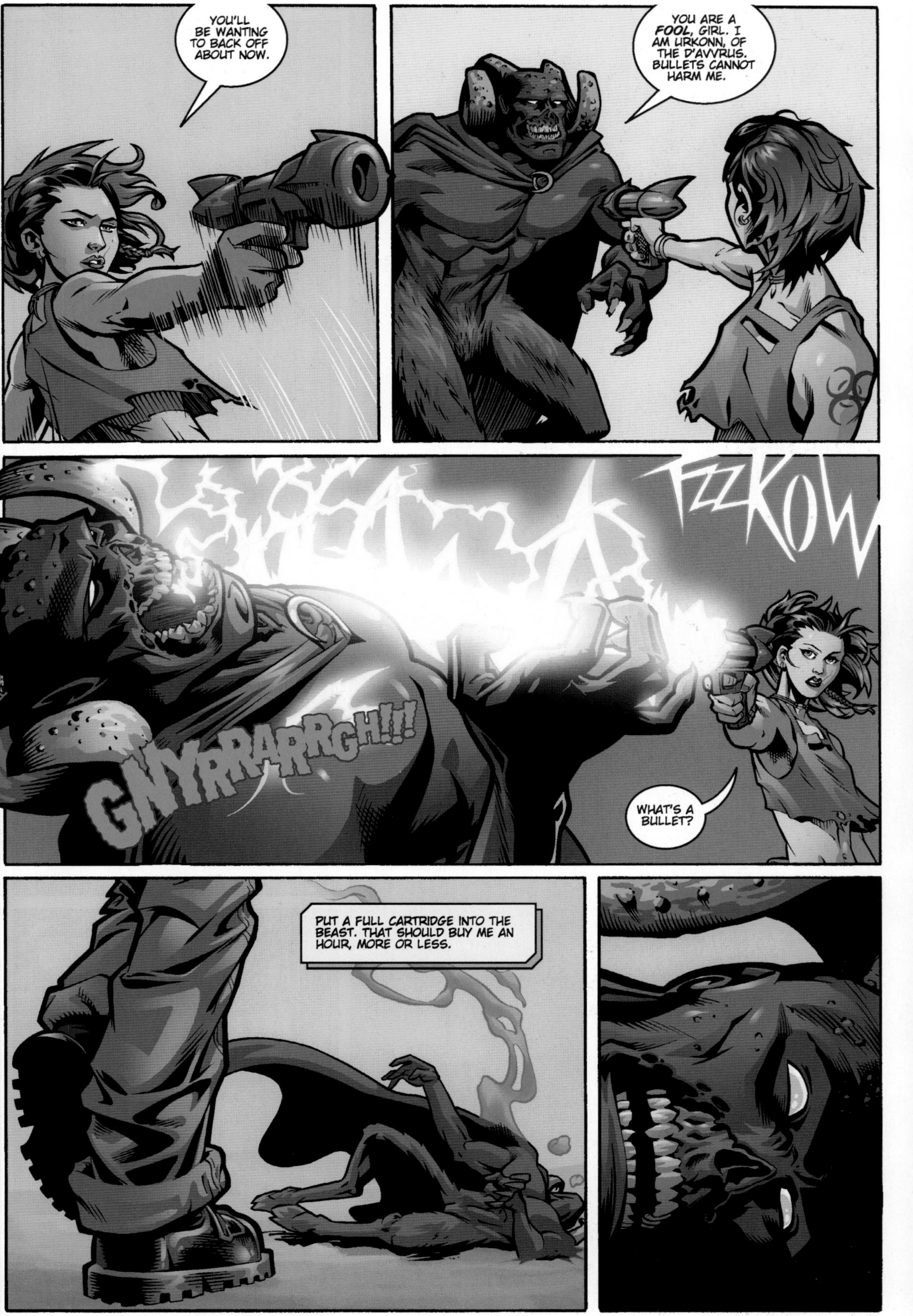
YOU'LL BE WANTING TO BACK OFF ABOUT NOW.
YOU ARE A FOOL, GIRL. I AM URKONN, OF THE D'AVVRUS. BULLETS CANNOT HARM ME.
FZZKOW
GNYRRARRGH!!!
WHAT'S A BULLET?
PUT A FULL CARTRIDGE INTO THE BEAST. THAT SHOULD BUY ME AN HOUR, MORE OR LESS.

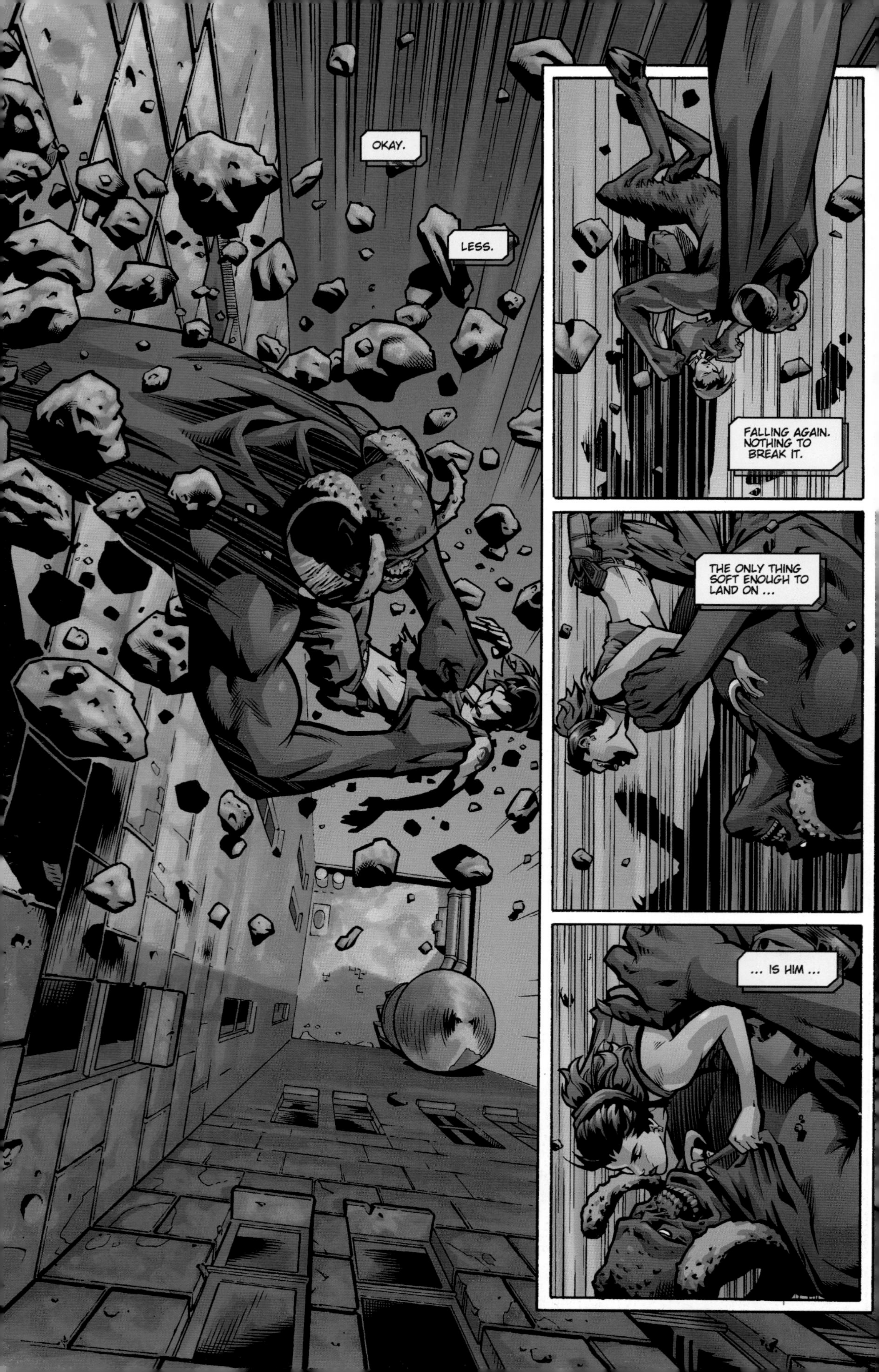
OKAY.
LESS.
FALLING AGAIN. NOTHING TO BREAK IT.
THE ONLY THING SOFT ENOUGH TO LAND ON ...
... IS HIM ...

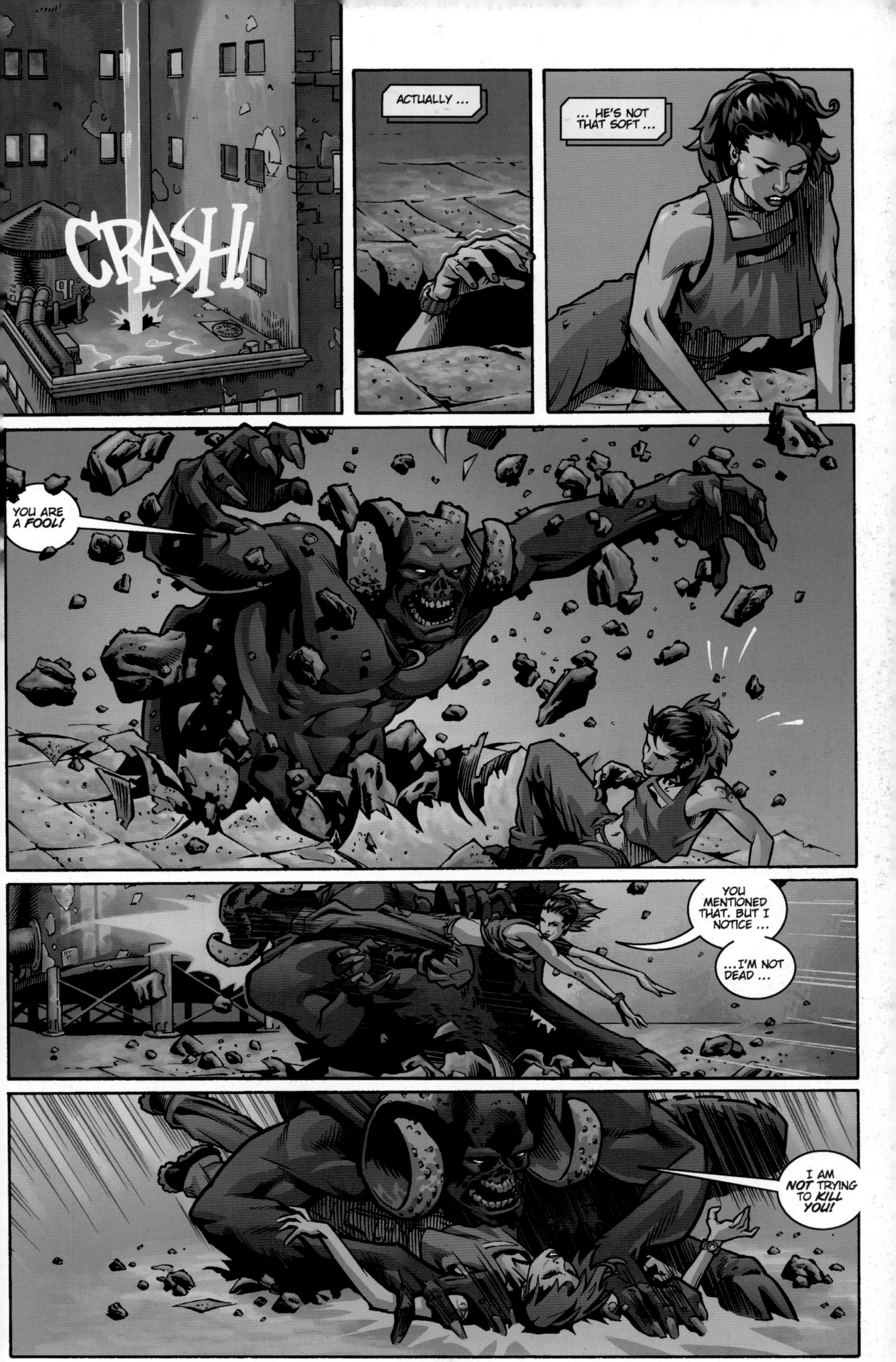
CRASH!!
ACTUALLY ...
... HE'S NOT THAT SOFT ...
YOU ARE A *FOOL!*
YOU MENTIONED THAT. BUT I NOTICE ...
...I'M NOT DEAD ...
I AM *NOT* TRYING TO *KILL YOU!*

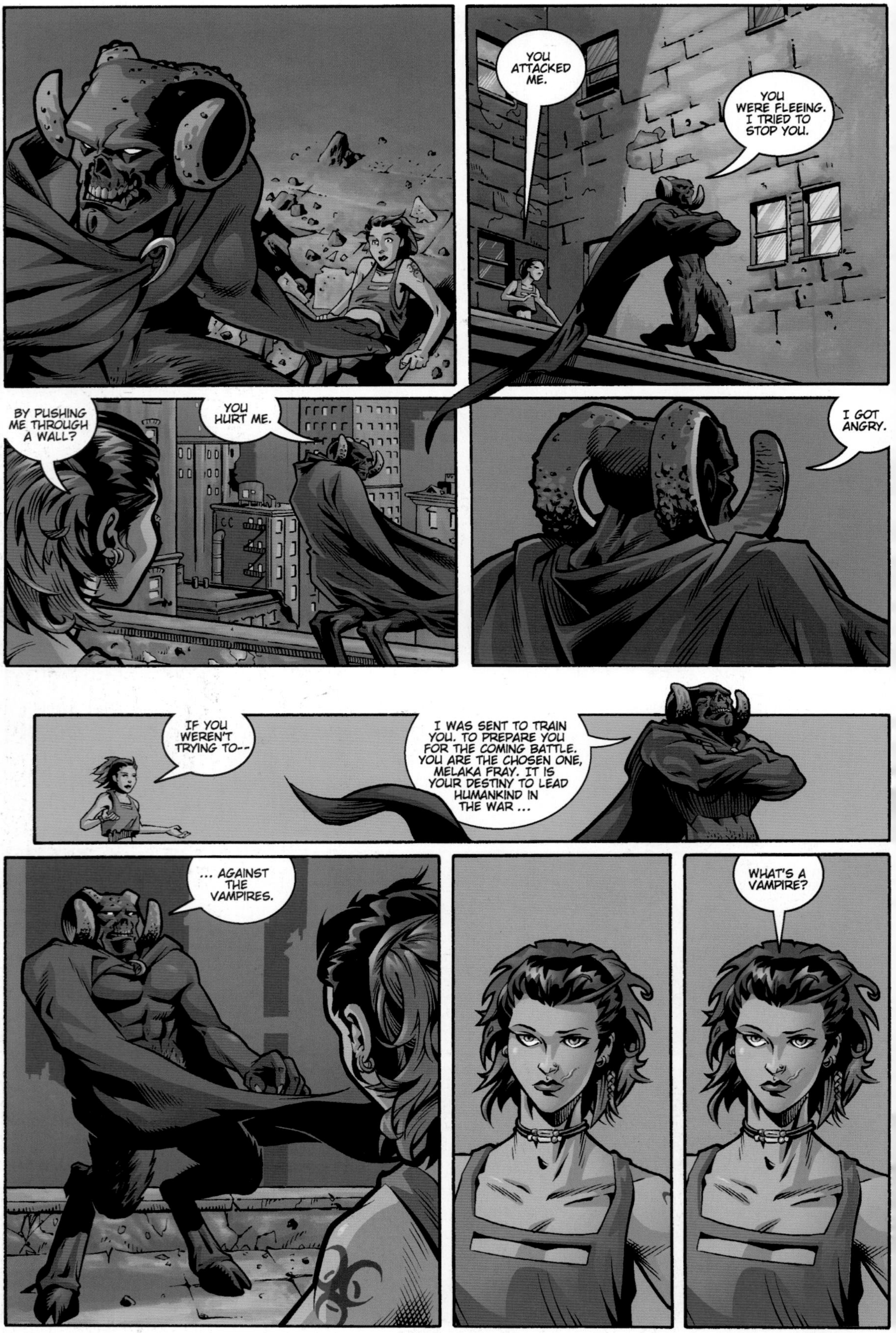
YOU ATTACKED ME.
YOU WERE FLEEING. I TRIED TO STOP YOU.
BY PUSHING ME THROUGH A WALL?
YOU HURT ME.
I GOT ANGRY.
IF YOU WEREN'T TRYING TO--
I WAS SENT TO TRAIN YOU. TO PREPARE YOU FOR THE COMING BATTLE. YOU ARE THE CHOSEN ONE, MELAKA FRAY. IT IS YOUR DESTINY TO LEAD HUMANKIND IN THE WAR ...
... AGAINST THE VAMPIRES.
WHAT'S A VAMPIRE?

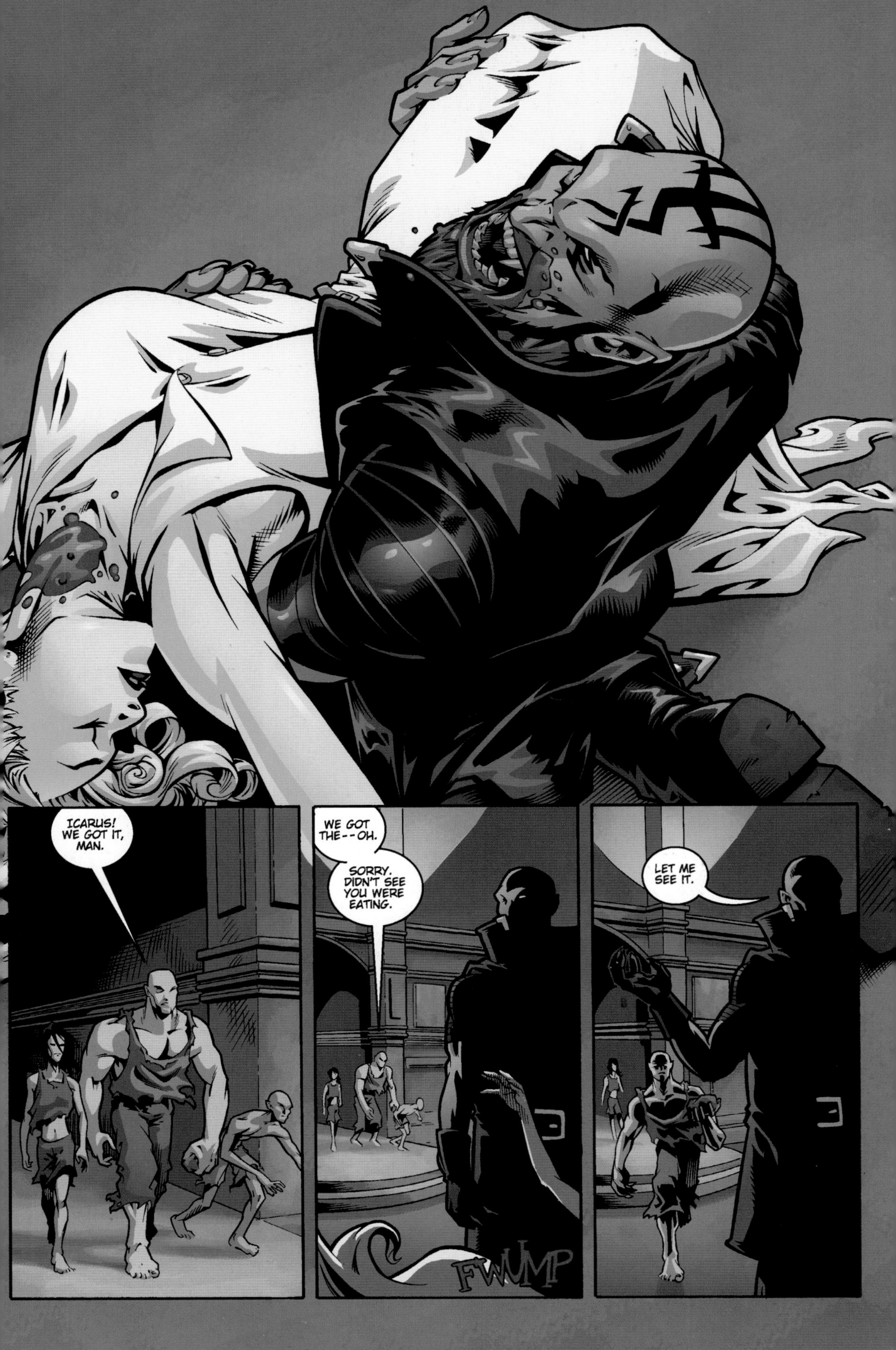
ICARUS! WE GOT IT, MAN.
WE GOT THE--OH.
SORRY. DIDN'T SEE YOU WERE EATING.
FWUMP
LET ME SEE IT.

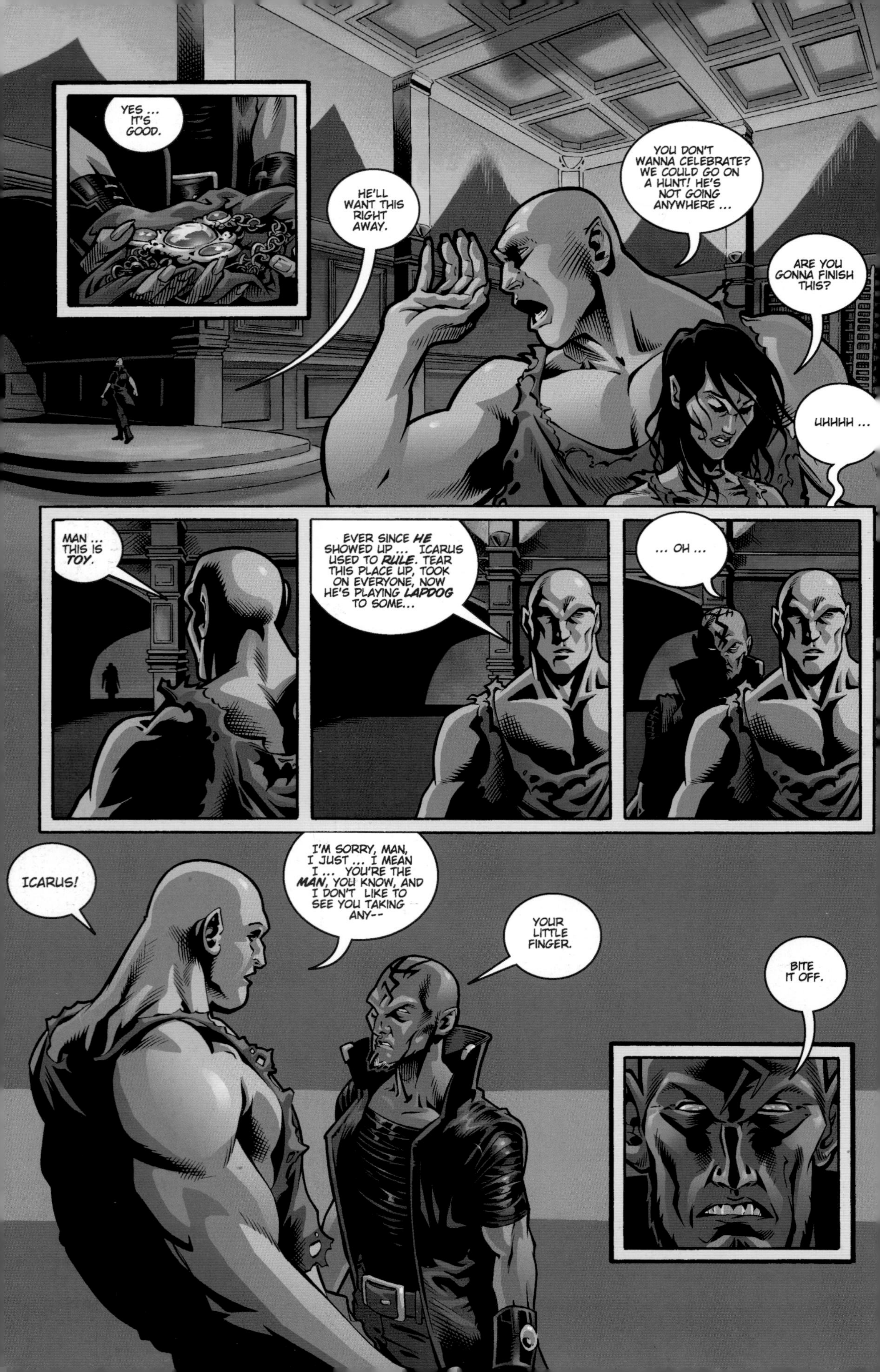
YES ... IT'S GOOD.
HE'LL WANT THIS RIGHT AWAY.
YOU DON'T WANNA CELEBRATE? WE COULD GO ON A HUNT! HE'S NOT GOING ANYWHERE ...
ARE YOU GONNA FINISH THIS?
UHHHH ...
MAN ... THIS IS TOY.
EVER SINCE HE SHOWED UP ... ICARUS USED TO RULE. TEAR THIS PLACE UP, TOOK ON EVERYONE, NOW HE'S PLAYING LAPDOG TO SOME...
... OH ...
ICARUS!
I'M SORRY, MAN, I JUST ... I MEAN I ... YOU'RE THE MAN, YOU KNOW, AND I DON'T LIKE TO SEE YOU TAKING ANY--
YOUR LITTLE FINGER.
BITE IT OFF.

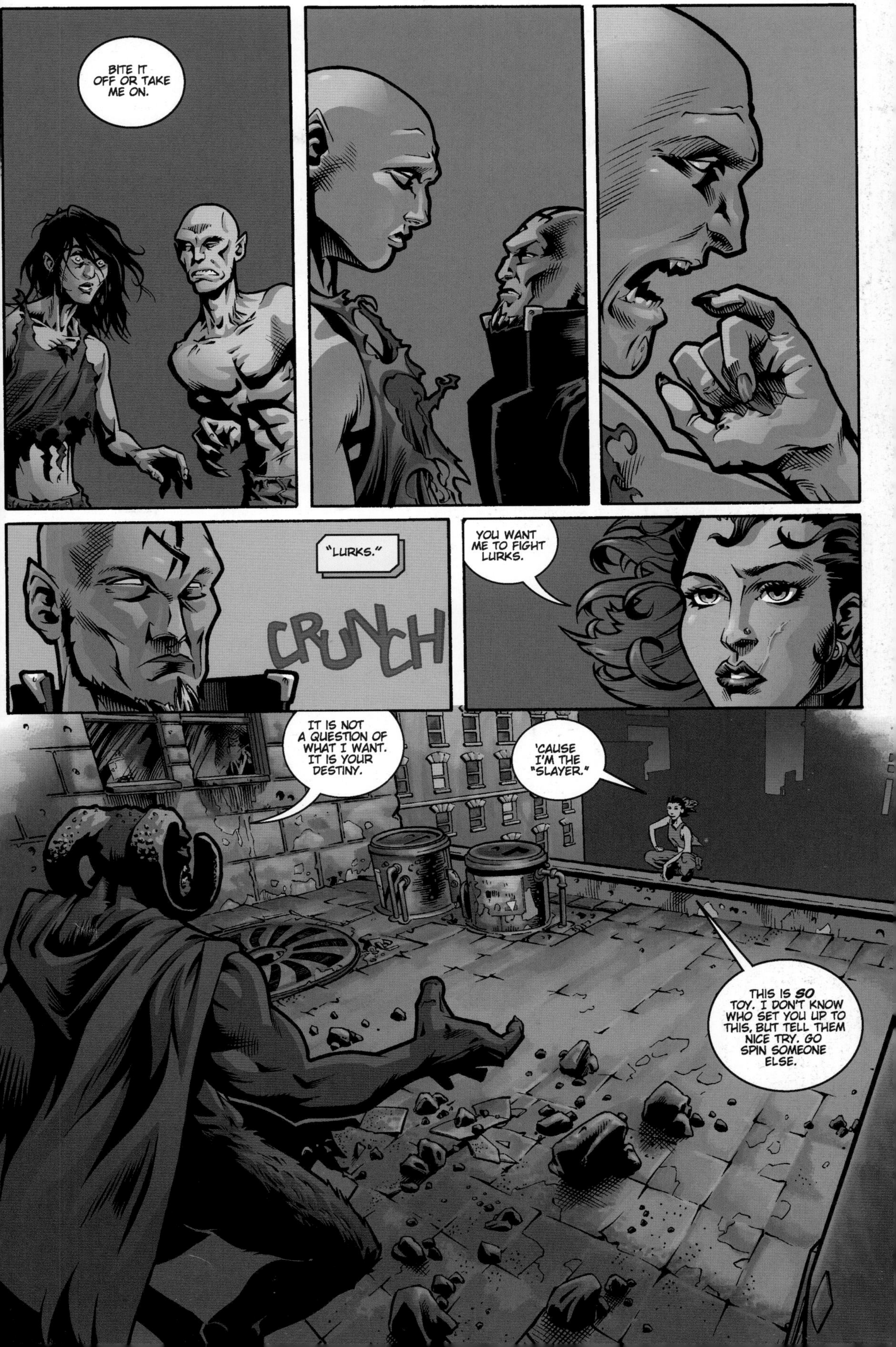
BITE IT OFF OR TAKE ME ON.
"LURKS."
CRUNCH
YOU WANT ME TO FIGHT LURKS.
IT IS NOT A QUESTION OF WHAT I WANT. IT IS YOUR DESTINY.
'CAUSE I'M THE "SLAYER."
THIS IS SO TOY. I DON'T KNOW WHO SET YOU UP TO THIS, BUT TELL THEM NICE TRY. GO SPIN SOMEONE ELSE.

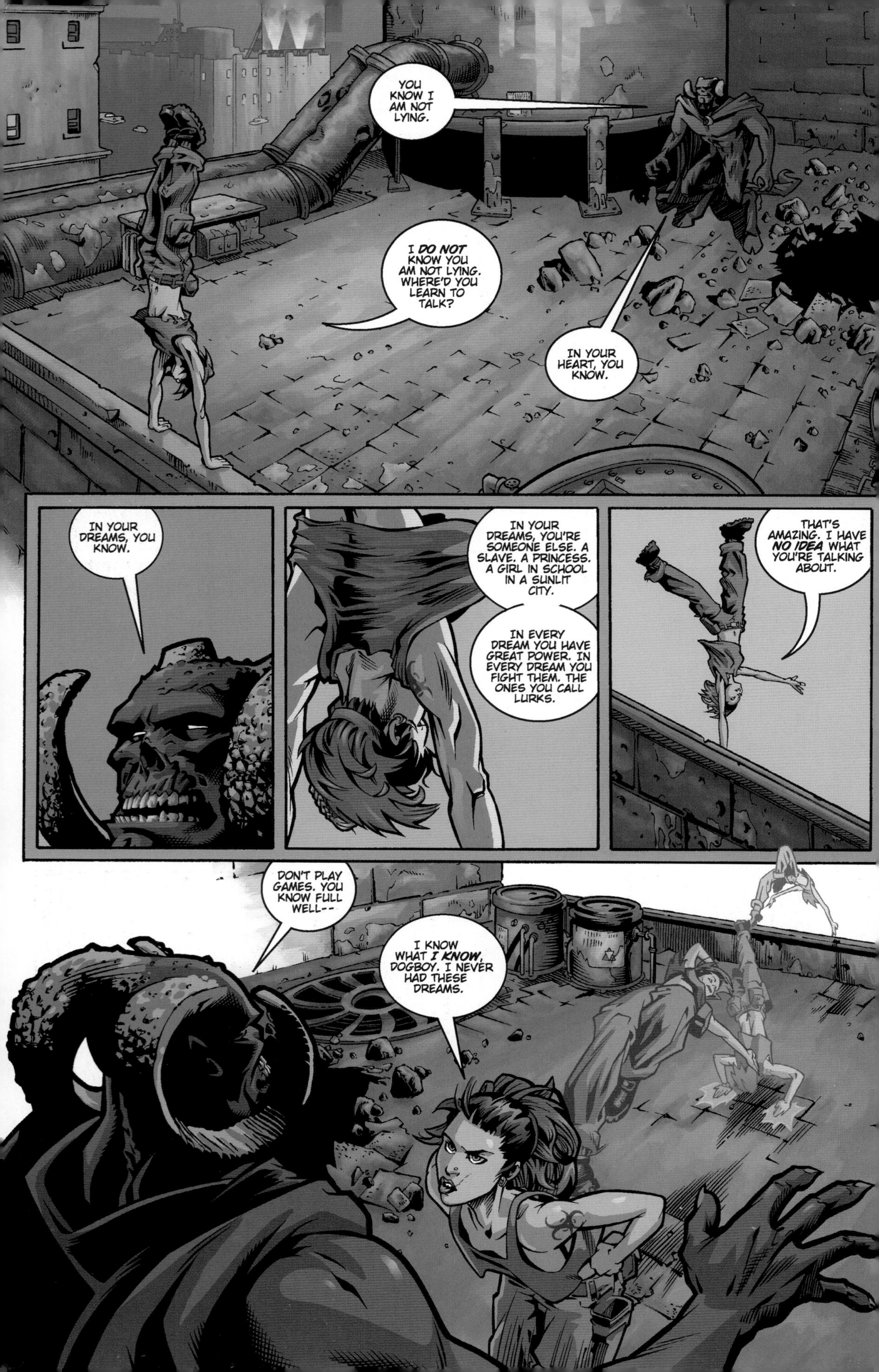

YOU KNOW I AM NOT LYING.
I DO NOT KNOW YOU AM NOT LYING. WHERE'D YOU LEARN TO TALK?
IN YOUR HEART, YOU KNOW.
IN YOUR DREAMS, YOU KNOW.
IN YOUR DREAMS, YOU'RE SOMEONE ELSE. A SLAVE. A PRINCESS. A GIRL IN SCHOOL IN A SUNLIT CITY.
IN EVERY DREAM YOU HAVE GREAT POWER. IN EVERY DREAM YOU FIGHT THEM. THE ONES YOU CALL LURKS.
THAT'S AMAZING. I HAVE NO IDEA WHAT YOU'RE TALKING ABOUT.
DON'T PLAY GAMES. YOU KNOW FULL WELL--
I KNOW WHAT I KNOW, DOGBOY. I NEVER HAD THESE DREAMS.

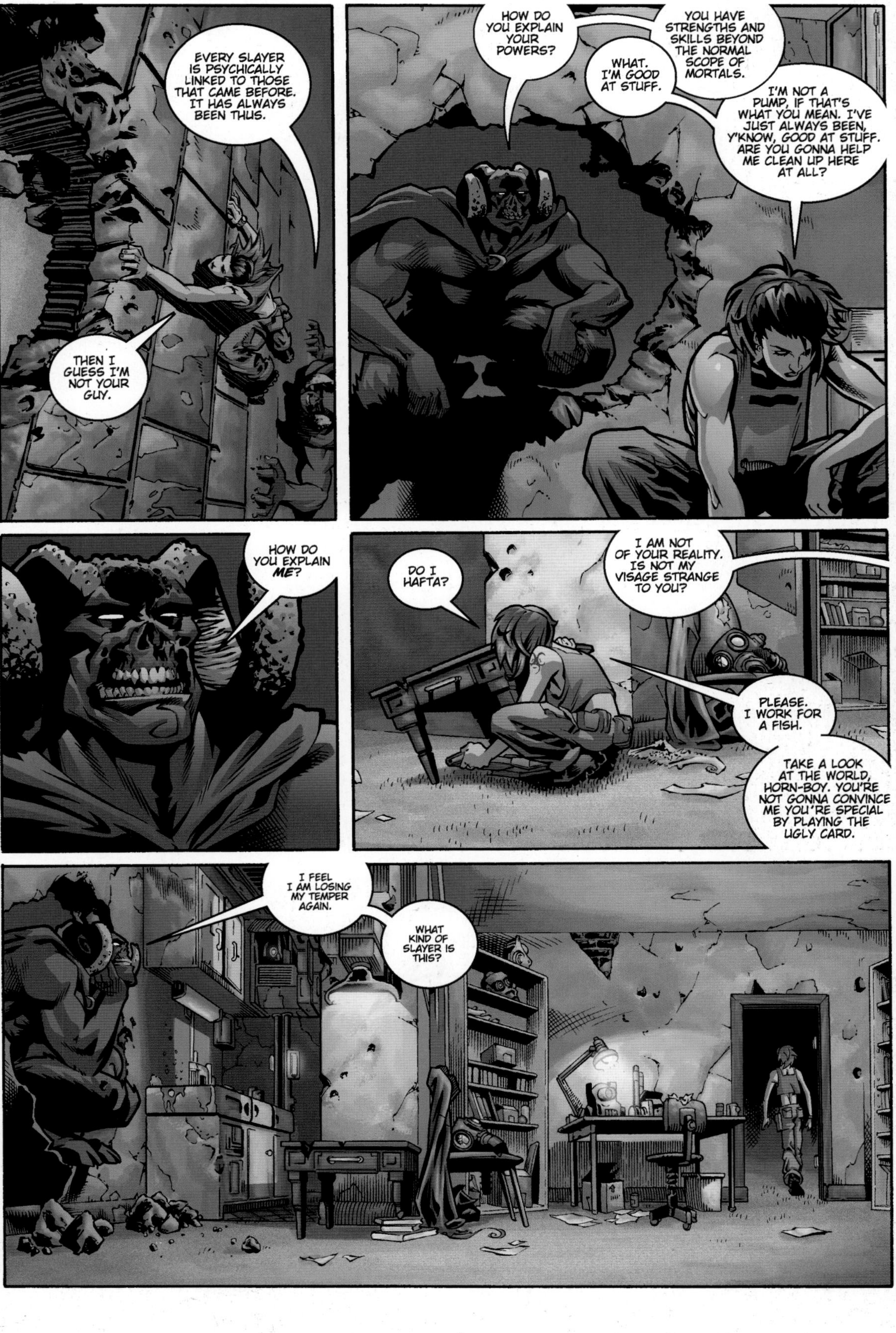

EVERY SLAYER IS PSYCHICALLY LINKED TO THOSE THAT CAME BEFORE. IT HAS ALWAYS BEEN THUS.
THEN I GUESS I'M NOT YOUR GUY.
HOW DO YOU EXPLAIN YOUR POWERS?
WHAT. I'M GOOD AT STUFF.
YOU HAVE STRENGTHS AND SKILLS BEYOND THE NORMAL SCOPE OF MORTALS.
I'M NOT A PUMP, IF THAT'S WHAT YOU MEAN. I'VE JUST ALWAYS BEEN, Y'KNOW, GOOD AT STUFF. ARE YOU GONNA HELP ME CLEAN UP HERE AT ALL?
HOW DO YOU EXPLAIN ME?
DO I HAFTA?
I AM NOT OF YOUR REALITY. IS NOT MY VISAGE STRANGE TO YOU?
PLEASE. I WORK FOR A FISH.
TAKE A LOOK AT THE WORLD, HORN-BOY. YOU'RE NOT GONNA CONVINCE ME YOU'RE SPECIAL BY PLAYING THE UGLY CARD.
I FEEL I AM LOSING MY TEMPER AGAIN.
WHAT KIND OF SLAYER IS THIS?

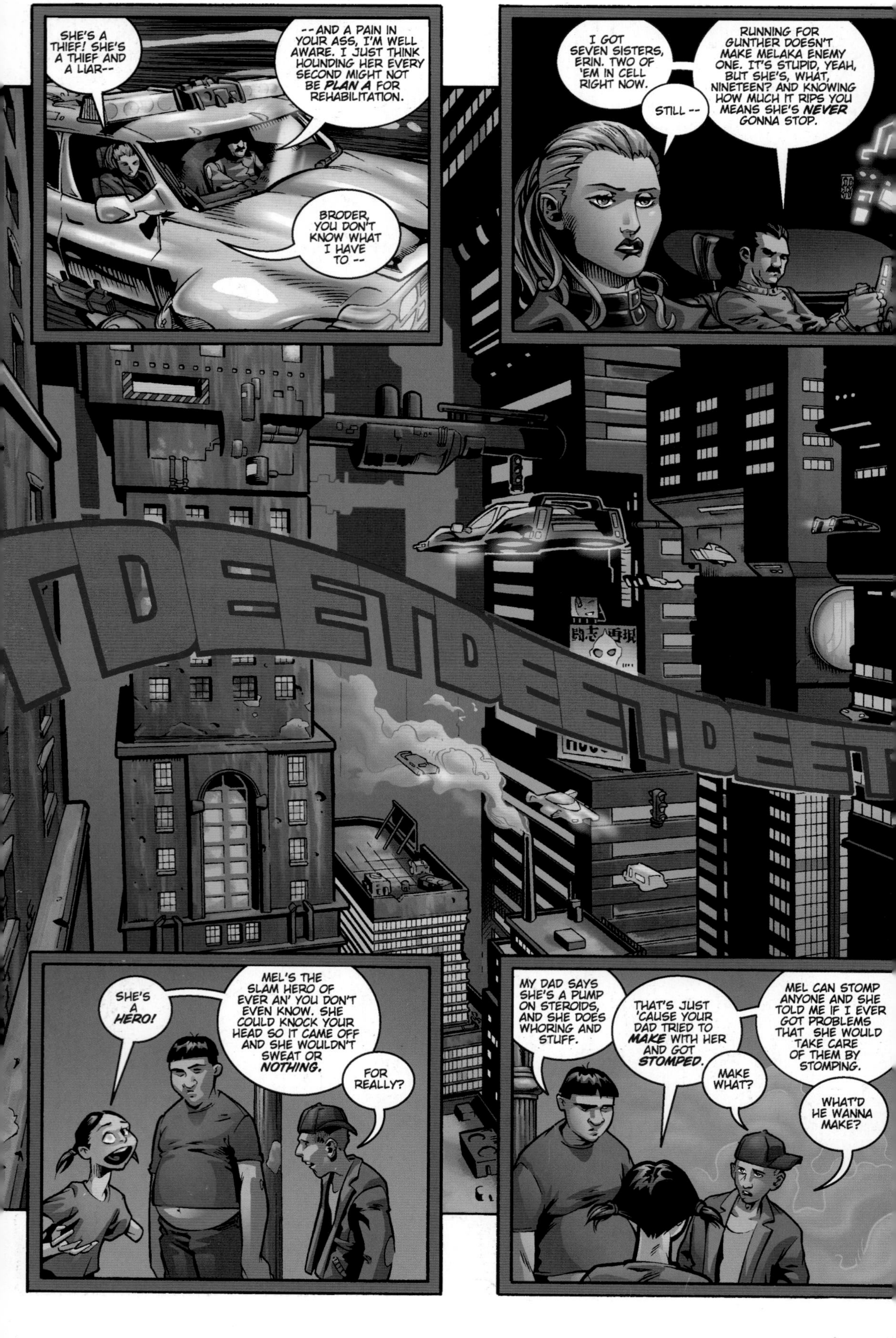
SHE'S A THIEF! SHE'S A THIEF AND A LIAR--
--AND A PAIN IN YOUR ASS, I'M WELL AWARE. I JUST THINK HOUNDING HER EVERY SECOND MIGHT NOT BE PLAN A FOR REHABILITATION.
BRODER, YOU DON'T KNOW WHAT I HAVE TO --
I GOT SEVEN SISTERS, ERIN. TWO OF 'EM IN CELL RIGHT NOW.
STILL --
RUNNING FOR GUNTHER DOESN'T MAKE MELAKA ENEMY ONE. IT'S STUPID, YEAH, BUT SHE'S, WHAT, NINETEEN? AND KNOWING HOW MUCH IT RIPS YOU MEANS SHE'S NEVER GONNA STOP.
DEETDEETDEETDEET
SHE'S A HERO!
MEL'S THE SLAM HERO OF EVER AN' YOU DON'T EVEN KNOW. SHE COULD KNOCK YOUR HEAD SO IT CAME OFF AND SHE WOULDN'T SWEAT OR NOTHING.
FOR REALLY?
MY DAD SAYS SHE'S A PUMP ON STEROIDS, AND SHE DOES WHORING AND STUFF.
THAT'S JUST 'CAUSE YOUR DAD TRIED TO MAKE WITH HER AND GOT STOMPED.
MAKE WHAT?
MEL CAN STOMP ANYONE AND SHE TOLD ME IF I EVER GOT PROBLEMS THAT SHE WOULD TAKE CARE OF THEM BY STOMPING.
WHAT'D HE WANNA MAKE?

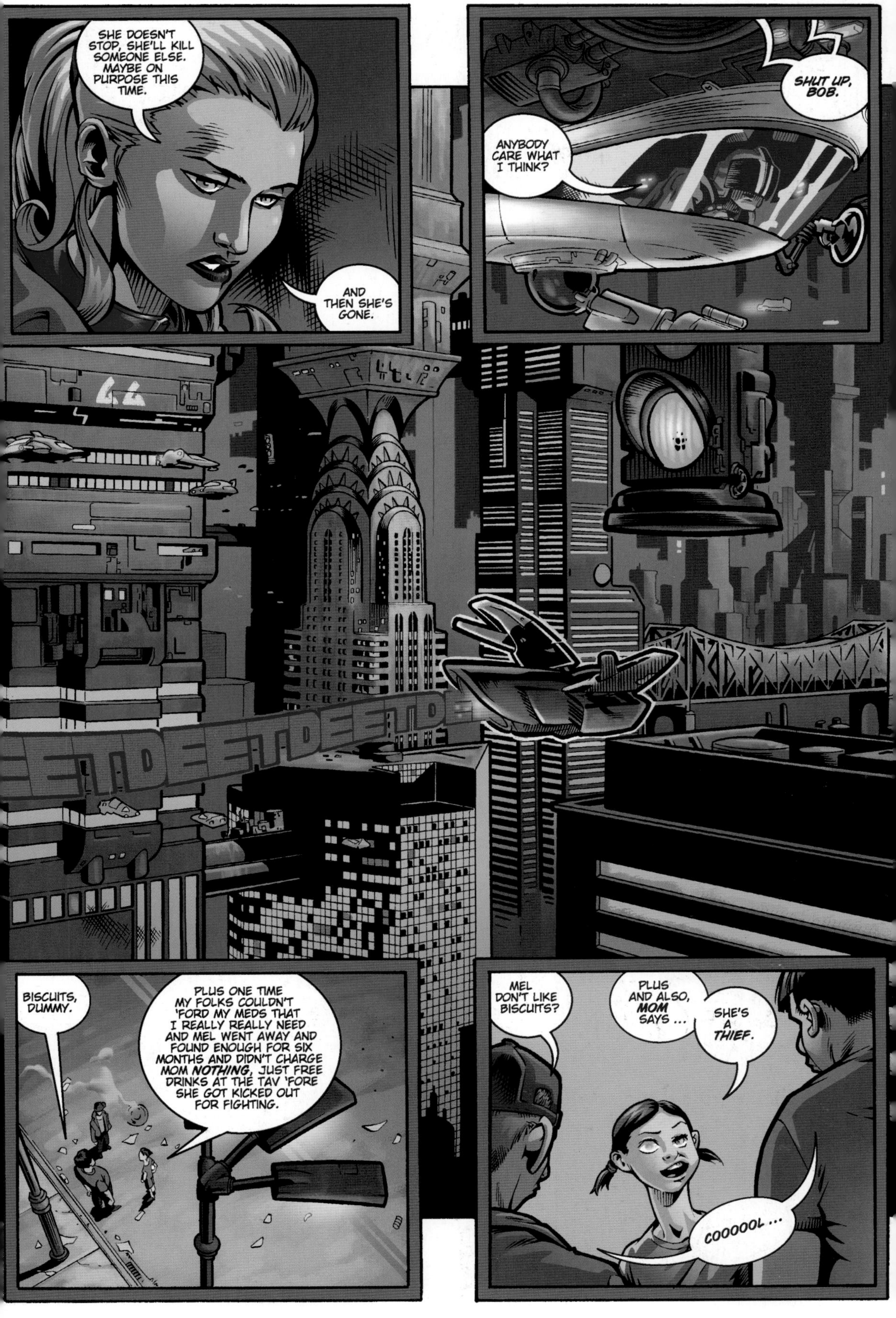
SHE DOESN'T STOP, SHE'LL KILL SOMEONE ELSE. MAYBE ON PURPOSE THIS TIME.
AND THEN SHE'S GONE.
SHUT UP, BOB.
ANYBODY CARE WHAT I THINK?
DEETDEETDEETDEE
BISCUITS, DUMMY.
PLUS ONE TIME MY FOLKS COULDN'T 'FORD MY MEDS THAT I REALLY REALLY NEED AND MEL WENT AWAY AND FOUND ENOUGH FOR SIX MONTHS AND DIDN'T CHARGE MOM NOTHING, JUST FREE DRINKS AT THE TAV 'FORE SHE GOT KICKED OUT FOR FIGHTING.
MEL DON'T LIKE BISCUITS?
PLUS AND ALSO, MOM SAYS ...
SHE'S A THIEF.
COOOOOL ...

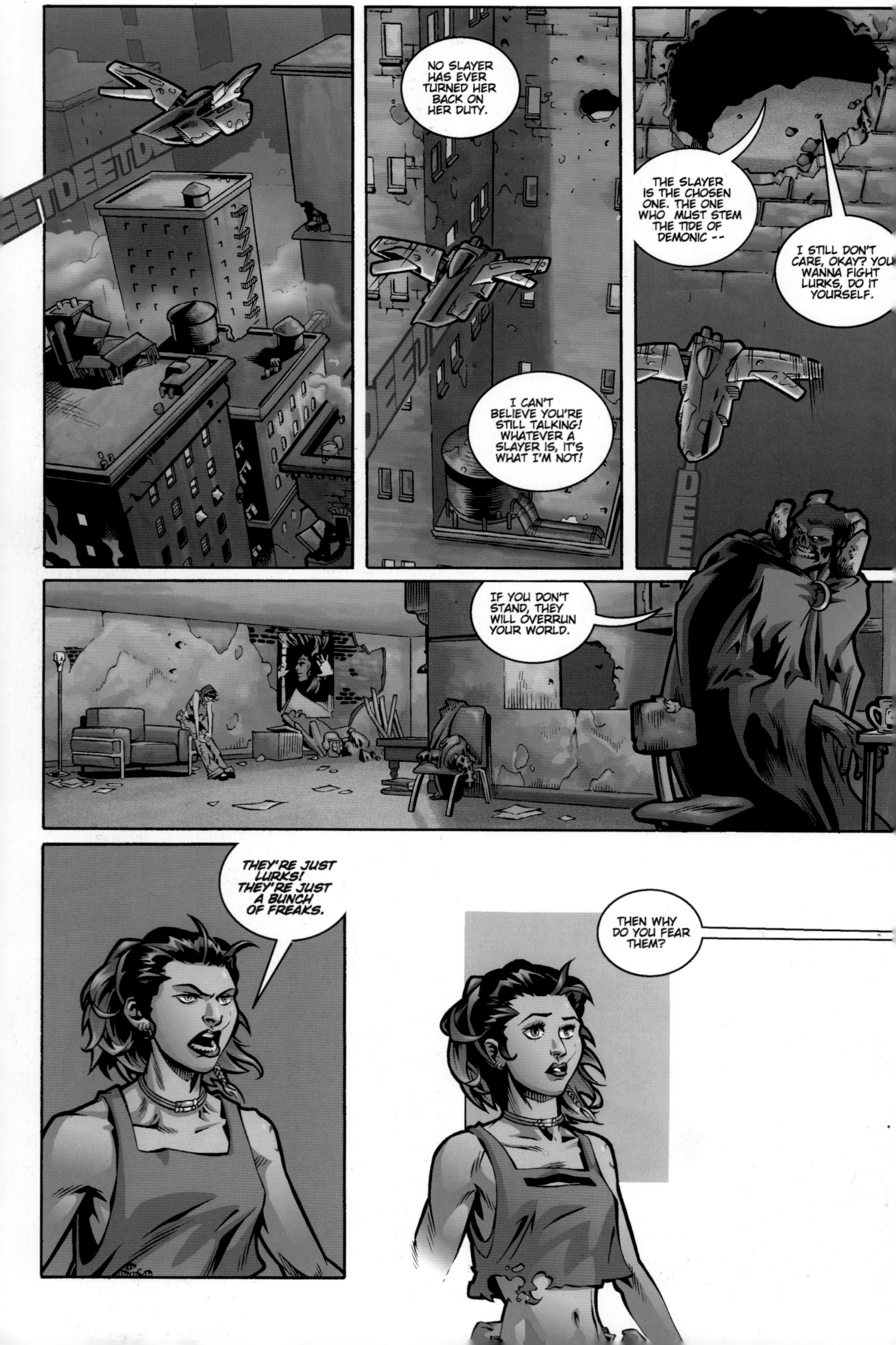
EETDEETD
NO SLAYER HAS EVER TURNED HER BACK ON HER DUTY.
DEEDL
I CAN'T BELIEVE YOU'RE STILL TALKING! WHATEVER A SLAYER IS, IT'S WHAT I'M NOT!
THE SLAYER IS THE CHOSEN ONE. THE ONE WHO MUST STEM THE TIDE OF DEMONIC --
I STILL DON'T CARE, OKAY? YOU WANNA FIGHT LURKS, DO IT YOURSELF.
DEE
IF YOU DON'T STAND, THEY WILL OVERRUN YOUR WORLD.
THEY'RE JUST LURKS! THEY'RE JUST A BUNCH OF FREAKS.
THEN WHY DO YOU FEAR THEM?

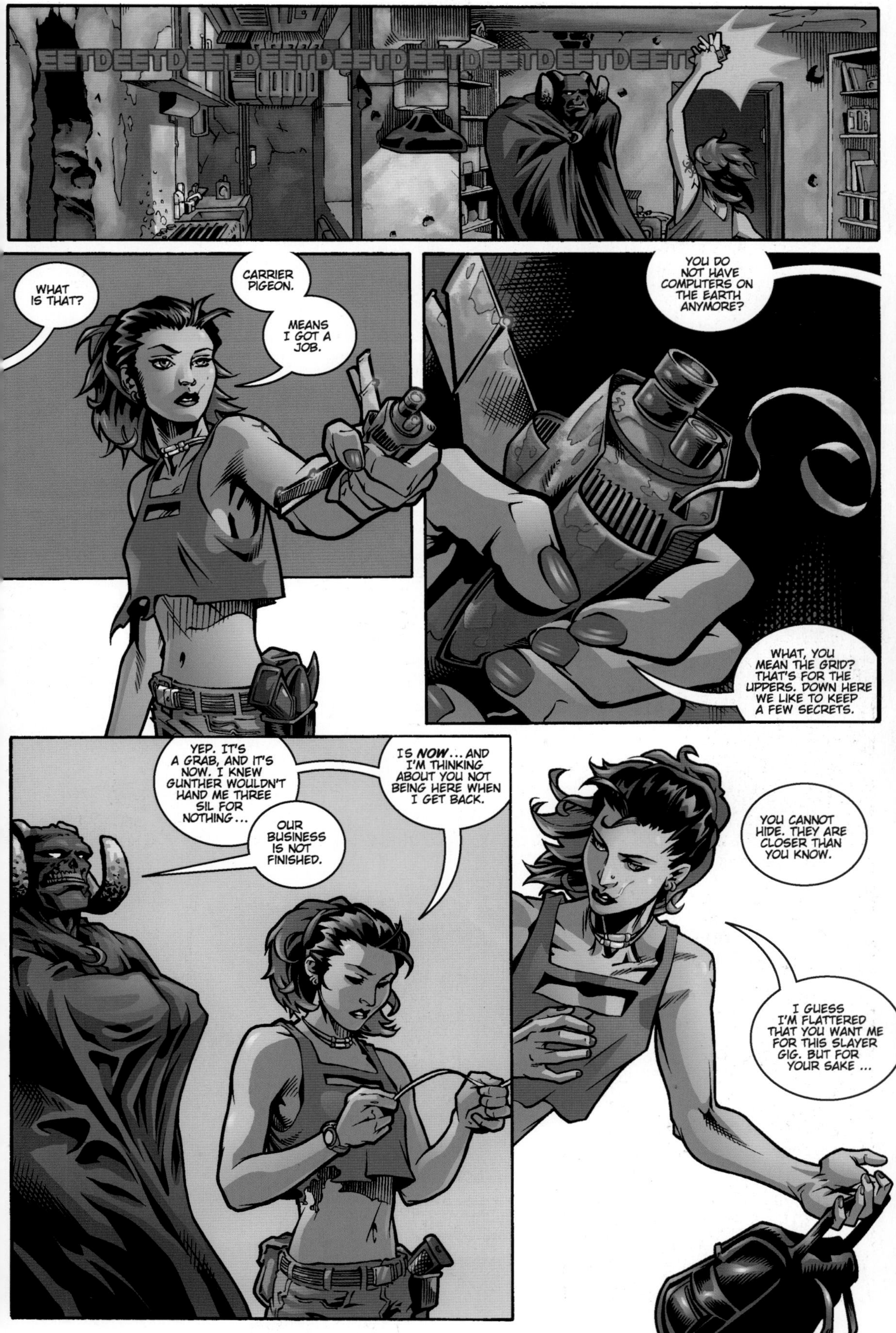
EETDEETDEETDEETDEETDEETDEETDEETDEETDEETDEET
WHAT IS THAT?
CARRIER PIGEON.
MEANS I GOT A JOB.
YOU DO NOT HAVE COMPUTERS ON THE EARTH ANYMORE?
WHAT, YOU MEAN THE GRID? THAT'S FOR THE UPPERS. DOWN HERE WE LIKE TO KEEP A FEW SECRETS.
YEP. IT'S A GRAB, AND IT'S NOW. I KNEW GUNTHER WOULDN'T HAND ME THREE SIL FOR NOTHING...
OUR BUSINESS IS NOT FINISHED.
IS *NOW*... AND I'M THINKING ABOUT YOU NOT BEING HERE WHEN I GET BACK.
YOU CANNOT HIDE. THEY ARE CLOSER THAN YOU KNOW.
I GUESS I'M FLATTERED THAT YOU WANT ME FOR THIS SLAYER GIG. BUT FOR YOUR SAKE ...

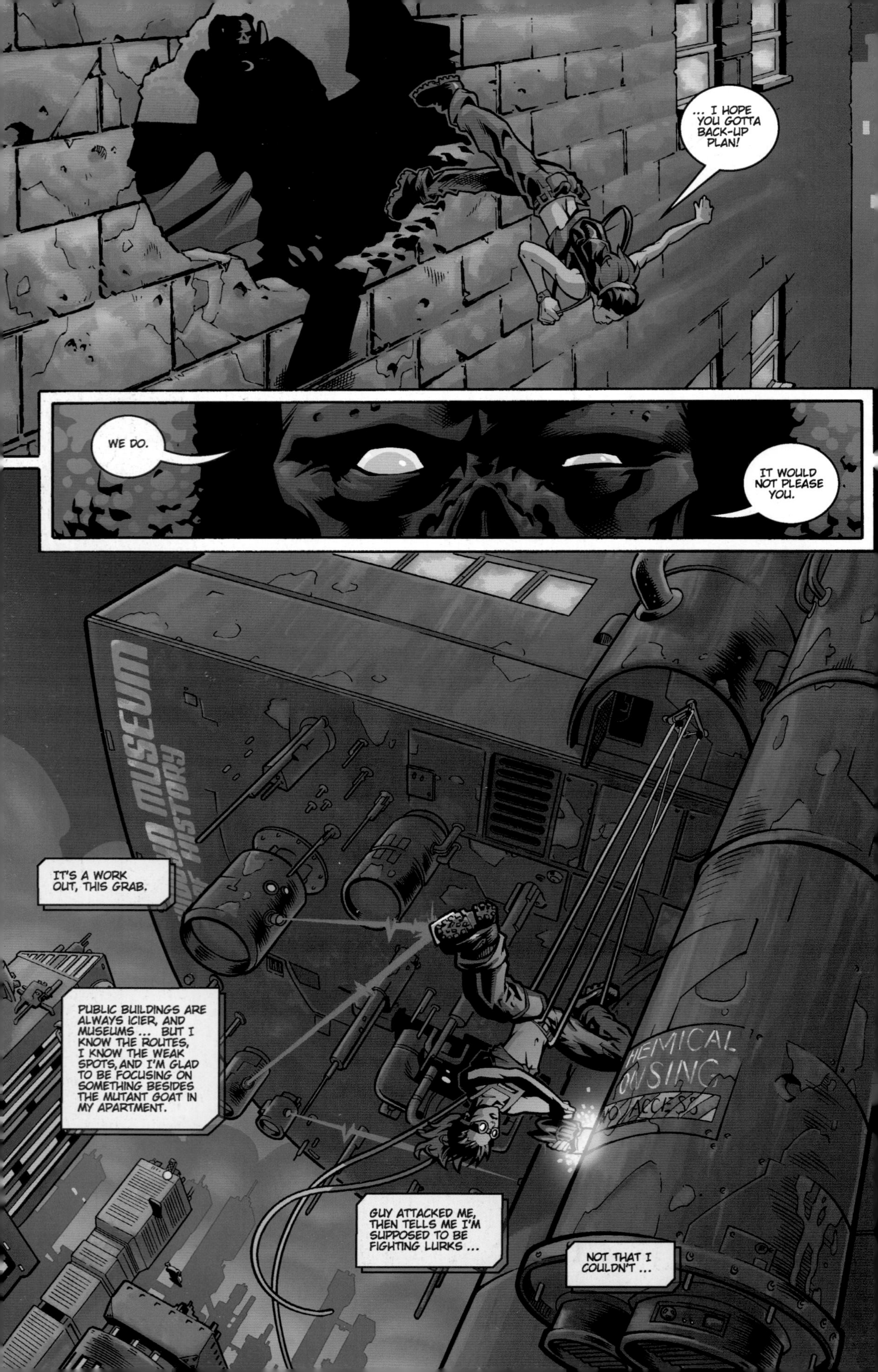
... I HOPE YOU GOTTA BACK-UP PLAN!
WE DO.
IT WOULD NOT PLEASE YOU.
MUSEUM
HISTORY
IT'S A WORK OUT, THIS GRAB.
PUBLIC BUILDINGS ARE ALWAYS ICIER, AND MUSEUMS ... BUT I KNOW THE ROUTES, I KNOW THE WEAK SPOTS, AND I'M GLAD TO BE FOCUSING ON SOMETHING BESIDES THE MUTANT GOAT IN MY APARTMENT.
HEMICAL
ONSING
NO ACCESS
GUY ATTACKED ME, THEN TELLS ME I'M SUPPOSED TO BE FIGHTING LURKS ...
NOT THAT I COULDN'T ...

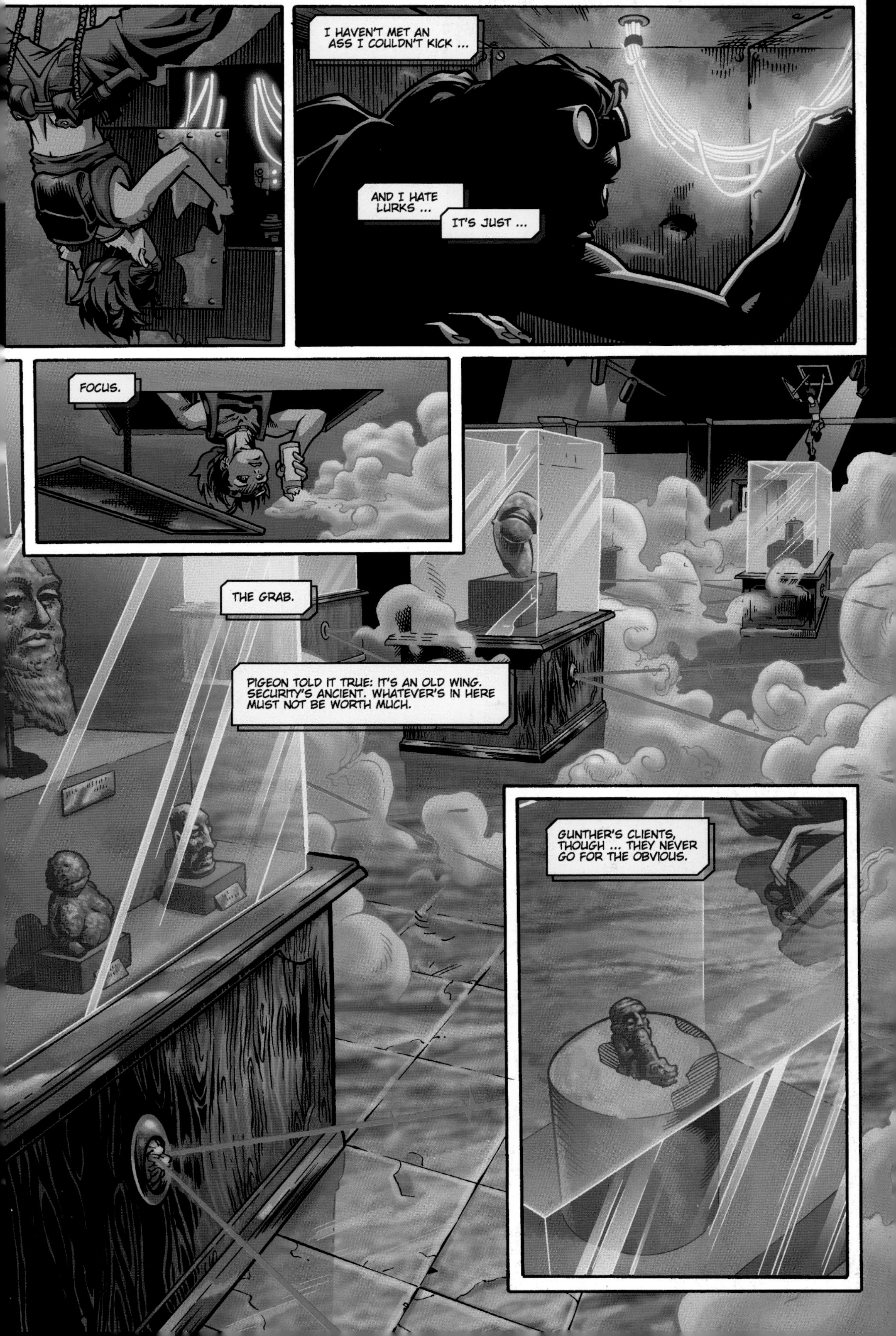
I HAVEN'T MET AN ASS I COULDN'T KICK ...
AND I HATE LURKS ...
IT'S JUST ...
FOCUS.
THE GRAB.
PIGEON TOLD IT TRUE: IT'S AN OLD WING. SECURITY'S ANCIENT. WHATEVER'S IN HERE MUST NOT BE WORTH MUCH.
GUNTHER'S CLIENTS, THOUGH ... THEY NEVER GO FOR THE OBVIOUS.

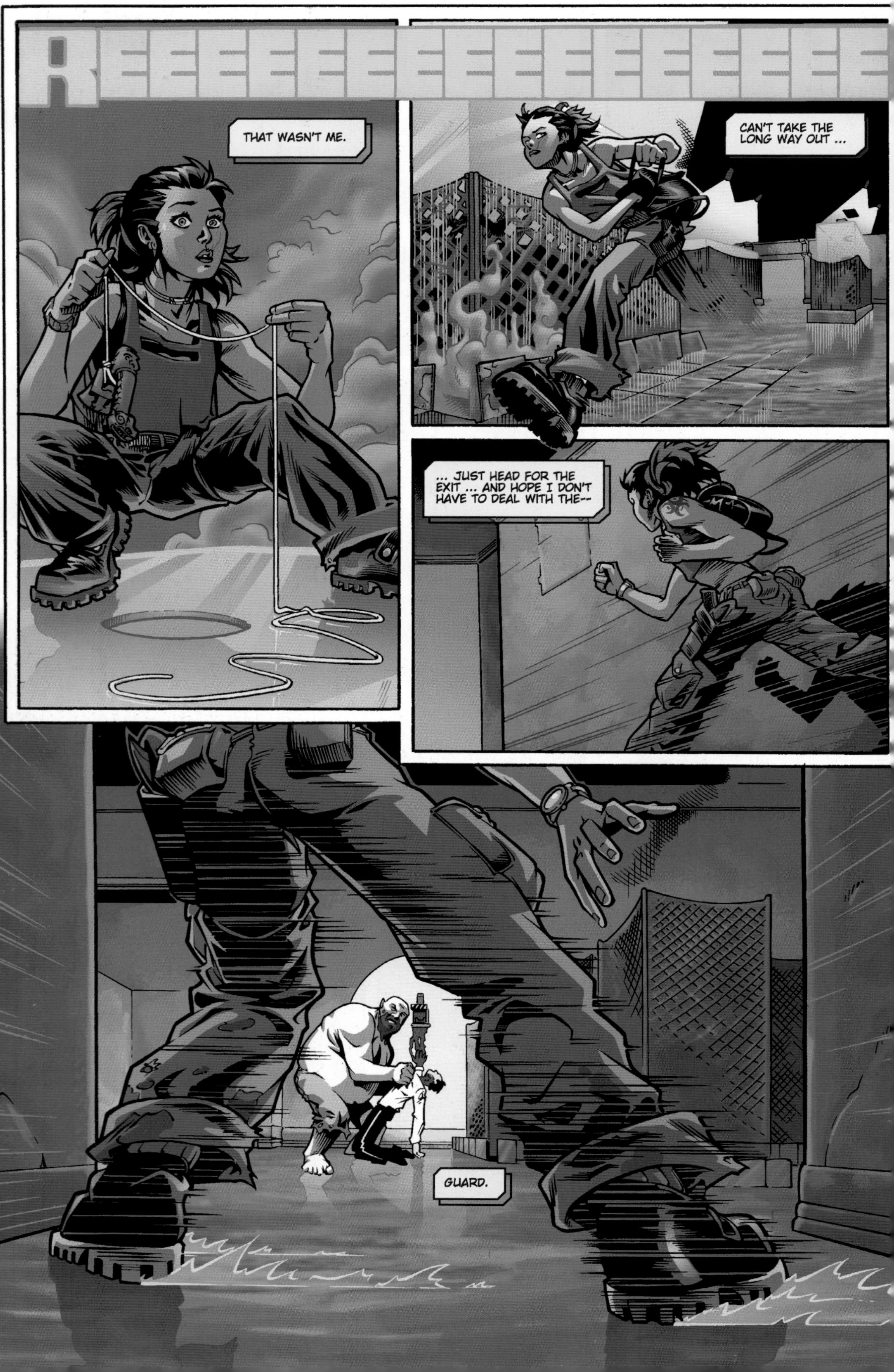
REEEEEEEEEEEEEEEEE
THAT WASN'T ME.
CAN'T TAKE THE LONG WAY OUT ...
... JUST HEAD FOR THE EXIT ... AND HOPE I DON'T HAVE TO DEAL WITH THE--
GUARD.

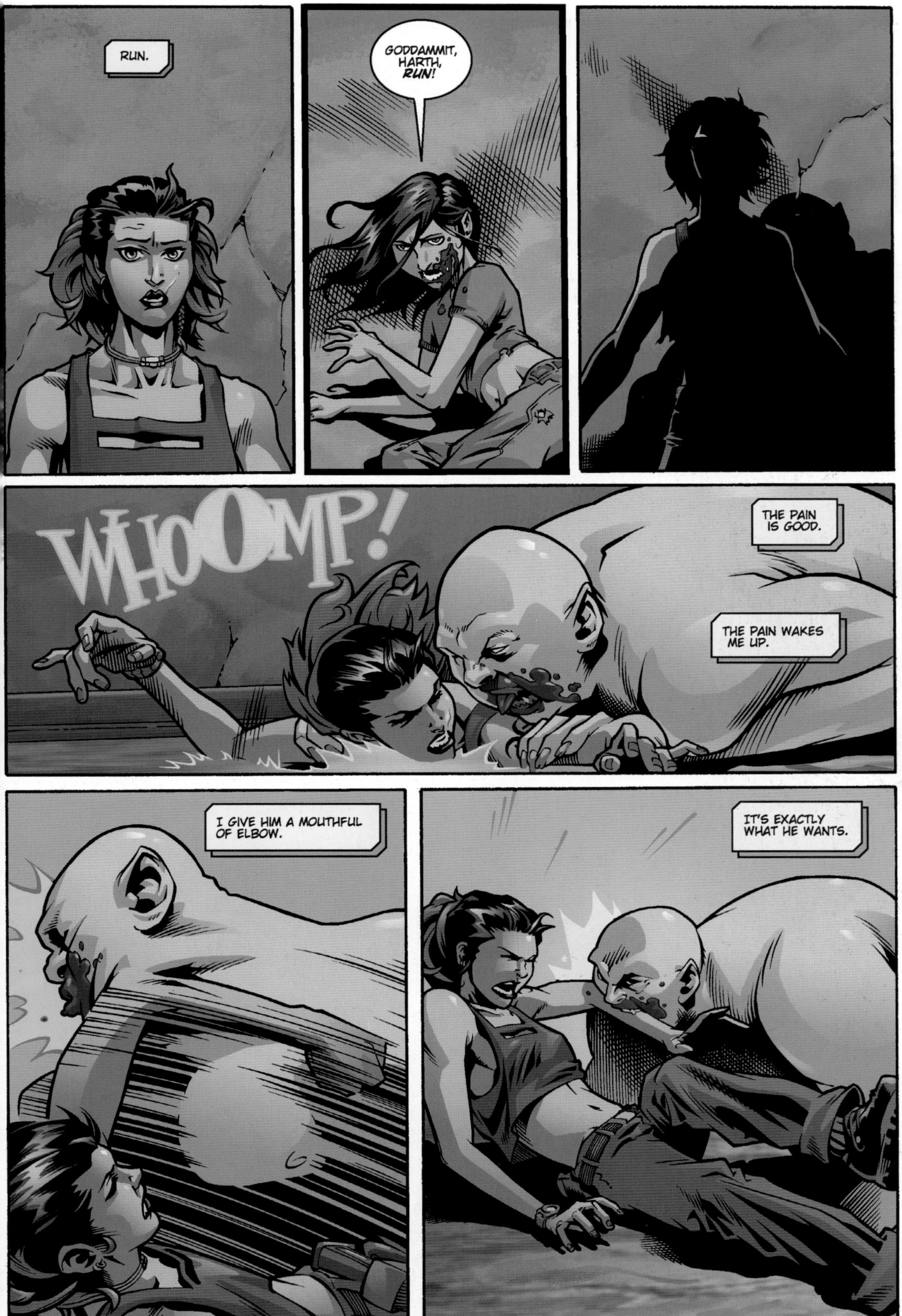
RUN.
GODDAMMIT, HARTH, RUN!
WHOOMP!
THE PAIN IS GOOD.
THE PAIN WAKES ME UP.
I GIVE HIM A MOUTHFUL OF ELBOW.
IT'S EXACTLY WHAT HE WANTS.

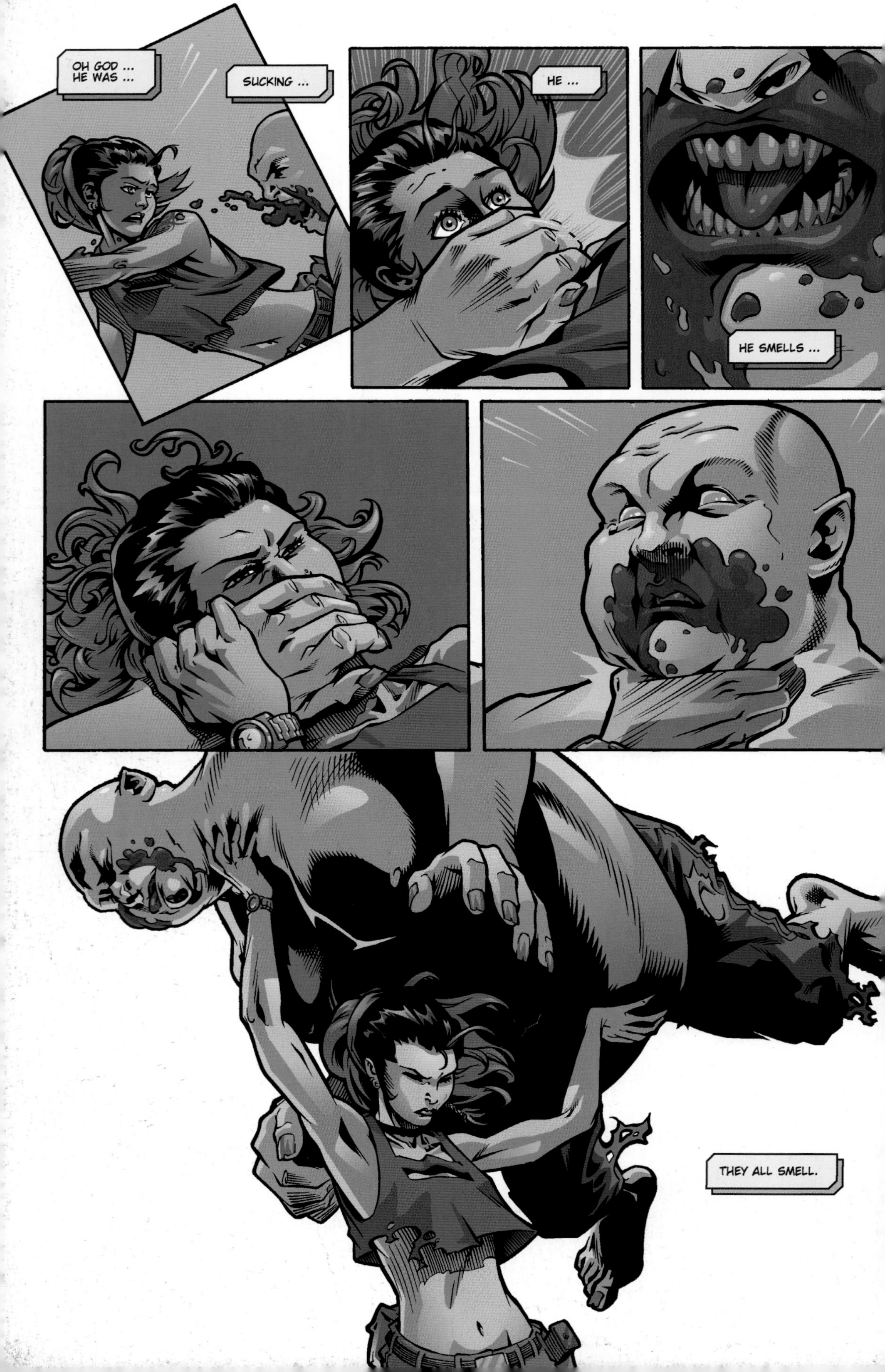
OH GOD ...
HE WAS ...
SUCKING ...
HE ...
HE SMELLS ...
THEY ALL SMELL.

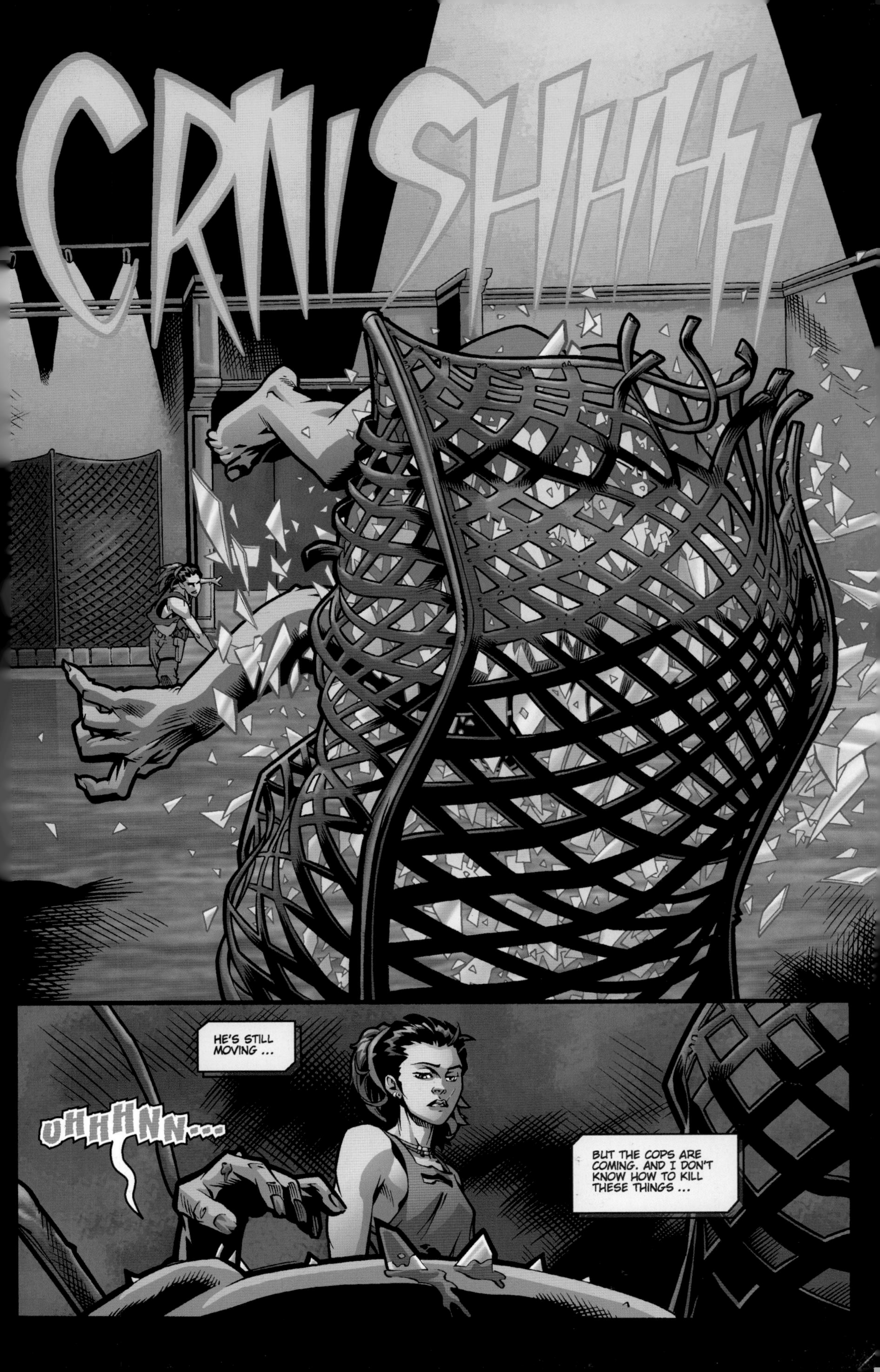
CRASHHHH
HE'S STILL MOVING ...
UHHHNN...
BUT THE COPS ARE COMING. AND I DON'T KNOW HOW TO KILL THESE THINGS ...

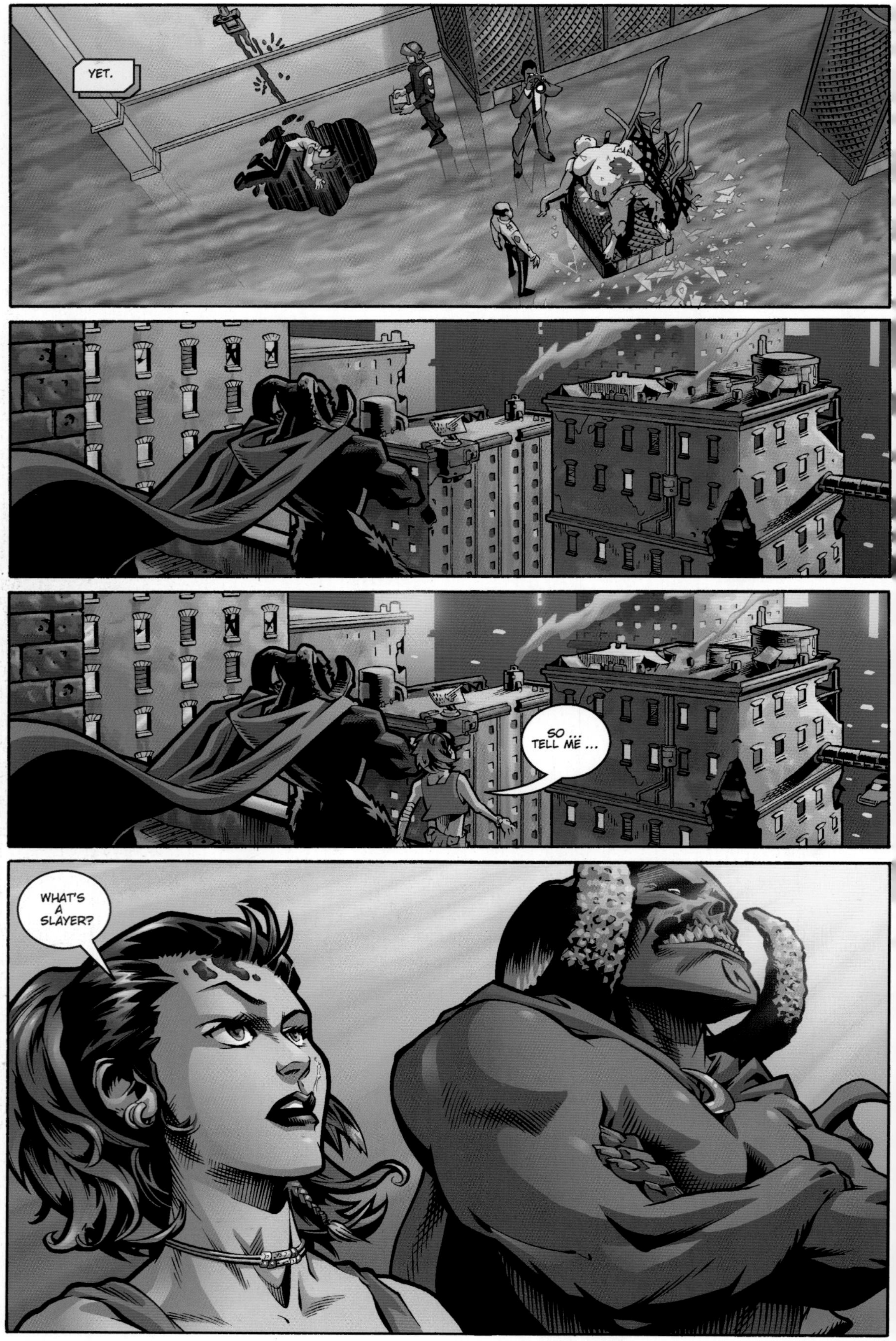
YET.
SO ... TELL ME ...
WHAT'S A SLAYER?

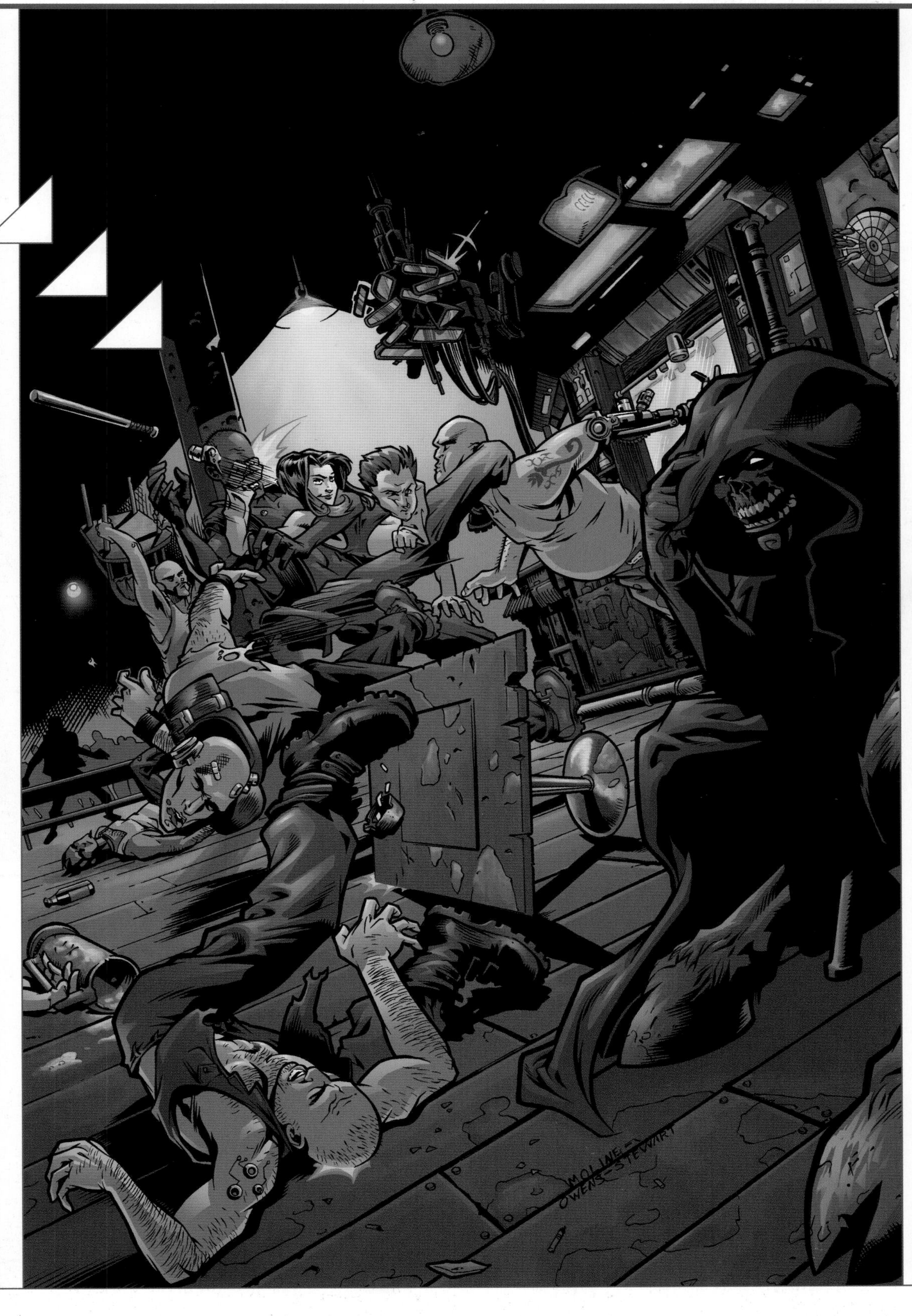
MOLINE
OWENS-STEWART

"He doesn't think I'm ready."

"He doesn't know me that well."

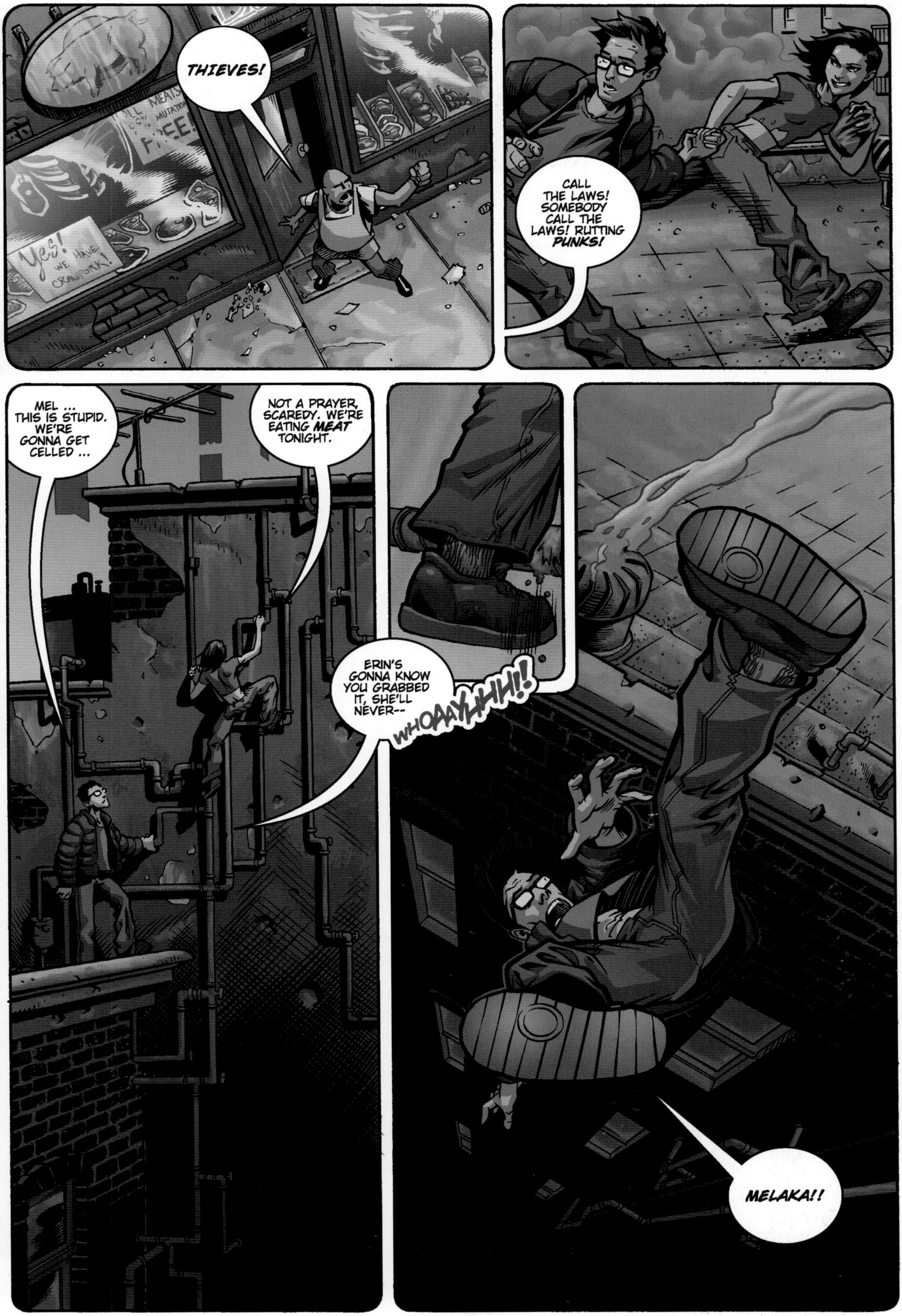
THIEVES!
CALL THE LAWS! SOMEBODY CALL THE LAWS! RUTTING PUNKS!
MEL ... THIS IS STUPID. WE'RE GONNA GET CELLED ...
NOT A PRAYER, SCAREDY. WE'RE EATING MEAT TONIGHT.
ERIN'S GONNA KNOW YOU GRABBED IT, SHE'LL NEVER--
WHOAAYHHH!!
MELAKA!!

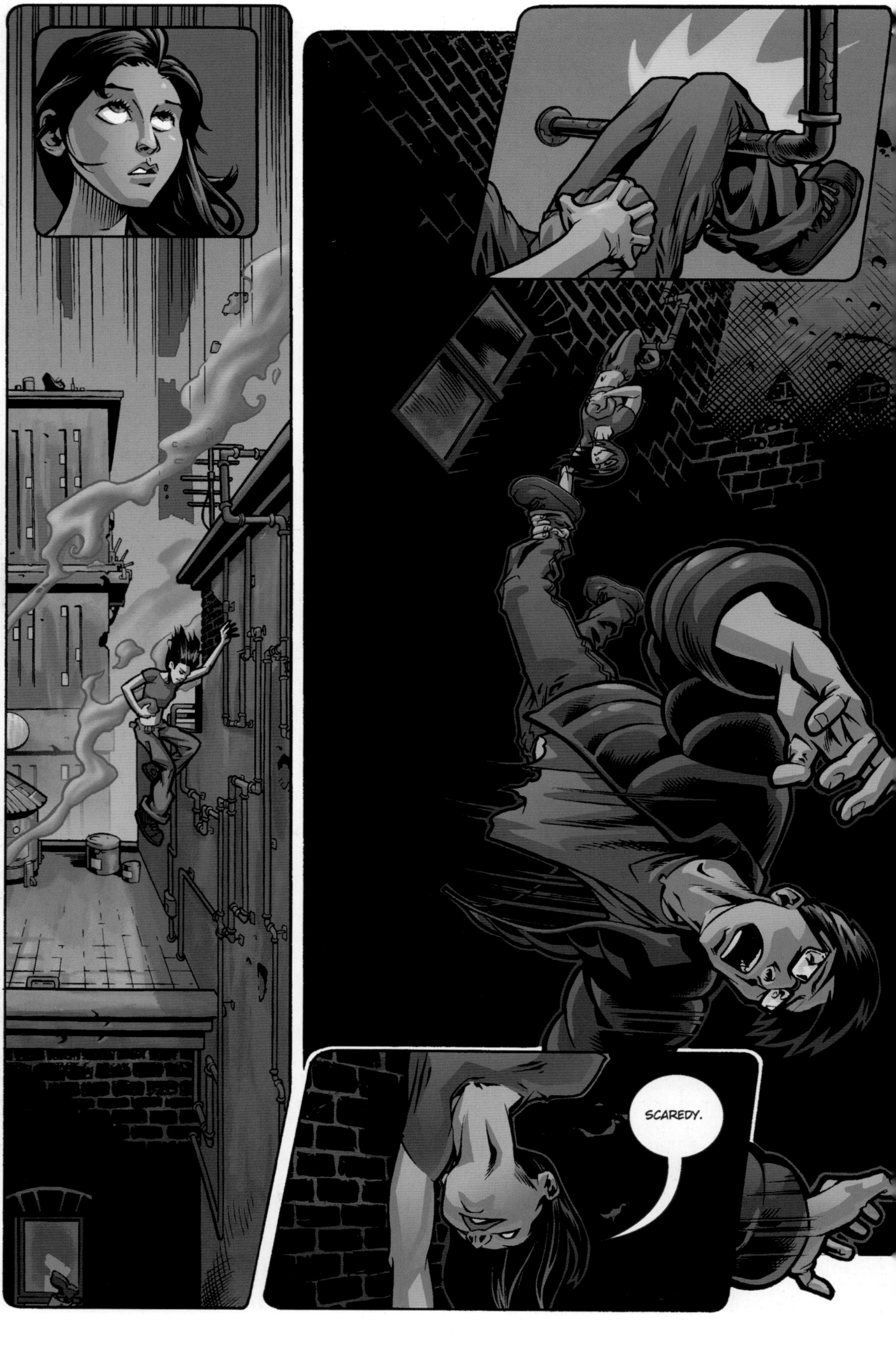
SCAREDY.

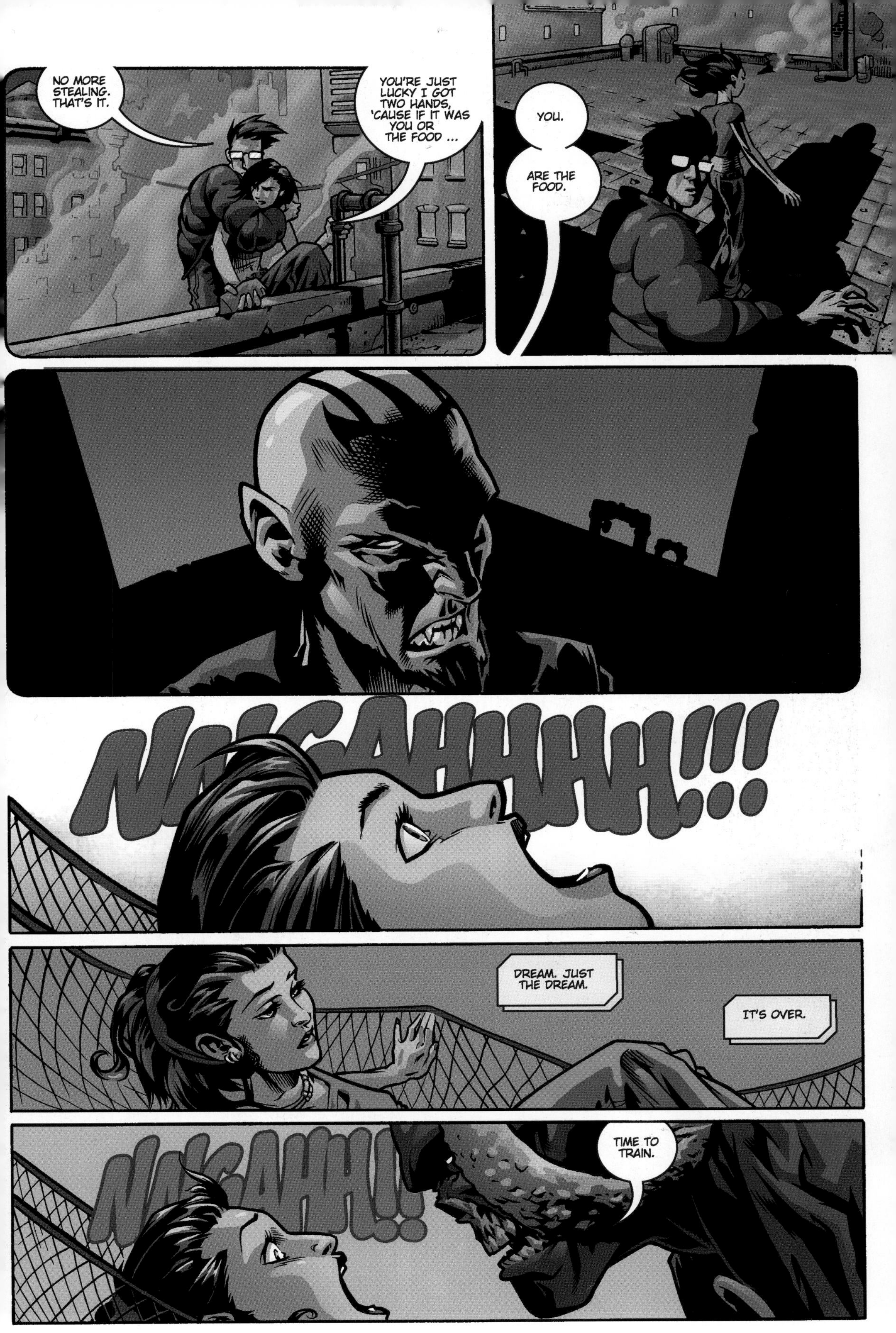
NO MORE STEALING. THAT'S IT.
YOU'RE JUST LUCKY I GOT TWO HANDS, 'CAUSE IF IT WAS YOU OR THE FOOD ...
YOU.
ARE THE FOOD.
NNGAHHHHH!!!
DREAM. JUST THE DREAM.
IT'S OVER.
NNGAHH!!!
TIME TO TRAIN.

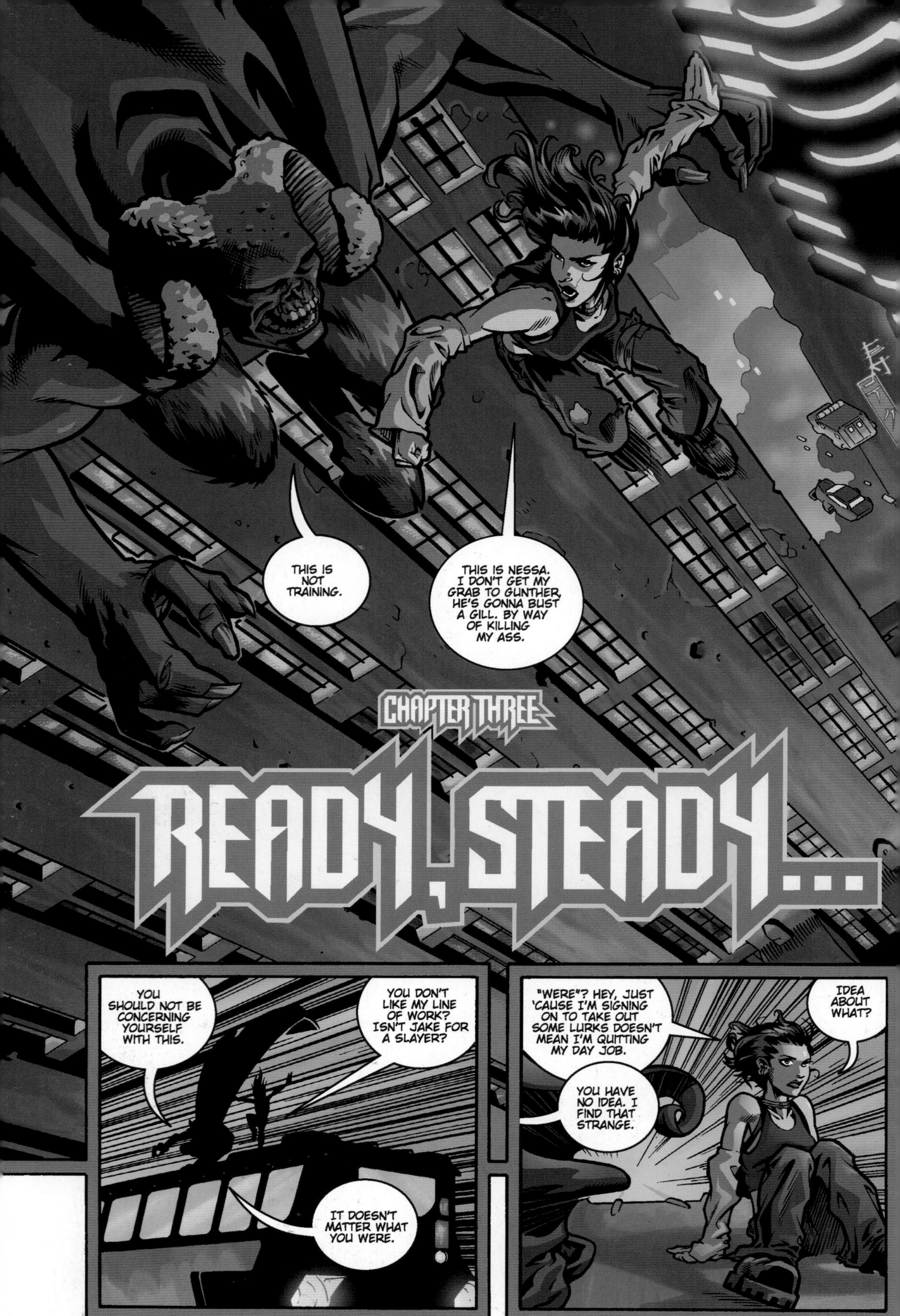
THIS IS NOT TRAINING.
THIS IS NESSA. I DON'T GET MY GRAB TO GUNTHER, HE'S GONNA BUST A GILL. BY WAY OF KILLING MY ASS.
CHAPTER THREE
READY, STEADY...
YOU SHOULD NOT BE CONCERNING YOURSELF WITH THIS.
YOU DON'T LIKE MY LINE OF WORK? ISN'T JAKE FOR A SLAYER?
IT DOESN'T MATTER WHAT YOU WERE.
"WERE"? HEY, JUST 'CAUSE I'M SIGNING ON TO TAKE OUT SOME LURKS DOESN'T MEAN I'M QUITTING MY DAY JOB.
YOU HAVE NO IDEA. I FIND THAT STRANGE.
IDEA ABOUT WHAT?

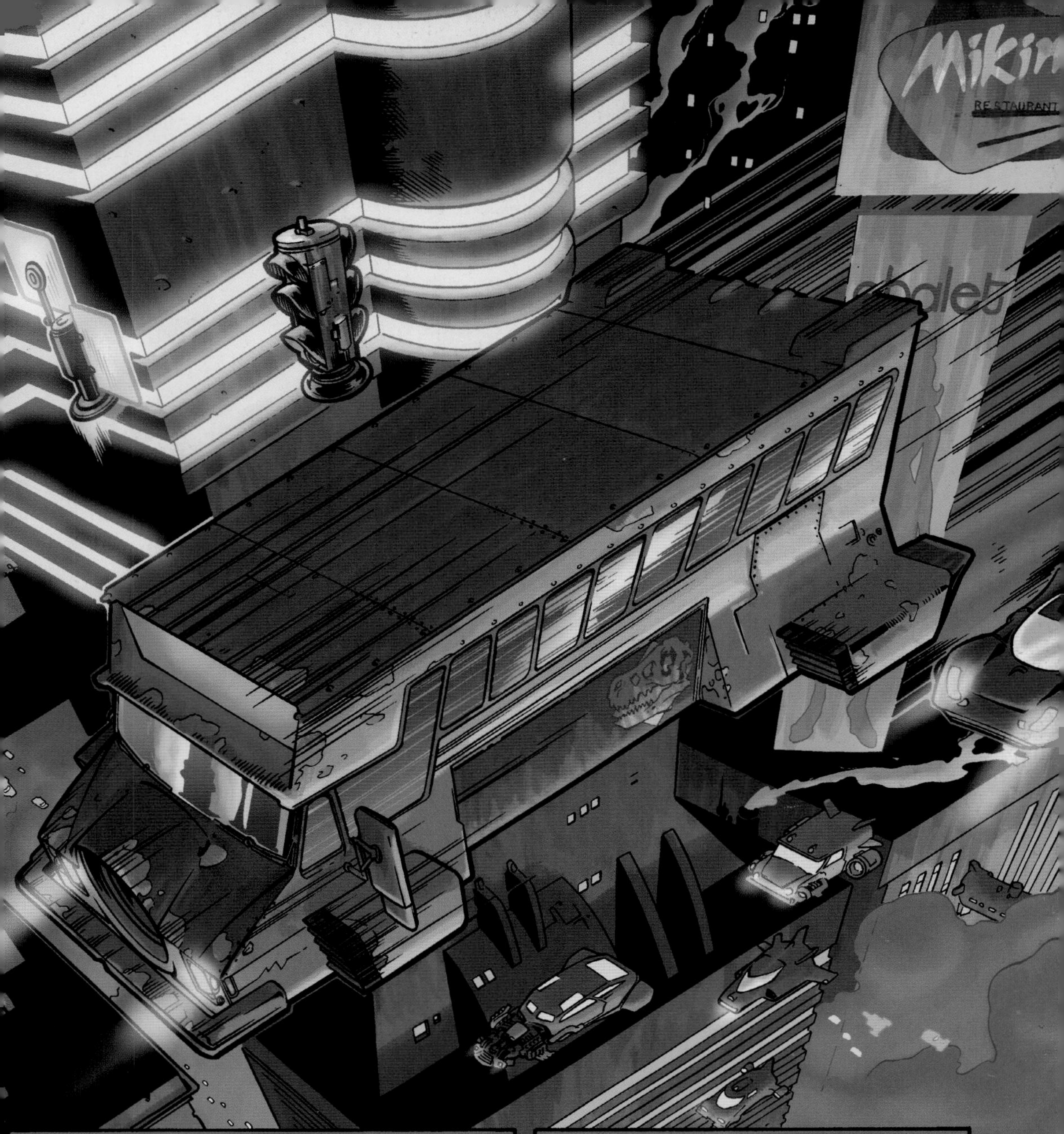
Mikin
RESTAURANT
chalet

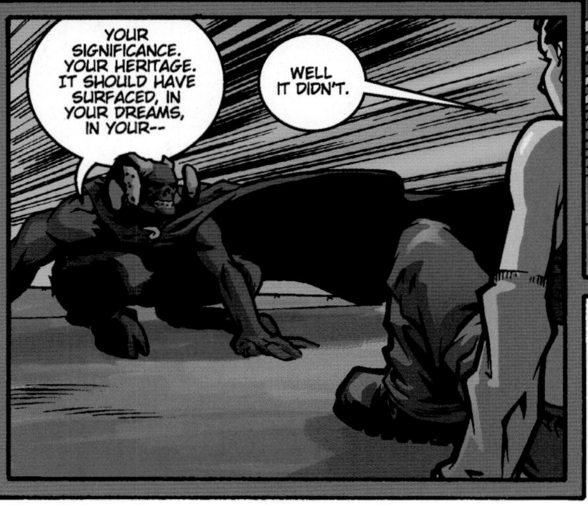
YOUR SIGNIFICANCE. YOUR HERITAGE. IT SHOULD HAVE SURFACED, IN YOUR DREAMS, IN YOUR--
WELL IT DIDN'T.

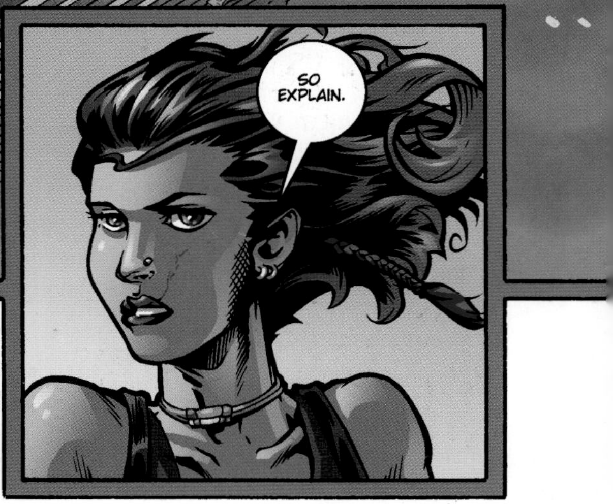
SO EXPLAIN.

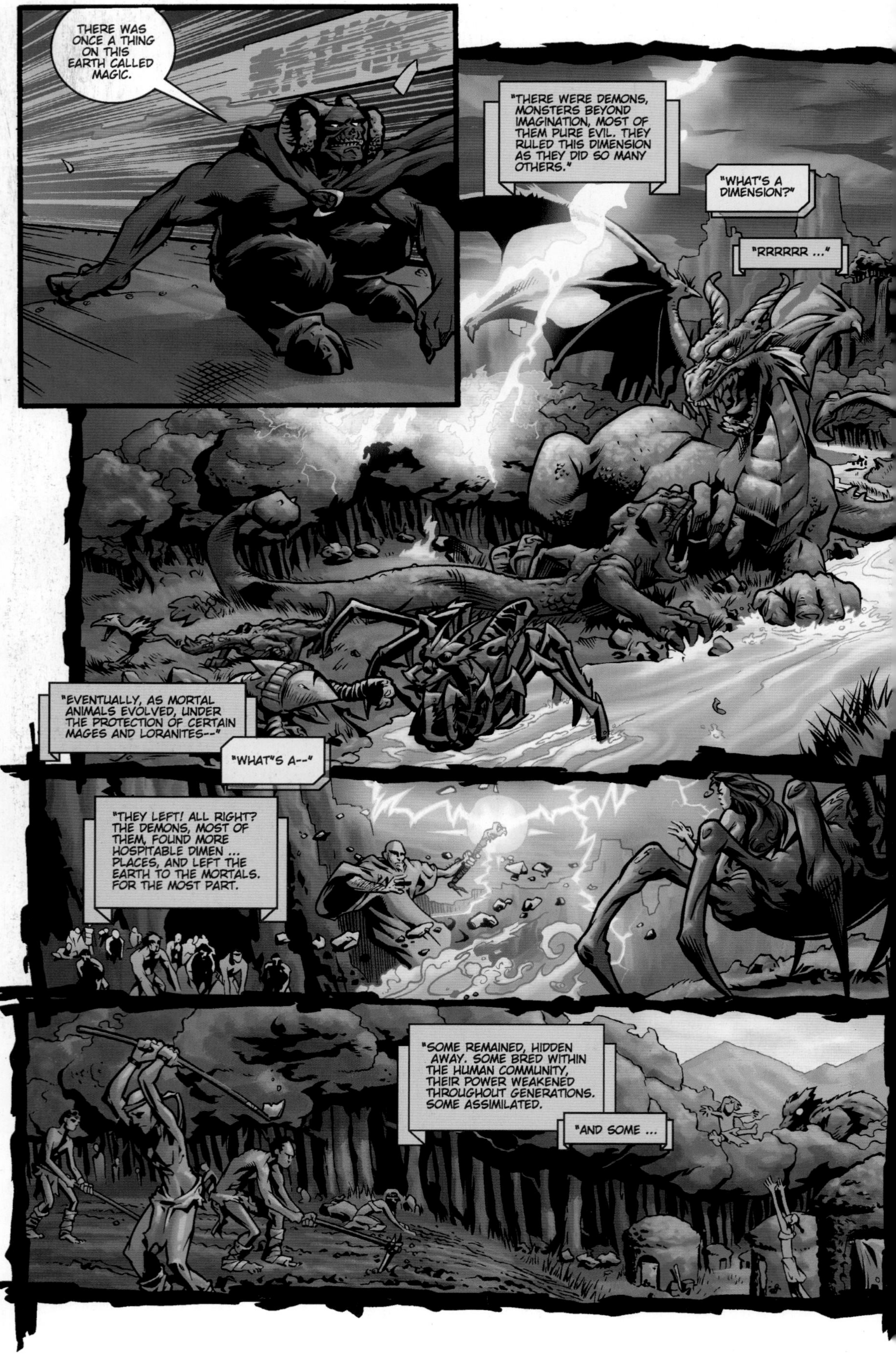

THERE WAS ONCE A THING ON THIS EARTH CALLED MAGIC.
"THERE WERE DEMONS, MONSTERS BEYOND IMAGINATION, MOST OF THEM PURE EVIL. THEY RULED THIS DIMENSION AS THEY DID SO MANY OTHERS."
"WHAT'S A DIMENSION?"
"RRRRRR ..."
"EVENTUALLY, AS MORTAL ANIMALS EVOLVED, UNDER THE PROTECTION OF CERTAIN MAGES AND LORANITES--"
"WHAT'S A--"
"THEY LEFT! ALL RIGHT? THE DEMONS, MOST OF THEM, FOUND MORE HOSPITABLE DIMEN ... PLACES, AND LEFT THE EARTH TO THE MORTALS. FOR THE MOST PART.
"SOME REMAINED, HIDDEN AWAY. SOME BRED WITHIN THE HUMAN COMMUNITY, THEIR POWER WEAKENED THROUGHOUT GENERATIONS. SOME ASSIMILATED.
"AND SOME ...

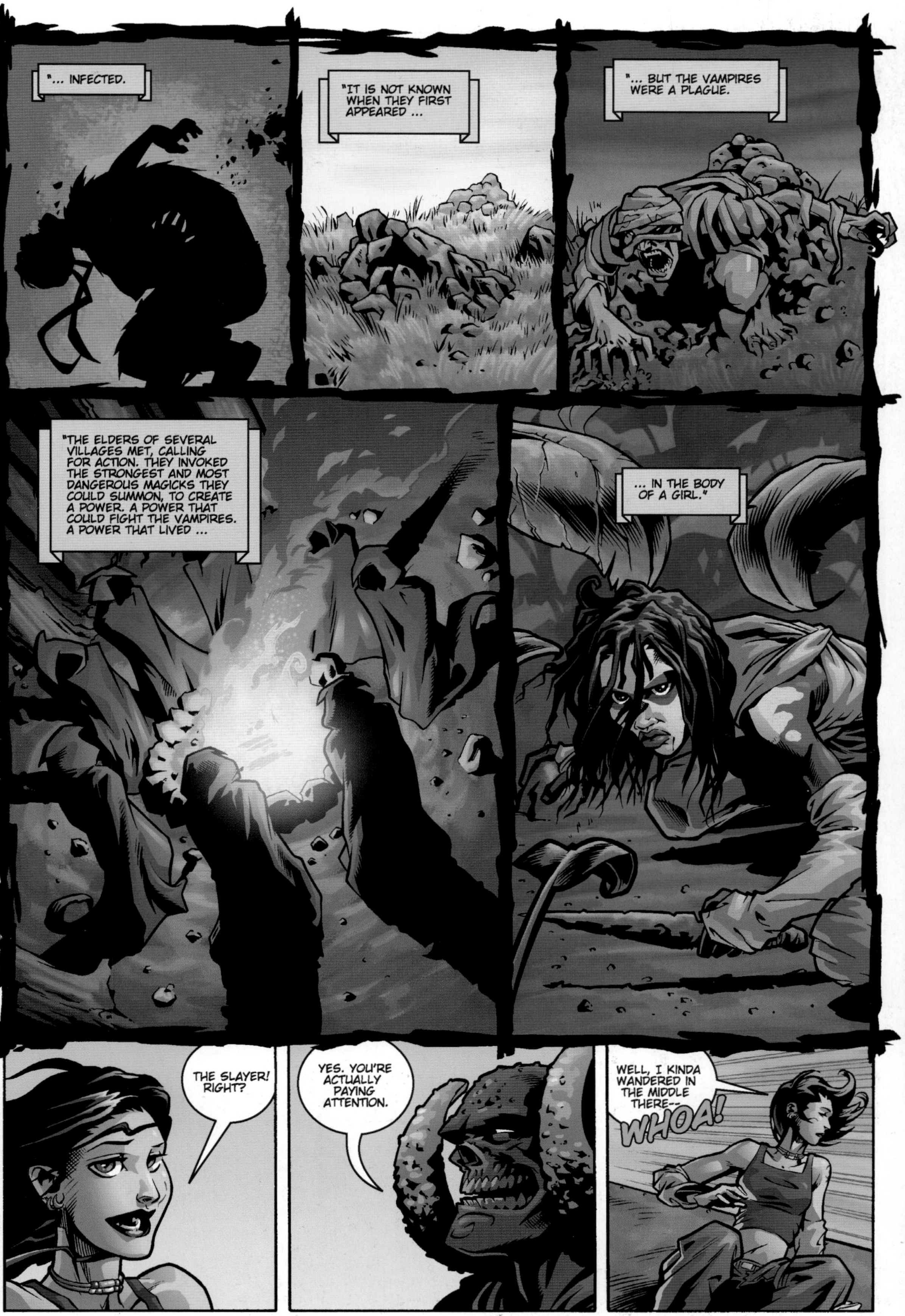
"... INFECTED.
"IT IS NOT KNOWN WHEN THEY FIRST APPEARED ...
"... BUT THE VAMPIRES WERE A PLAGUE.
"THE ELDERS OF SEVERAL VILLAGES MET, CALLING FOR ACTION. THEY INVOKED THE STRONGEST AND MOST DANGEROUS MAGICKS THEY COULD SUMMON, TO CREATE A POWER. A POWER THAT COULD FIGHT THE VAMPIRES. A POWER THAT LIVED ...
... IN THE BODY OF A GIRL."
THE SLAYER! RIGHT?
YES. YOU'RE ACTUALLY PAYING ATTENTION.
WELL, I KINDA WANDERED IN THE MIDDLE THERE--
WHOA!

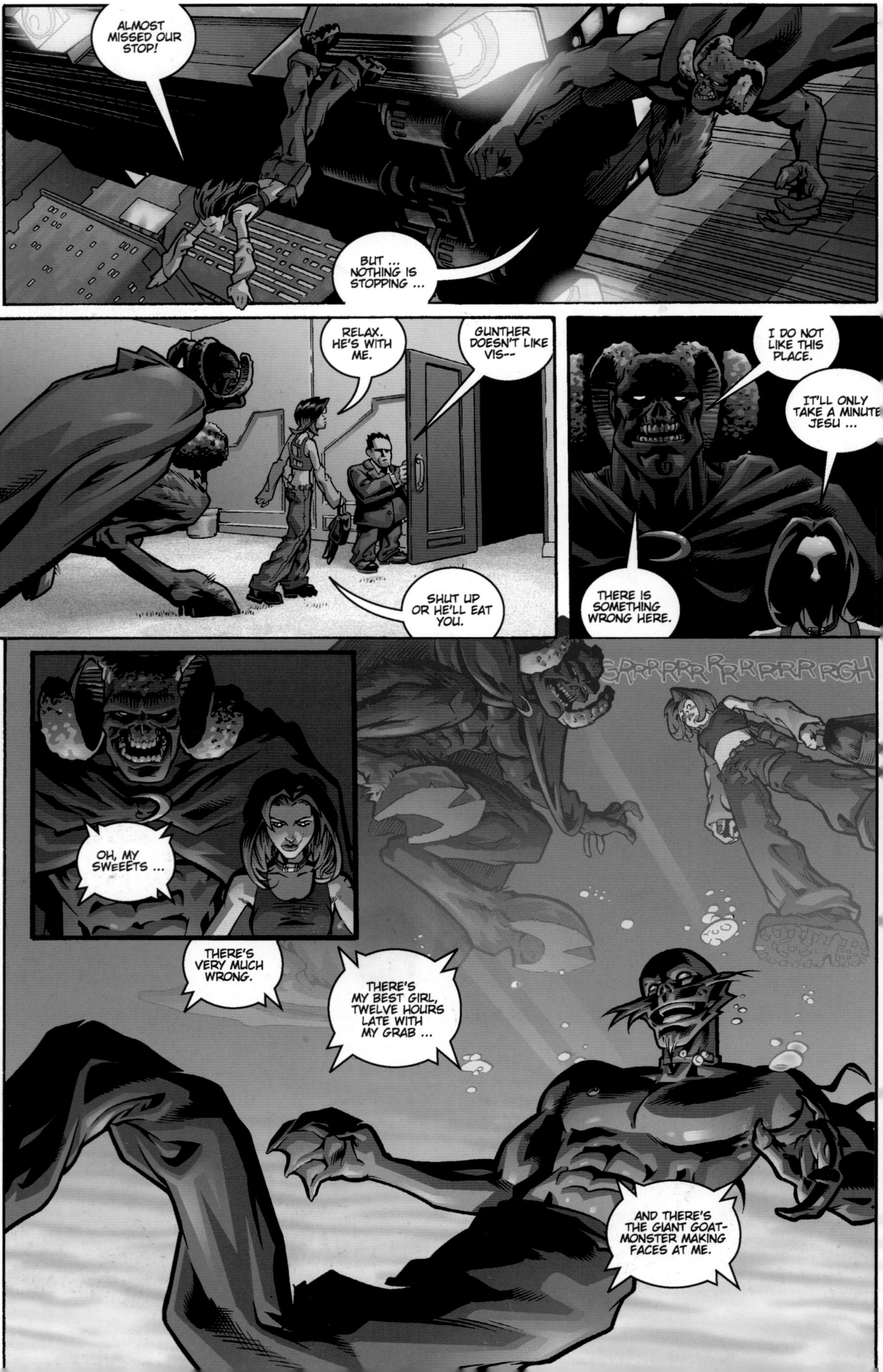
ALMOST MISSED OUR STOP!
BUT ... NOTHING IS STOPPING ...
RELAX. HE'S WITH ME.
GUNTHER DOESN'T LIKE VIS--
SHUT UP OR HE'LL EAT YOU.
I DO NOT LIKE THIS PLACE.
IT'LL ONLY TAKE A MINUTE JESU ...
THERE IS SOMETHING WRONG HERE.
GRRRRRRRRRRRRRRGH
OH, MY SWEEETS ...
THERE'S VERY MUCH WRONG.
THERE'S MY BEST GIRL, TWELVE HOURS LATE WITH MY GRAB ...
AND THERE'S THE GIANT GOAT-MONSTER MAKING FACES AT ME.

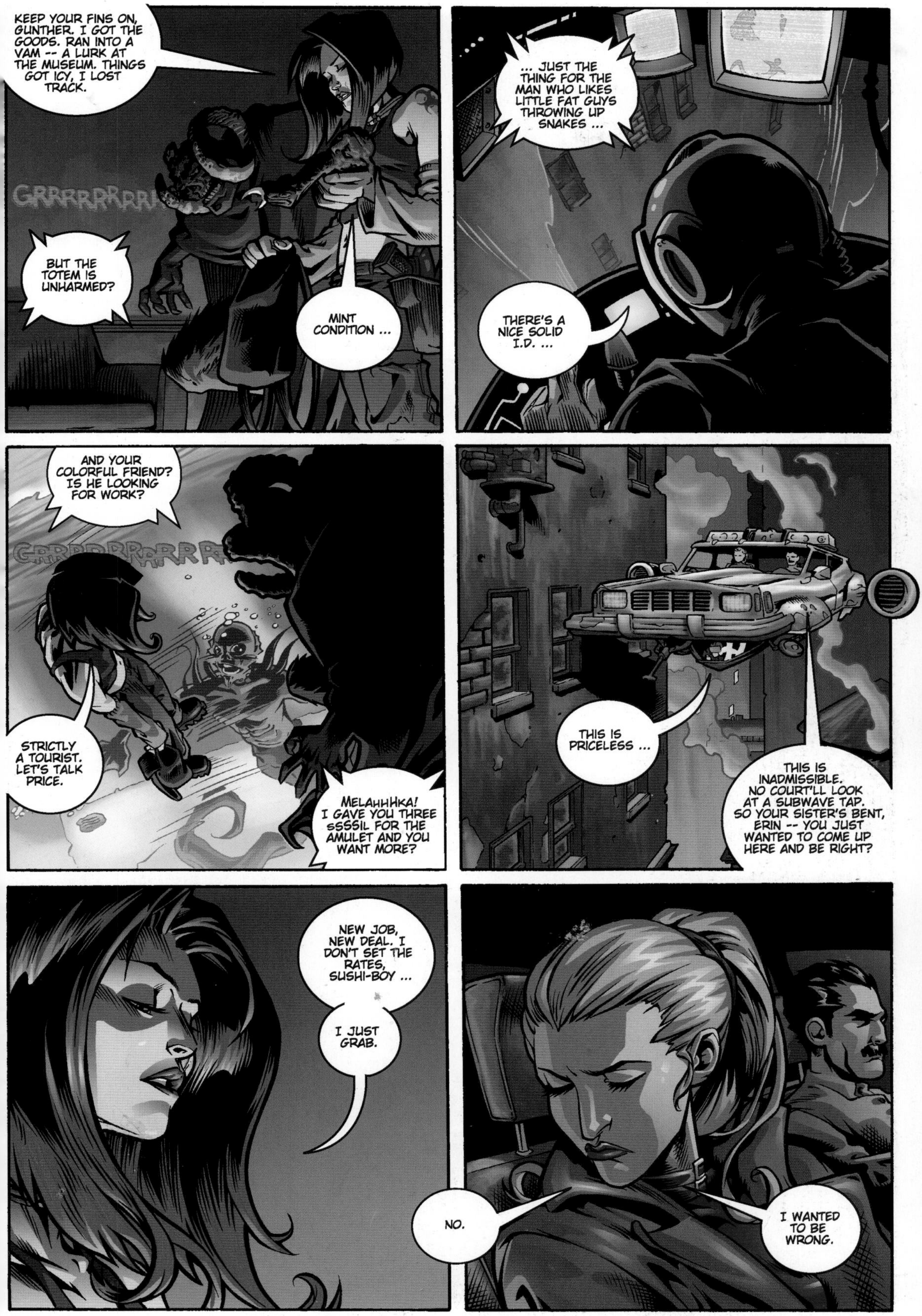
KEEP YOUR FINS ON, GUNTHER. I GOT THE GOODS. RAN INTO A VAM -- A LURK AT THE MUSEUM. THINGS GOT ICY, I LOST TRACK.
GRRRRRRRR
BUT THE TOTEM IS UNHARMED?
MINT CONDITION ...
... JUST THE THING FOR THE MAN WHO LIKES LITTLE FAT GUYS THROWING UP SNAKES ...
THERE'S A NICE SOLID I.D. ...
AND YOUR COLORFUL FRIEND? IS HE LOOKING FOR WORK?
GRRRRRRARRRR
STRICTLY A TOURIST. LET'S TALK PRICE.
MELAHHHKA! I GAVE YOU THREE sSSSIL FOR THE AMULET AND YOU WANT MORE?
THIS IS PRICELESS ...
THIS IS INADMISSIBLE. NO COURT'LL LOOK AT A SUBWAVE TAP. SO YOUR SISTER'S BENT, ERIN -- YOU JUST WANTED TO COME UP HERE AND BE RIGHT?
NEW JOB, NEW DEAL. I DON'T SET THE RATES, SUSHI-BOY ...
I JUST GRAB.
NO.
I WANTED TO BE WRONG.

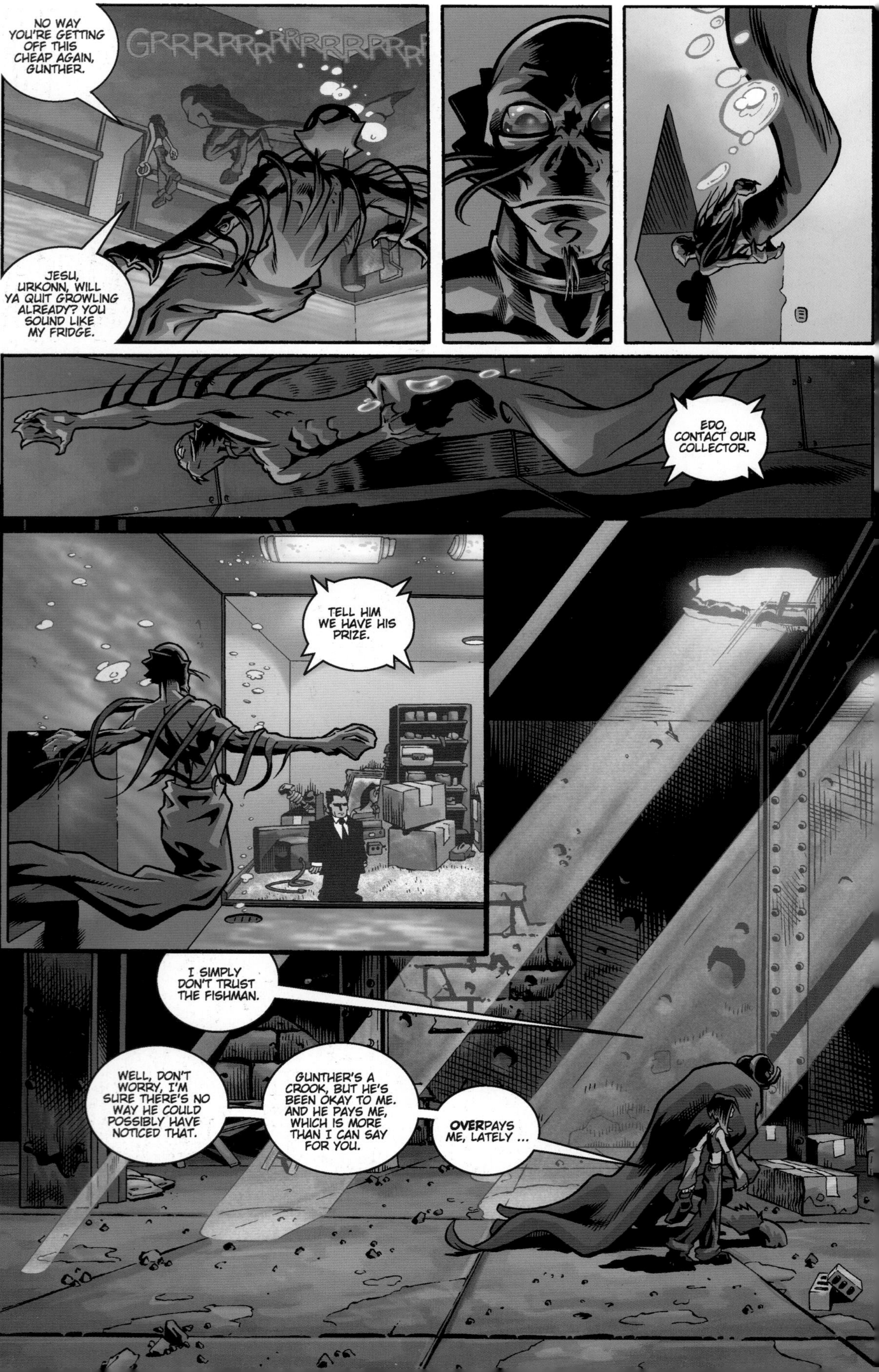
NO WAY YOU'RE GETTING OFF THIS CHEAP AGAIN, GUNTHER.
GRRRRRRRRRRRRRRRRR
JESU, URKONN, WILL YA QUIT GROWLING ALREADY? YOU SOUND LIKE MY FRIDGE.
EDO, CONTACT OUR COLLECTOR.
TELL HIM WE HAVE HIS PRIZE.
I SIMPLY DON'T TRUST THE FISHMAN.
WELL, DON'T WORRY, I'M SURE THERE'S NO WAY HE COULD POSSIBLY HAVE NOTICED THAT.
GUNTHER'S A CROOK, BUT HE'S BEEN OKAY TO ME. AND HE PAYS ME, WHICH IS MORE THAN I CAN SAY FOR YOU.
OVERPAYS ME, LATELY ...

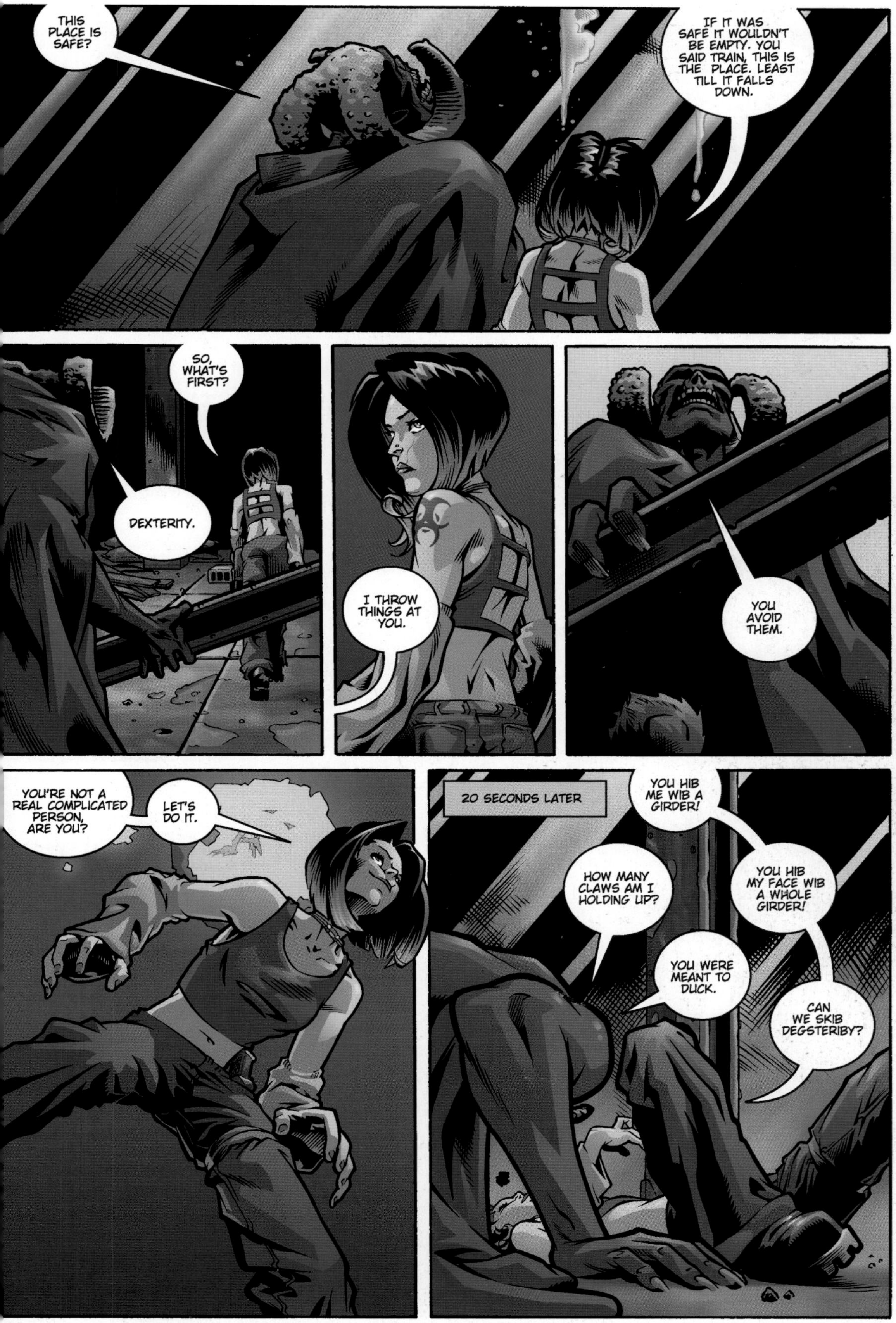
THIS PLACE IS SAFE?
IF IT WAS SAFE IT WOULDN'T BE EMPTY. YOU SAID TRAIN, THIS IS THE PLACE. LEAST TILL IT FALLS DOWN.
SO, WHAT'S FIRST?
DEXTERITY.
I THROW THINGS AT YOU.
YOU AVOID THEM.
YOU'RE NOT A REAL COMPLICATED PERSON, ARE YOU?
LET'S DO IT.
20 SECONDS LATER
YOU HIB ME WIB A GIRDER!
YOU HIB MY FACE WIB A WHOLE GIRDER!
HOW MANY CLAWS AM I HOLDING UP?
YOU WERE MEANT TO DUCK.
CAN WE SKIB DEGSTERIBY?

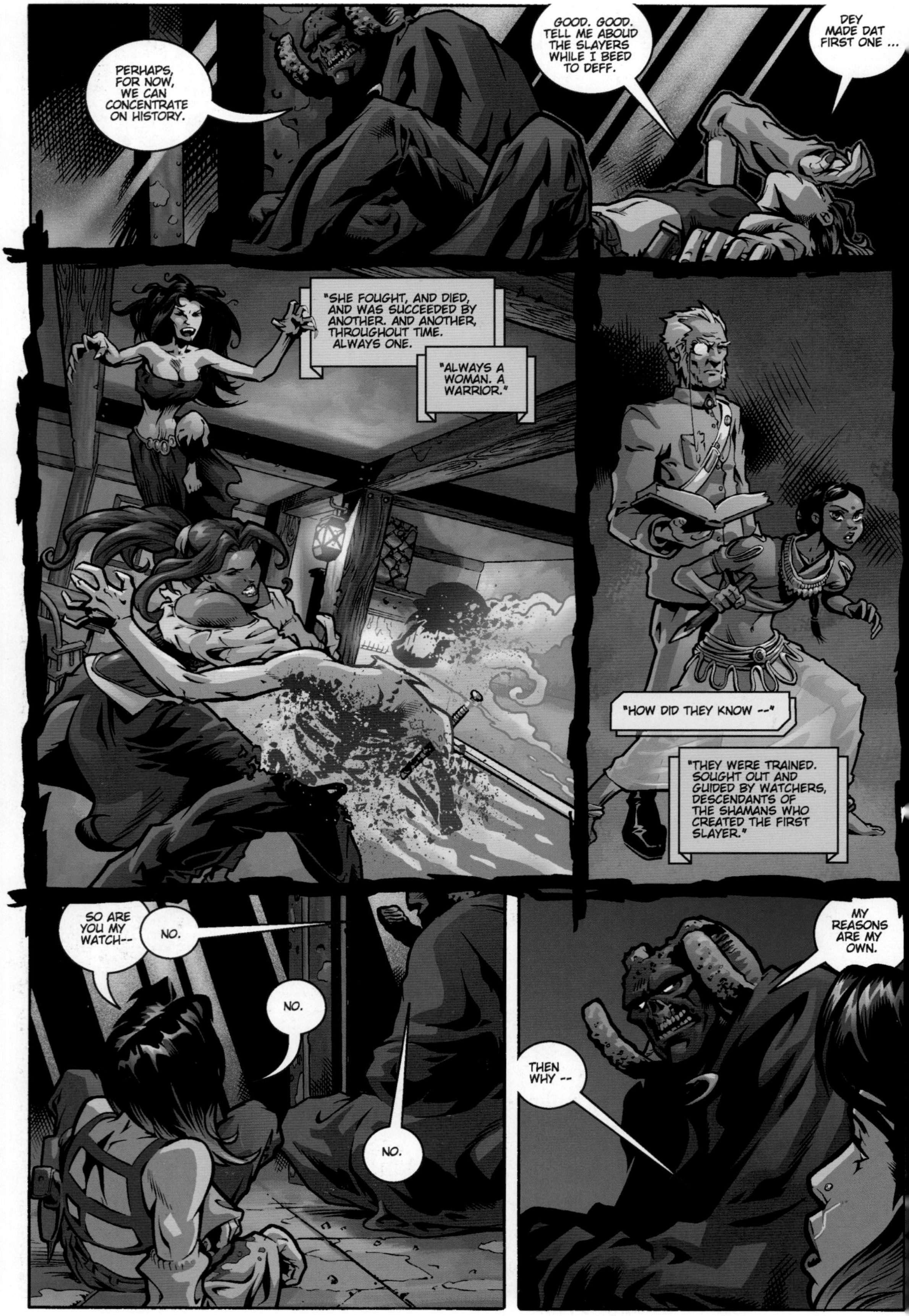
PERHAPS, FOR NOW, WE CAN CONCENTRATE ON HISTORY.
GOOD. GOOD. TELL ME ABOUD THE SLAYERS WHILE I BEED TO DEFF.
DEY MADE DAT FIRST ONE ...
"SHE FOUGHT, AND DIED, AND WAS SUCCEEDED BY ANOTHER. AND ANOTHER, THROUGHOUT TIME. ALWAYS ONE.
"ALWAYS A WOMAN. A WARRIOR."
"HOW DID THEY KNOW --"
"THEY WERE TRAINED. SOUGHT OUT AND GUIDED BY WATCHERS, DESCENDANTS OF THE SHAMANS WHO CREATED THE FIRST SLAYER."
SO ARE YOU MY WATCH--
NO.
NO.
NO.
MY REASONS ARE MY OWN.
THEN WHY --

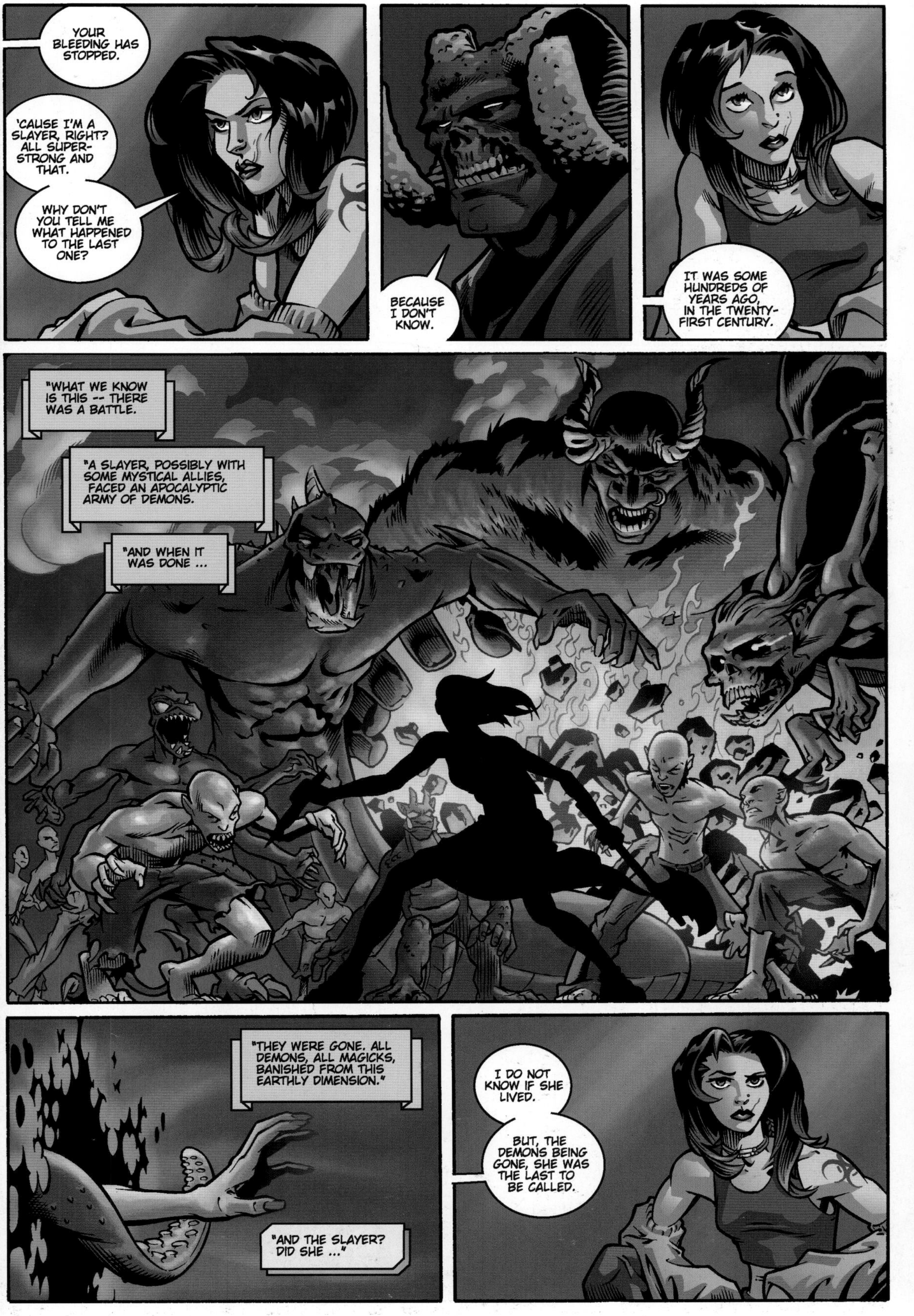
YOUR BLEEDING HAS STOPPED.
'CAUSE I'M A SLAYER, RIGHT? ALL SUPER-STRONG AND THAT.
WHY DON'T YOU TELL ME WHAT HAPPENED TO THE LAST ONE?
BECAUSE I DON'T KNOW.
IT WAS SOME HUNDREDS OF YEARS AGO, IN THE TWENTY-FIRST CENTURY.
"WHAT WE KNOW IS THIS -- THERE WAS A BATTLE.
"A SLAYER, POSSIBLY WITH SOME MYSTICAL ALLIES, FACED AN APOCALYPTIC ARMY OF DEMONS.
"AND WHEN IT WAS DONE ...
"THEY WERE GONE. ALL DEMONS, ALL MAGICKS, BANISHED FROM THIS EARTHLY DIMENSION."
"AND THE SLAYER? DID SHE ..."
I DO NOT KNOW IF SHE LIVED.
BUT, THE DEMONS BEING GONE, SHE WAS THE LAST TO BE CALLED.

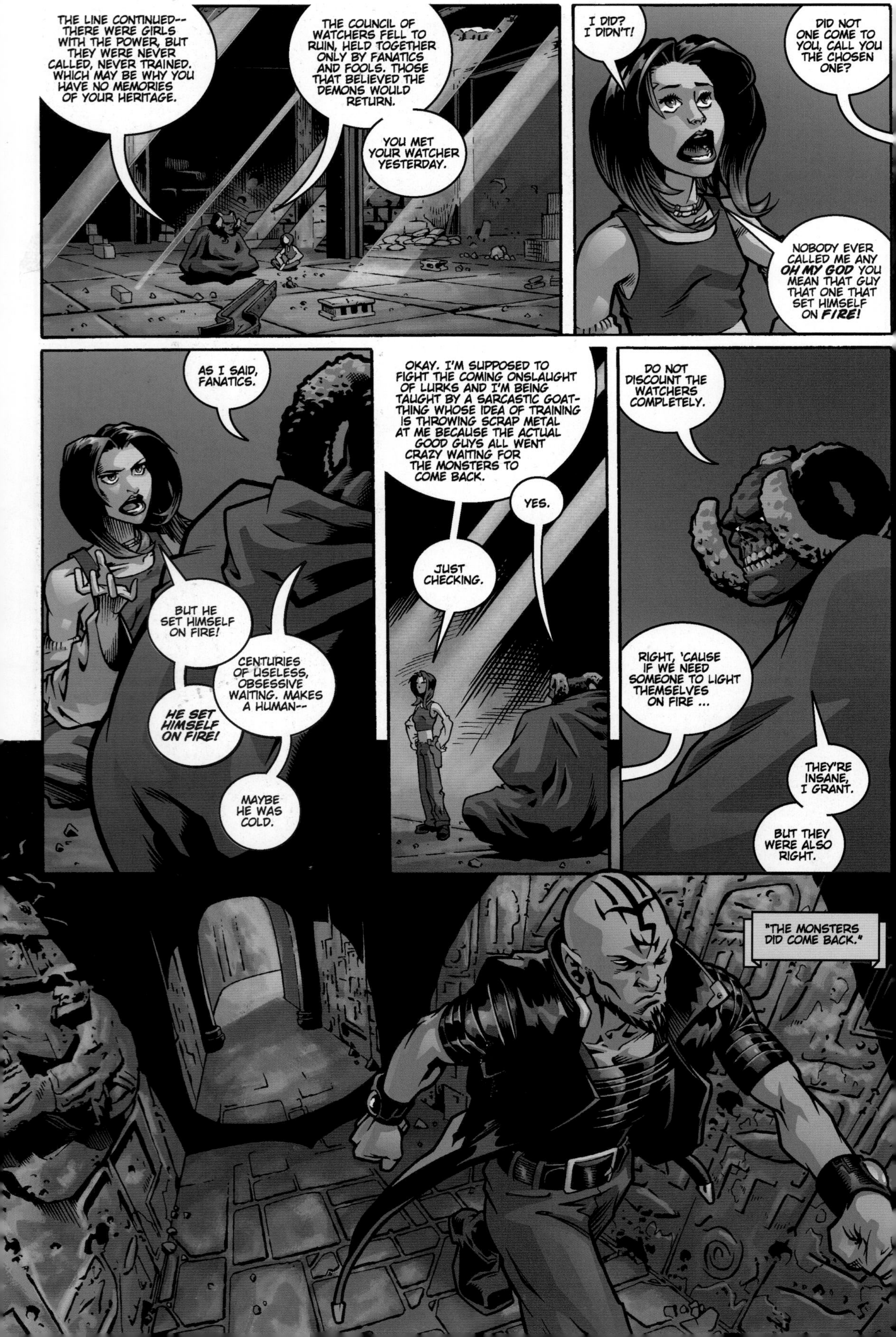
THE LINE CONTINUED-- THERE WERE GIRLS WITH THE POWER, BUT THEY WERE NEVER CALLED, NEVER TRAINED. WHICH MAY BE WHY YOU HAVE NO MEMORIES OF YOUR HERITAGE.
THE COUNCIL OF WATCHERS FELL TO RUIN, HELD TOGETHER ONLY BY FANATICS AND FOOLS. THOSE THAT BELIEVED THE DEMONS WOULD RETURN.
YOU MET YOUR WATCHER YESTERDAY.
I DID? I DIDN'T!
DID NOT ONE COME TO YOU, CALL YOU THE CHOSEN ONE?
NOBODY EVER CALLED ME ANY **OH MY GOD** YOU MEAN THAT GUY THAT ONE THAT SET HIMSELF ON **FIRE!**
AS I SAID, FANATICS.
BUT HE SET HIMSELF ON FIRE!
CENTURIES OF USELESS, OBSESSIVE WAITING. MAKES A HUMAN--
HE SET HIMSELF ON FIRE!
MAYBE HE WAS COLD.
OKAY. I'M SUPPOSED TO FIGHT THE COMING ONSLAUGHT OF LURKS AND I'M BEING TAUGHT BY A SARCASTIC GOAT-THING WHOSE IDEA OF TRAINING IS THROWING SCRAP METAL AT ME BECAUSE THE ACTUAL GOOD GUYS ALL WENT CRAZY WAITING FOR THE MONSTERS TO COME BACK.
YES.
JUST CHECKING.
DO NOT DISCOUNT THE WATCHERS COMPLETELY.
RIGHT, 'CAUSE IF WE NEED SOMEONE TO LIGHT THEMSELVES ON FIRE ...
THEY'RE INSANE, I GRANT.
BUT THEY WERE ALSO RIGHT.
"THE MONSTERS DID COME BACK."

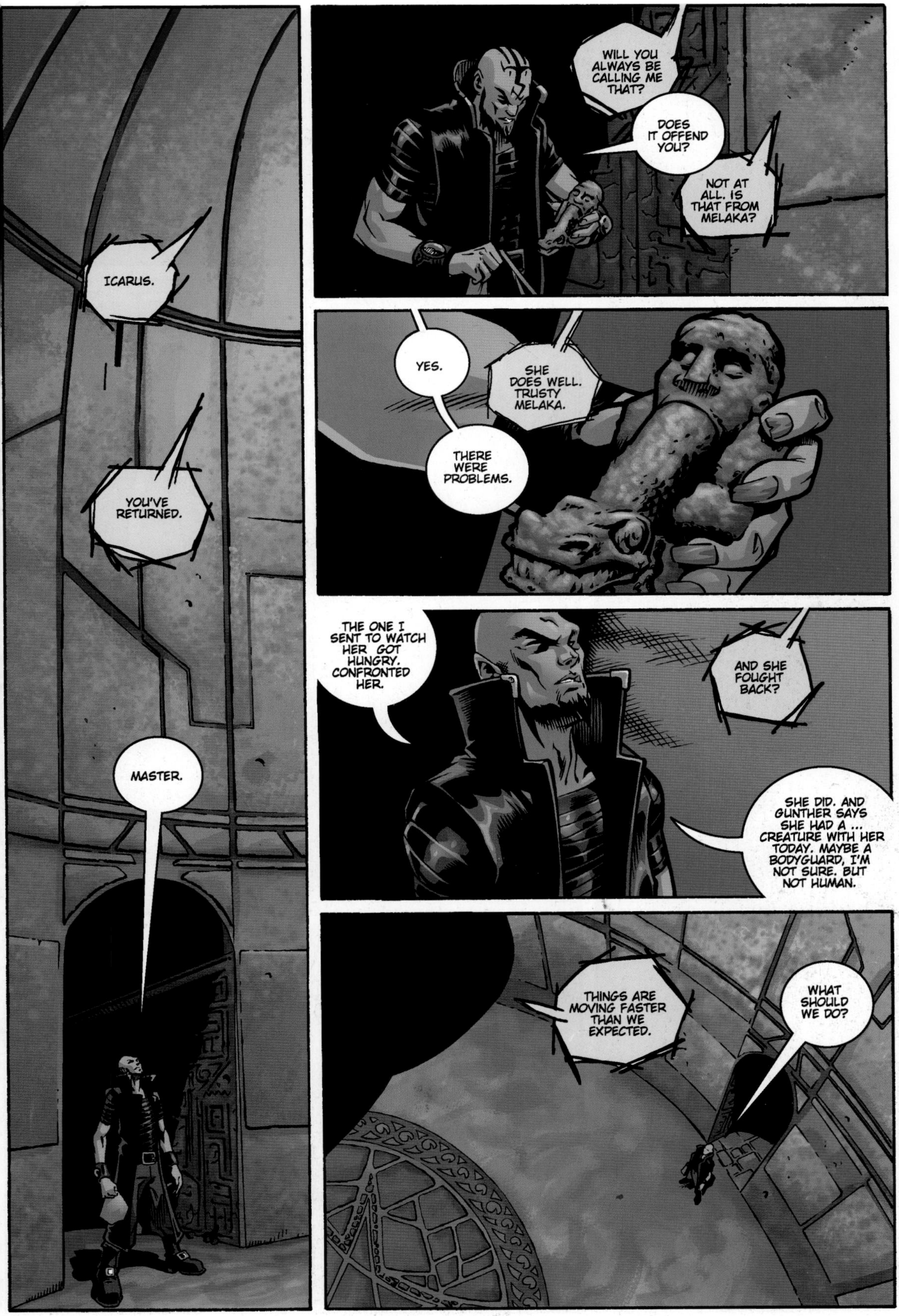
ICARUS.
YOU'VE RETURNED.
MASTER.
WILL YOU ALWAYS BE CALLING ME THAT?
DOES IT OFFEND YOU?
NOT AT ALL. IS THAT FROM MELAKA?
YES.
SHE DOES WELL. TRUSTY MELAKA.
THERE WERE PROBLEMS.
THE ONE I SENT TO WATCH HER GOT HUNGRY. CONFRONTED HER.
AND SHE FOUGHT BACK?
SHE DID. AND GUNTHER SAYS SHE HAD A ... CREATURE WITH HER TODAY. MAYBE A BODYGUARD, I'M NOT SURE. BUT NOT HUMAN.
THINGS ARE MOVING FASTER THAN WE EXPECTED.
WHAT SHOULD WE DO?

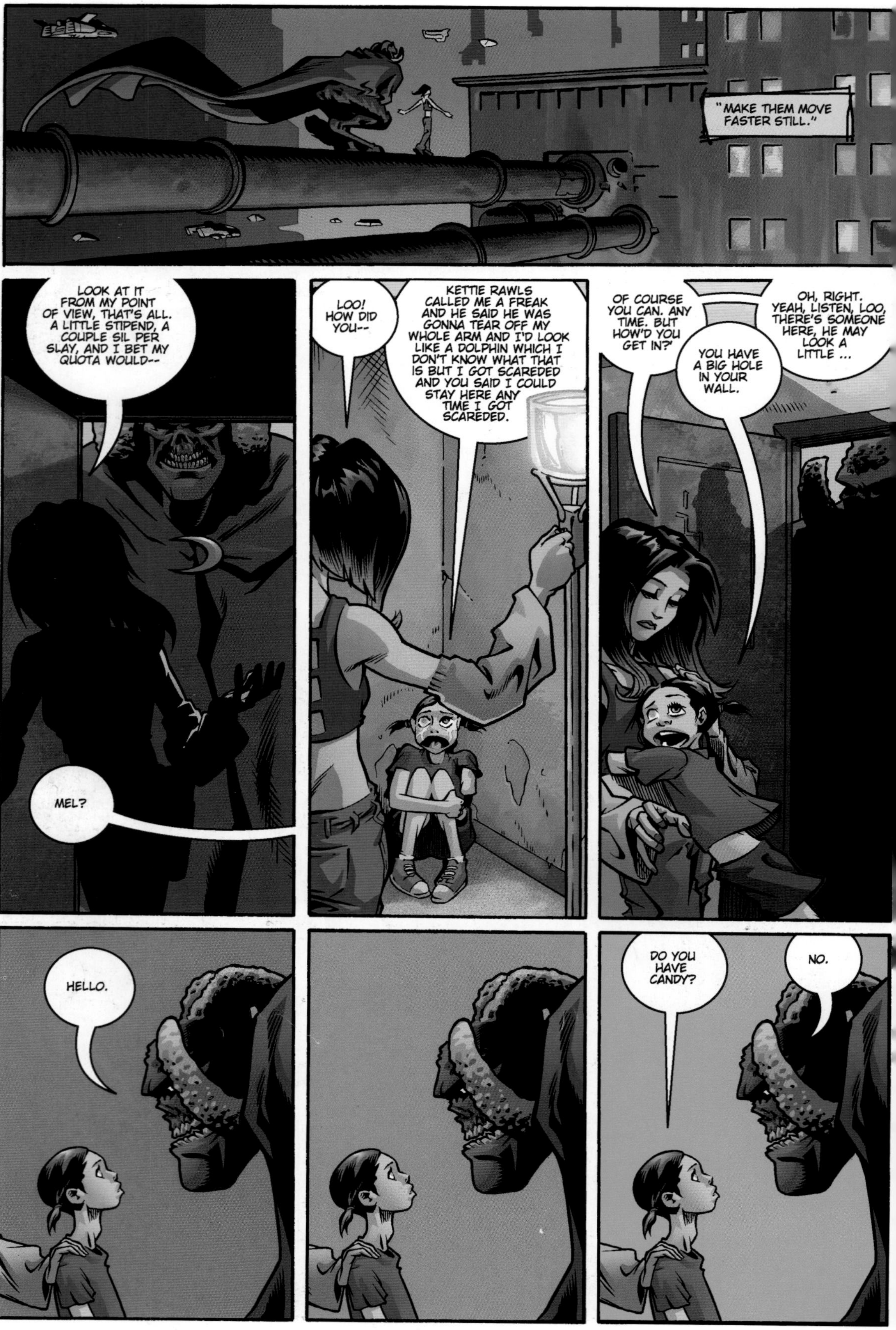
"MAKE THEM MOVE FASTER STILL."
LOOK AT IT FROM MY POINT OF VIEW, THAT'S ALL. A LITTLE STIPEND, A COUPLE SIL PER SLAY, AND I BET MY QUOTA WOULD--
MEL?
LOO! HOW DID YOU--
KETTIE RAWLS CALLED ME A FREAK AND HE SAID HE WAS GONNA TEAR OFF MY WHOLE ARM AND I'D LOOK LIKE A DOLPHIN WHICH I DON'T KNOW WHAT THAT IS BUT I GOT SCAREDED AND YOU SAID I COULD STAY HERE ANY TIME I GOT SCAREDED.
OF COURSE YOU CAN. ANY TIME. BUT HOW'D YOU GET IN?'
YOU HAVE A BIG HOLE IN YOUR WALL.
OH, RIGHT. YEAH, LISTEN, LOO, THERE'S SOMEONE HERE, HE MAY LOOK A LITTLE ...
HELLO.
DO YOU HAVE CANDY?
NO.

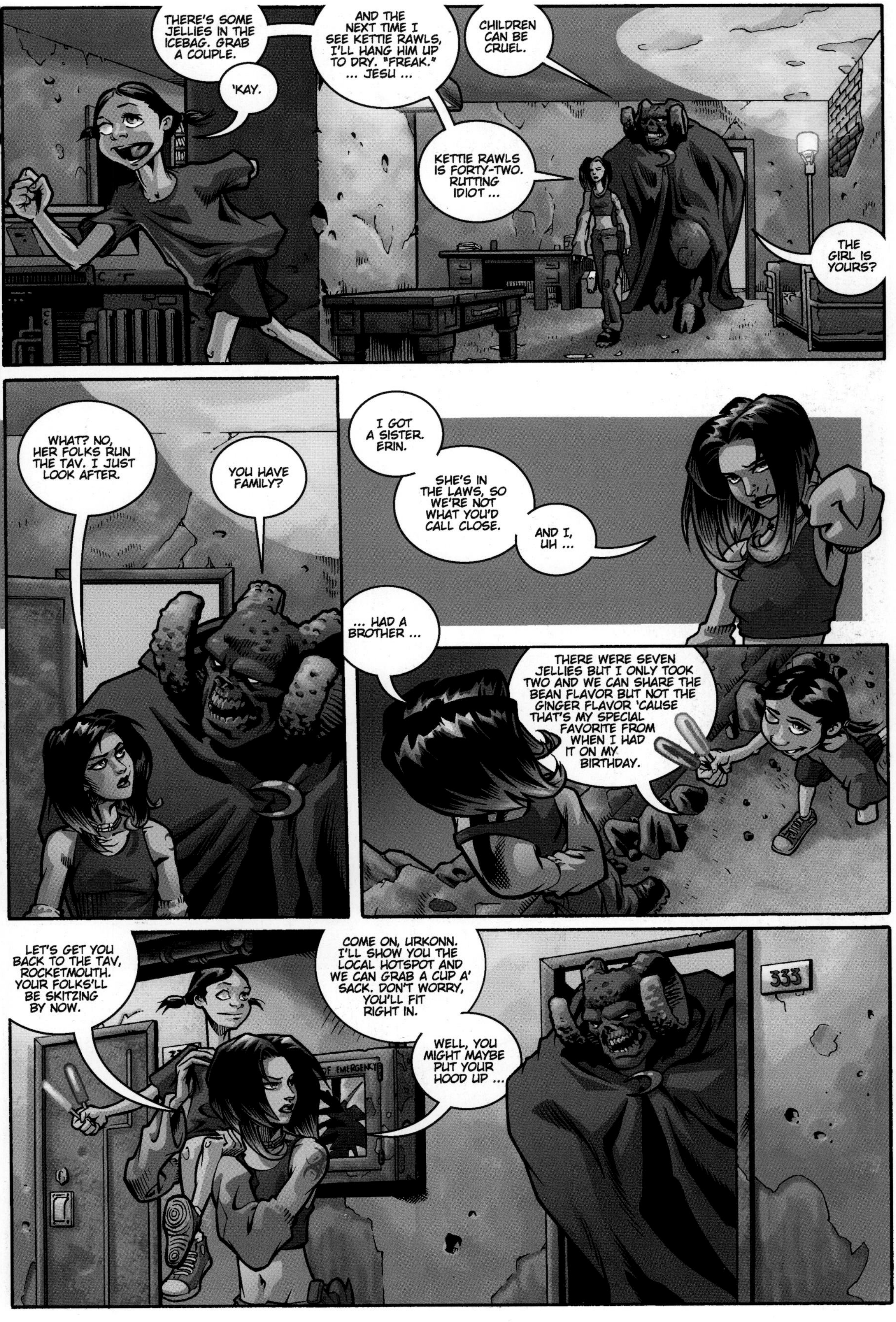
THERE'S SOME JELLIES IN THE ICEBAG. GRAB A COUPLE.
'KAY.
AND THE NEXT TIME I SEE KETTIE RAWLS, I'LL HANG HIM UP TO DRY. "FREAK." ... JESU ...
KETTIE RAWLS IS FORTY-TWO. RUTTING IDIOT ...
CHILDREN CAN BE CRUEL.
THE GIRL IS YOURS?
WHAT? NO, HER FOLKS RUN THE TAV. I JUST LOOK AFTER.
YOU HAVE FAMILY?
I GOT A SISTER. ERIN.
SHE'S IN THE LAWS, SO WE'RE NOT WHAT YOU'D CALL CLOSE.
AND I, UH ...
... HAD A BROTHER ...
THERE WERE SEVEN JELLIES BUT I ONLY TOOK TWO AND WE CAN SHARE THE BEAN FLAVOR BUT NOT THE GINGER FLAVOR 'CAUSE THAT'S MY SPECIAL FAVORITE FROM WHEN I HAD IT ON MY BIRTHDAY.
LET'S GET YOU BACK TO THE TAV, ROCKETMOUTH. YOUR FOLKS'LL BE SKITZING BY NOW.
COME ON, URKONN. I'LL SHOW YOU THE LOCAL HOTSPOT AND WE CAN GRAB A CUP A' SACK. DON'T WORRY, YOU'LL FIT RIGHT IN.
WELL, YOU MIGHT MAYBE PUT YOUR HOOD UP ...
333

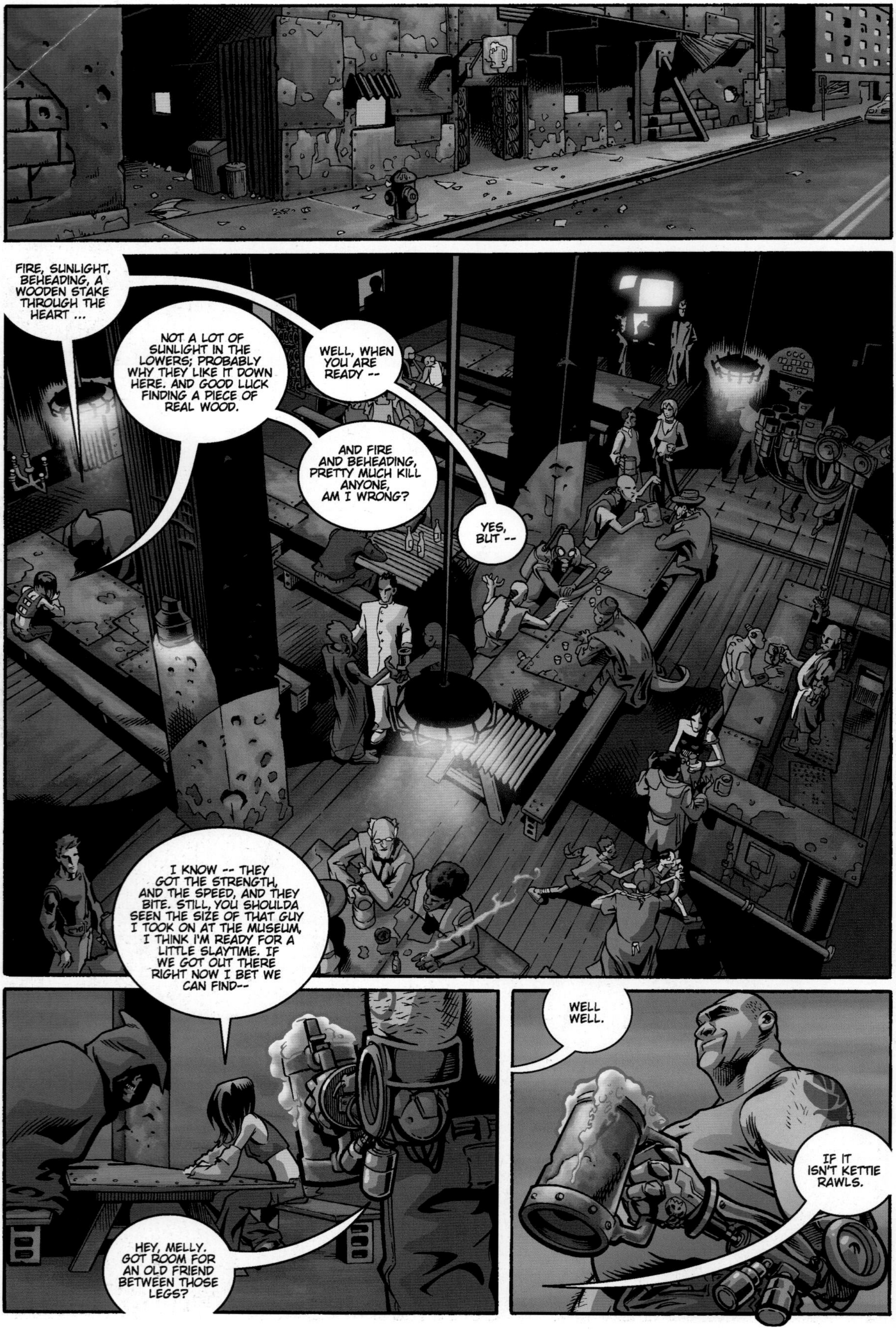
FIRE, SUNLIGHT, BEHEADING, A WOODEN STAKE THROUGH THE HEART ...
NOT A LOT OF SUNLIGHT IN THE LOWERS; PROBABLY WHY THEY LIKE IT DOWN HERE. AND GOOD LUCK FINDING A PIECE OF REAL WOOD.
WELL, WHEN YOU ARE READY --
AND FIRE AND BEHEADING, PRETTY MUCH KILL ANYONE, AM I WRONG?
YES, BUT --
I KNOW -- THEY GOT THE STRENGTH, AND THE SPEED, AND THEY BITE. STILL, YOU SHOULDA SEEN THE SIZE OF THAT GUY I TOOK ON AT THE MUSEUM, I THINK I'M READY FOR A LITTLE SLAYTIME. IF WE GOT OUT THERE RIGHT NOW I BET WE CAN FIND--
HEY, MELLY. GOT ROOM FOR AN OLD FRIEND BETWEEN THOSE LEGS?
WELL WELL.
IF IT ISN'T KETTIE RAWLS.

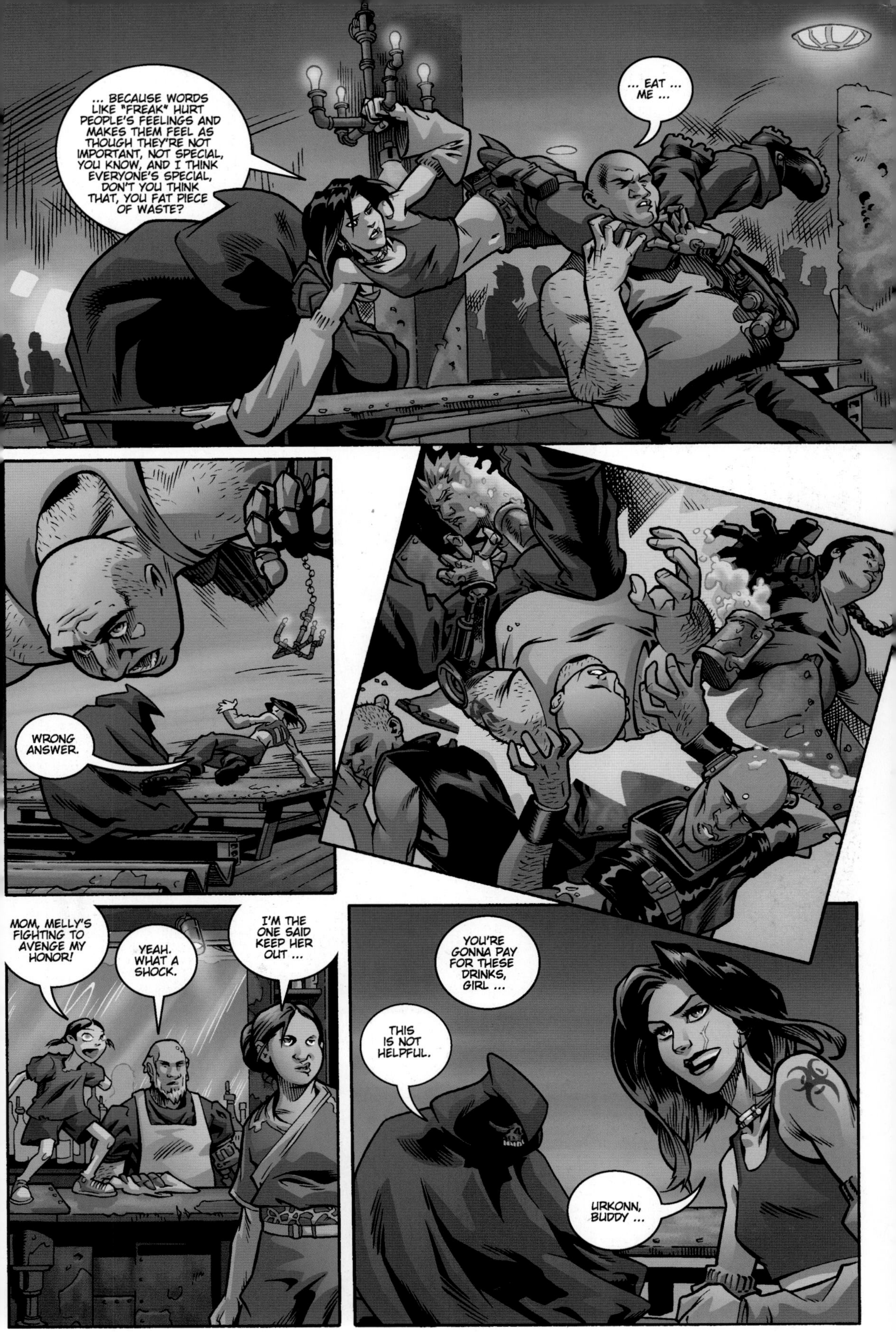

... BECAUSE WORDS LIKE "FREAK" HURT PEOPLE'S FEELINGS AND MAKES THEM FEEL AS THOUGH THEY'RE NOT IMPORTANT, NOT SPECIAL, YOU KNOW, AND I THINK EVERYONE'S SPECIAL, DON'T YOU THINK THAT, YOU FAT PIECE OF WASTE?
... EAT ... ME ...
WRONG ANSWER.
MOM, MELLY'S FIGHTING TO AVENGE MY HONOR!
YEAH. WHAT A SHOCK.
I'M THE ONE SAID KEEP HER OUT ...
YOU'RE GONNA PAY FOR THESE DRINKS, GIRL ...
THIS IS NOT HELPFUL.
URKONN, BUDDY ...

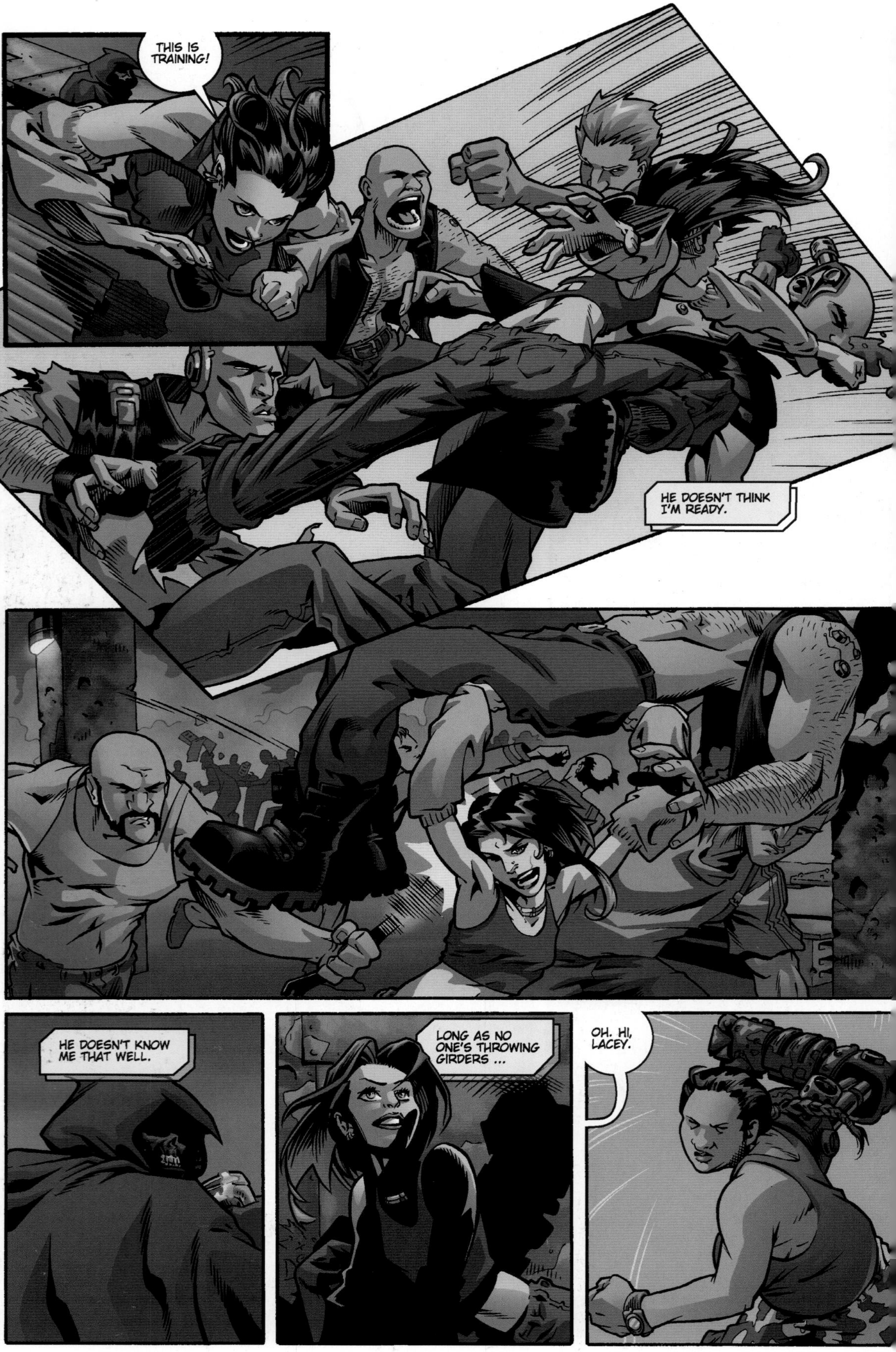
THIS IS TRAINING!
HE DOESN'T THINK I'M READY.
HE DOESN'T KNOW ME THAT WELL.
LONG AS NO ONE'S THROWING GIRDERS ...
OH. HI, LACEY.

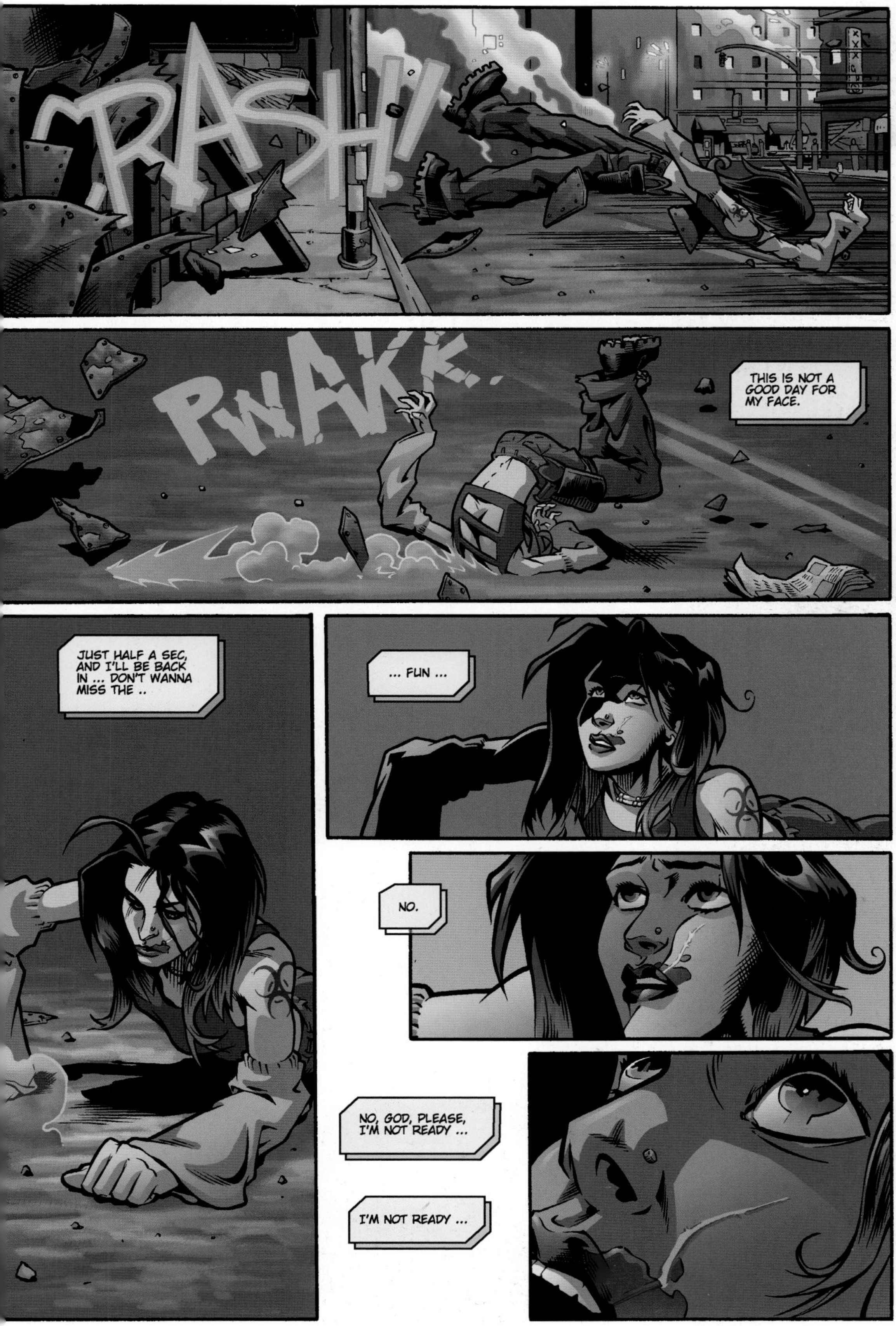
CRASH!!
PWAKK
THIS IS NOT A GOOD DAY FOR MY FACE.
JUST HALF A SEC, AND I'LL BE BACK IN ... DON'T WANNA MISS THE ..
... FUN ...
NO.
NO, GOD, PLEASE, I'M NOT READY ...
I'M NOT READY ...

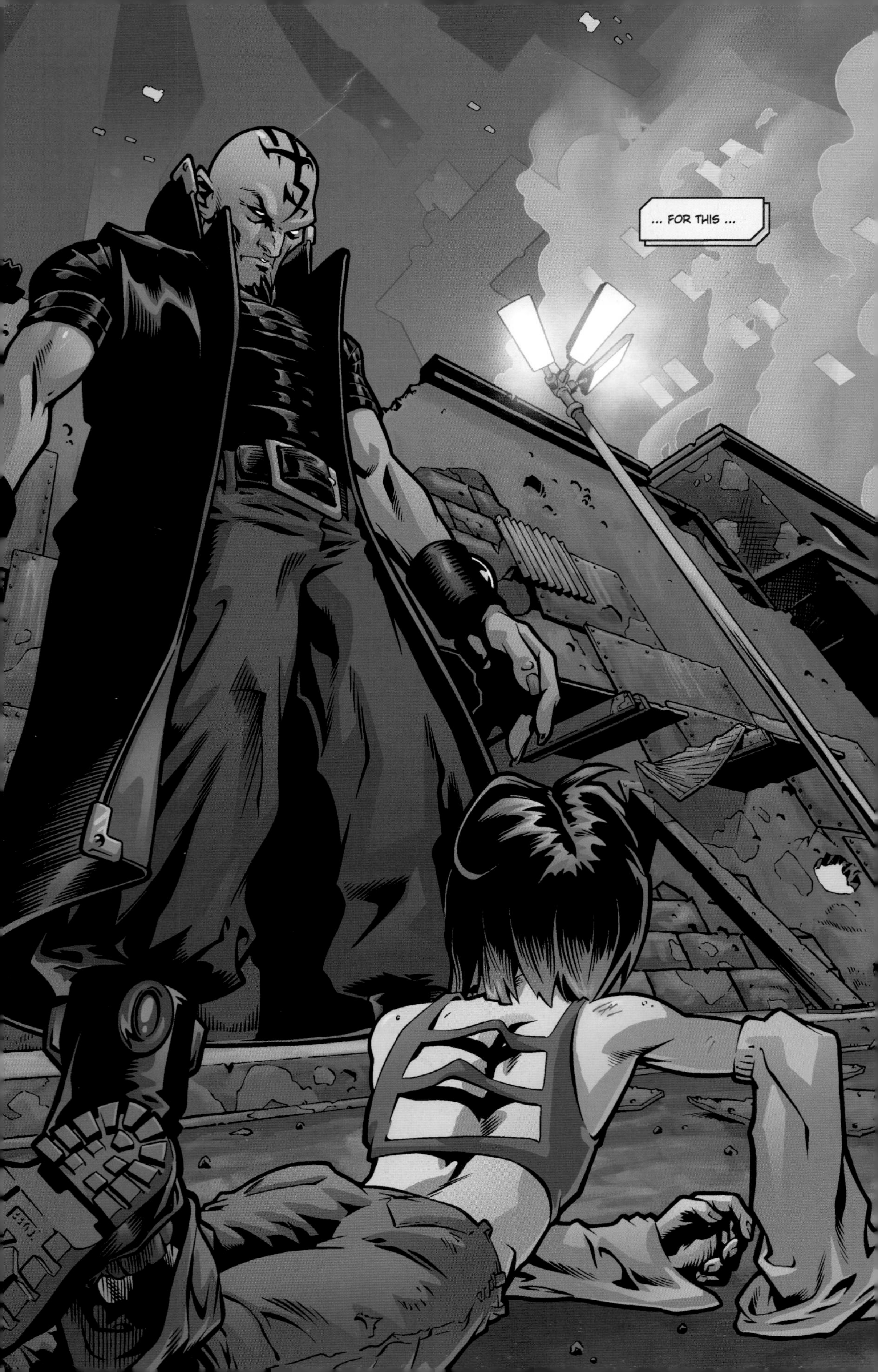
... FOR THIS ...

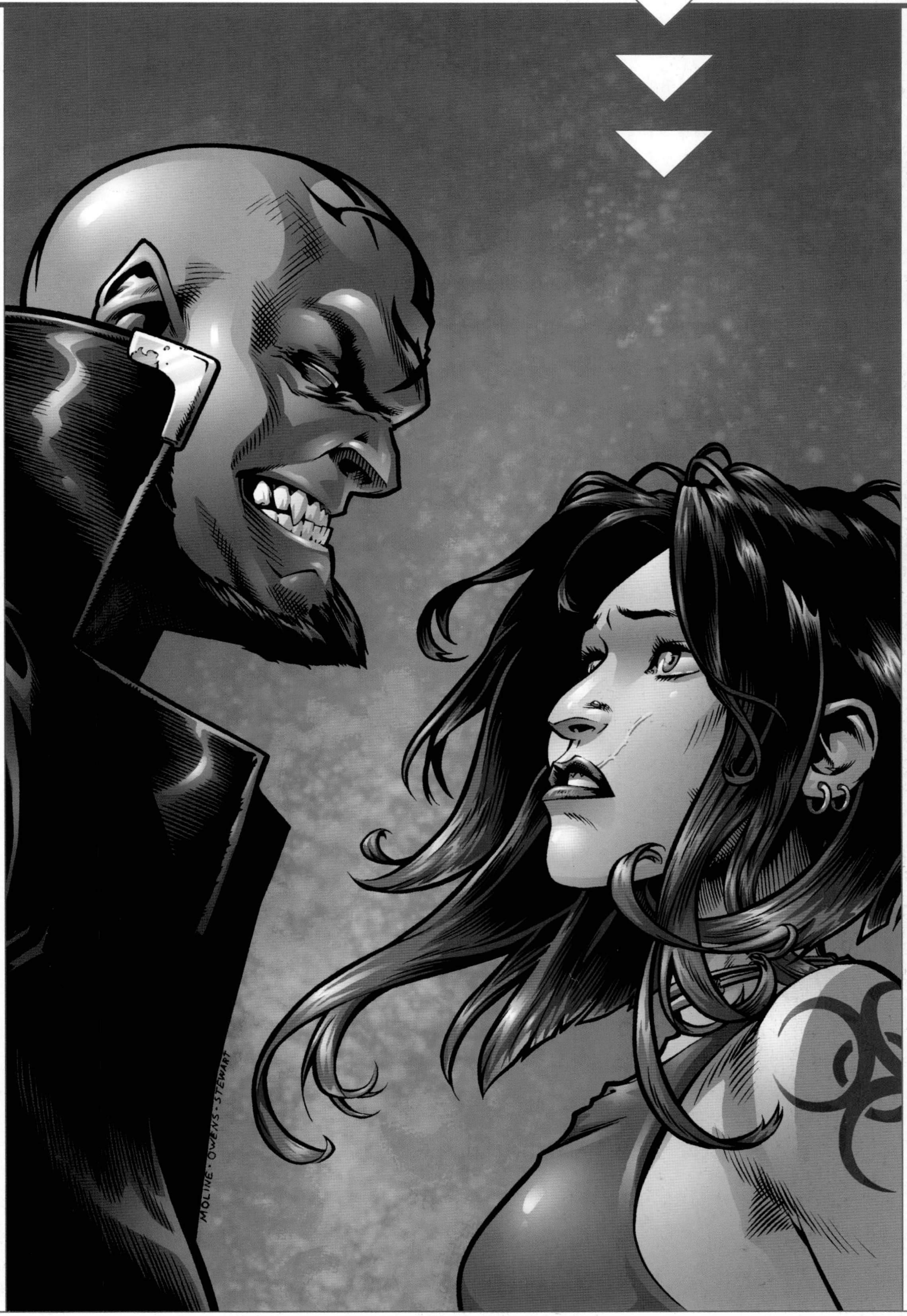
MOLINE • OWENS • STEWART

"I've met you ten thousand times.
I've killed you a hundred ways—in a rage,
cool as ice, giggling like a schoolgirl..."

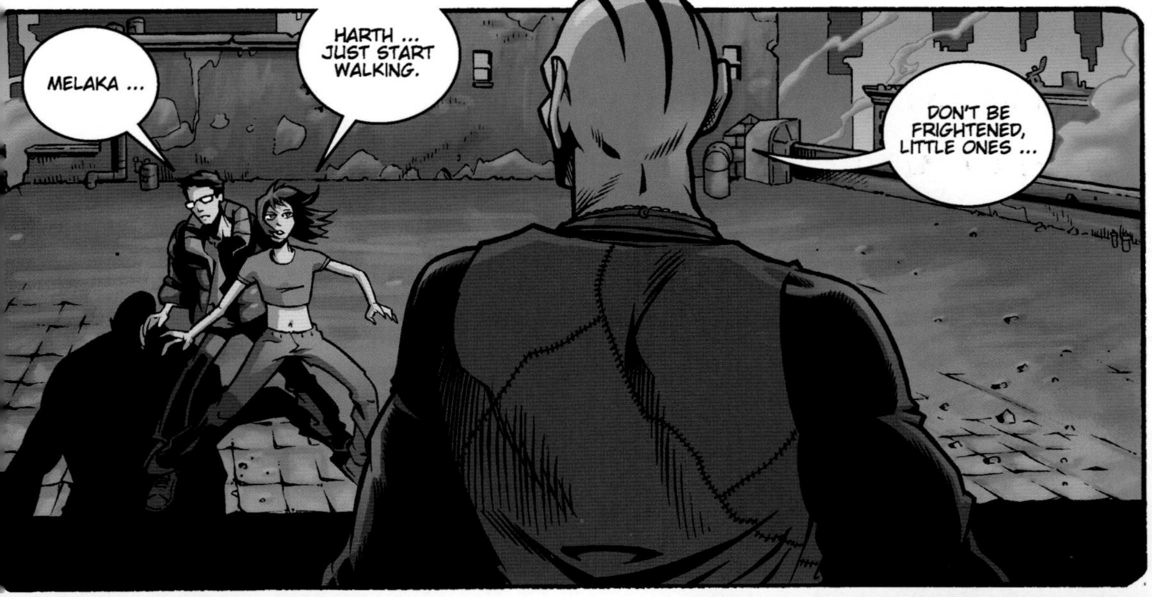
MELAKA ...
HARTH ... JUST START WALKING.
DON'T BE FRIGHTENED, LITTLE ONES ...

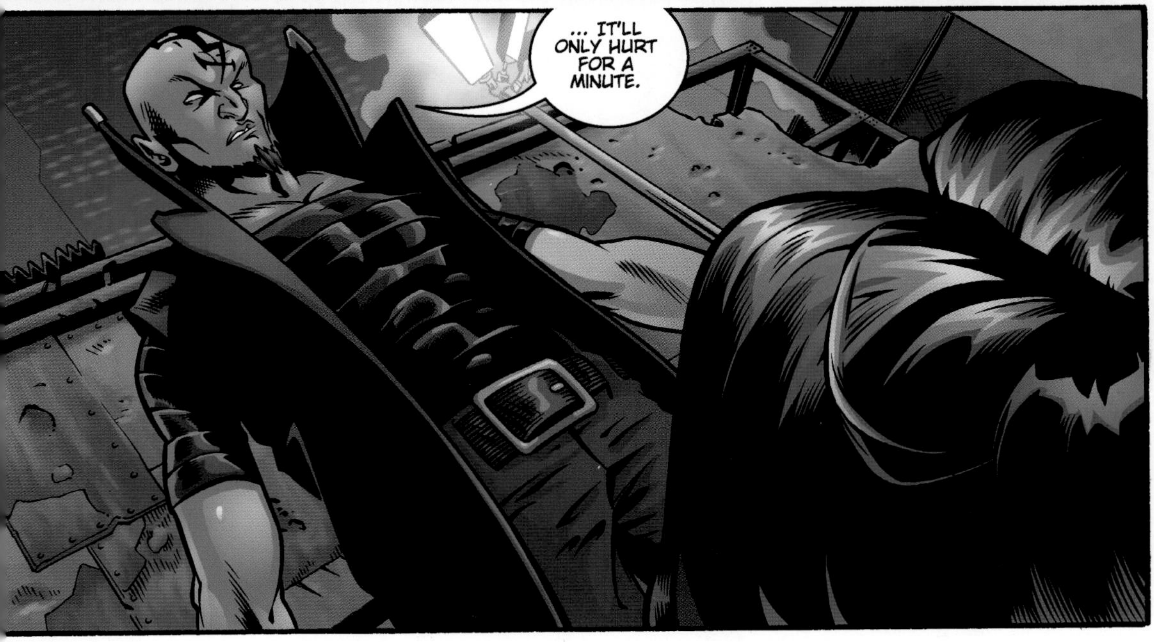
... IT'LL ONLY HURT FOR A MINUTE.

CHAPTER FOUR

OUT OF THE PAST

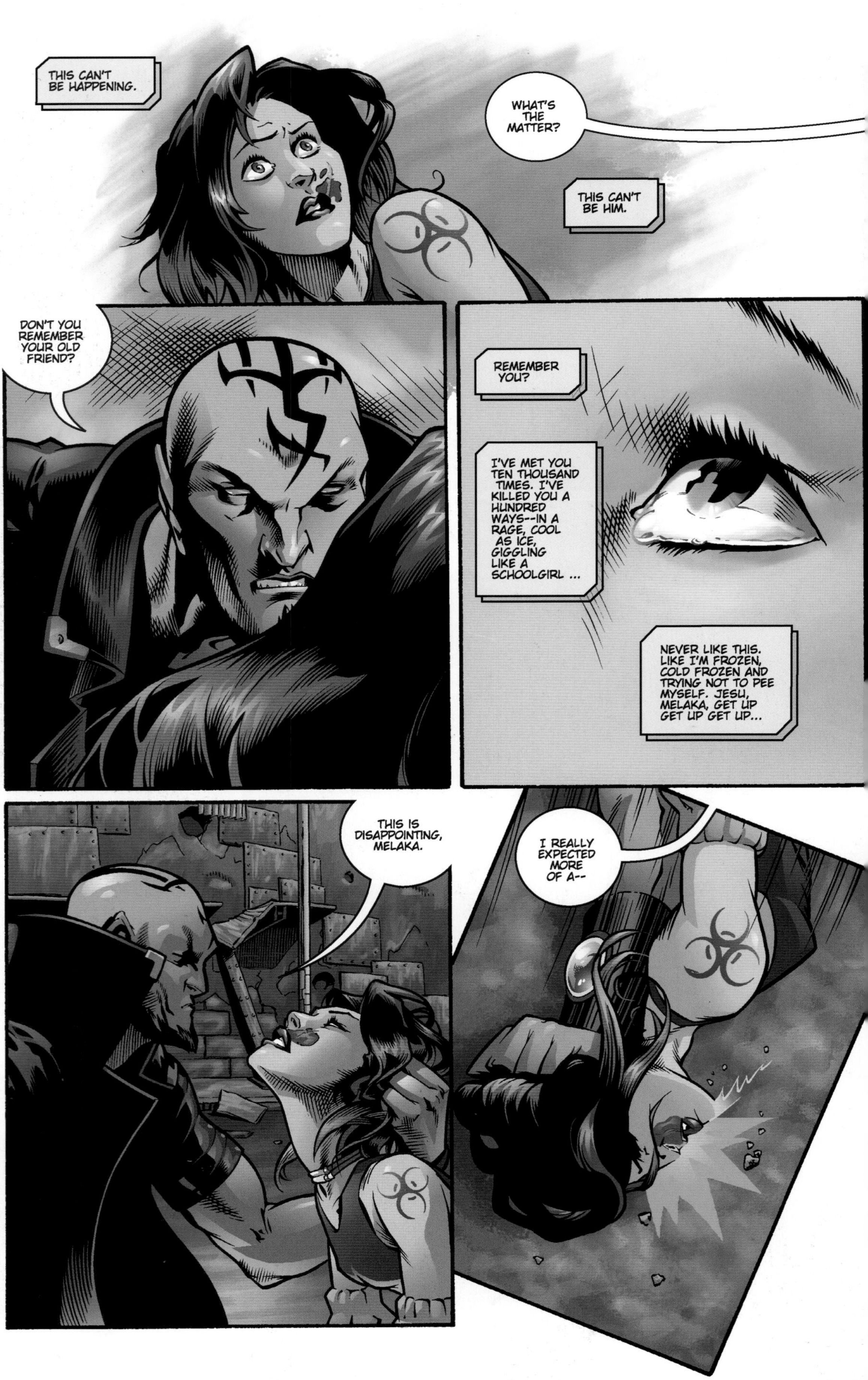
THIS CAN'T BE HAPPENING.
WHAT'S THE MATTER?
THIS CAN'T BE HIM.
DON'T YOU REMEMBER YOUR OLD FRIEND?
REMEMBER YOU?
I'VE MET YOU TEN THOUSAND TIMES. I'VE KILLED YOU A HUNDRED WAYS--IN A RAGE, COOL AS ICE, GIGGLING LIKE A SCHOOLGIRL ...
NEVER LIKE THIS. LIKE I'M FROZEN, COLD FROZEN AND TRYING NOT TO PEE MYSELF. JESU, MELAKA, GET UP GET UP GET UP...
THIS IS DISAPPOINTING, MELAKA.
I REALLY EXPECTED MORE OF A--

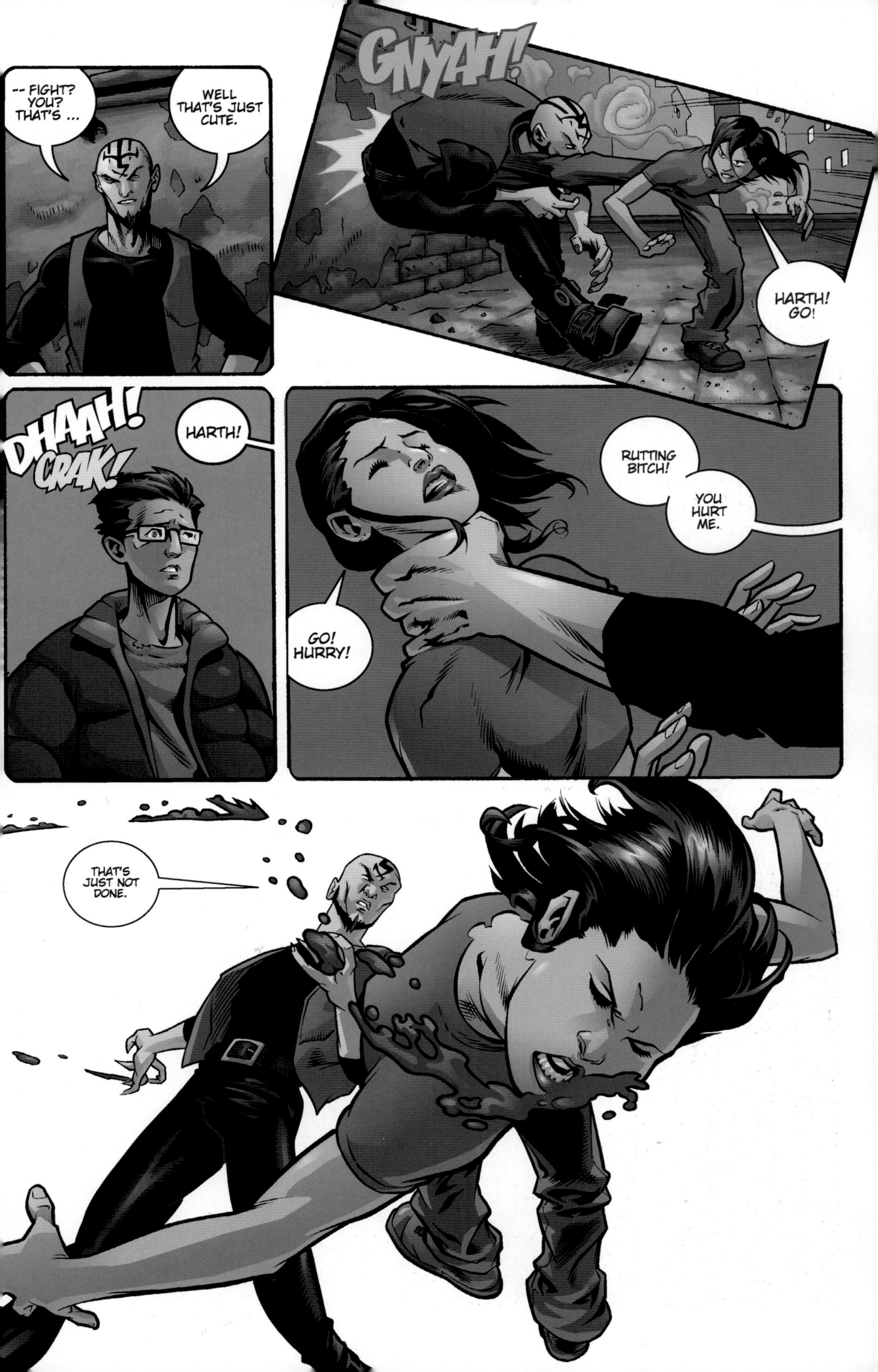
-- FIGHT? YOU? THAT'S ...
WELL THAT'S JUST CUTE.
GNYAH!
HARTH! GO!
DHAAH!
CRAK!
HARTH!
RUTTING BITCH!
YOU HURT ME.
GO! HURRY!
THAT'S JUST NOT DONE.

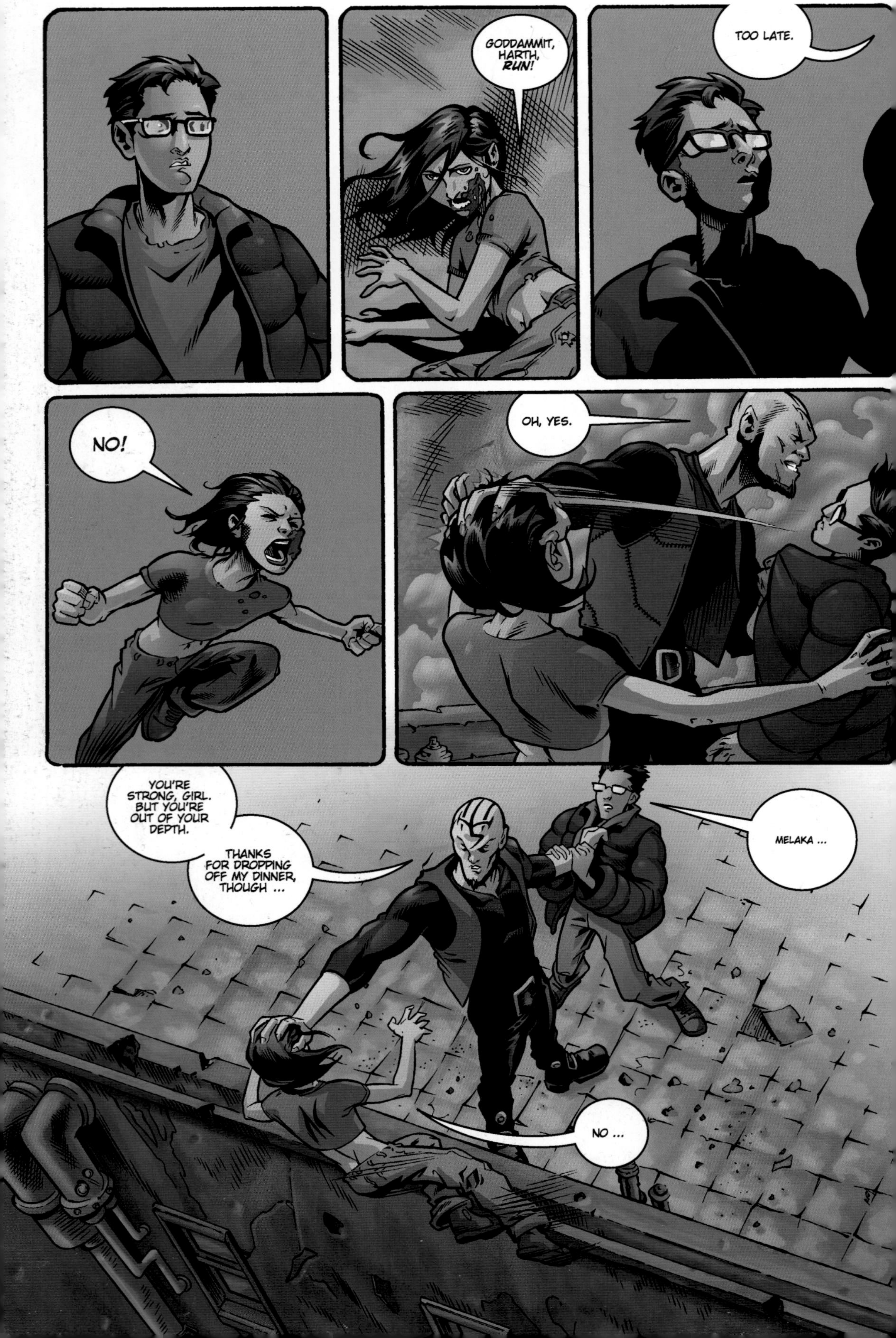
GODDAMMIT, HARTH, RUN!
TOO LATE.
NO!
OH, YES.
YOU'RE STRONG, GIRL. BUT YOU'RE OUT OF YOUR DEPTH.
THANKS FOR DROPPING OFF MY DINNER, THOUGH ...
MELAKA ...
NO ...

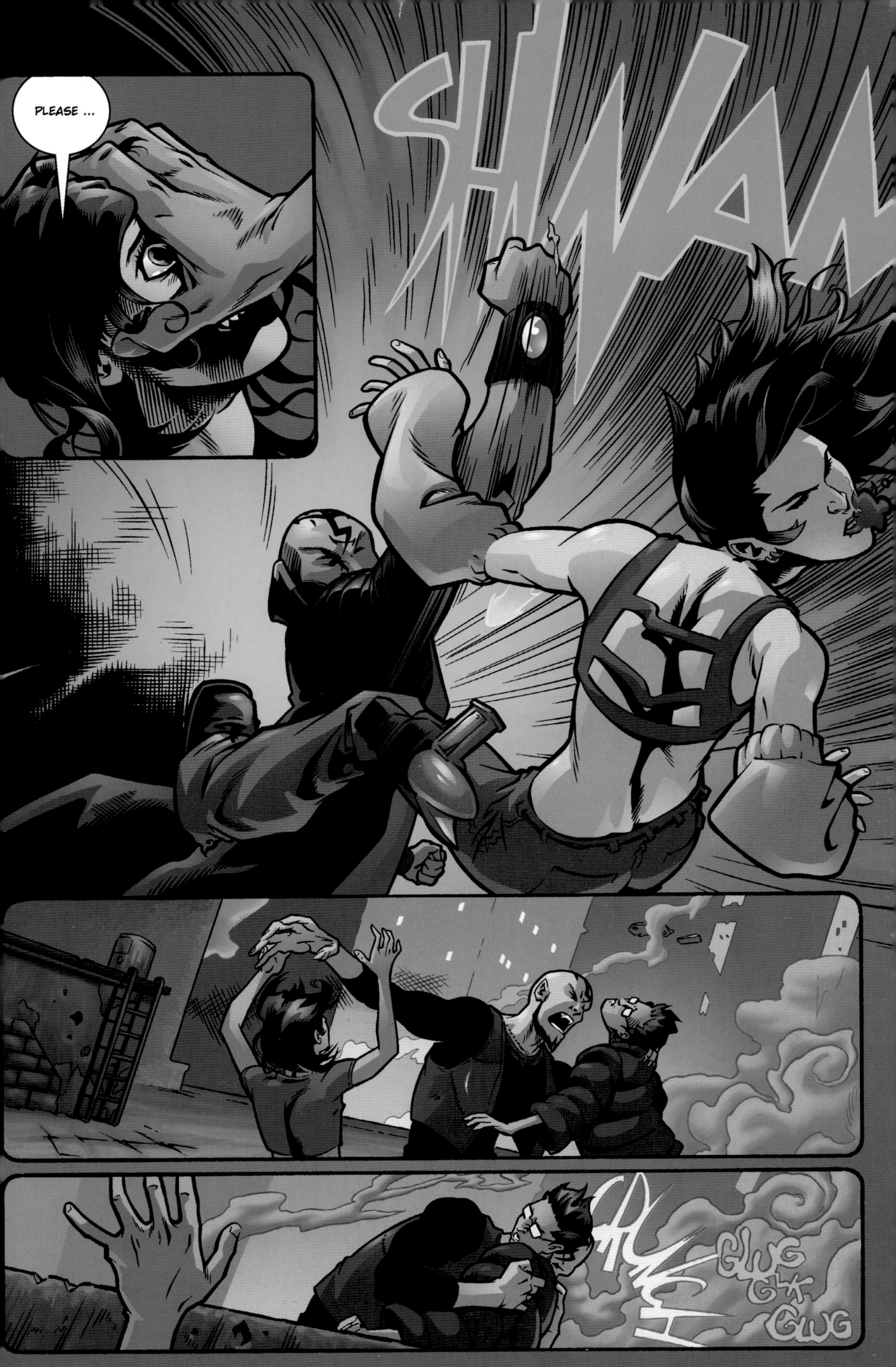
PLEASE ...
GLUG
GLK
GLUG

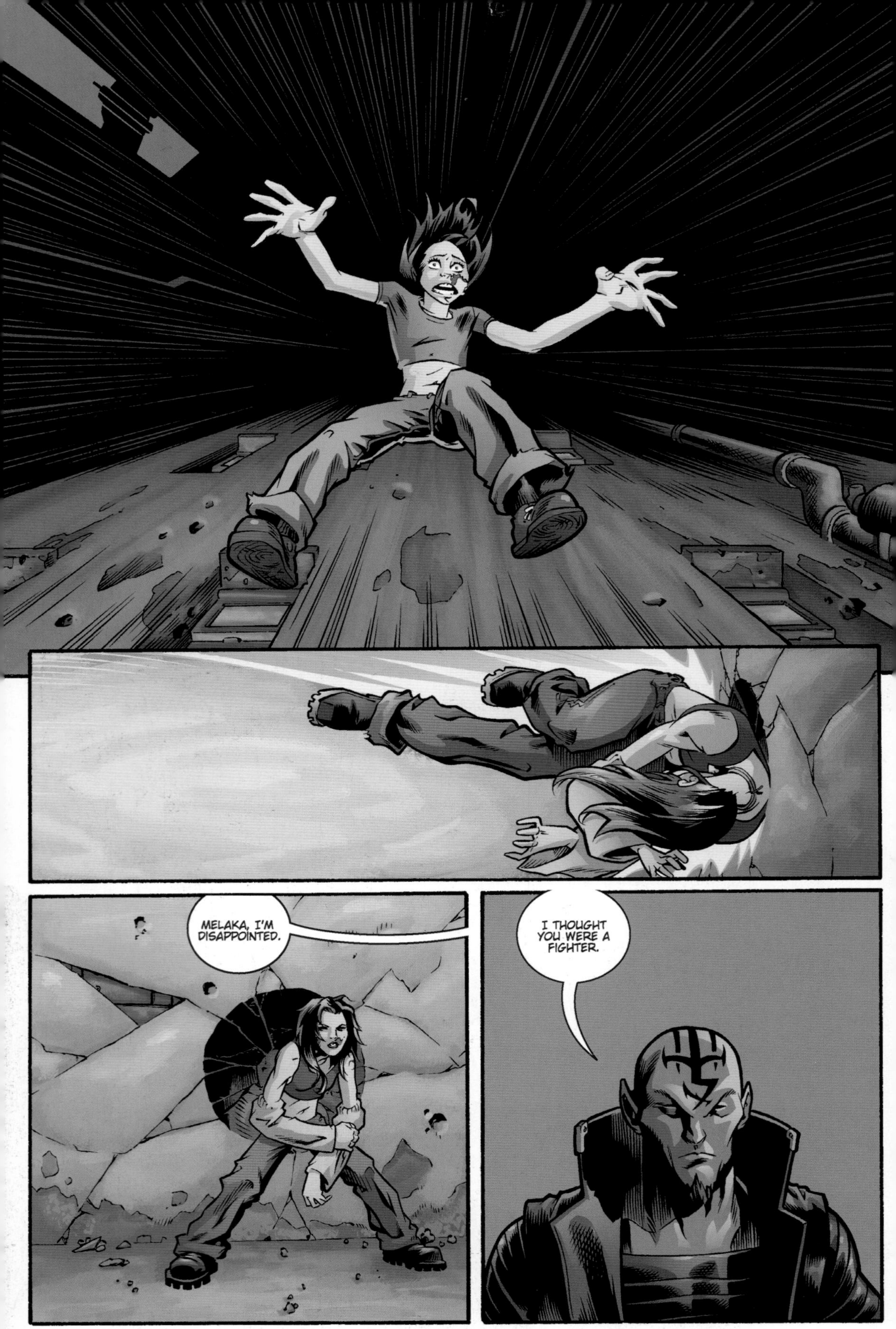
MELAKA, I'M DISAPPOINTED.
I THOUGHT YOU WERE A FIGHTER.

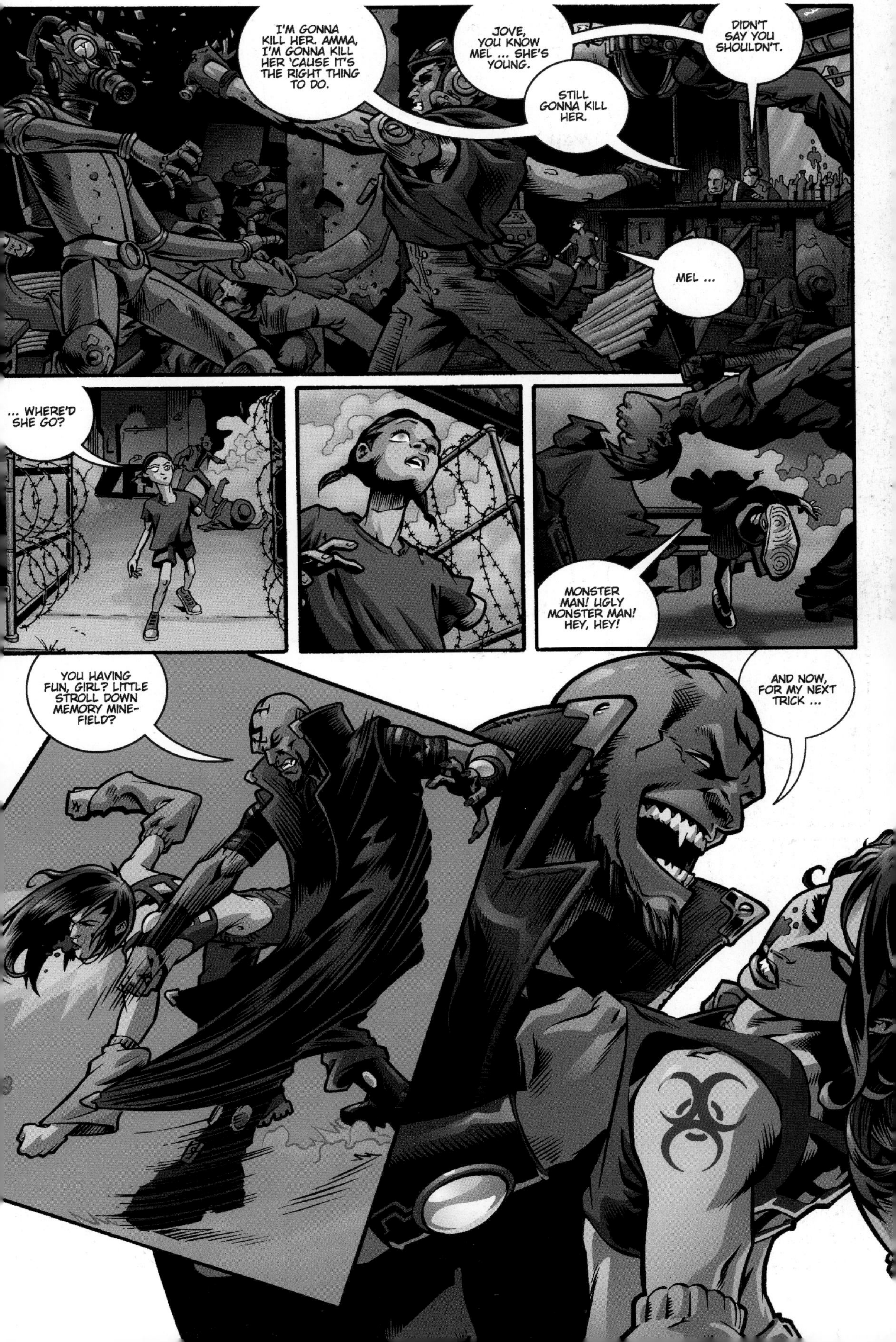
I'M GONNA KILL HER. AMMA, I'M GONNA KILL HER 'CAUSE IT'S THE RIGHT THING TO DO.
JOVE, YOU KNOW MEL ... SHE'S YOUNG.
STILL GONNA KILL HER.
DIDN'T SAY YOU SHOULDN'T.
MEL ...
... WHERE'D SHE GO?
MONSTER MAN! UGLY MONSTER MAN! HEY, HEY!
YOU HAVING FUN, GIRL? LITTLE STROLL DOWN MEMORY MINE-FIELD?
AND NOW, FOR MY NEXT TRICK ...

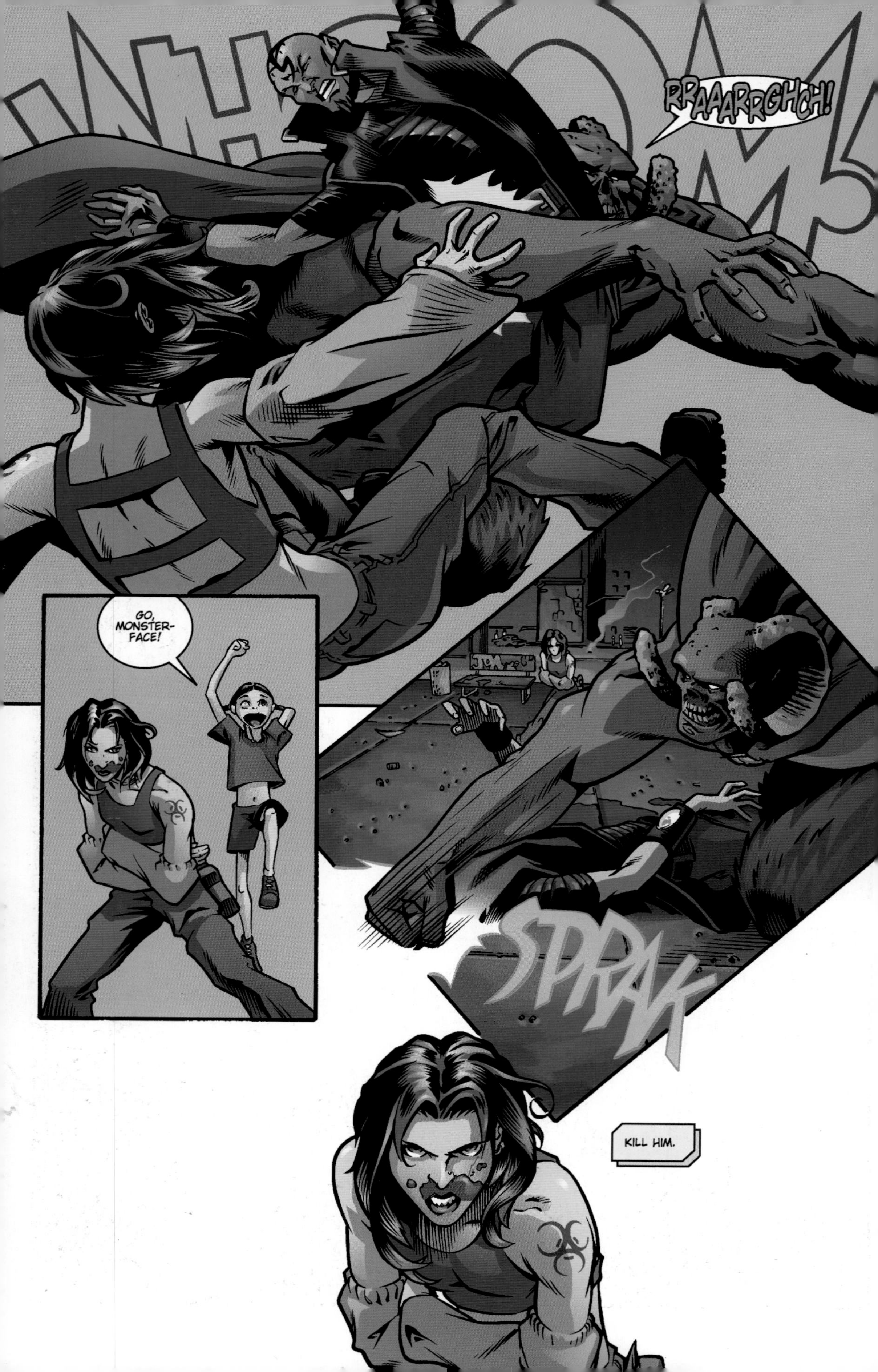
RRAAARRGHCH!
GO, MONSTER-FACE!
SPRAK
KILL HIM.

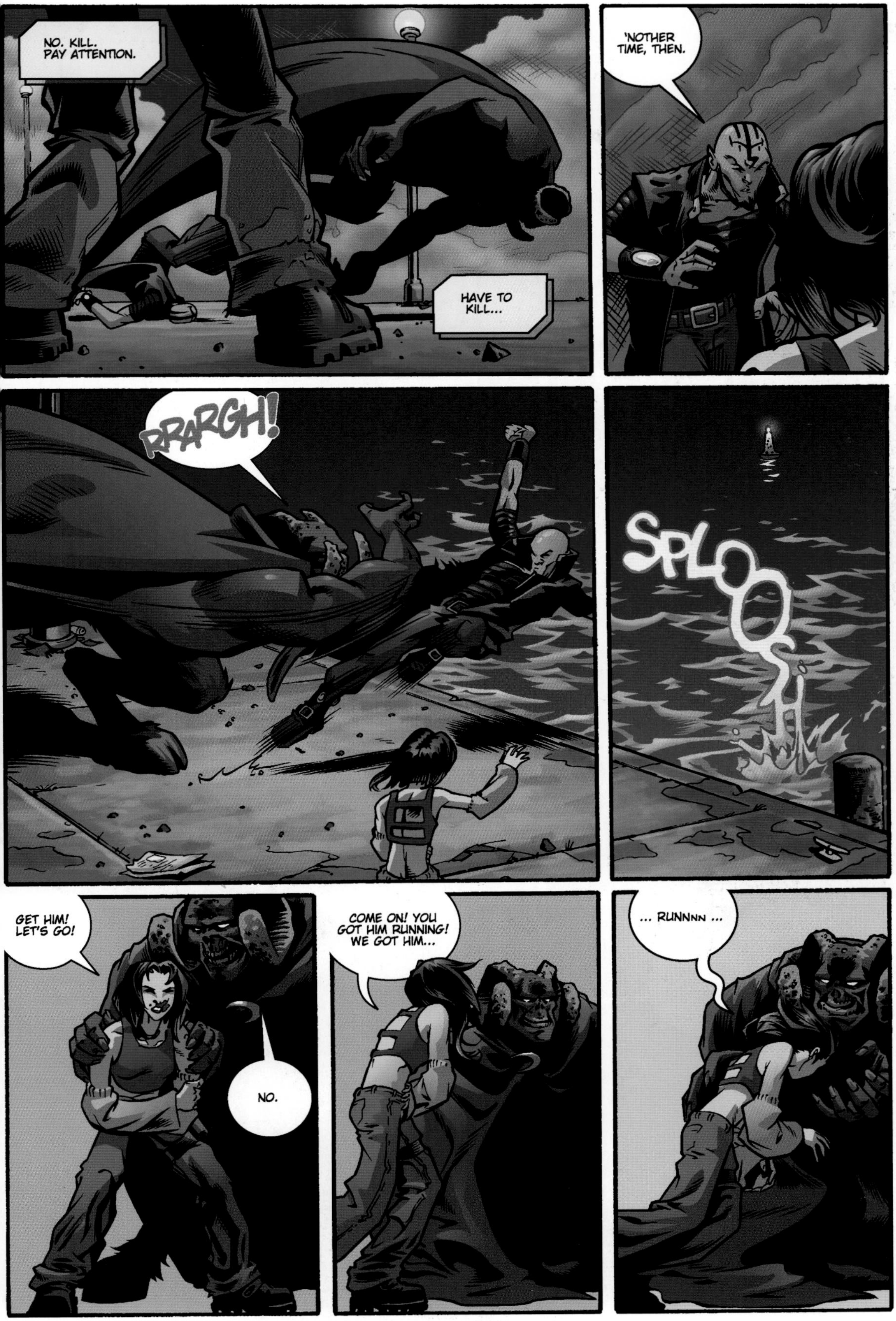

NO. KILL.
PAY ATTENTION.
HAVE TO KILL...
'NOTHER TIME, THEN.
RRARGH!
SPLOOSH
GET HIM! LET'S GO!
NO.
COME ON! YOU GOT HIM RUNNING! WE GOT HIM...
... RUNNNN ...

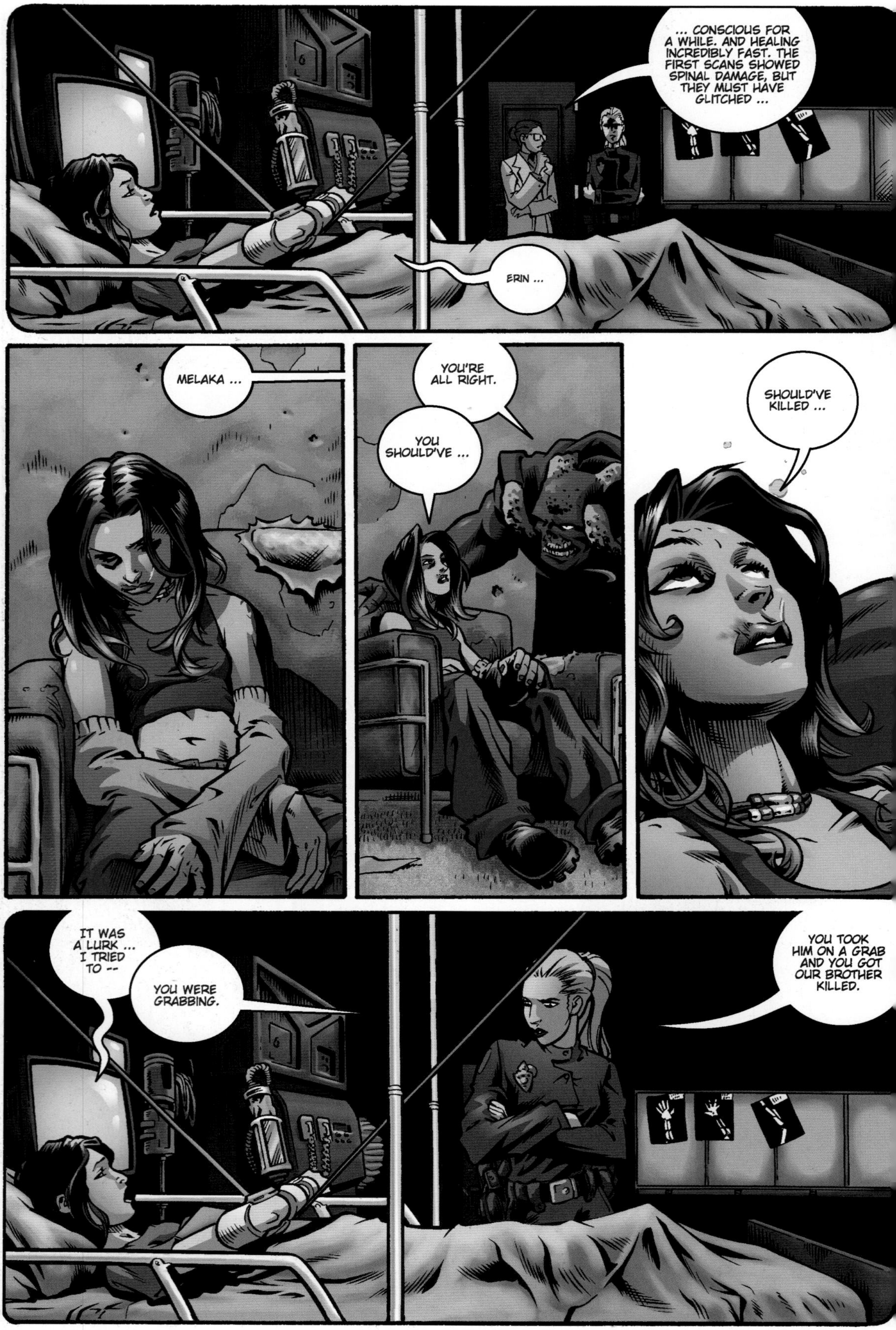
... CONSCIOUS FOR A WHILE. AND HEALING INCREDIBLY FAST. THE FIRST SCANS SHOWED SPINAL DAMAGE, BUT THEY MUST HAVE GLITCHED ...
ERIN ...
MELAKA ...
YOU'RE ALL RIGHT.
YOU SHOULD'VE ...
SHOULD'VE KILLED ...
IT WAS A LURK ... I TRIED TO --
YOU WERE GRABBING.
YOU TOOK HIM ON A GRAB AND YOU GOT OUR BROTHER KILLED.

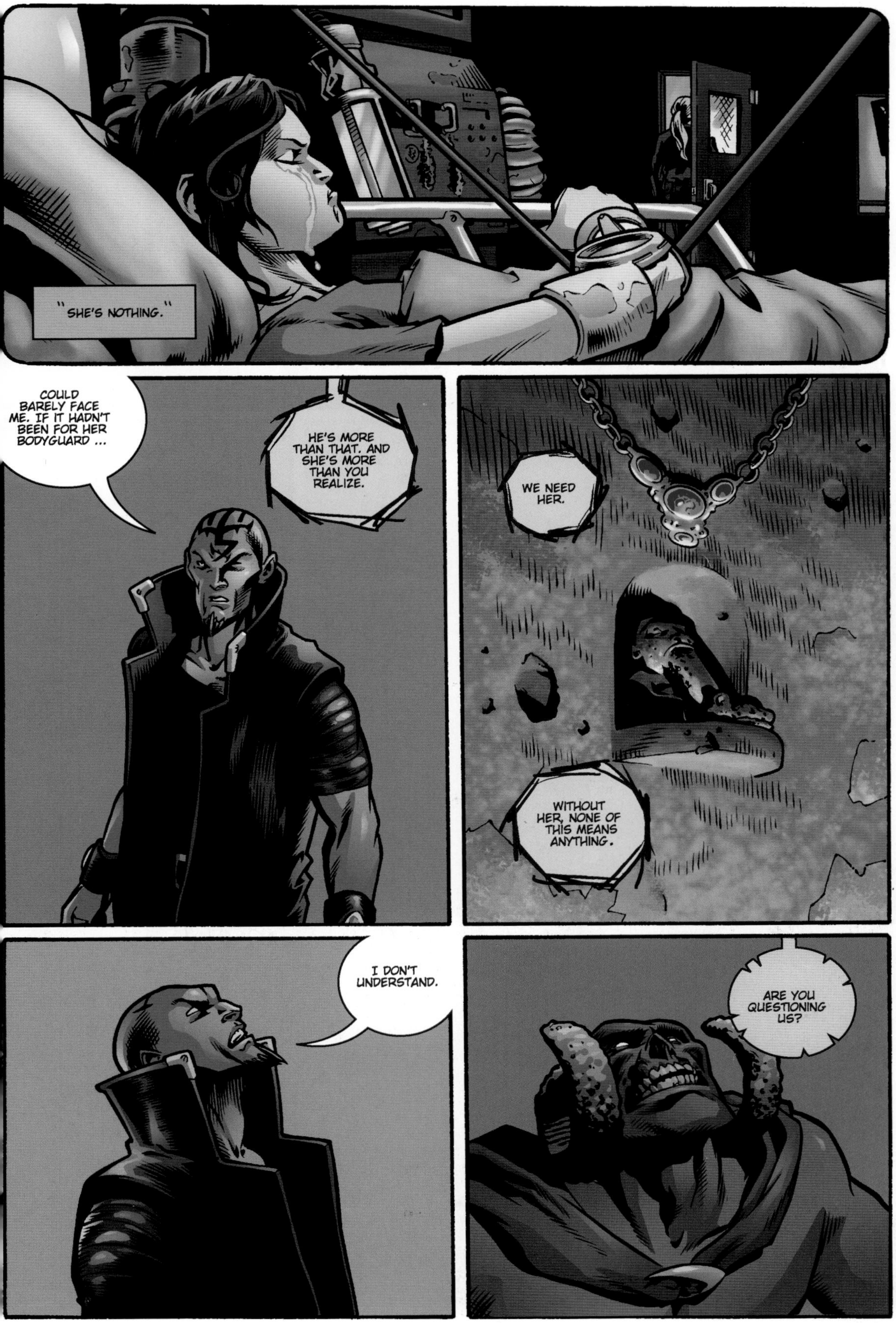
"SHE'S NOTHING."
COULD BARELY FACE ME. IF IT HADN'T BEEN FOR HER BODYGUARD ...
HE'S MORE THAN THAT. AND SHE'S MORE THAN YOU REALIZE.
WE NEED HER.
WITHOUT HER, NONE OF THIS MEANS ANYTHING.
I DON'T UNDERSTAND.
ARE YOU QUESTIONING US?

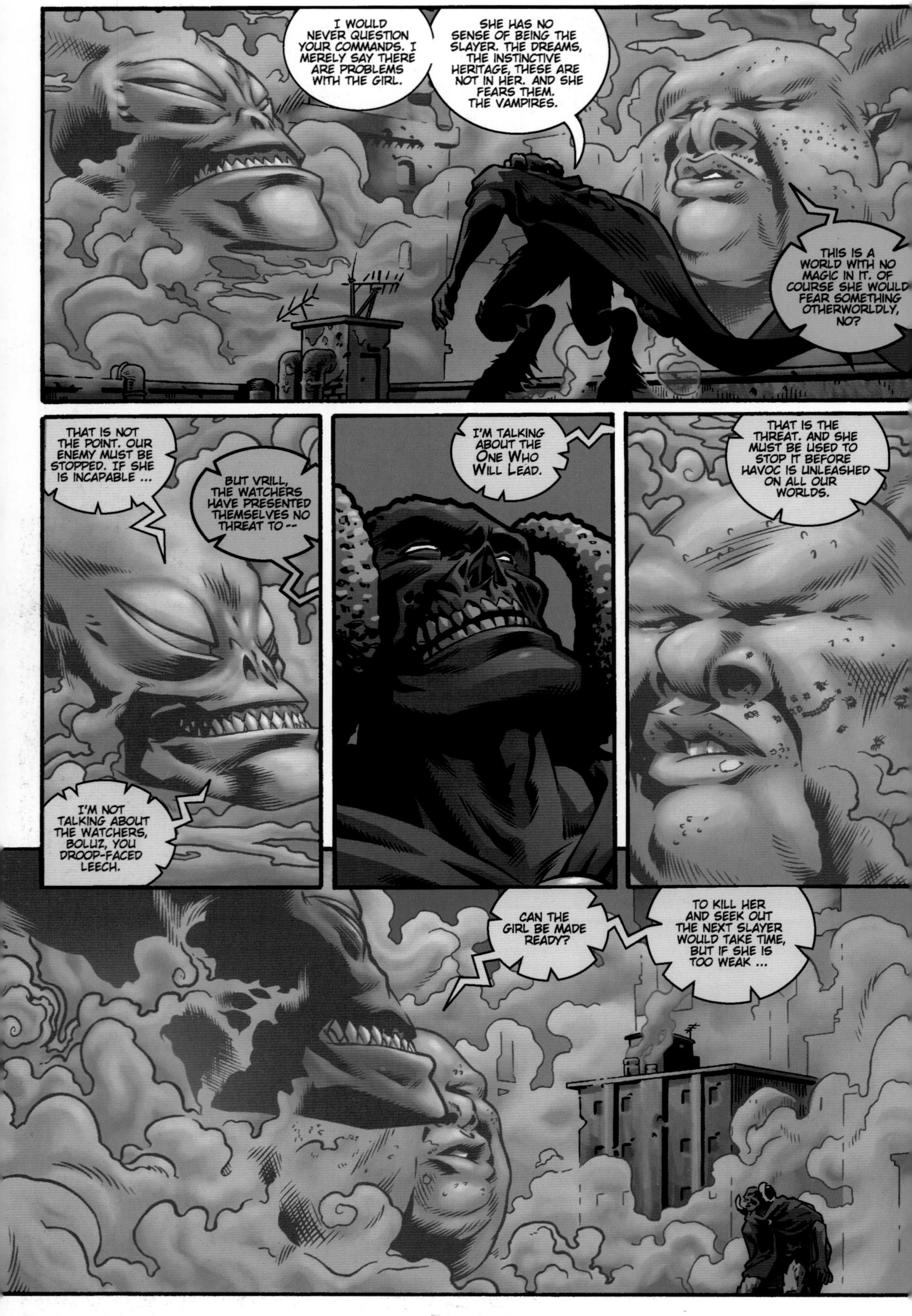
I WOULD NEVER QUESTION YOUR COMMANDS. I MERELY SAY THERE ARE PROBLEMS WITH THE GIRL.
SHE HAS NO SENSE OF BEING THE SLAYER. THE DREAMS, THE INSTINCTIVE HERITAGE, THESE ARE NOT IN HER. AND SHE FEARS THEM. THE VAMPIRES.
THIS IS A WORLD WITH NO MAGIC IN IT. OF COURSE SHE WOULD FEAR SOMETHING OTHERWORLDLY, NO?
THAT IS NOT THE POINT. OUR ENEMY MUST BE STOPPED. IF SHE IS INCAPABLE ...
BUT VRILL, THE WATCHERS HAVE PRESENTED THEMSELVES NO THREAT TO --
I'M NOT TALKING ABOUT THE WATCHERS, BOLUZ, YOU DROOP-FACED LEECH.
I'M TALKING ABOUT THE ONE WHO WILL LEAD.
THAT IS THE THREAT. AND SHE MUST BE USED TO STOP IT BEFORE HAVOC IS UNLEASHED ON ALL OUR WORLDS.
CAN THE GIRL BE MADE READY?
TO KILL HER AND SEEK OUT THE NEXT SLAYER WOULD TAKE TIME, BUT IF SHE IS TOO WEAK ...

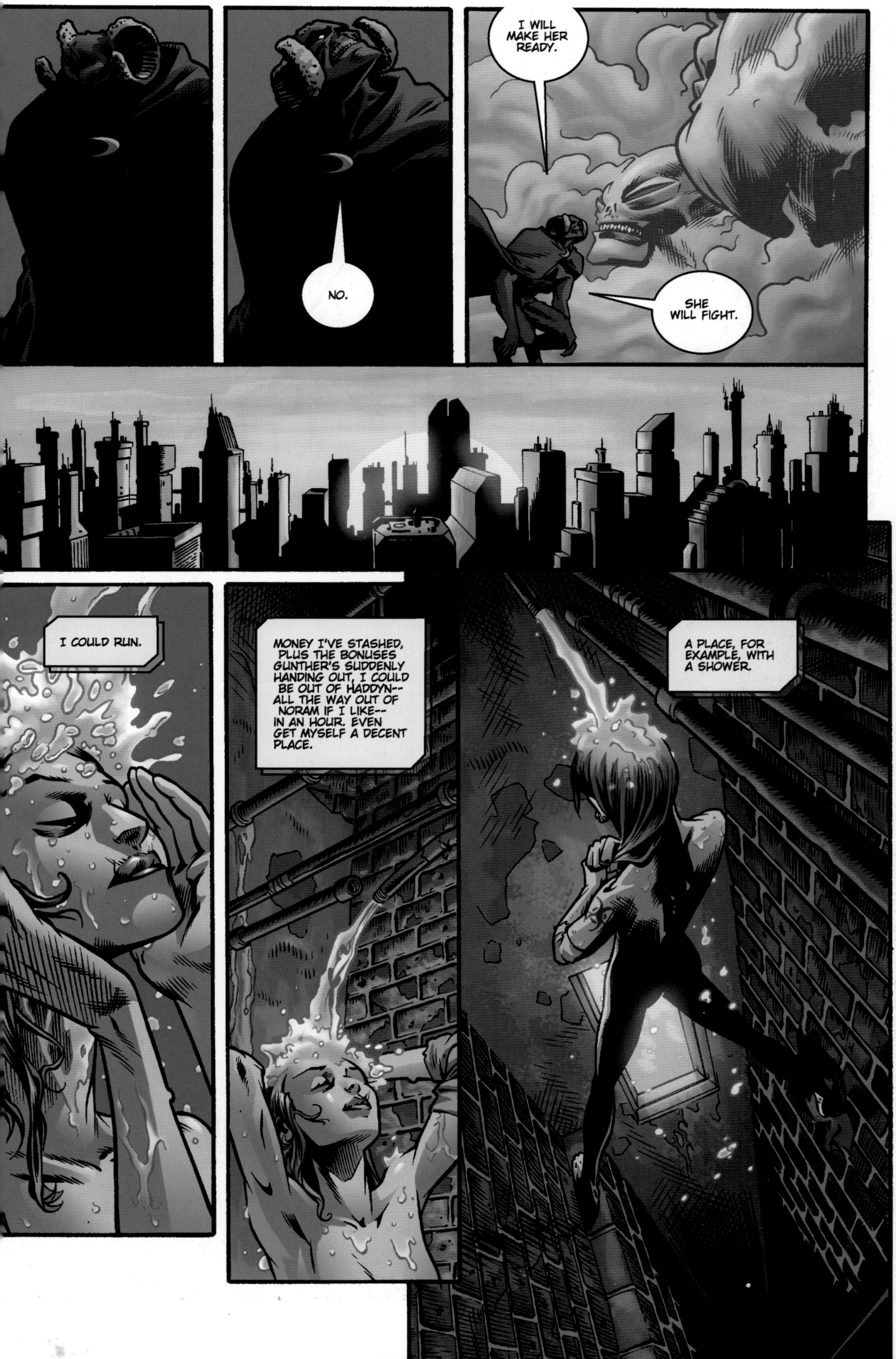
NO.
I WILL MAKE HER READY.
SHE WILL FIGHT.
I COULD RUN.
MONEY I'VE STASHED, PLUS THE BONUSES GUNTHER'S SUDDENLY HANDING OUT, I COULD BE OUT OF HADDYN-- ALL THE WAY OUT OF NORAM IF I LIKE-- IN AN HOUR. EVEN GET MYSELF A DECENT PLACE.
A PLACE, FOR EXAMPLE, WITH A SHOWER.

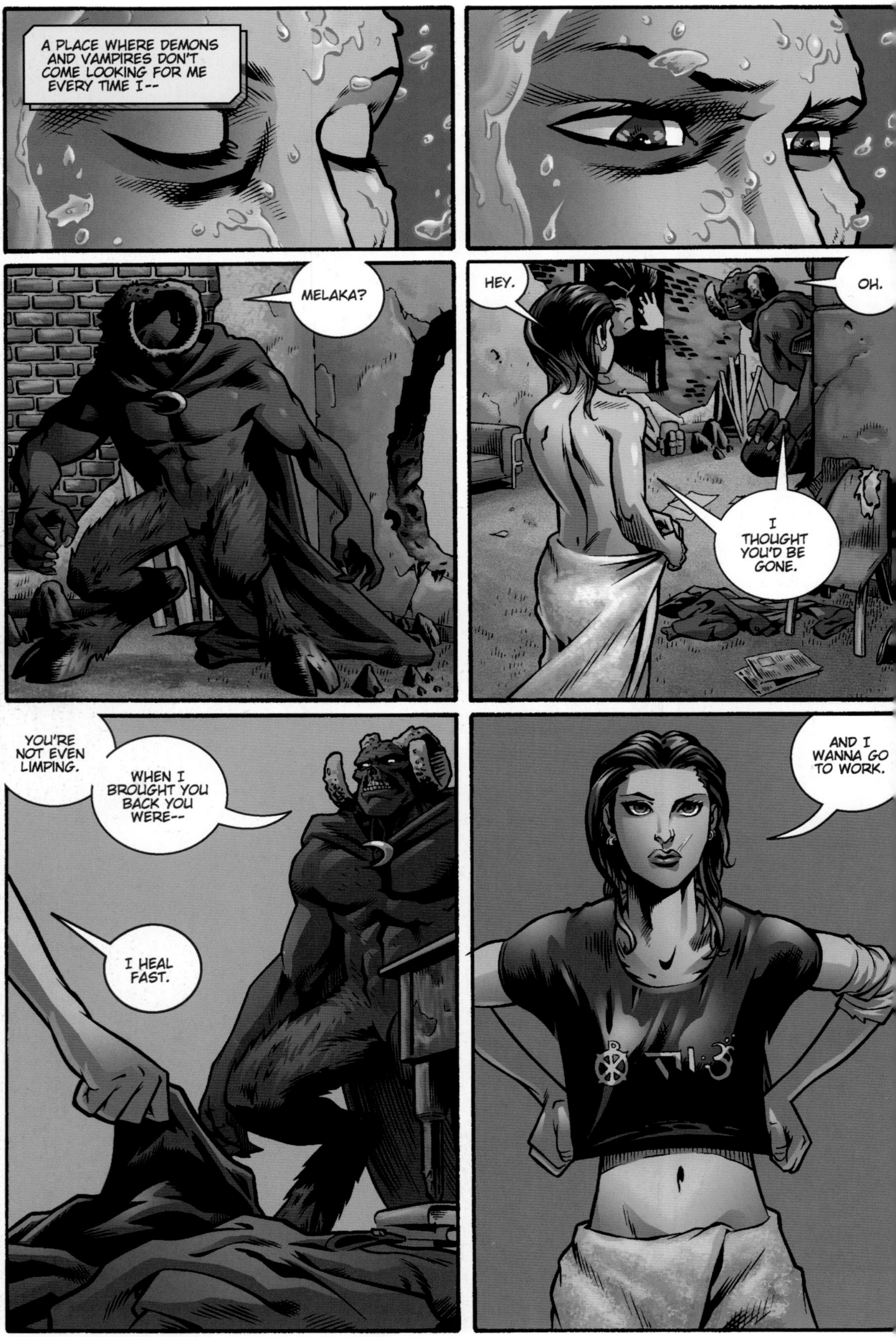
A PLACE WHERE DEMONS AND VAMPIRES DON'T COME LOOKING FOR ME EVERY TIME I--
MELAKA?
HEY.
OH.
I THOUGHT YOU'D BE GONE.
YOU'RE NOT EVEN LIMPING.
WHEN I BROUGHT YOU BACK YOU WERE--
I HEAL FAST.
AND I WANNA GO TO WORK.

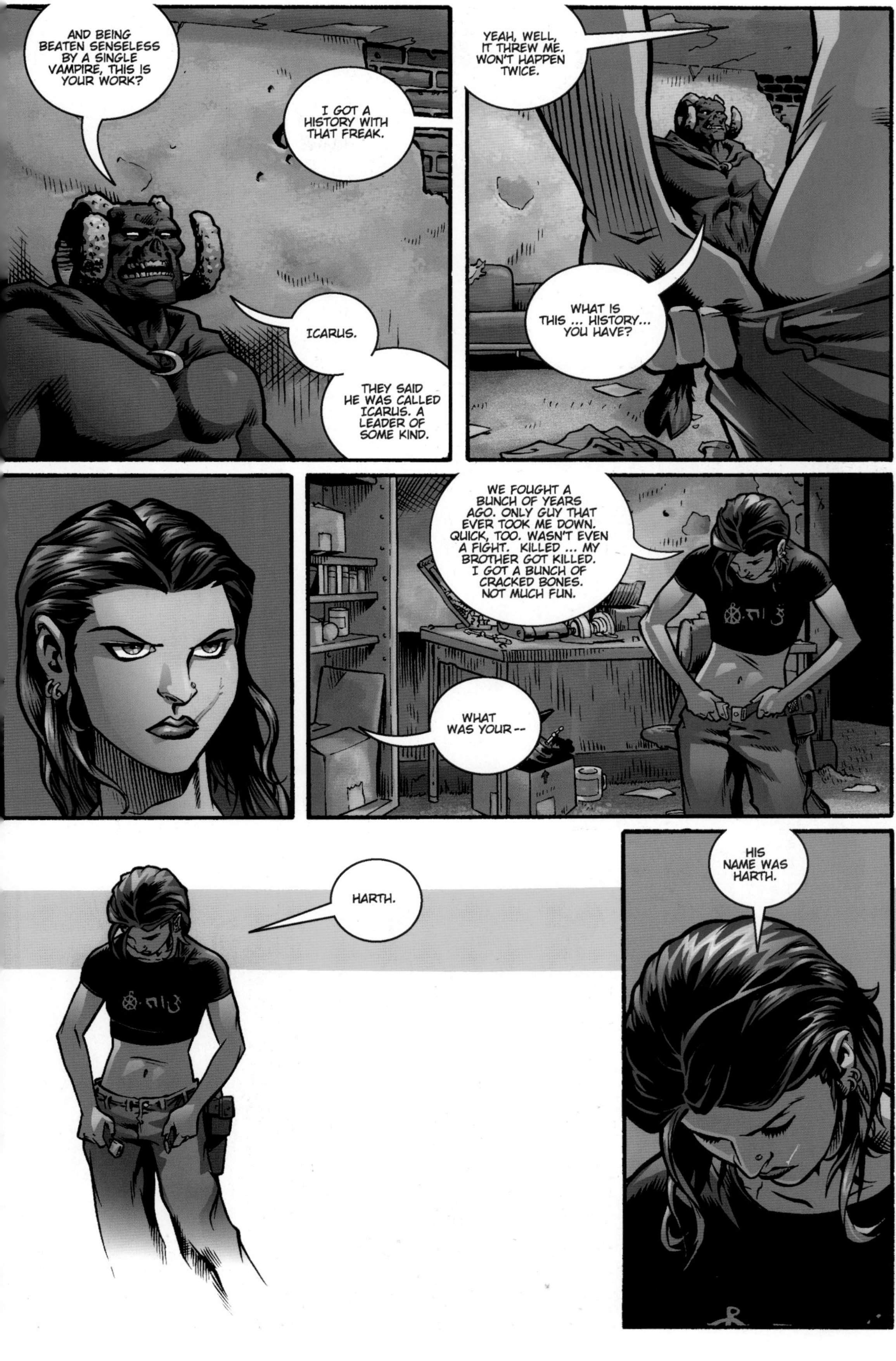
AND BEING BEATEN SENSELESS BY A SINGLE VAMPIRE, THIS IS YOUR WORK?
I GOT A HISTORY WITH THAT FREAK.
ICARUS.
THEY SAID HE WAS CALLED ICARUS. A LEADER OF SOME KIND.
YEAH, WELL, IT THREW ME. WON'T HAPPEN TWICE.
WHAT IS THIS ... HISTORY... YOU HAVE?
WE FOUGHT A BUNCH OF YEARS AGO. ONLY GUY THAT EVER TOOK ME DOWN. QUICK, TOO. WASN'T EVEN A FIGHT. KILLED ... MY BROTHER GOT KILLED. I GOT A BUNCH OF CRACKED BONES. NOT MUCH FUN.
WHAT WAS YOUR --
HARTH.
HIS NAME WAS HARTH.

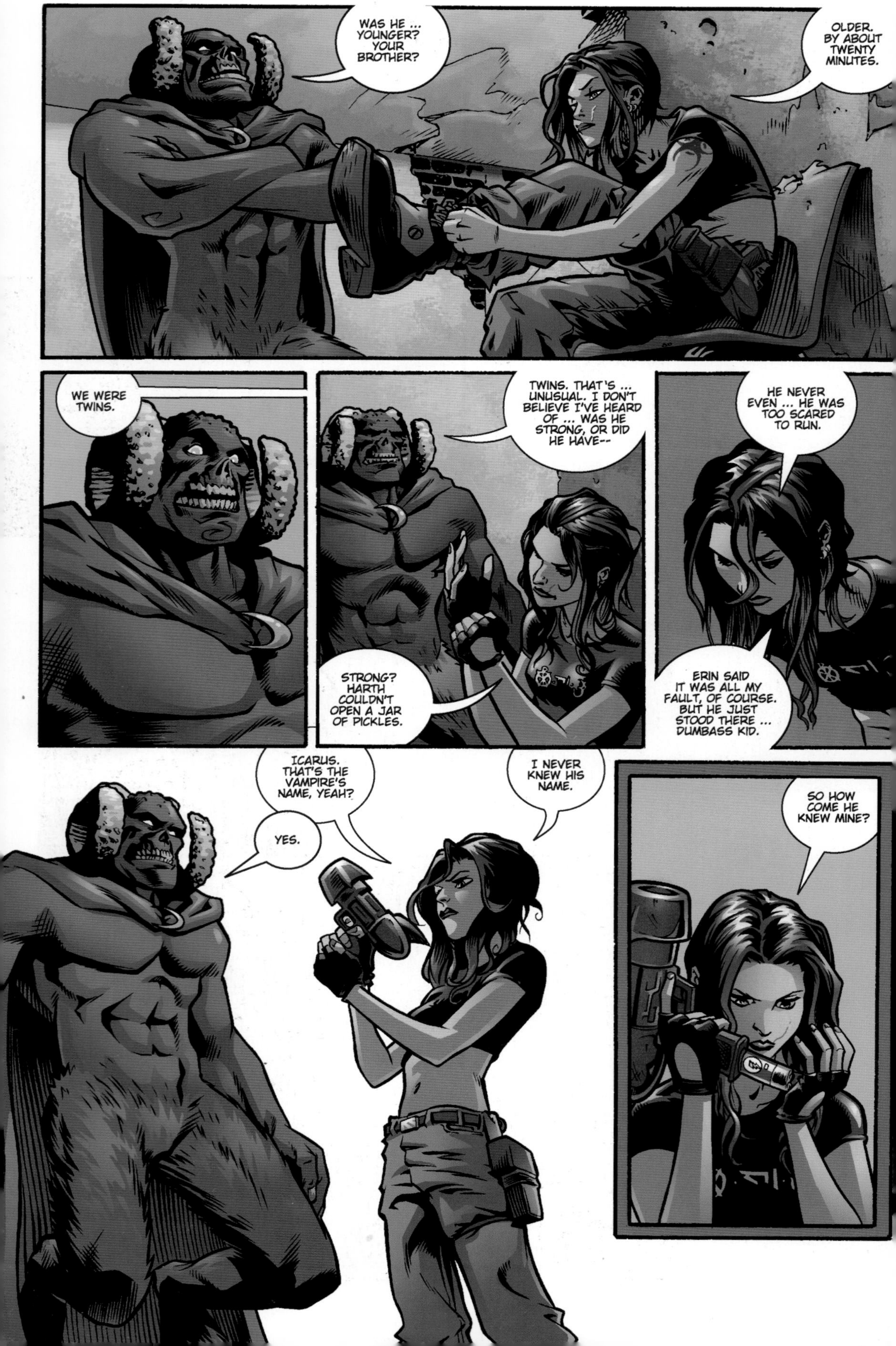
WAS HE ... YOUNGER? YOUR BROTHER?
OLDER. BY ABOUT TWENTY MINUTES.
WE WERE TWINS.
TWINS. THAT'S ... UNUSUAL. I DON'T BELIEVE I'VE HEARD OF ... WAS HE STRONG, OR DID HE HAVE--
STRONG? HARTH COULDN'T OPEN A JAR OF PICKLES.
HE NEVER EVEN ... HE WAS TOO SCARED TO RUN.
ERIN SAID IT WAS ALL MY FAULT, OF COURSE. BUT HE JUST STOOD THERE ... DUMBASS KID.
ICARUS. THAT'S THE VAMPIRE'S NAME, YEAH?
YES.
I NEVER KNEW HIS NAME.
SO HOW COME HE KNEW MINE?

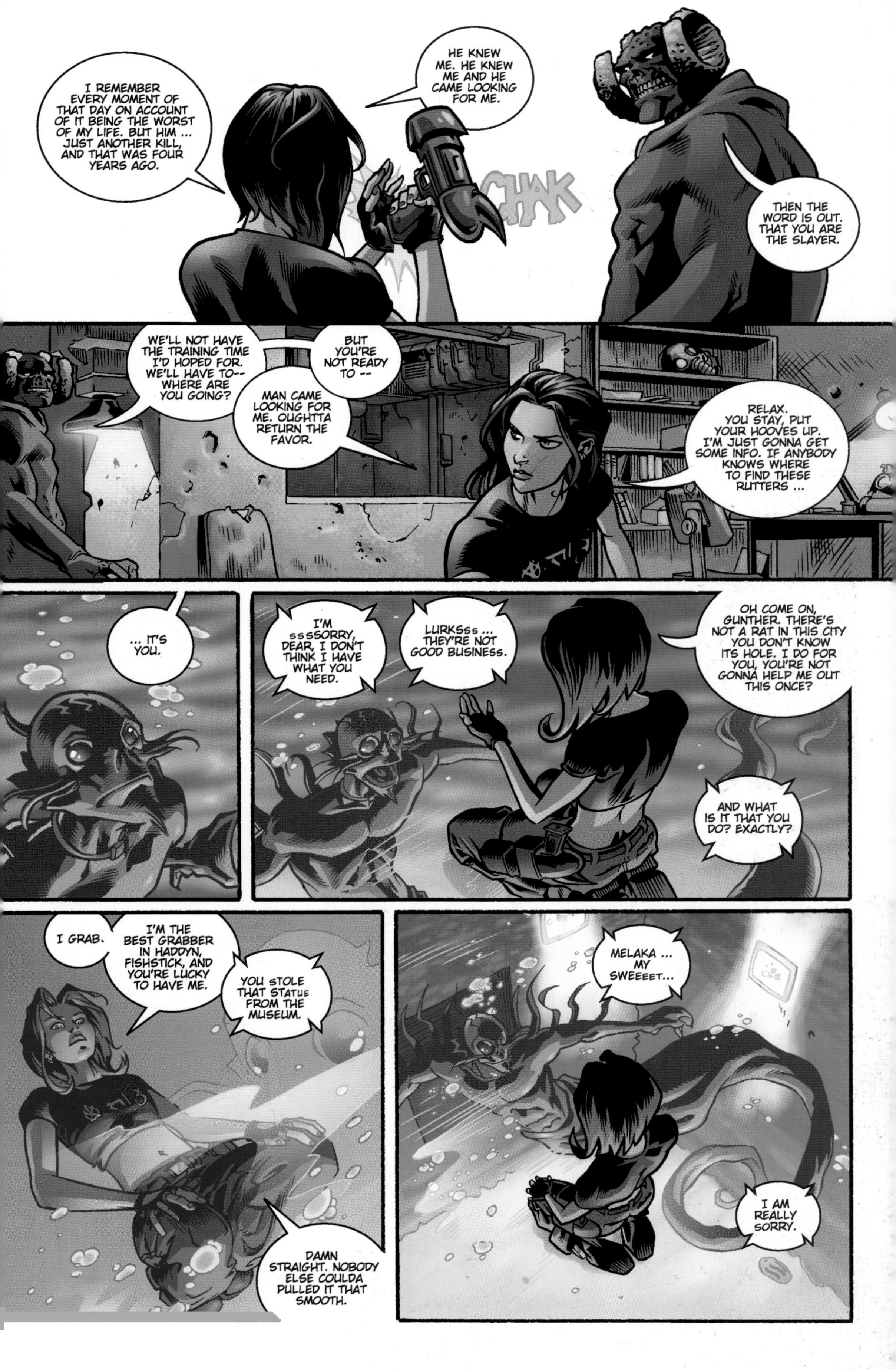
I REMEMBER EVERY MOMENT OF THAT DAY ON ACCOUNT OF IT BEING THE WORST OF MY LIFE. BUT HIM ... JUST ANOTHER KILL, AND THAT WAS FOUR YEARS AGO.
HE KNEW ME. HE KNEW ME AND HE CAME LOOKING FOR ME.
CHAK
THEN THE WORD IS OUT. THAT YOU ARE THE SLAYER.
WE'LL NOT HAVE THE TRAINING TIME I'D HOPED FOR. WE'LL HAVE TO-- WHERE ARE YOU GOING?
MAN CAME LOOKING FOR ME. OUGHTTA RETURN THE FAVOR.
BUT YOU'RE NOT READY TO --
RELAX. YOU STAY, PUT YOUR HOOVES UP. I'M JUST GONNA GET SOME INFO. IF ANYBODY KNOWS WHERE TO FIND THESE RUTTERS ...
... IT'S YOU.
I'M sssSORRY, DEAR, I DON'T THINK I HAVE WHAT YOU NEED.
LURKSss ... THEY'RE NOT GOOD BUSINESS.
OH COME ON, GUNTHER. THERE'S NOT A RAT IN THIS CITY YOU DON'T KNOW ITS HOLE. I DO FOR YOU, YOU'RE NOT GONNA HELP ME OUT THIS ONCE?
AND WHAT IS IT THAT YOU DO? EXACTLY?
I GRAB.
I'M THE BEST GRABBER IN HADDYN, FISHSTICK, AND YOU'RE LUCKY TO HAVE ME.
YOU STOLE THAT STATUE FROM THE MUSEUM.
DAMN STRAIGHT. NOBODY ELSE COULDA PULLED IT THAT SMOOTH.
MELAKA ... MY SWEEEEET...
I AM REALLY SORRY.

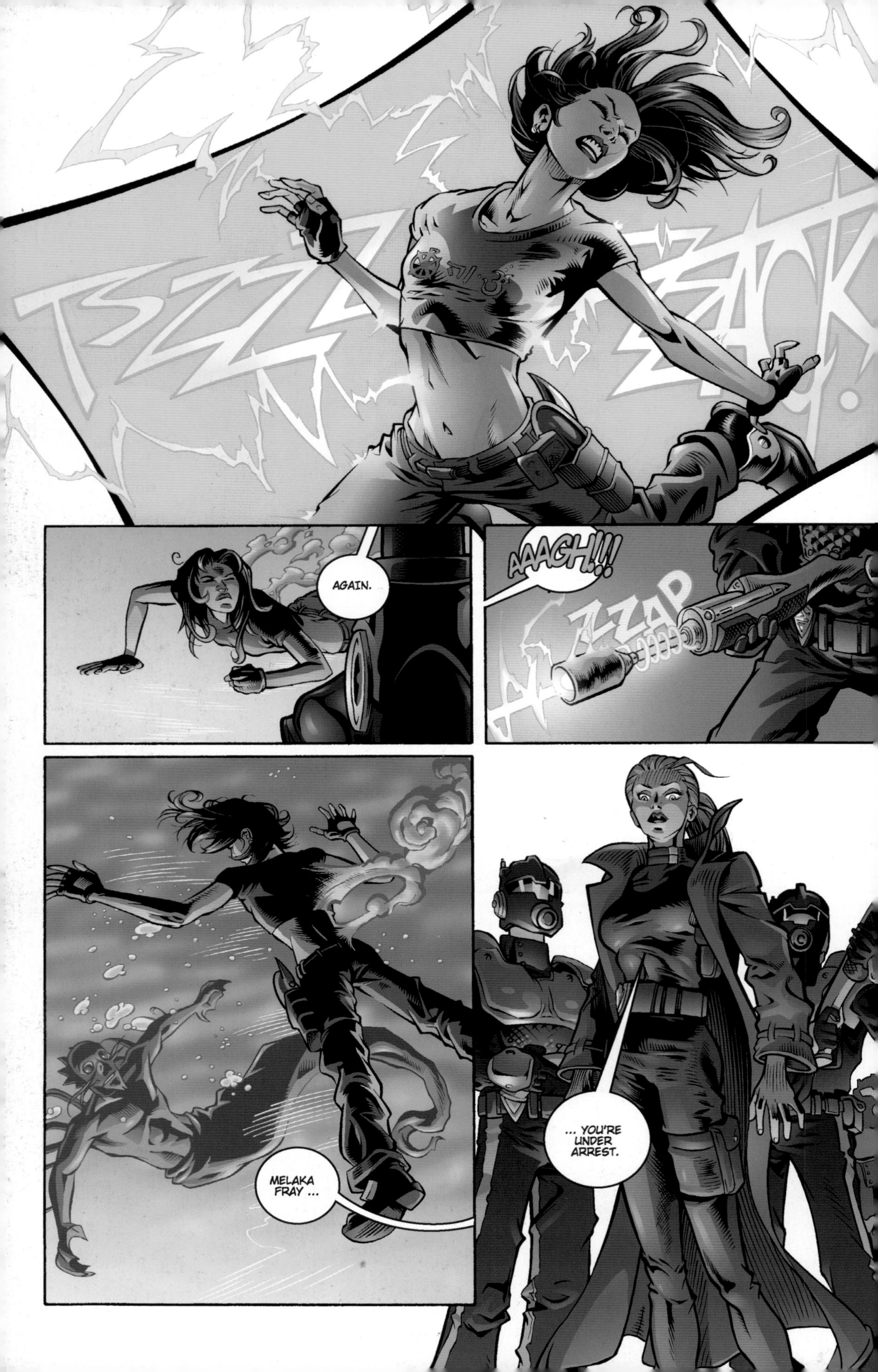
TSZZZZZZZAACK!
AGAIN.
AAAGH!!!
ZZZAP
MELAKA FRAY ...
... YOU'RE UNDER ARREST.

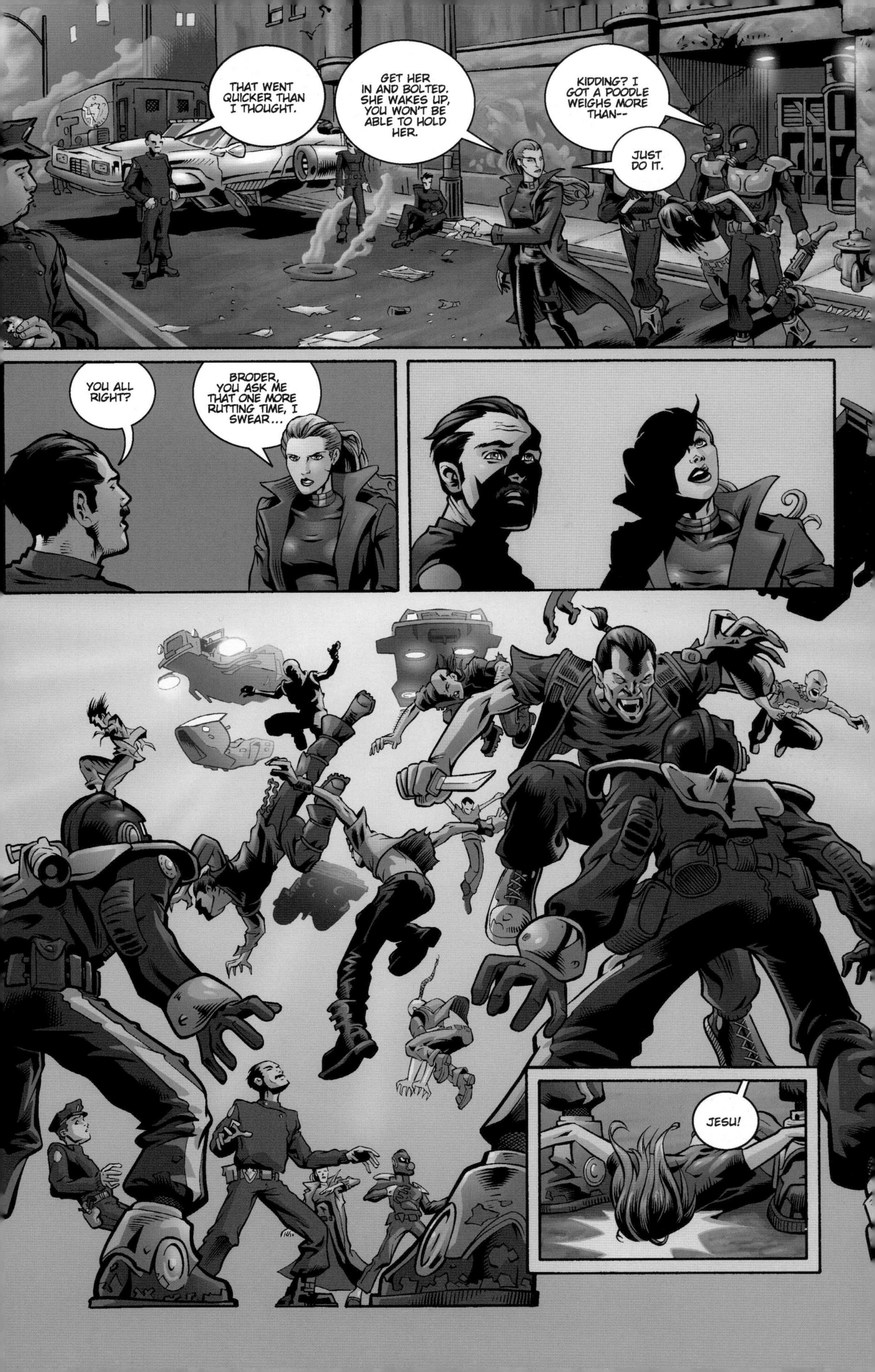
THAT WENT QUICKER THAN I THOUGHT.
GET HER IN AND BOLTED. SHE WAKES UP, YOU WON'T BE ABLE TO HOLD HER.
KIDDING? I GOT A POODLE WEIGHS MORE THAN--
JUST DO IT.
YOU ALL RIGHT?
BRODER, YOU ASK ME THAT ONE MORE RUTTING TIME, I SWEAR...
JESU!

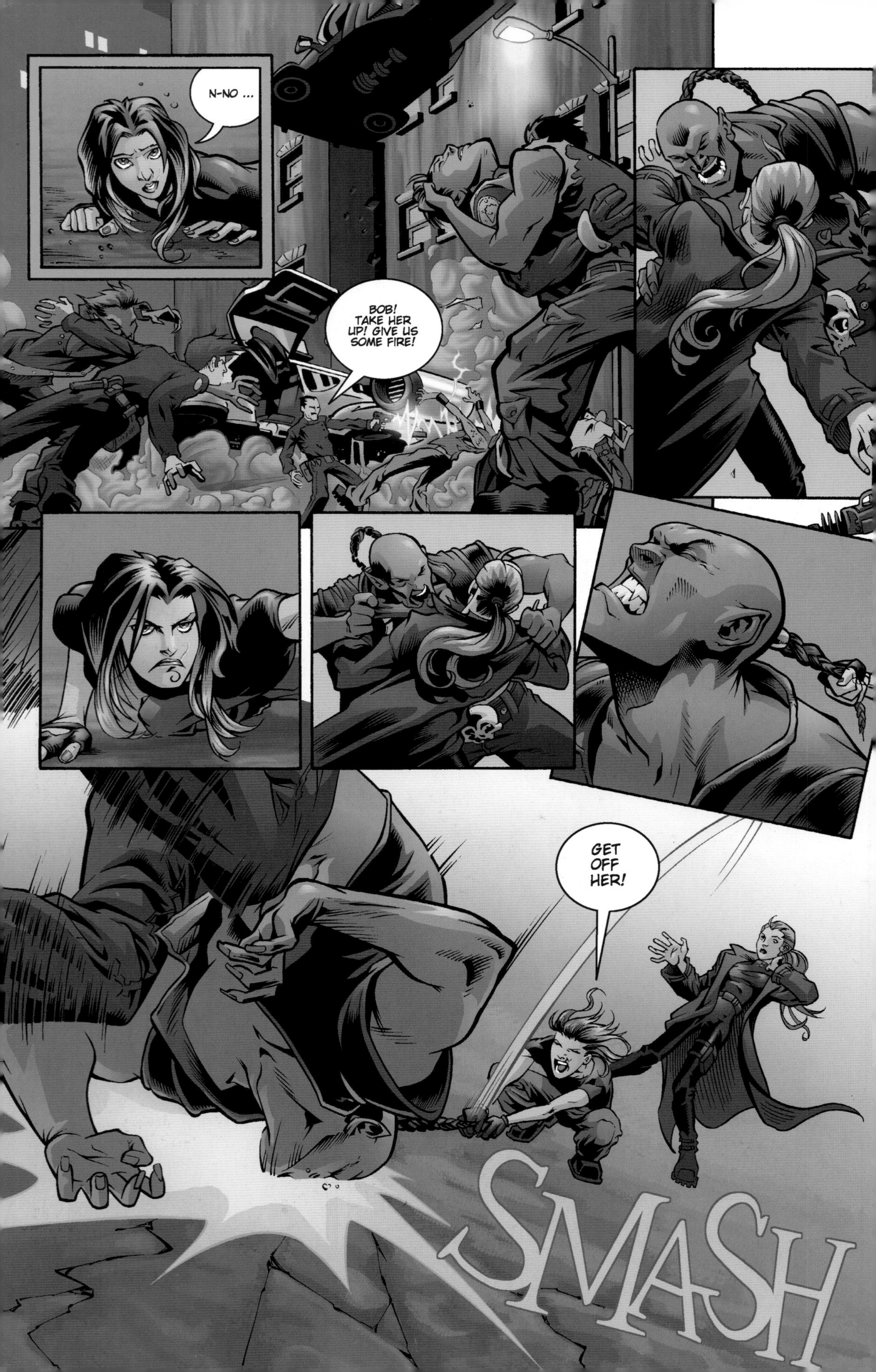
N-NO ...
BOB! TAKE HER UP! GIVE US SOME FIRE!
GET OFF HER!
SMASH

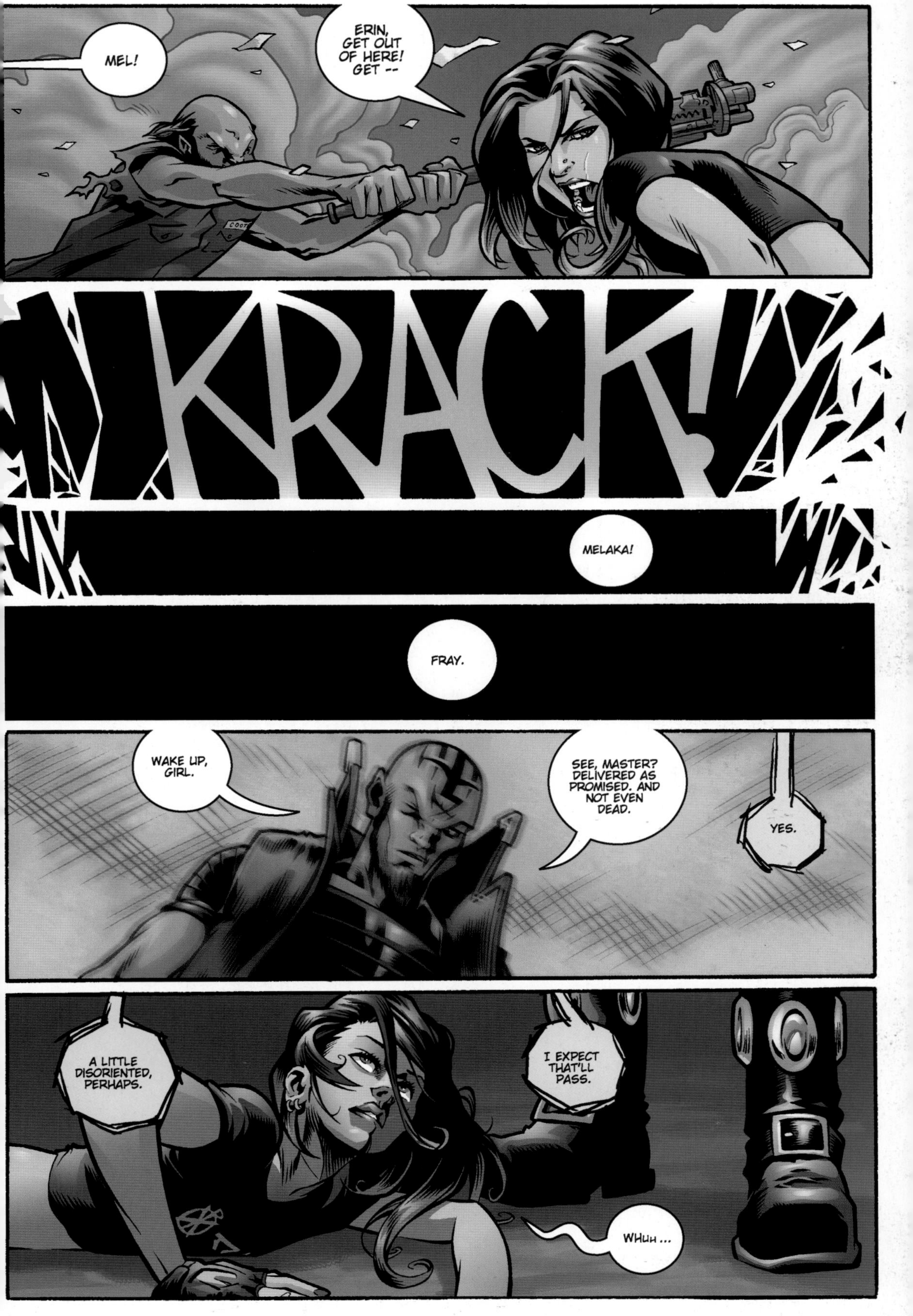
MEL!
ERIN, GET OUT OF HERE! GET --
KRACK!
MELAKA!
FRAY.
WAKE UP, GIRL.
SEE, MASTER? DELIVERED AS PROMISED. AND NOT EVEN DEAD.
YES.
A LITTLE DISORIENTED, PERHAPS.
I EXPECT THAT'LL PASS.
WHUH ...

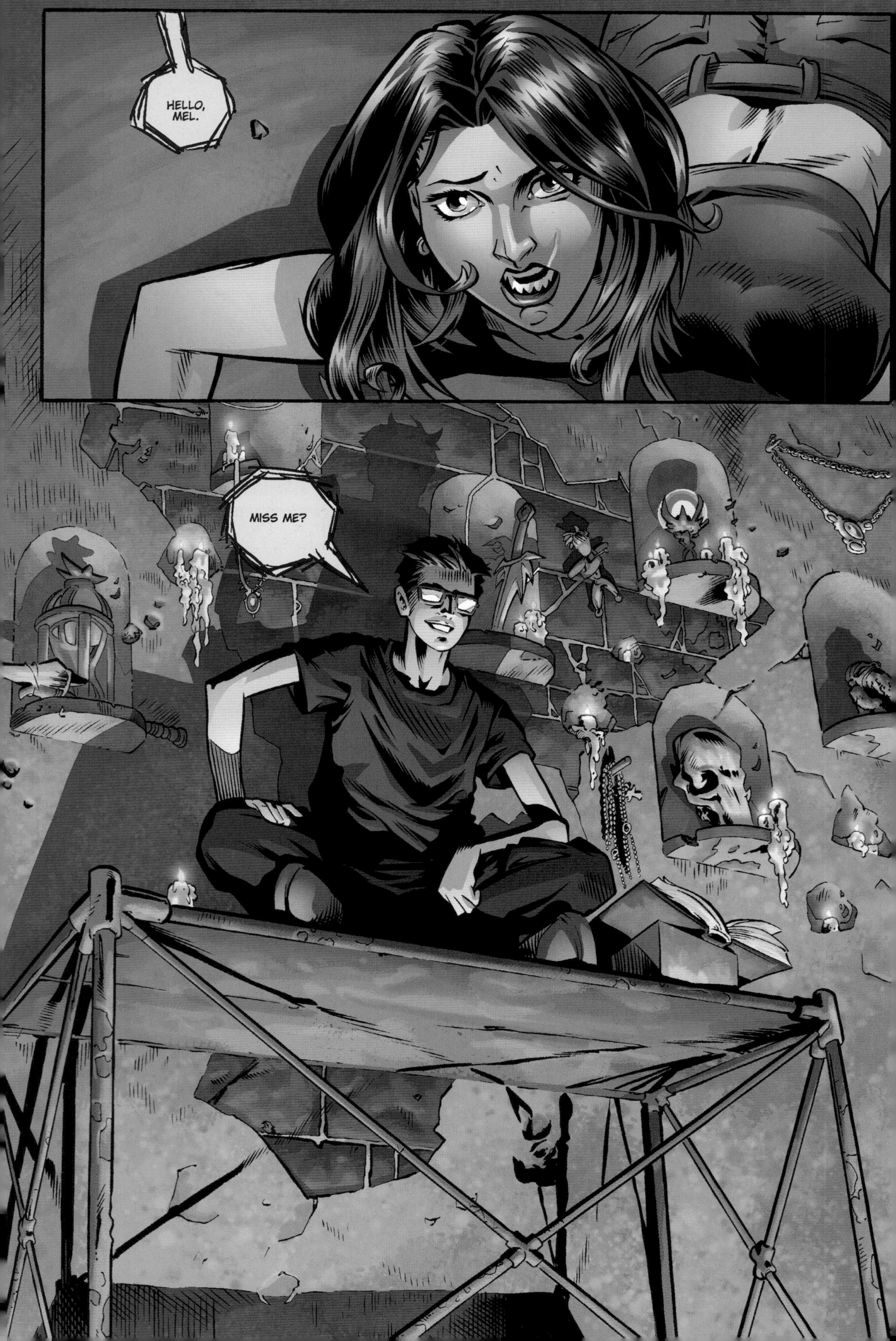
HELLO, MEL.
MISS ME?

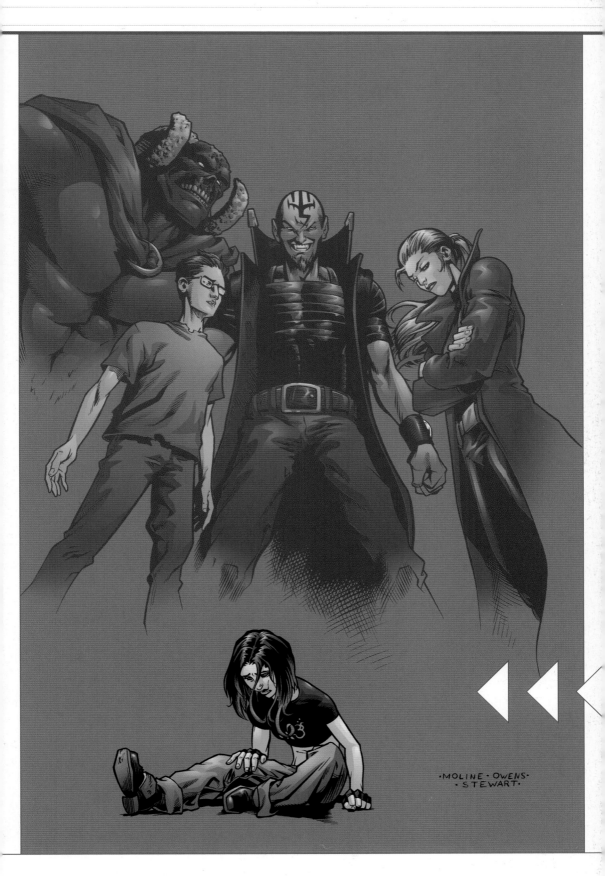

MOLINE · OWENS
· STEWART ·

"Mel, Mel, you can't protect anyone.

Haven't you learned that by now?"

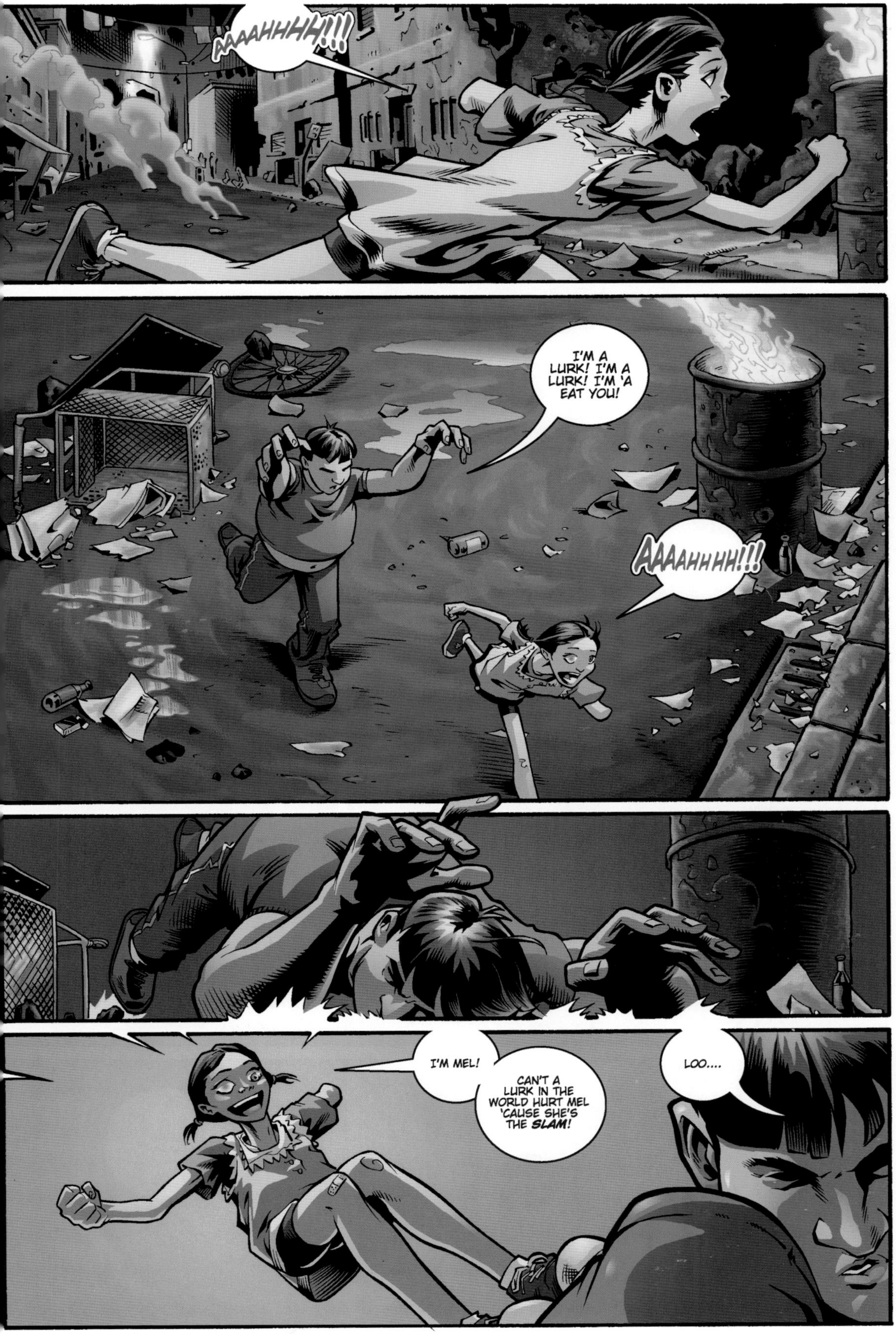
AAAAHHHH!!!
I'M A LURK! I'M A LURK! I'M 'A EAT YOU!
AAAAHHHH!!!
I'M MEL!
CAN'T A LURK IN THE WORLD HURT MEL 'CAUSE SHE'S THE *SLAM*!
LOO....

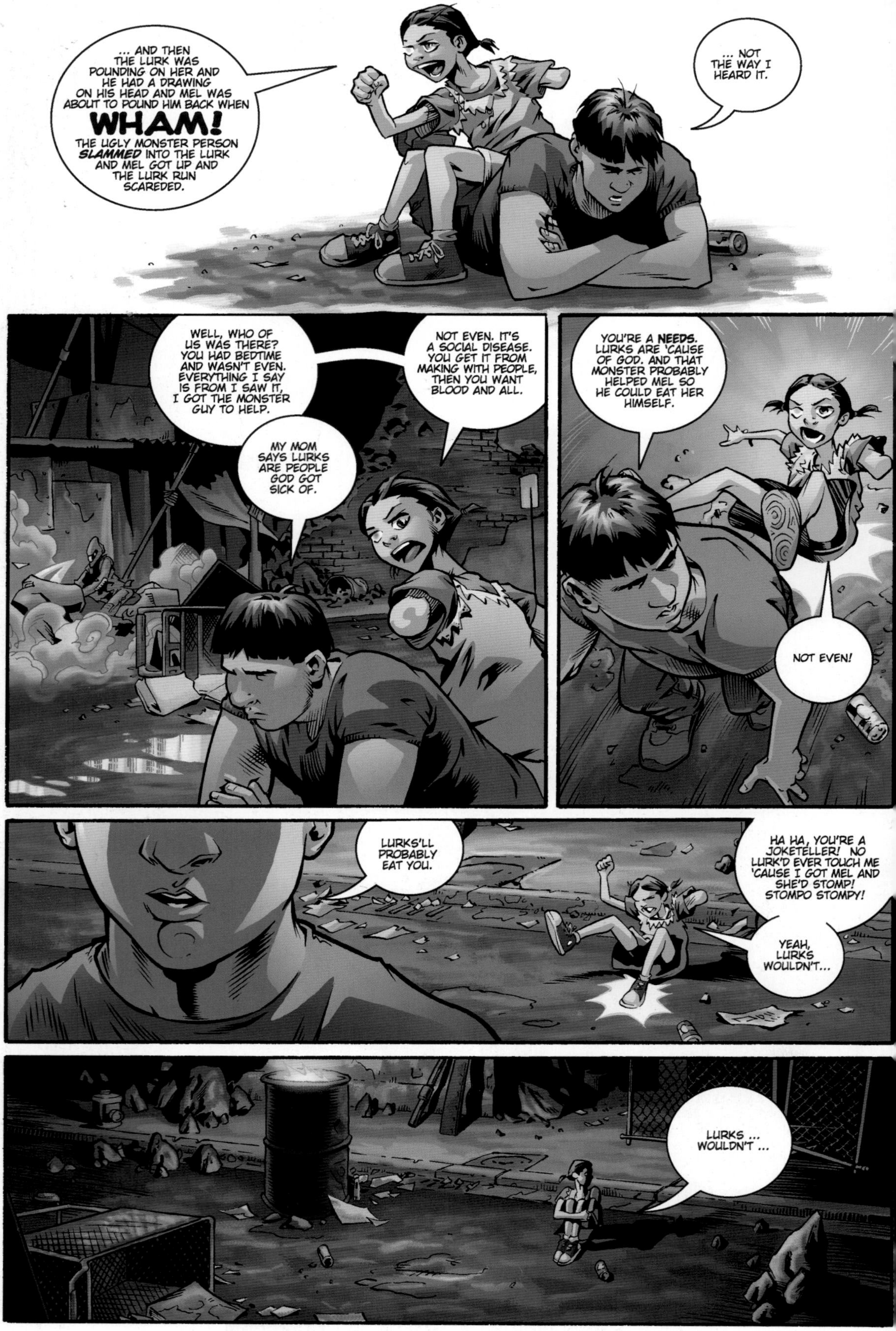

... AND THEN THE LURK WAS POUNDING ON HER AND HE HAD A DRAWING ON HIS HEAD AND MEL WAS ABOUT TO POUND HIM BACK WHEN WHAM! THE UGLY MONSTER PERSON SLAMMED INTO THE LURK AND MEL GOT UP AND THE LURK RUN SCAREDED.
... NOT THE WAY I HEARD IT.
WELL, WHO OF US WAS THERE? YOU HAD BEDTIME AND WASN'T EVEN. EVERYTHING I SAY IS FROM I SAW IT, I GOT THE MONSTER GUY TO HELP.
MY MOM SAYS LURKS ARE PEOPLE GOD GOT SICK OF.
NOT EVEN. IT'S A SOCIAL DISEASE. YOU GET IT FROM MAKING WITH PEOPLE, THEN YOU WANT BLOOD AND ALL.
YOU'RE A NEEDS. LURKS ARE 'CAUSE OF GOD. AND THAT MONSTER PROBABLY HELPED MEL SO HE COULD EAT HER HIMSELF.
NOT EVEN!
LURKS'LL PROBABLY EAT YOU.
HA HA, YOU'RE A JOKETELLER! NO LURK'D EVER TOUCH ME 'CAUSE I GOT MEL AND SHE'D STOMP! STOMPO STOMPY!
YEAH, LURKS WOULDN'T...
LURKS ... WOULDN'T ...

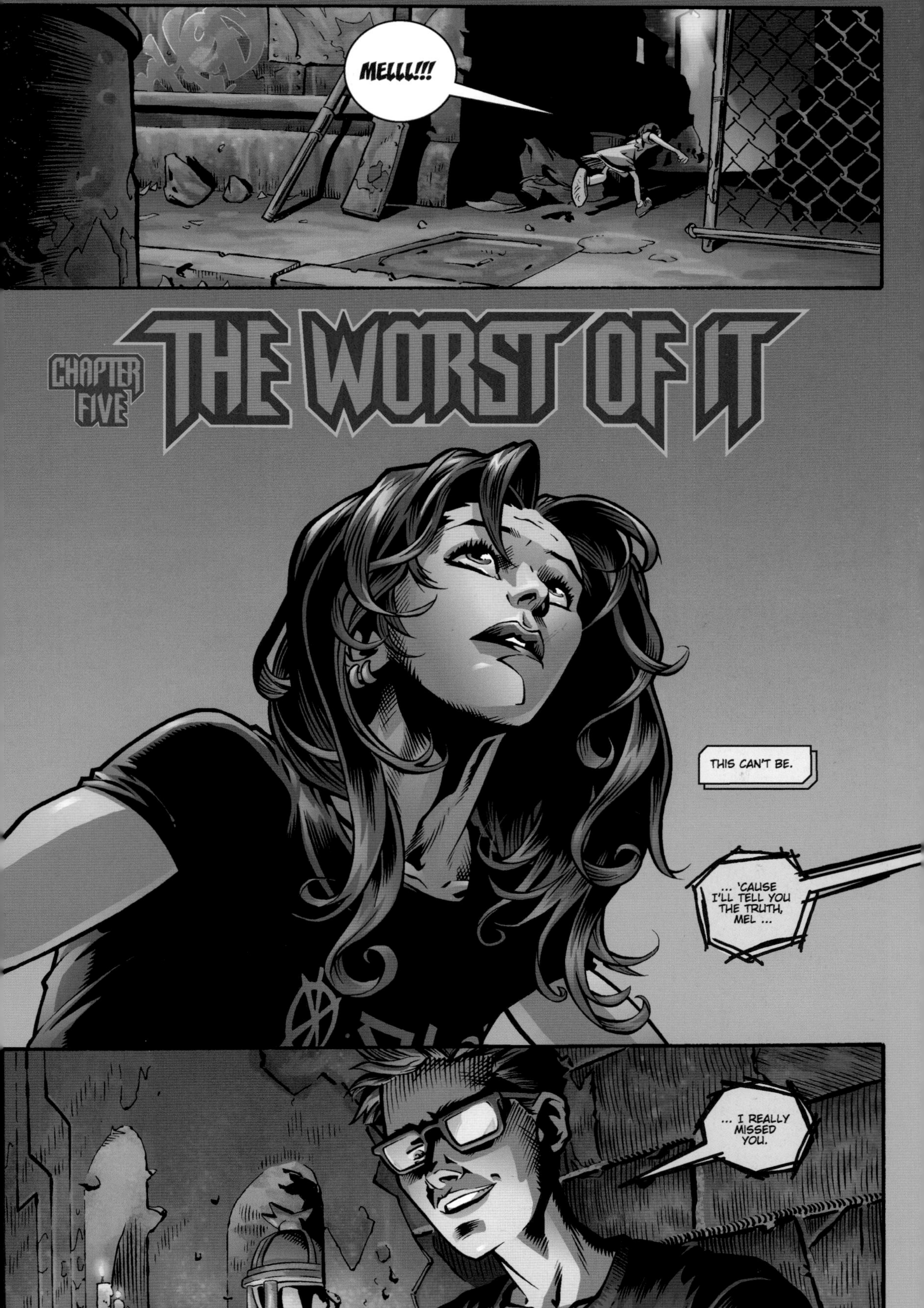
MELLL!!!
CHAPTER FIVE
THE WORST OF IT
THIS CAN'T BE.
... 'CAUSE I'LL TELL YOU THE TRUTH, MEL ...
... I REALLY MISSED YOU.

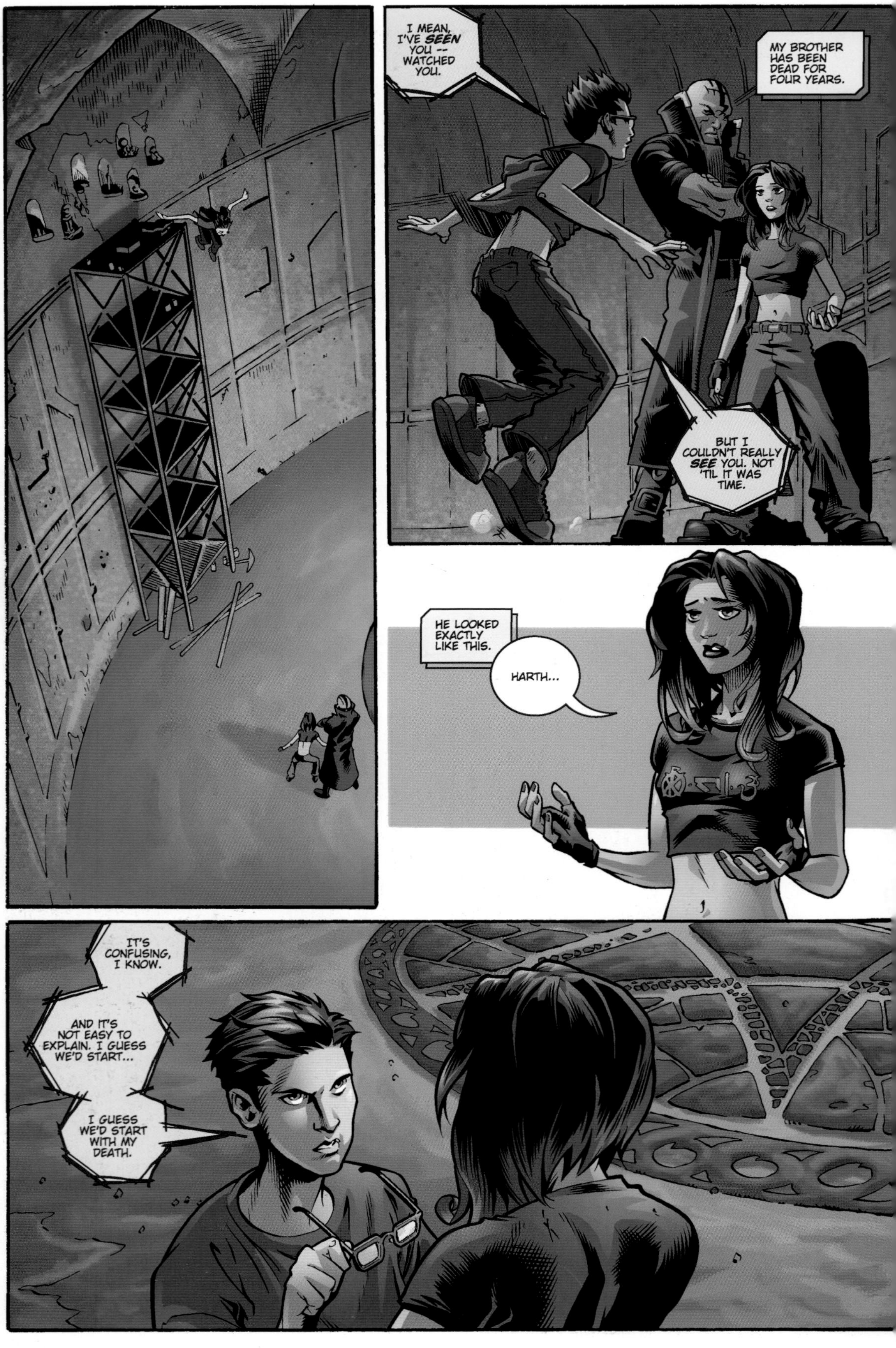
I MEAN, I'VE SEEN YOU -- WATCHED YOU.
MY BROTHER HAS BEEN DEAD FOR FOUR YEARS.
BUT I COULDN'T REALLY SEE YOU. NOT 'TIL IT WAS TIME.
HE LOOKED EXACTLY LIKE THIS.
HARTH...
IT'S CONFUSING, I KNOW.
AND IT'S NOT EASY TO EXPLAIN. I GUESS WE'D START...
I GUESS WE'D START WITH MY DEATH.

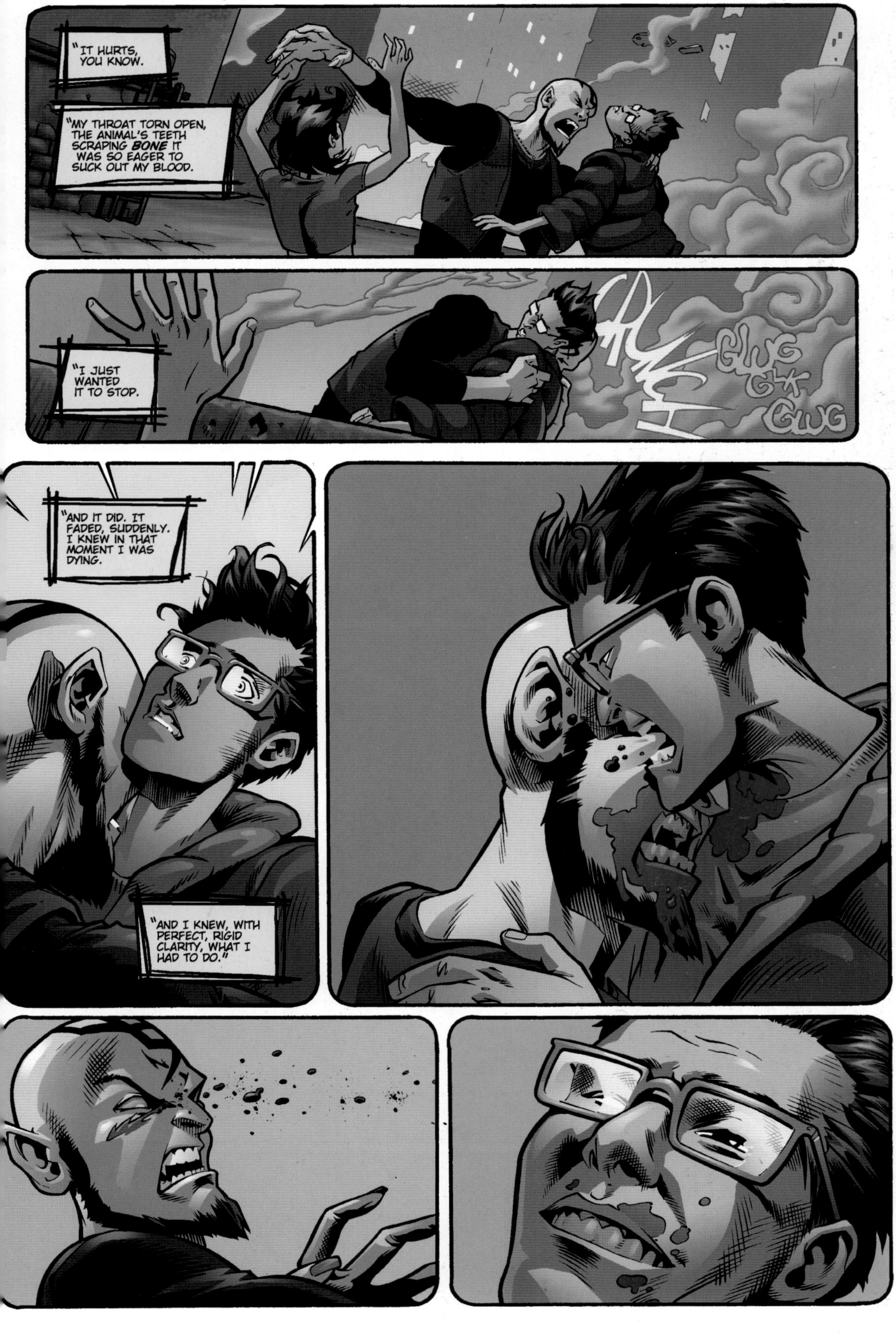
"IT HURTS, YOU KNOW.
"MY THROAT TORN OPEN, THE ANIMAL'S TEETH SCRAPING BONE IT WAS SO EAGER TO SUCK OUT MY BLOOD.
"I JUST WANTED IT TO STOP.
GLUG GLK GLUG
"AND IT DID. IT FADED, SUDDENLY. I KNEW IN THAT MOMENT I WAS DYING.
"AND I KNEW, WITH PERFECT, RIGID CLARITY, WHAT I HAD TO DO."

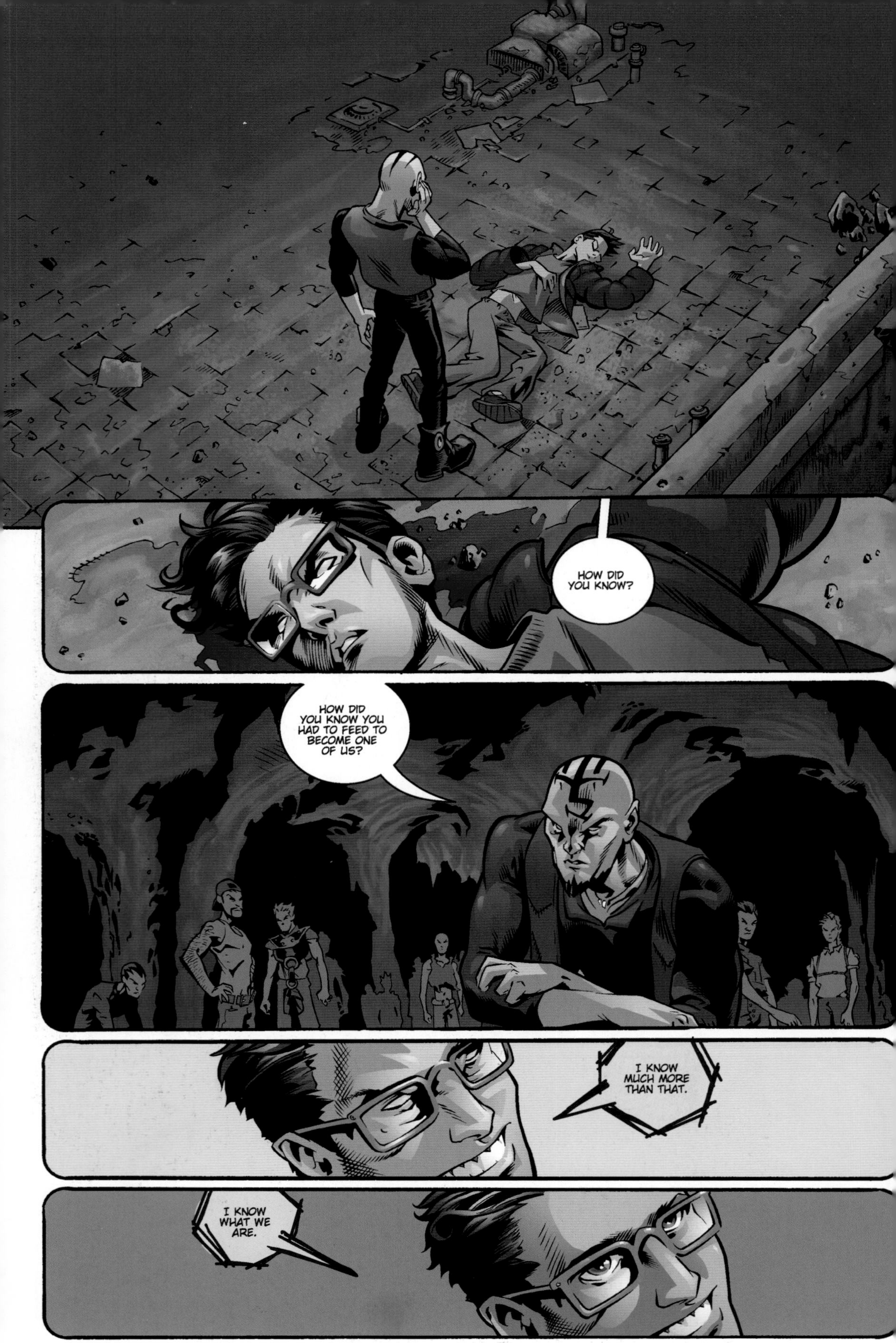
HOW DID YOU KNOW?
HOW DID YOU KNOW YOU HAD TO FEED TO BECOME ONE OF US?
I KNOW MUCH MORE THAN THAT.
I KNOW WHAT WE ARE.

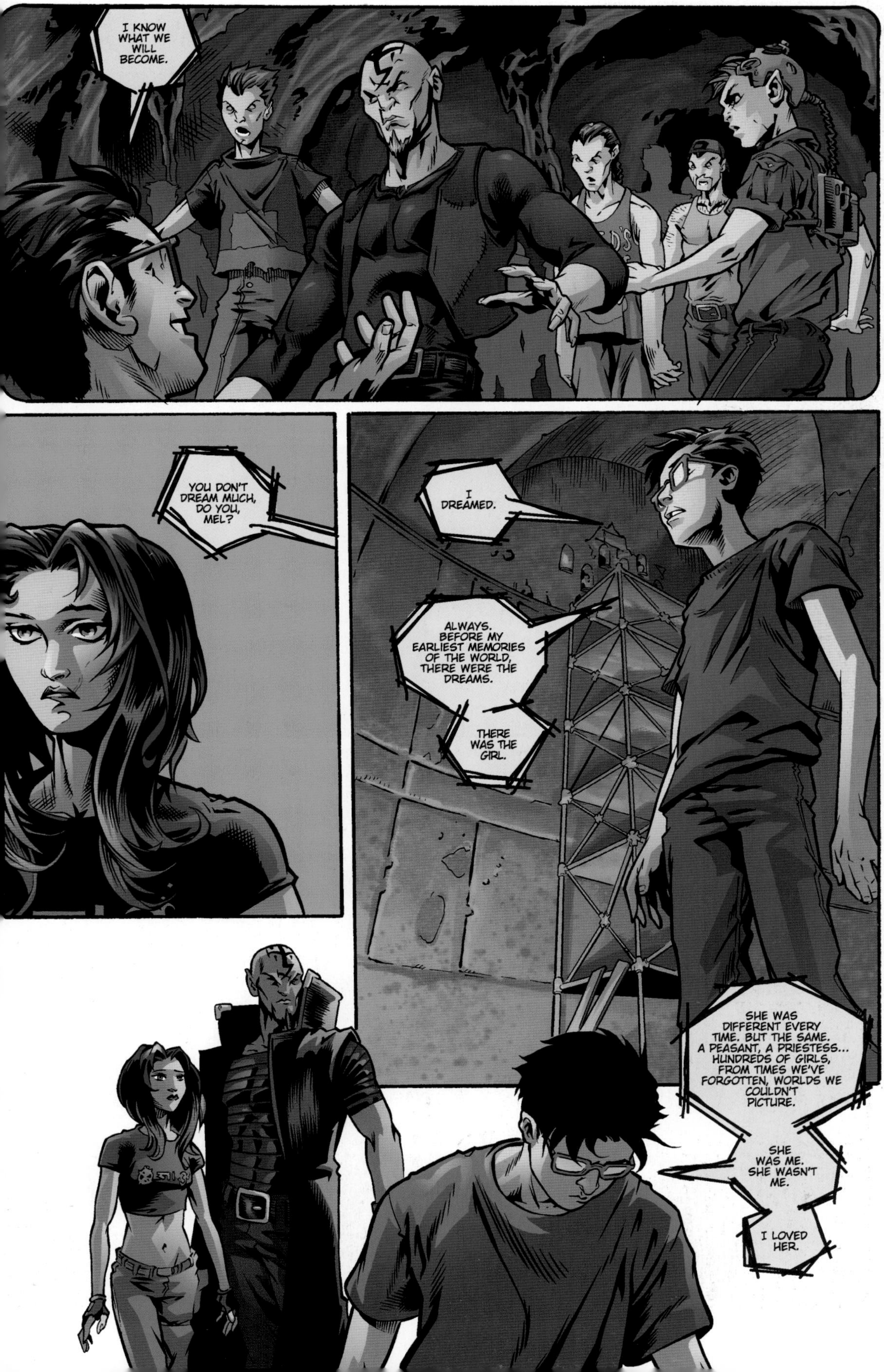
I KNOW WHAT WE WILL BECOME.
YOU DON'T DREAM MUCH, DO YOU, MEL?
I DREAMED.
ALWAYS. BEFORE MY EARLIEST MEMORIES OF THE WORLD, THERE WERE THE DREAMS.
THERE WAS THE GIRL.
SHE WAS DIFFERENT EVERY TIME. BUT THE SAME. A PEASANT, A PRIESTESS... HUNDREDS OF GIRLS, FROM TIMES WE'VE FORGOTTEN, WORLDS WE COULDN'T PICTURE.
SHE WAS ME. SHE WASN'T ME.
I LOVED HER.

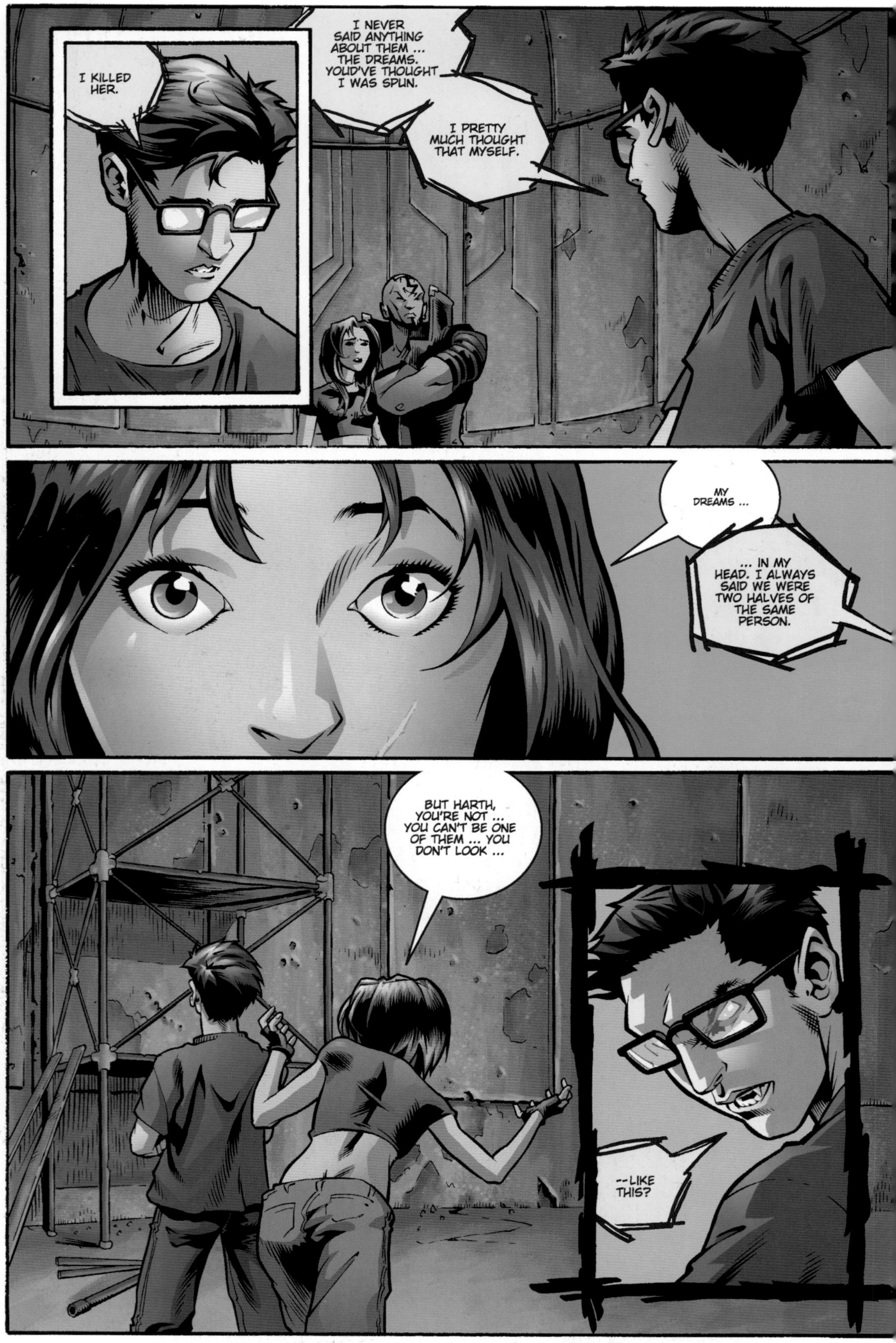
I KILLED HER.
I NEVER SAID ANYTHING ABOUT THEM ... THE DREAMS. YOUD'VE THOUGHT I WAS SPUN.
I PRETTY MUCH THOUGHT THAT MYSELF.
MY DREAMS ...
... IN MY HEAD. I ALWAYS SAID WE WERE TWO HALVES OF THE SAME PERSON.
BUT HARTH, YOU'RE NOT ... YOU CAN'T BE ONE OF THEM ... YOU DON'T LOOK ...
--LIKE THIS?

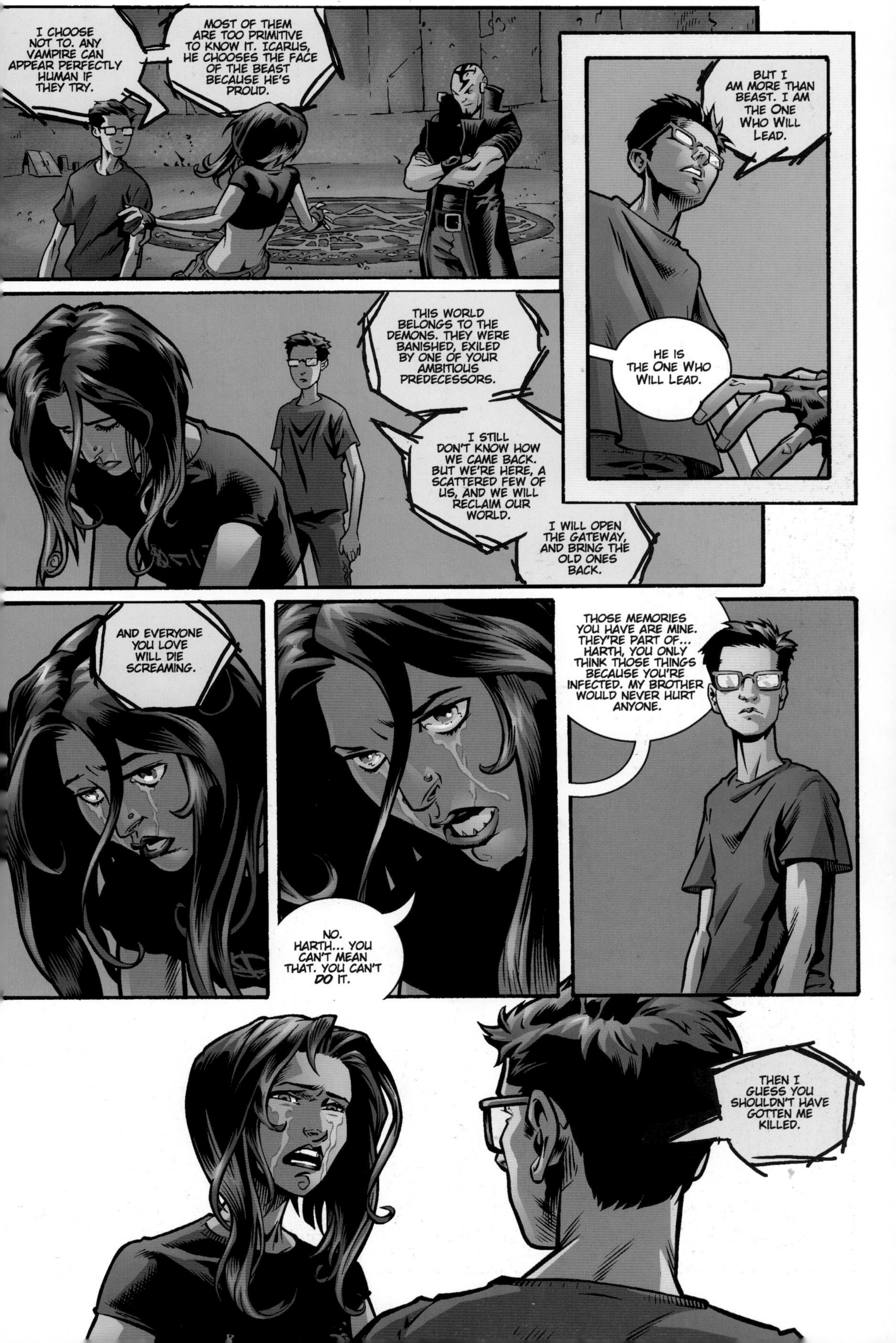
I CHOOSE NOT TO. ANY VAMPIRE CAN APPEAR PERFECTLY HUMAN IF THEY TRY.
MOST OF THEM ARE TOO PRIMITIVE TO KNOW IT. ICARUS, HE CHOOSES THE FACE OF THE BEAST BECAUSE HE'S PROUD.
BUT I AM MORE THAN BEAST. I AM THE ONE WHO WILL LEAD.
HE IS THE ONE WHO WILL LEAD.
THIS WORLD BELONGS TO THE DEMONS. THEY WERE BANISHED, EXILED BY ONE OF YOUR AMBITIOUS PREDECESSORS.
I STILL DON'T KNOW HOW WE CAME BACK. BUT WE'RE HERE, A SCATTERED FEW OF US, AND WE WILL RECLAIM OUR WORLD.
I WILL OPEN THE GATEWAY, AND BRING THE OLD ONES BACK.
AND EVERYONE YOU LOVE WILL DIE SCREAMING.
NO. HARTH... YOU CAN'T MEAN THAT. YOU CAN'T ***DO*** IT.
THOSE MEMORIES YOU HAVE ARE MINE. THEY'RE PART OF... HARTH, YOU ONLY THINK THOSE THINGS BECAUSE YOU'RE INFECTED. MY BROTHER WOULD NEVER HURT ANYONE.
THEN I GUESS YOU SHOULDN'T HAVE GOTTEN ME KILLED.

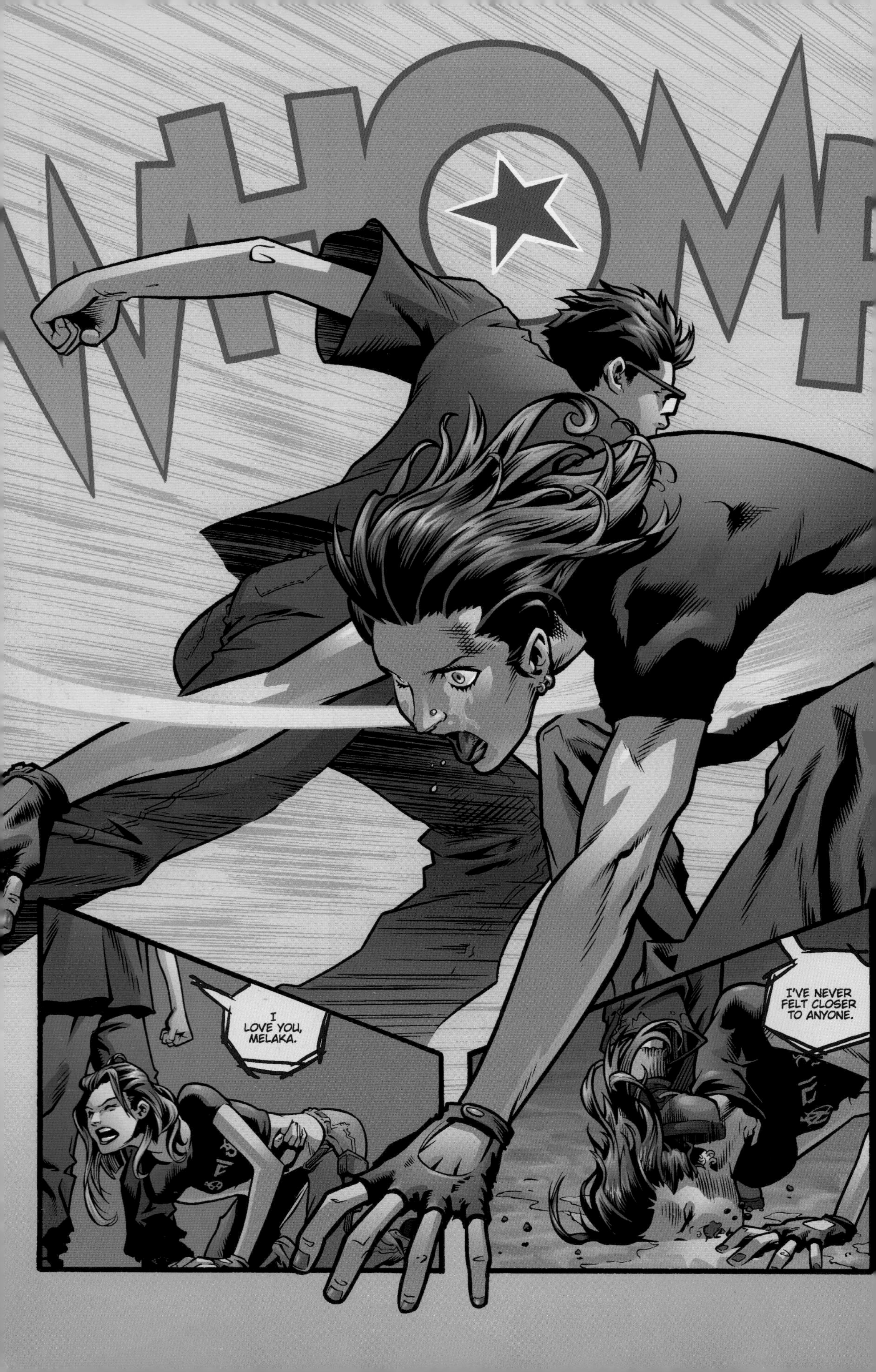
WHOMP
I LOVE YOU, MELAKA.
I'VE NEVER FELT CLOSER TO ANYONE.

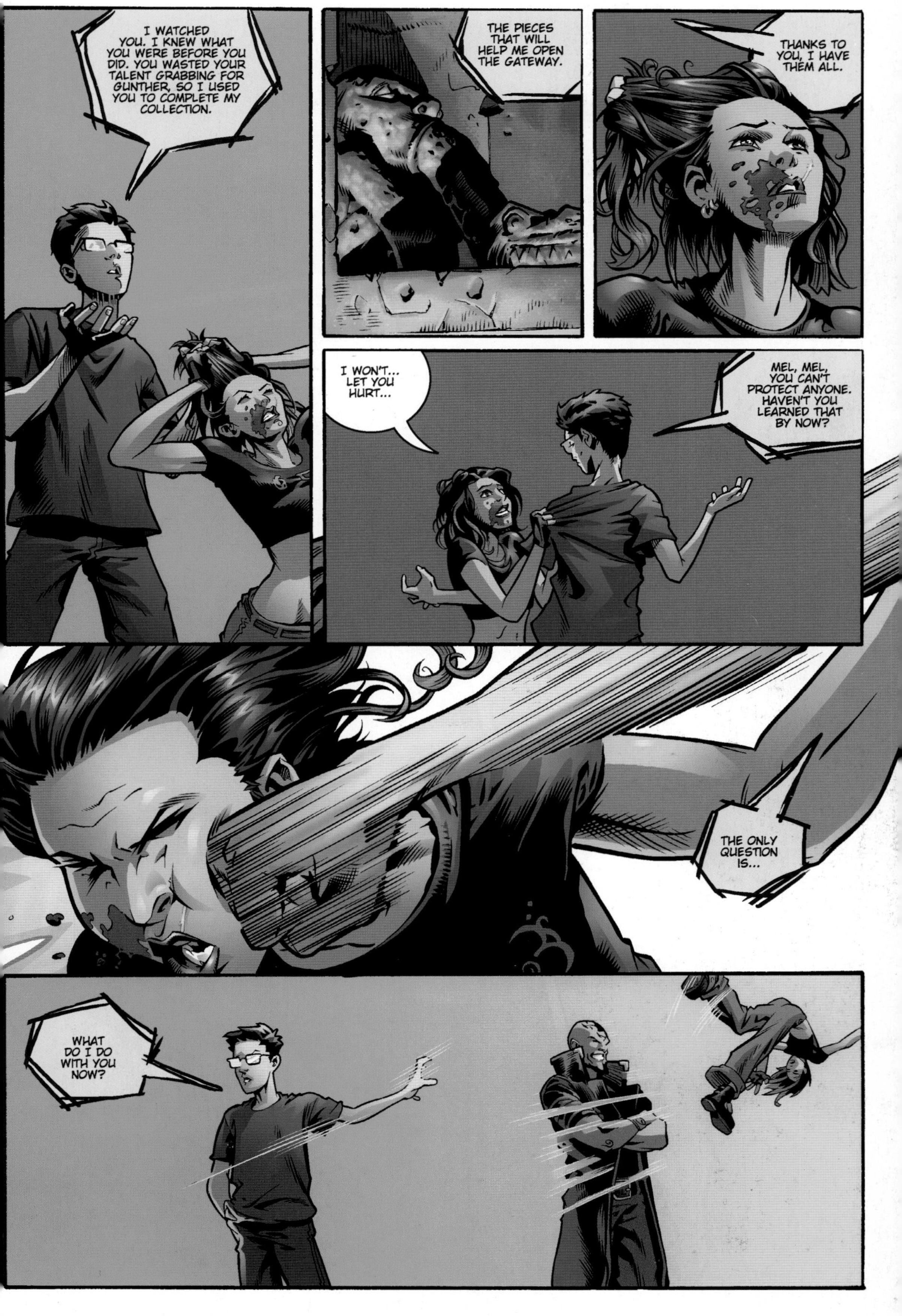
I WATCHED YOU. I KNEW WHAT YOU WERE BEFORE YOU DID. YOU WASTED YOUR TALENT GRABBING FOR GUNTHER, SO I USED YOU TO COMPLETE MY COLLECTION.
THE PIECES THAT WILL HELP ME OPEN THE GATEWAY.
THANKS TO YOU, I HAVE THEM ALL.
I WON'T... LET YOU HURT...
MEL, MEL, YOU CAN'T PROTECT ANYONE. HAVEN'T YOU LEARNED THAT BY NOW?
THE ONLY QUESTION IS...
WHAT DO I DO WITH YOU NOW?

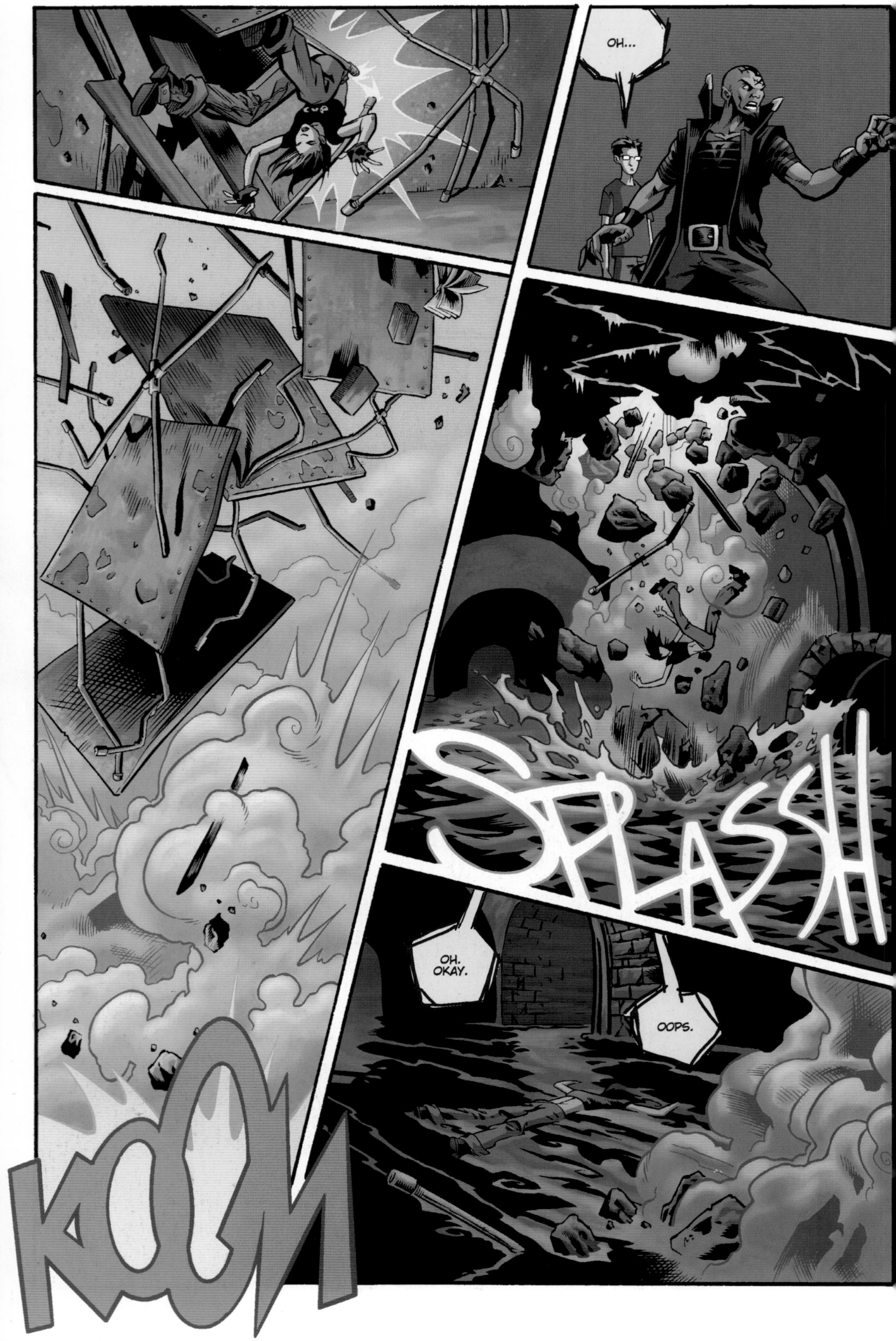
OH...
SPLASSH
KROOM
OH. OKAY.
OOPS.

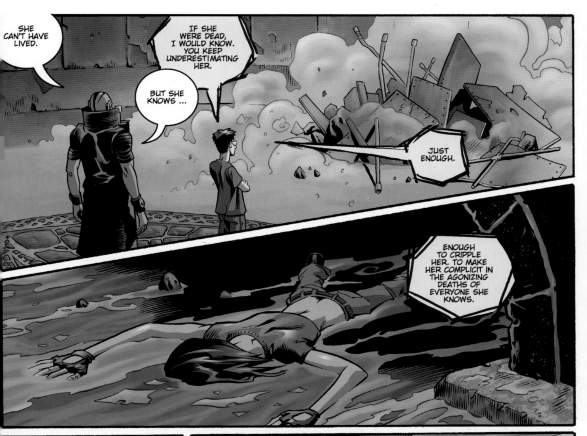

SHE CAN'T HAVE LIVED.

IF SHE WERE DEAD, I WOULD KNOW. YOU KEEP UNDERESTIMATING HER.

BUT SHE KNOWS ...

JUST ENOUGH.

ENOUGH TO CRIPPLE HER. TO MAKE HER COMPLICIT IN THE AGONIZING DEATHS OF EVERYONE SHE KNOWS.

ENOUGH TO PROVE MY LOVE.

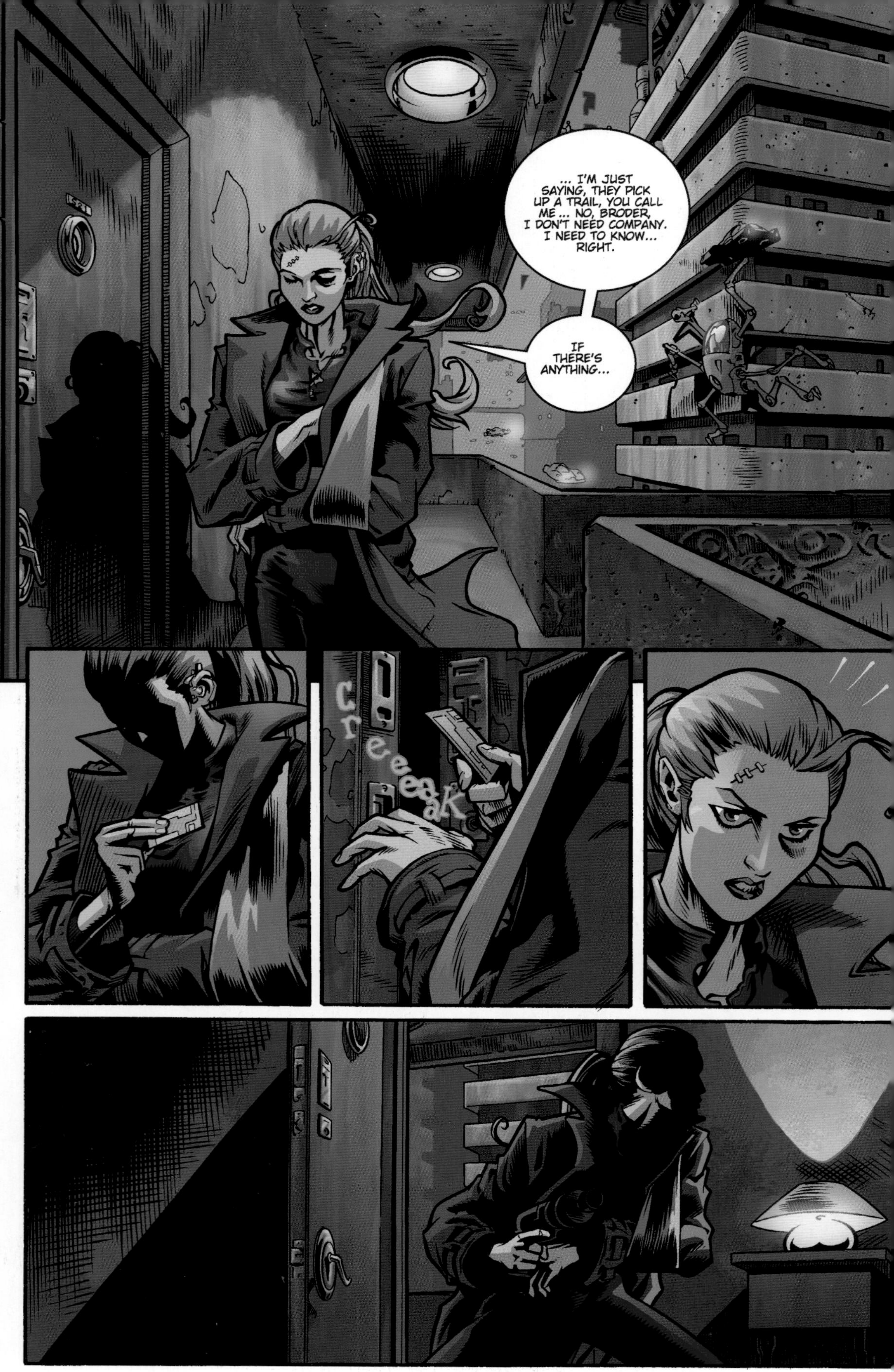
... I'M JUST SAYING, THEY PICK UP A TRAIL, YOU CALL ME ... NO, BRODER, I DON'T NEED COMPANY. I NEED TO KNOW... RIGHT.
IF THERE'S ANYTHING...
creeeaK

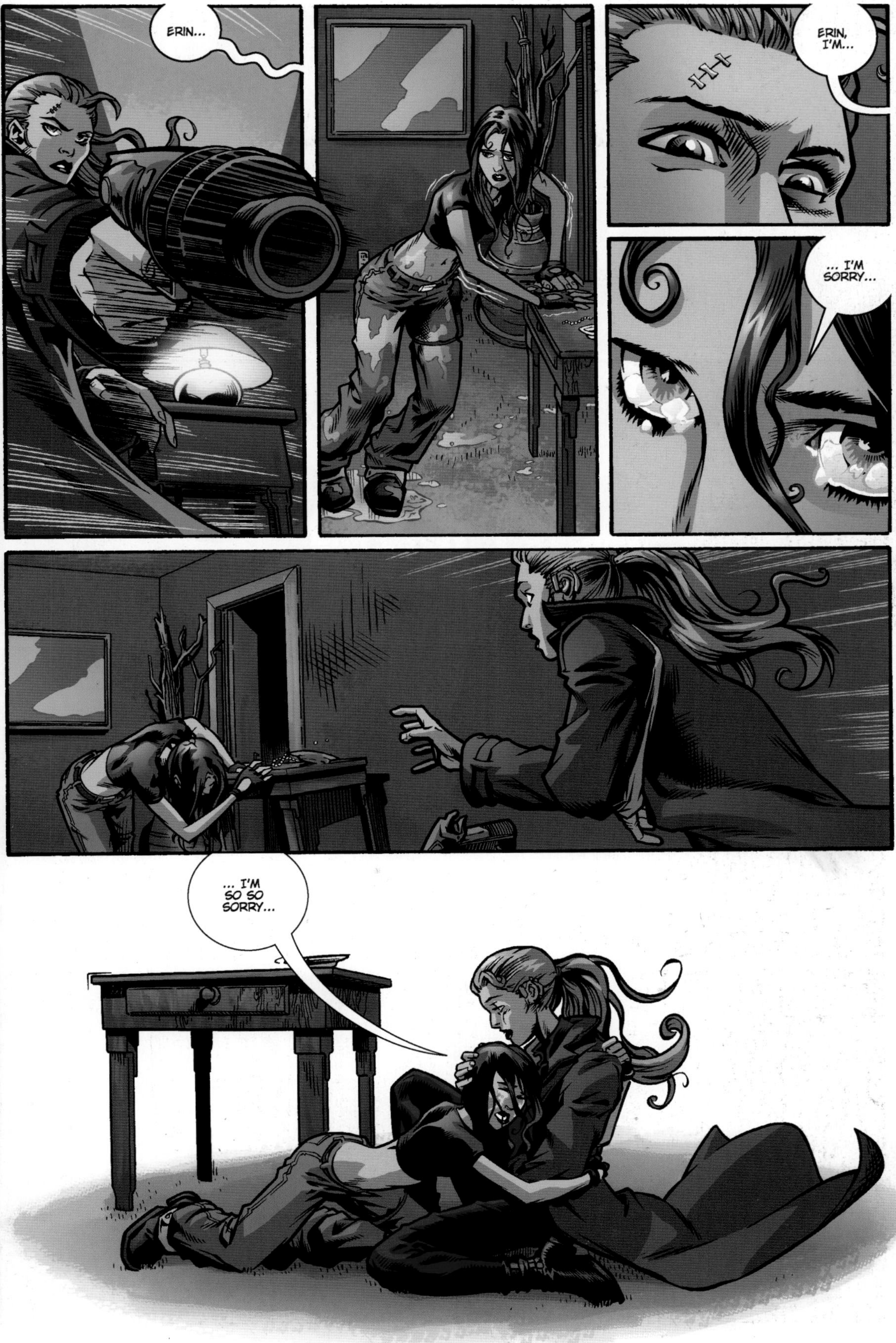
ERIN...
ERIN, I'M...
... I'M SORRY...
... I'M SO SO SORRY...

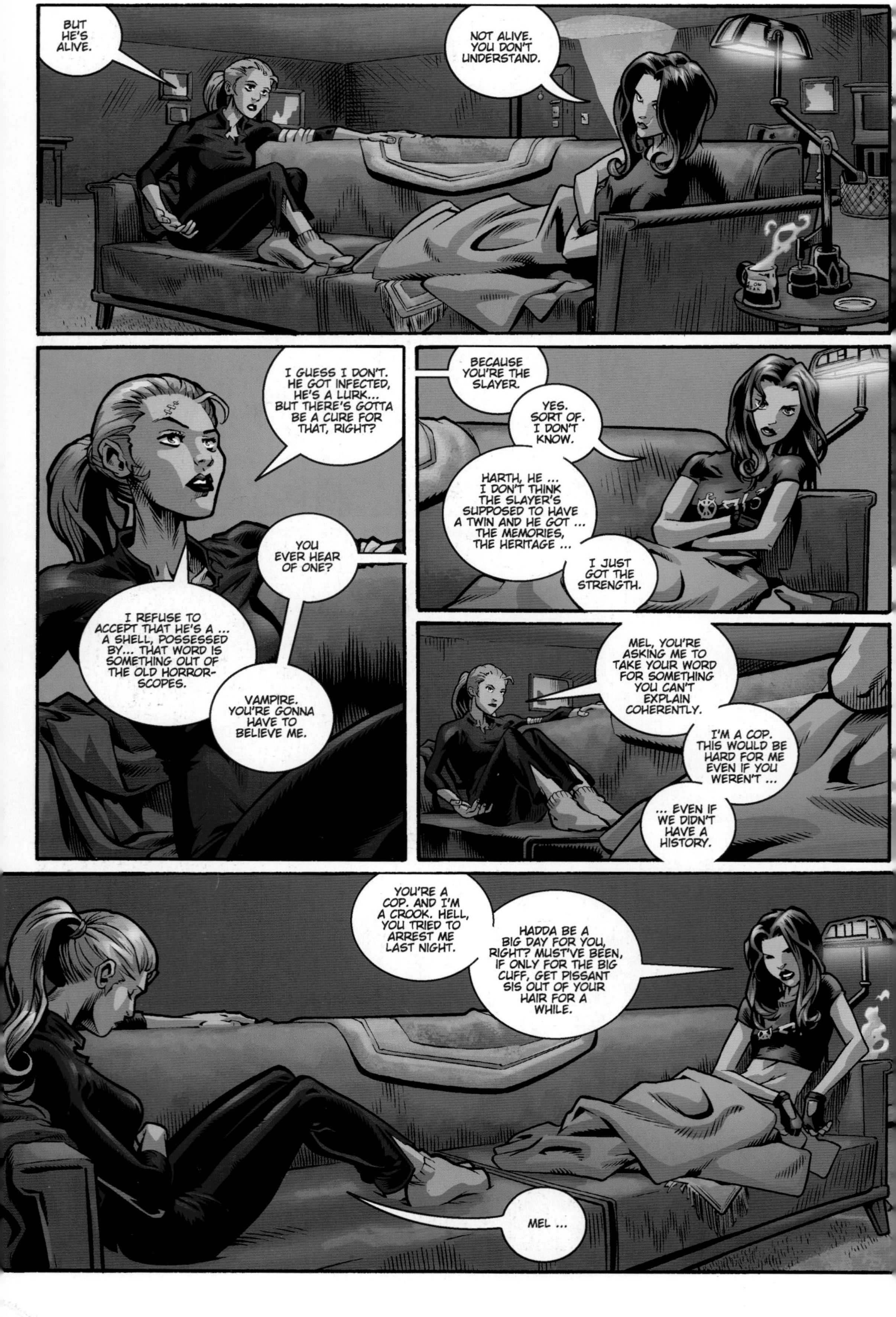
BUT HE'S ALIVE.
NOT ALIVE. YOU DON'T UNDERSTAND.
I GUESS I DON'T. HE GOT INFECTED, HE'S A LURK... BUT THERE'S GOTTA BE A CURE FOR THAT, RIGHT?
BECAUSE YOU'RE THE SLAYER.
YES. SORT OF. I DON'T KNOW.
HARTH, HE ... I DON'T THINK THE SLAYER'S SUPPOSED TO HAVE A TWIN AND HE GOT ... THE MEMORIES, THE HERITAGE ...
I JUST GOT THE STRENGTH.
YOU EVER HEAR OF ONE?
I REFUSE TO ACCEPT THAT HE'S A ... A SHELL, POSSESSED BY... THAT WORD IS SOMETHING OUT OF THE OLD HORROR-SCOPES.
VAMPIRE. YOU'RE GONNA HAVE TO BELIEVE ME.
MEL, YOU'RE ASKING ME TO TAKE YOUR WORD FOR SOMETHING YOU CAN'T EXPLAIN COHERENTLY.
I'M A COP. THIS WOULD BE HARD FOR ME EVEN IF YOU WEREN'T ...
... EVEN IF WE DIDN'T HAVE A HISTORY.
YOU'RE A COP. AND I'M A CROOK. HELL, YOU TRIED TO ARREST ME LAST NIGHT.
HADDA BE A BIG DAY FOR YOU, RIGHT? MUST'VE BEEN, IF ONLY FOR THE BIG CUFF, GET PISSANT SIS OUT OF YOUR HAIR FOR A WHILE.
MEL ...

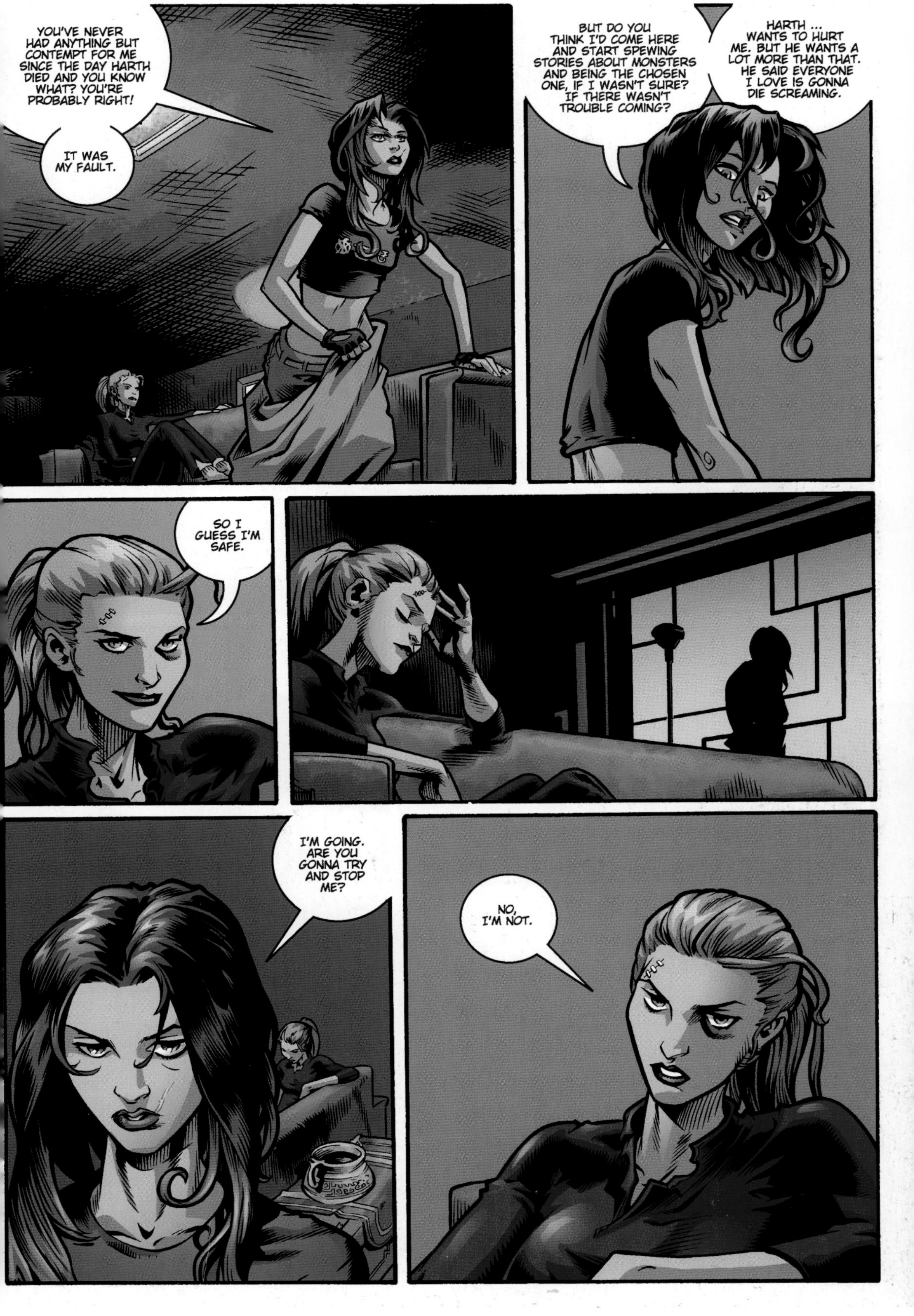
YOU'VE NEVER HAD ANYTHING BUT CONTEMPT FOR ME SINCE THE DAY HARTH DIED AND YOU KNOW WHAT? YOU'RE PROBABLY RIGHT!
IT WAS MY FAULT.
BUT DO YOU THINK I'D COME HERE AND START SPEWING STORIES ABOUT MONSTERS AND BEING THE CHOSEN ONE, IF I WASN'T SURE? IF THERE WASN'T TROUBLE COMING?
HARTH ... WANTS TO HURT ME. BUT HE WANTS A LOT MORE THAN THAT. HE SAID EVERYONE I LOVE IS GONNA DIE SCREAMING.
SO I GUESS I'M SAFE.
I'M GOING. ARE YOU GONNA TRY AND STOP ME?
NO, I'M NOT.

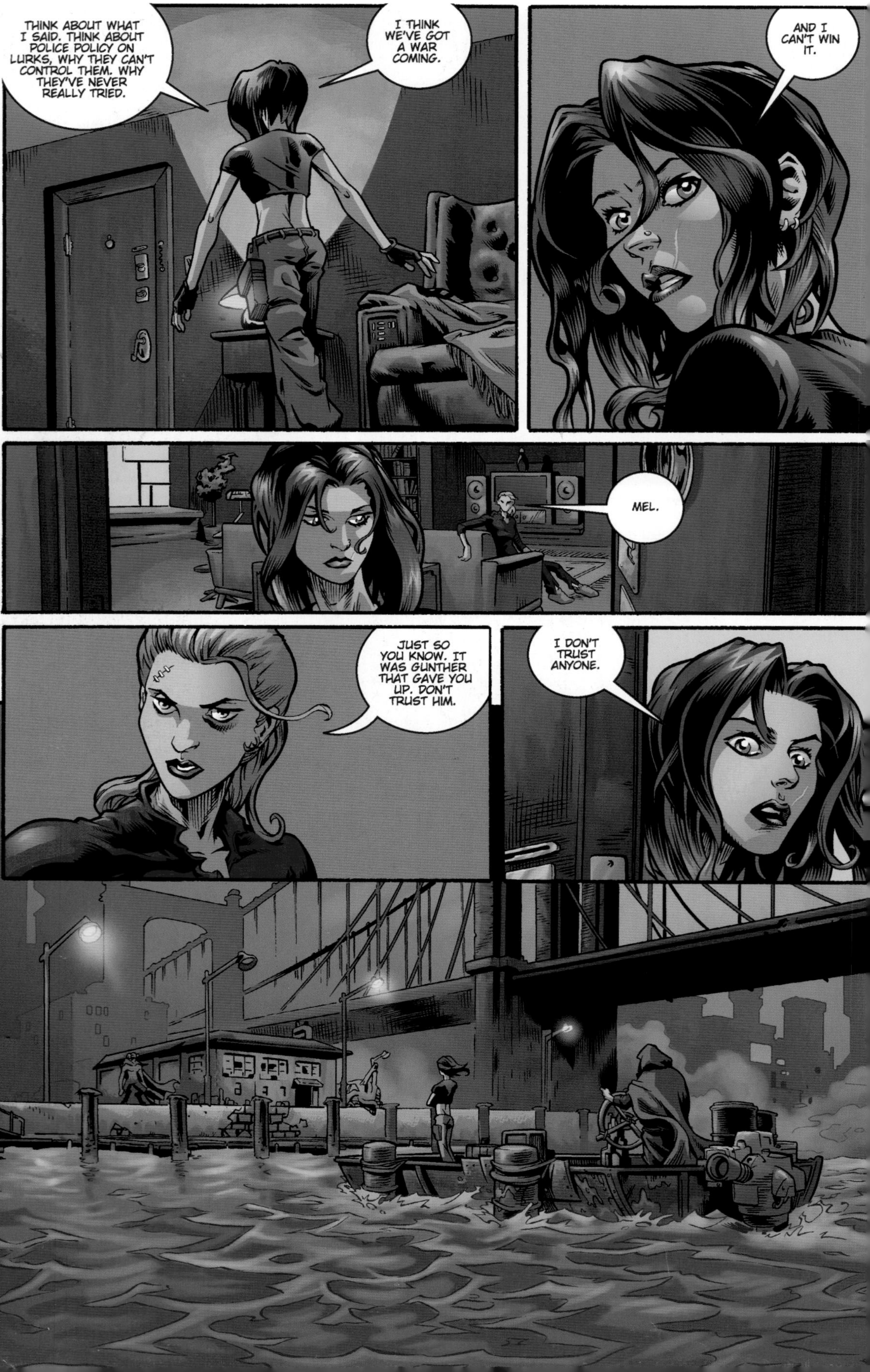
THINK ABOUT WHAT I SAID. THINK ABOUT POLICE POLICY ON LURKS, WHY THEY CAN'T CONTROL THEM. WHY THEY'VE NEVER REALLY TRIED.
I THINK WE'VE GOT A WAR COMING.
AND I CAN'T WIN IT.
MEL.
JUST SO YOU KNOW. IT WAS GUNTHER THAT GAVE YOU UP. DON'T TRUST HIM.
I DON'T TRUST ANYONE.

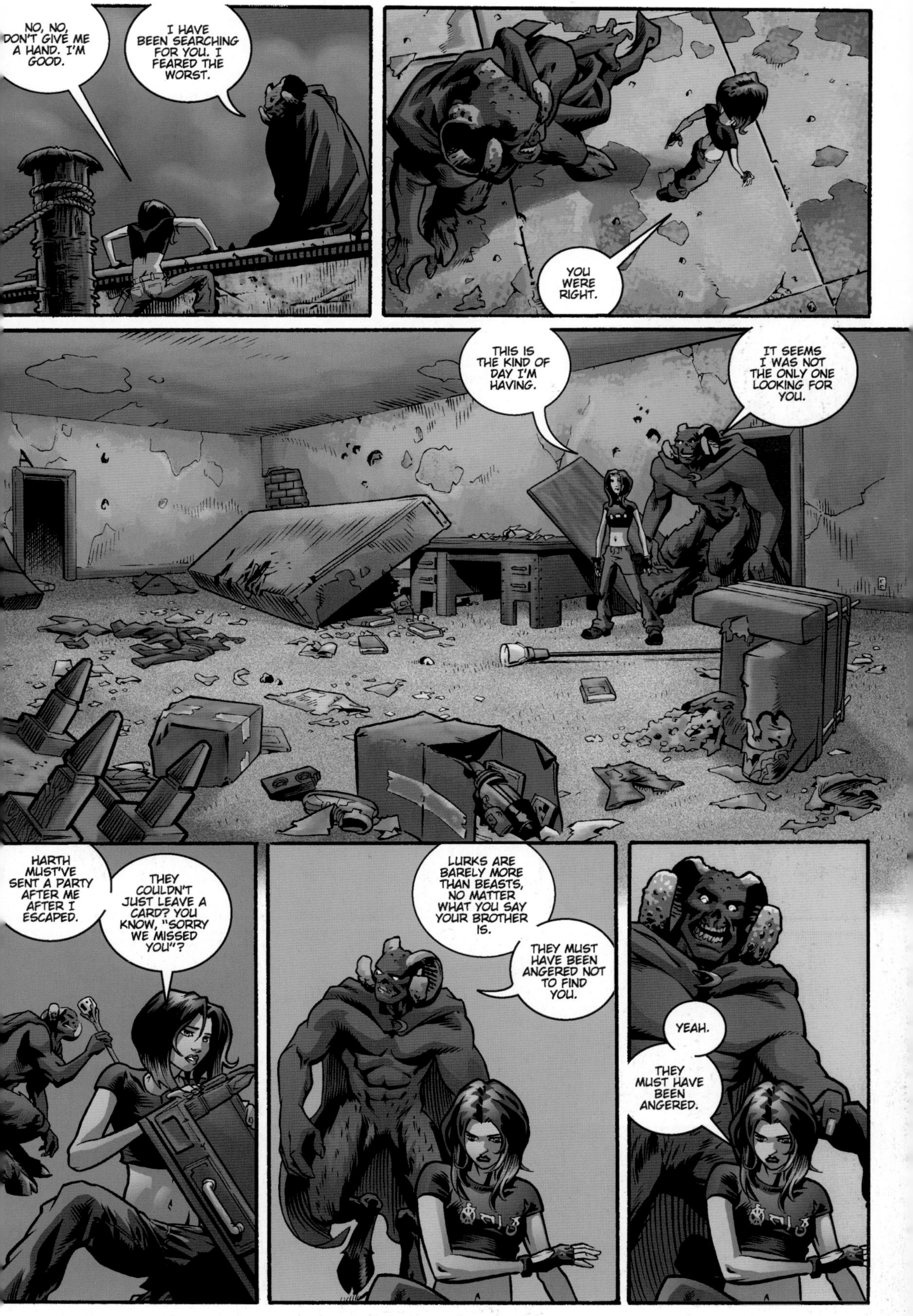

NO, NO, DON'T GIVE ME A HAND. I'M GOOD.
I HAVE BEEN SEARCHING FOR YOU. I FEARED THE WORST.
YOU WERE RIGHT.
THIS IS THE KIND OF DAY I'M HAVING.
IT SEEMS I WAS NOT THE ONLY ONE LOOKING FOR YOU.
HARTH MUST'VE SENT A PARTY AFTER ME AFTER I ESCAPED.
THEY COULDN'T JUST LEAVE A CARD? YOU KNOW, "SORRY WE MISSED YOU"?
LURKS ARE BARELY MORE THAN BEASTS, NO MATTER WHAT YOU SAY YOUR BROTHER IS.
THEY MUST HAVE BEEN ANGERED NOT TO FIND YOU.
YEAH.
THEY MUST HAVE BEEN ANGERED.

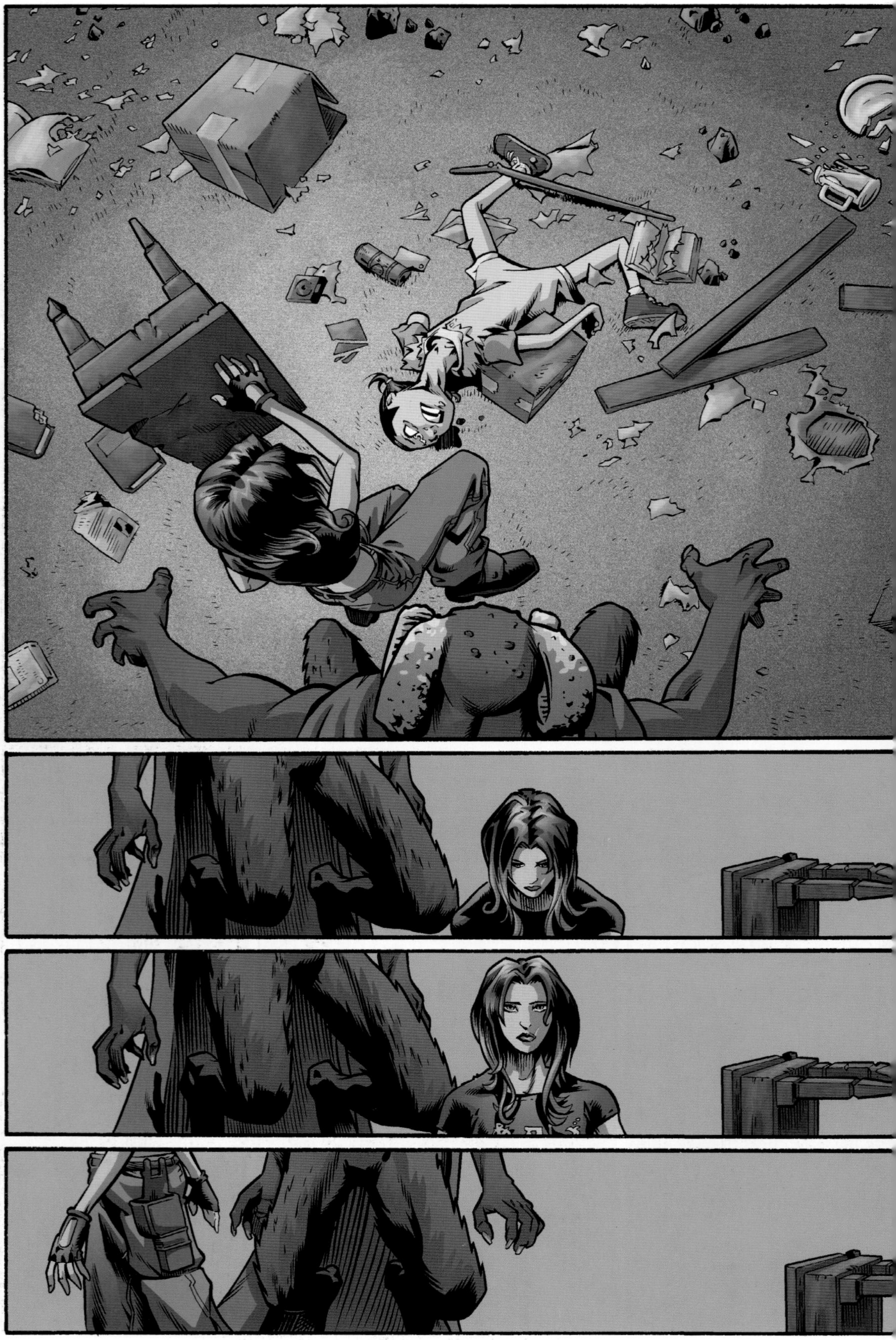

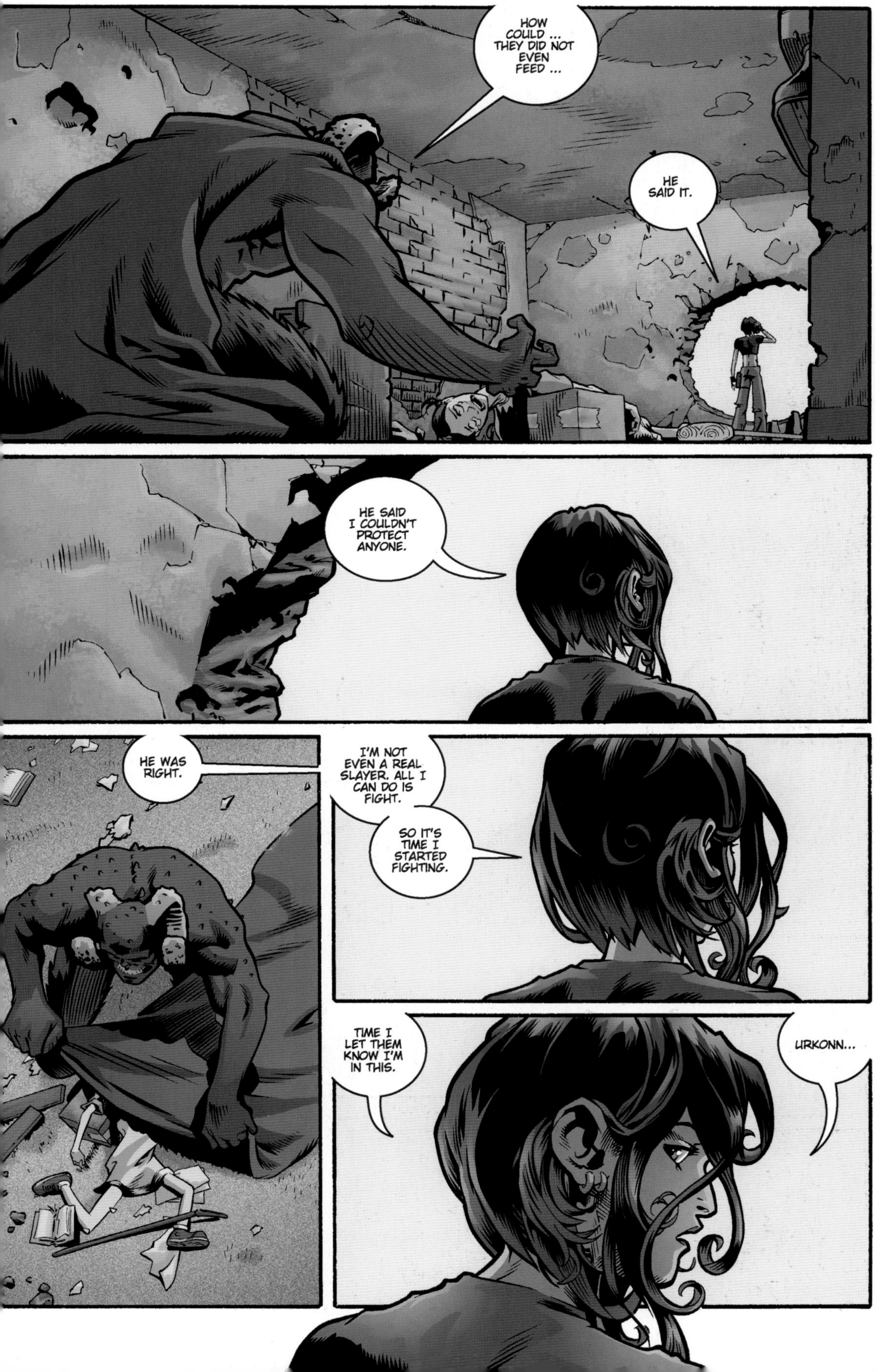

HOW COULD ... THEY DID NOT EVEN FEED ...
HE SAID IT.
HE SAID I COULDN'T PROTECT ANYONE.
HE WAS RIGHT.
I'M NOT EVEN A REAL SLAYER. ALL I CAN DO IS FIGHT.
SO IT'S TIME I STARTED FIGHTING.
TIME I LET THEM KNOW I'M IN THIS.
URKONN...

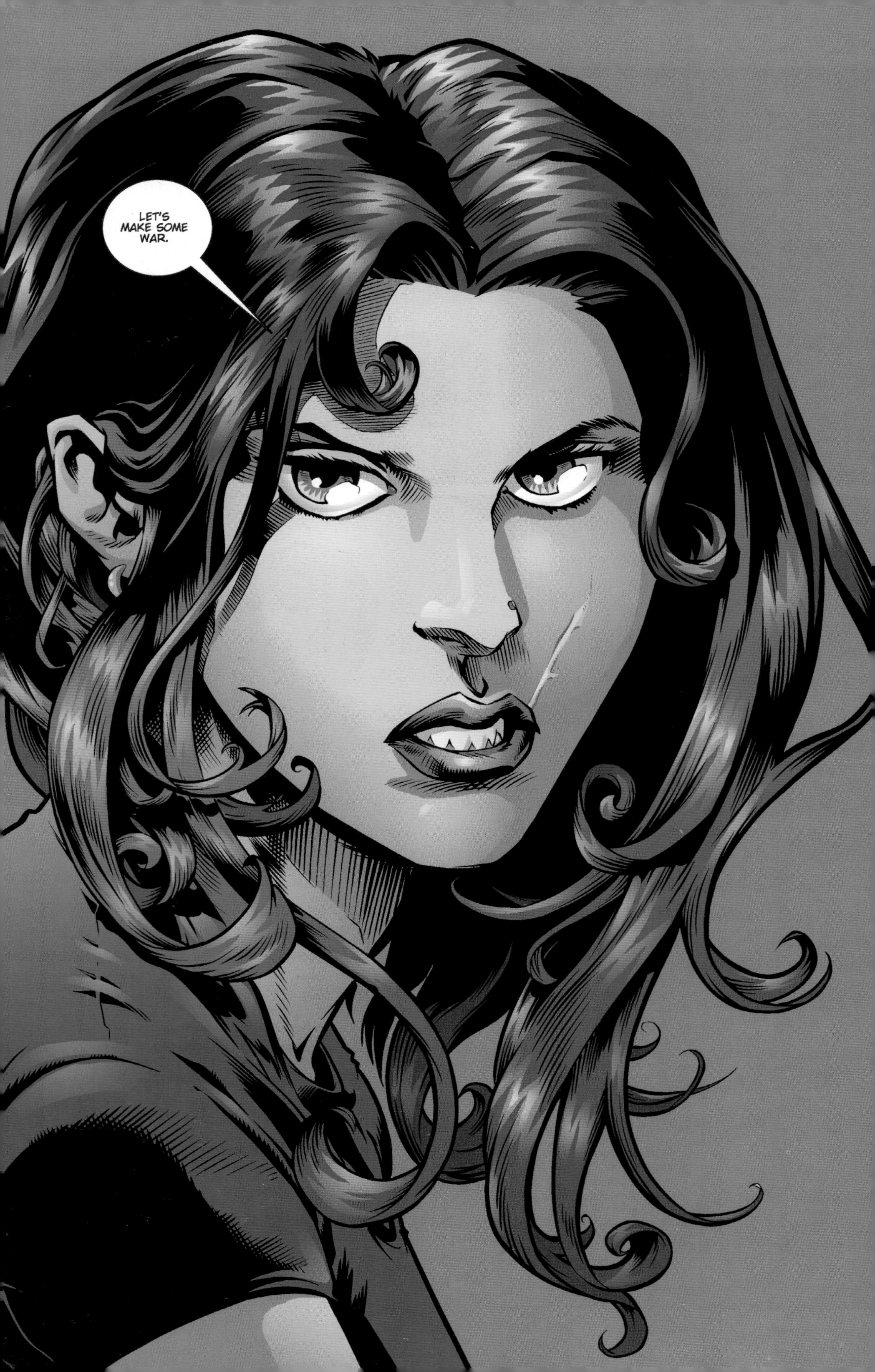
LET'S MAKE SOME WAR.

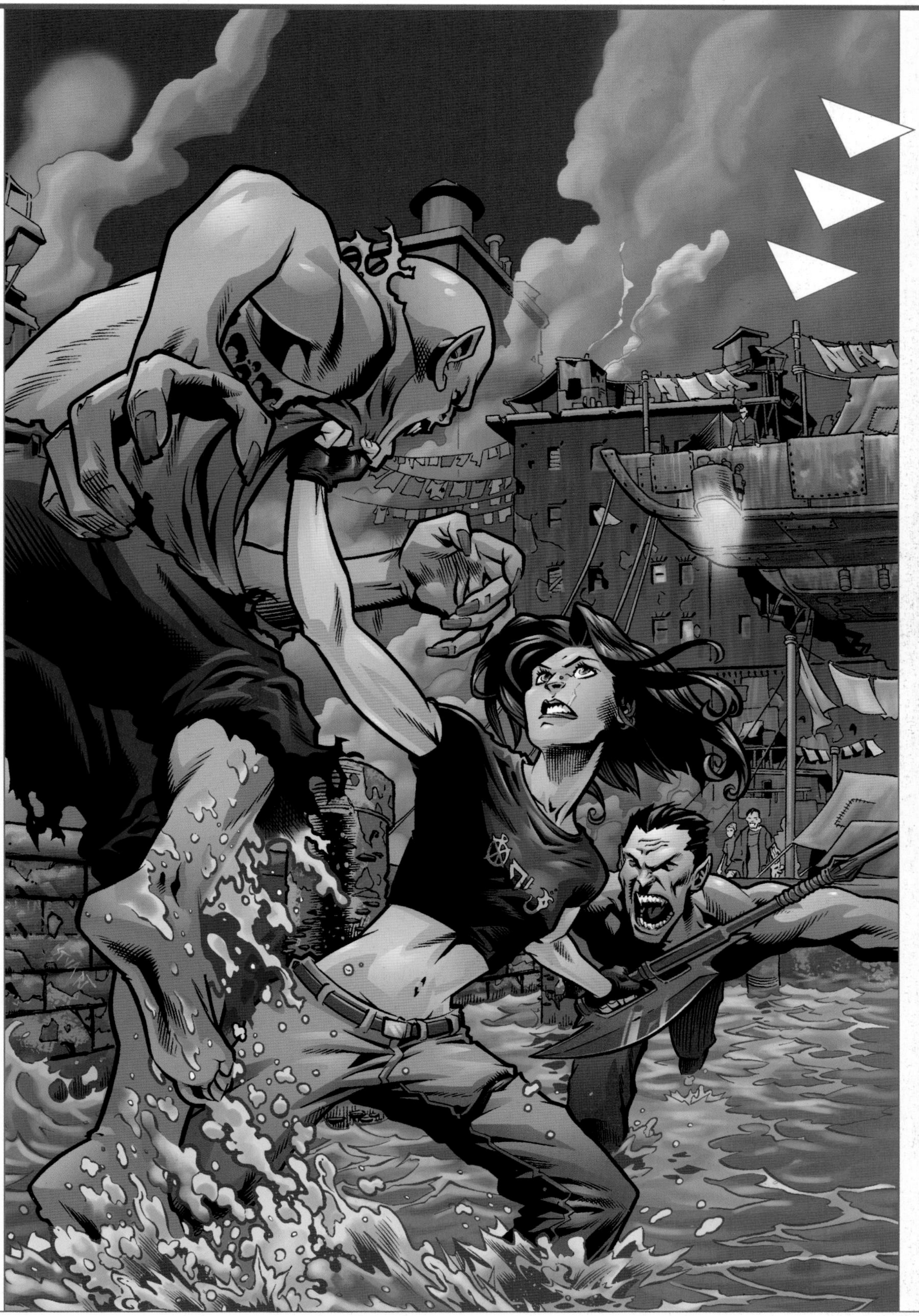

"Finally. Things get clearer.
This is how I begin."

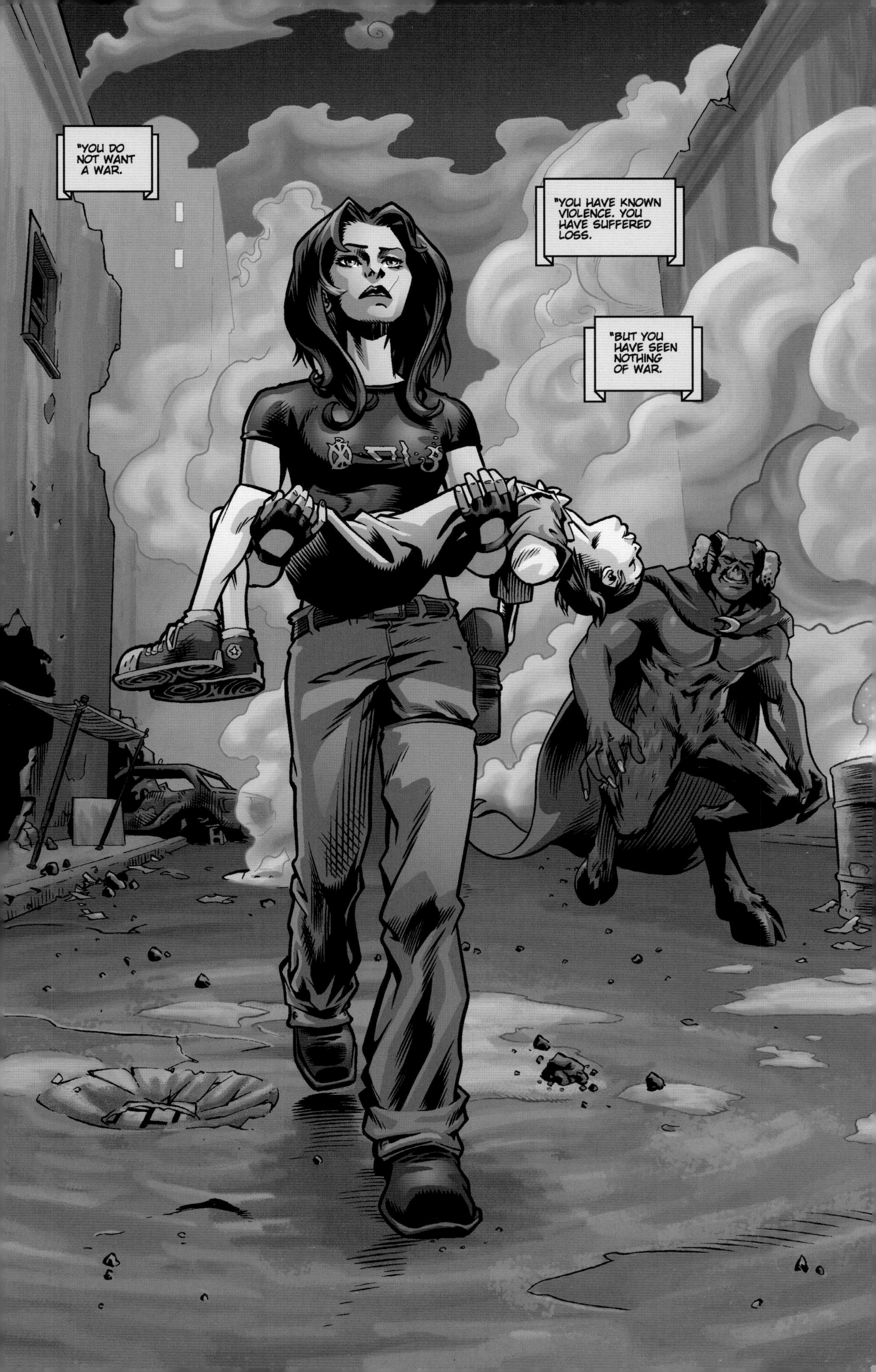
"YOU DO NOT WANT A WAR.
"YOU HAVE KNOWN VIOLENCE. YOU HAVE SUFFERED LOSS.
"BUT YOU HAVE SEEN NOTHING OF WAR.

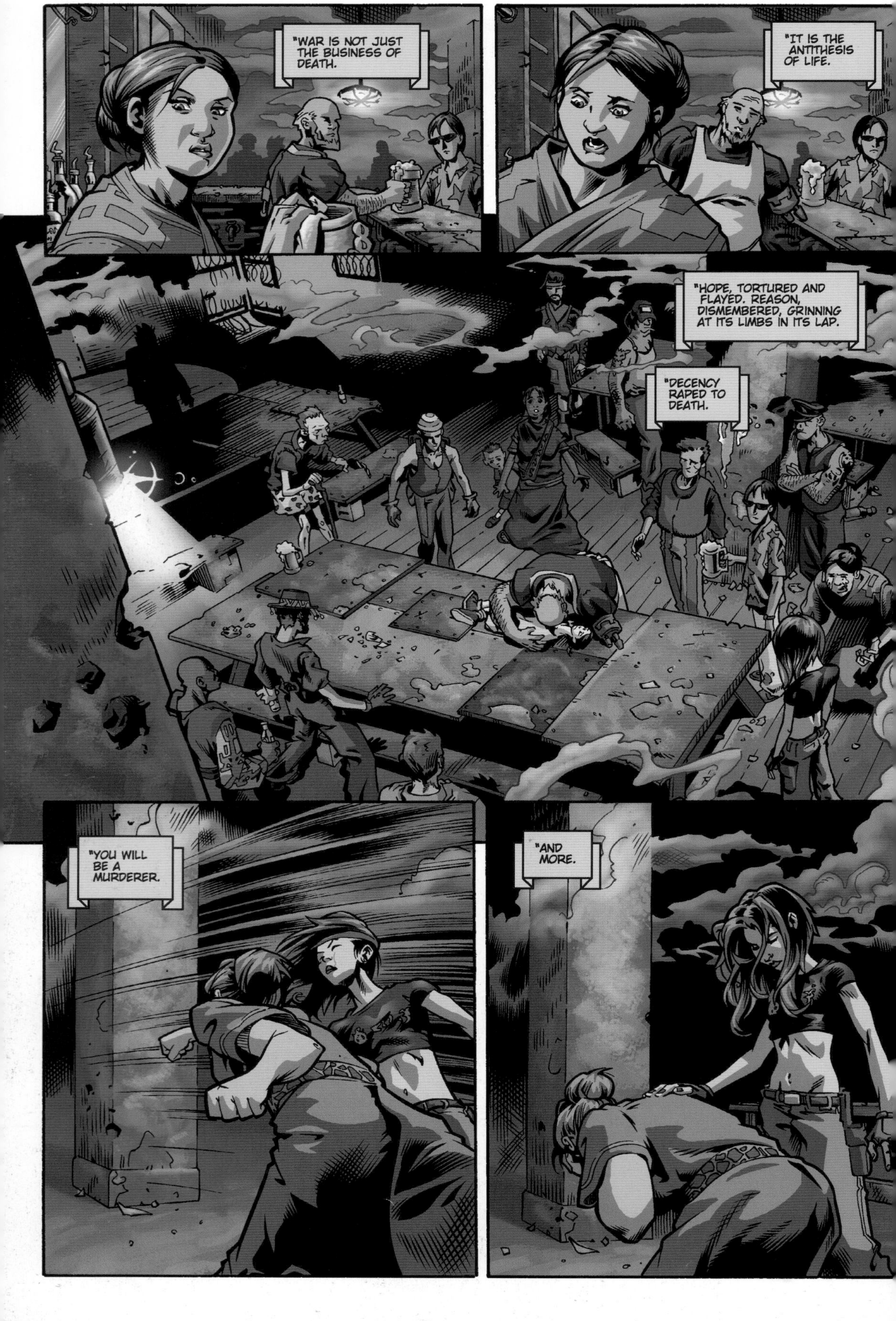
"WAR IS NOT JUST THE BUSINESS OF DEATH.
"IT IS THE ANTITHESIS OF LIFE.
"HOPE, TORTURED AND FLAYED. REASON, DISMEMBERED, GRINNING AT ITS LIMBS IN ITS LAP.
"DECENCY RAPED TO DEATH.
"YOU WILL BE A MURDERER.
"AND MORE.

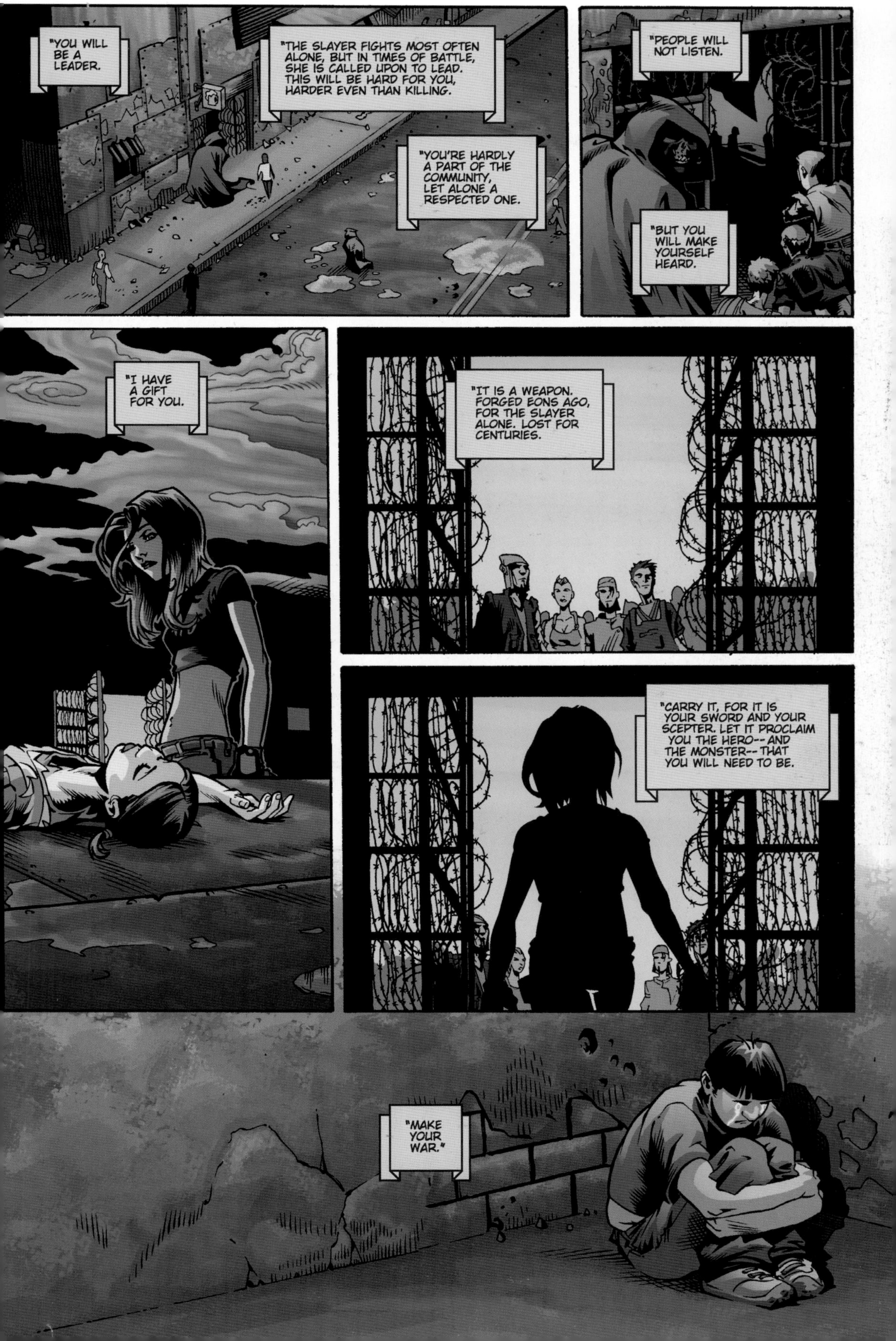
"YOU WILL BE A LEADER.
"THE SLAYER FIGHTS MOST OFTEN ALONE, BUT IN TIMES OF BATTLE, SHE IS CALLED UPON TO LEAD. THIS WILL BE HARD FOR YOU, HARDER EVEN THAN KILLING.
"YOU'RE HARDLY A PART OF THE COMMUNITY, LET ALONE A RESPECTED ONE.
"PEOPLE WILL NOT LISTEN.
"BUT YOU WILL MAKE YOURSELF HEARD.
"I HAVE A GIFT FOR YOU.
"IT IS A WEAPON. FORGED EONS AGO, FOR THE SLAYER ALONE. LOST FOR CENTURIES.
"CARRY IT, FOR IT IS YOUR SWORD AND YOUR SCEPTER. LET IT PROCLAIM YOU THE HERO-- AND THE MONSTER-- THAT YOU WILL NEED TO BE.
"MAKE YOUR WAR."

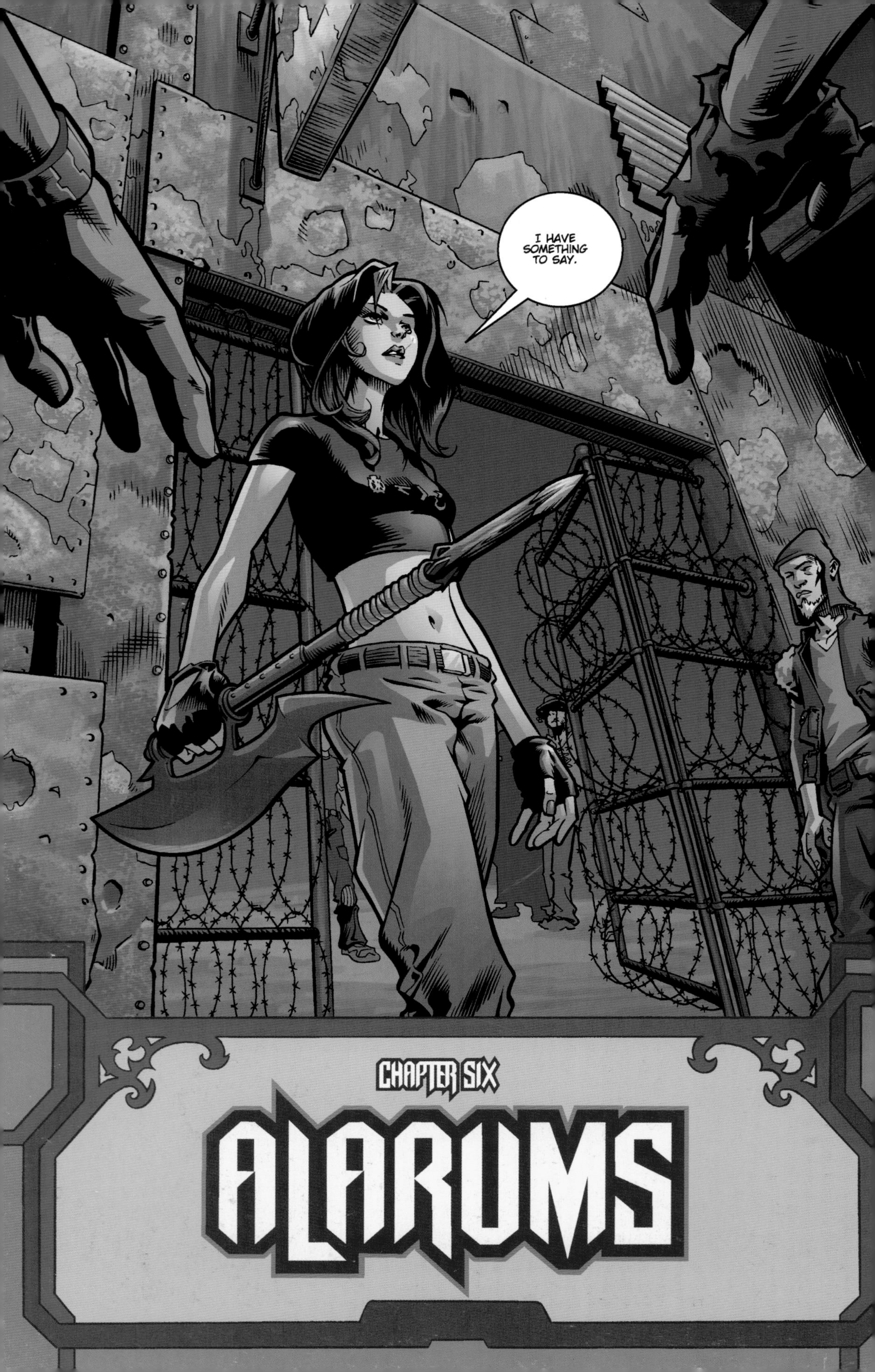

I HAVE SOMETHING TO SAY.
CHAPTER SIX
ALARUMS

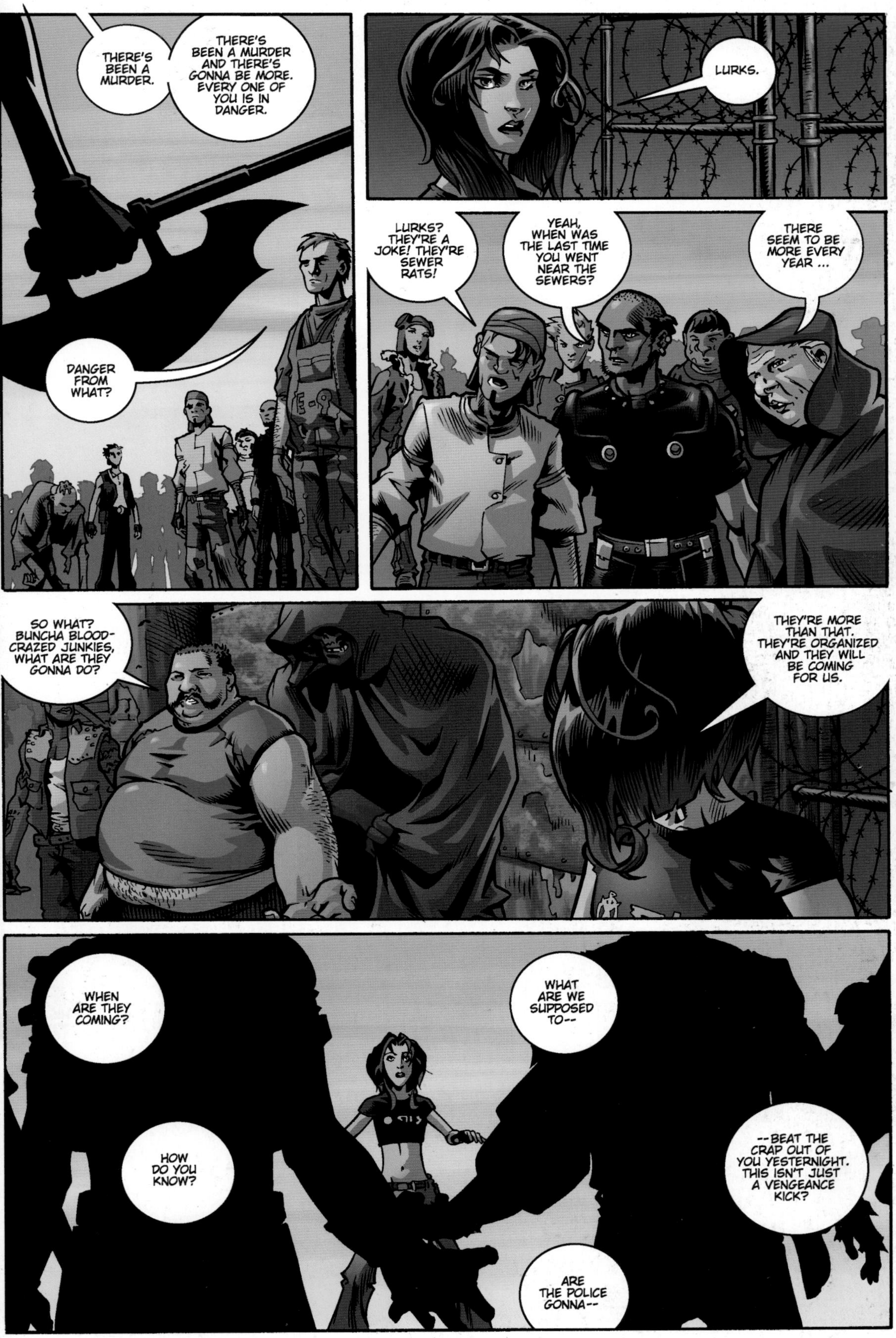
THERE'S BEEN A MURDER.
THERE'S BEEN A MURDER AND THERE'S GONNA BE MORE. EVERY ONE OF YOU IS IN DANGER.
DANGER FROM WHAT?
LURKS.
LURKS? THEY'RE A JOKE! THEY'RE SEWER RATS!
YEAH, WHEN WAS THE LAST TIME YOU WENT NEAR THE SEWERS?
THERE SEEM TO BE MORE EVERY YEAR ...
SO WHAT? BUNCHA BLOOD-CRAZED JUNKIES, WHAT ARE THEY GONNA DO?
THEY'RE MORE THAN THAT. THEY'RE ORGANIZED AND THEY WILL BE COMING FOR US.
WHEN ARE THEY COMING?
HOW DO YOU KNOW?
WHAT ARE WE SUPPOSED TO--
--BEAT THE CRAP OUT OF YOU YESTERNIGHT. THIS ISN'T JUST A VENGEANCE KICK?
ARE THE POLICE GONNA--

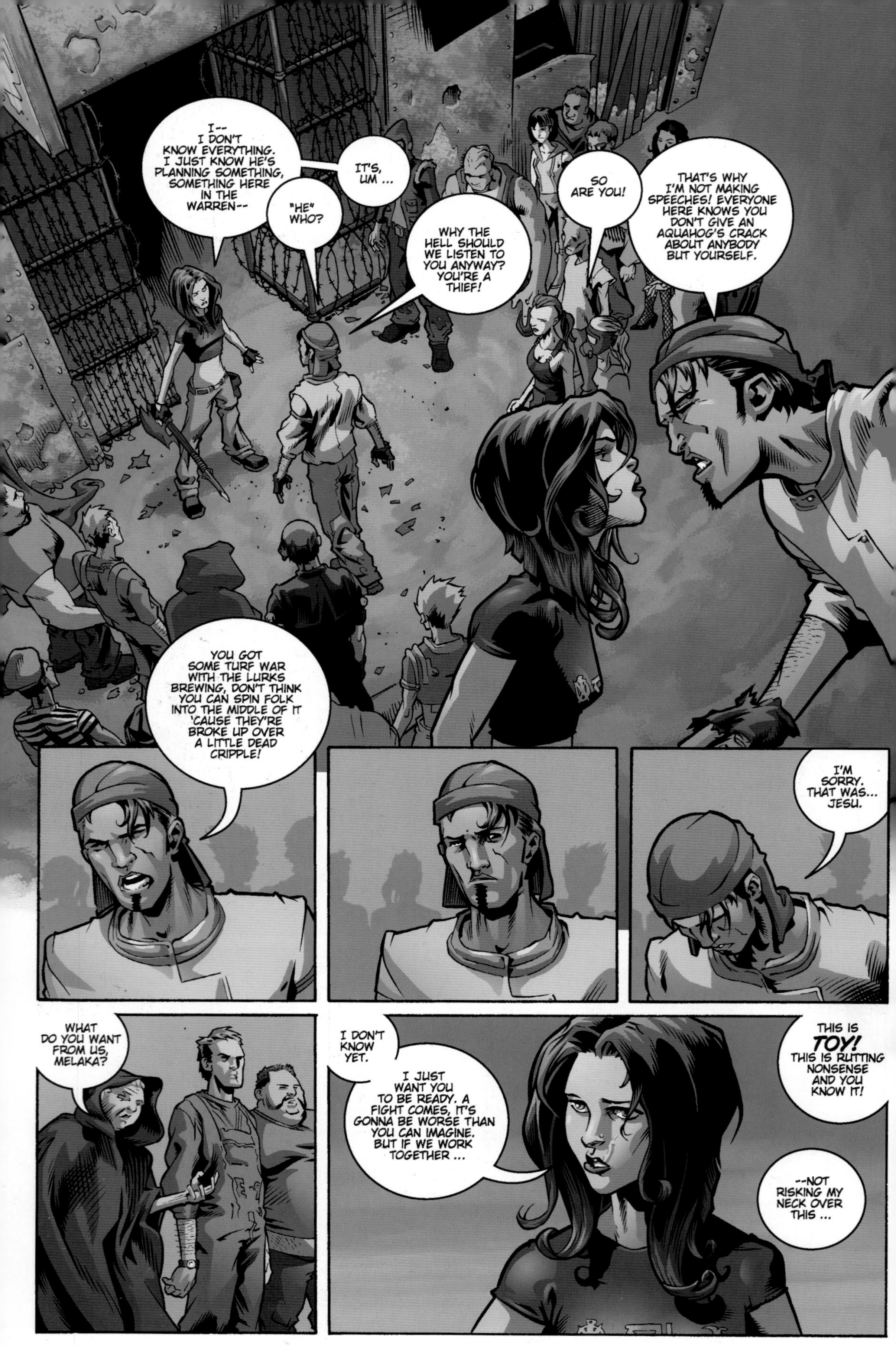
I-- I DON'T KNOW EVERYTHING. I JUST KNOW HE'S PLANNING SOMETHING, SOMETHING HERE IN THE WARREN--
"HE" WHO?
IT'S, UM ...
WHY THE HELL SHOULD WE LISTEN TO YOU ANYWAY? YOU'RE A THIEF!
SO ARE YOU!
THAT'S WHY I'M NOT MAKING SPEECHES! EVERYONE HERE KNOWS YOU DON'T GIVE AN AQUAHOG'S CRACK ABOUT ANYBODY BUT YOURSELF.
YOU GOT SOME TURF WAR WITH THE LURKS BREWING, DON'T THINK YOU CAN SPIN FOLK INTO THE MIDDLE OF IT 'CAUSE THEY'RE BROKE UP OVER A LITTLE DEAD CRIPPLE!
I'M SORRY. THAT WAS... JESU.
WHAT DO YOU WANT FROM US, MELAKA?
I DON'T KNOW YET.
I JUST WANT YOU TO BE READY. A FIGHT COMES, IT'S GONNA BE WORSE THAN YOU CAN IMAGINE. BUT IF WE WORK TOGETHER ...
THIS IS TOY! THIS IS RUTTING NONSENSE AND YOU KNOW IT!
--NOT RISKING MY NECK OVER THIS ...

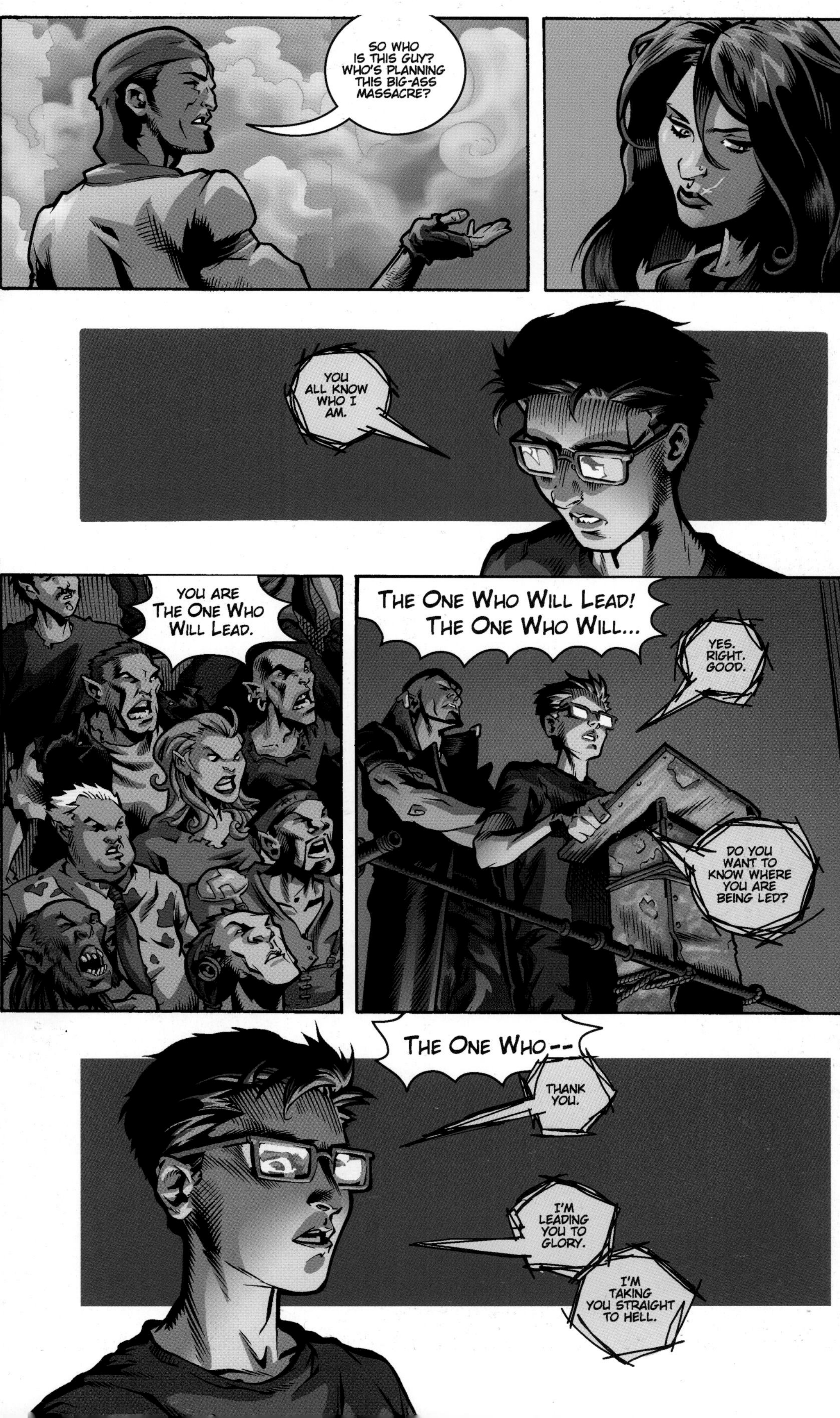
SO WHO IS THIS GUY? WHO'S PLANNING THIS BIG-ASS MASSACRE?
YOU ALL KNOW WHO I AM.
YOU ARE THE ONE WHO WILL LEAD.
THE ONE WHO WILL LEAD! THE ONE WHO WILL...
YES. RIGHT. GOOD.
DO YOU WANT TO KNOW WHERE YOU ARE BEING LED?
THE ONE WHO--
THANK YOU.
I'M LEADING YOU TO GLORY.
I'M TAKING YOU STRAIGHT TO HELL.

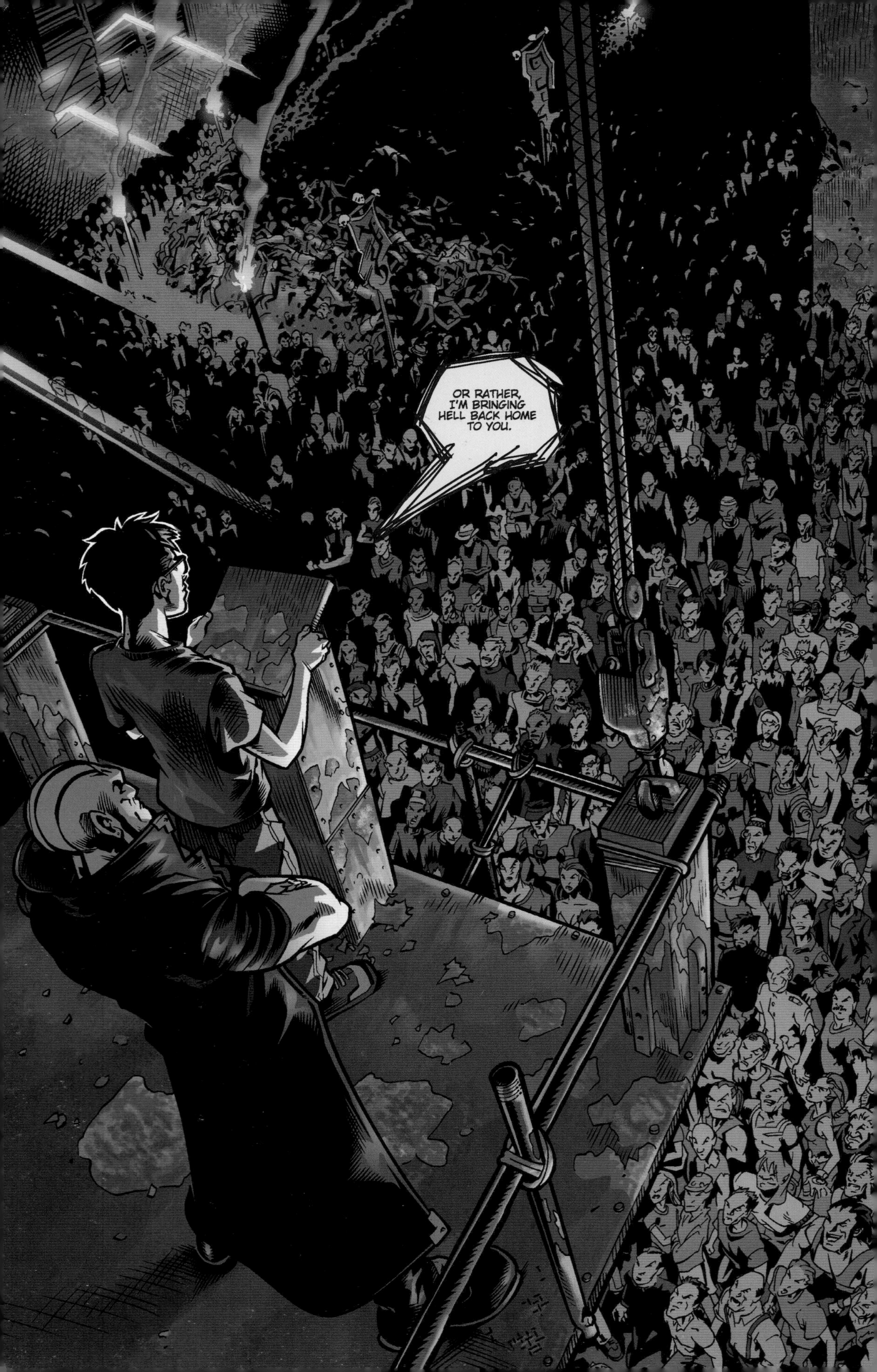
OR RATHER, I'M BRINGING HELL BACK HOME TO YOU.

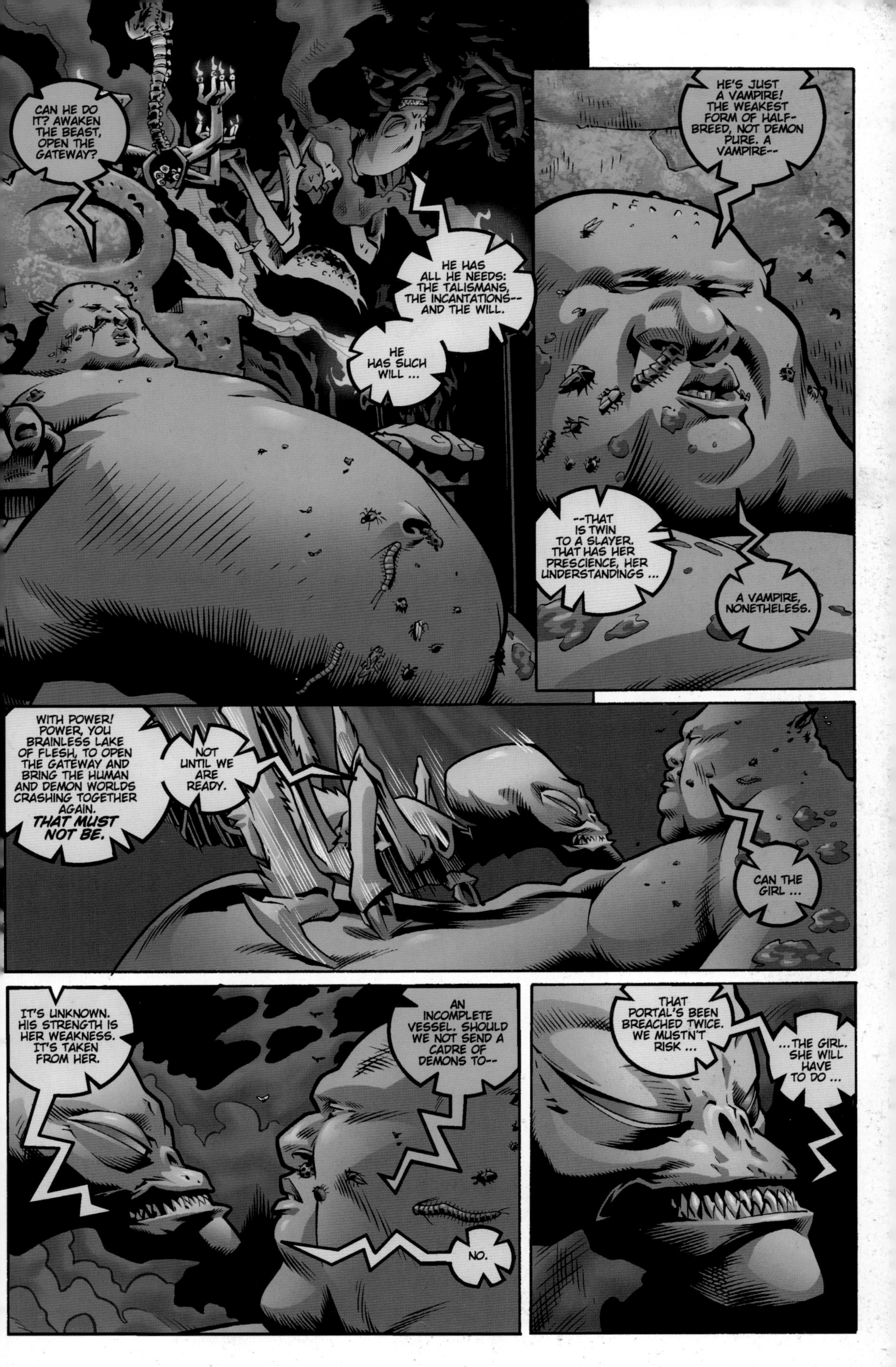
CAN HE DO IT? AWAKEN THE BEAST, OPEN THE GATEWAY?
HE HAS ALL HE NEEDS: THE TALISMANS, THE INCANTATIONS-- AND THE WILL.
HE HAS SUCH WILL ...
HE'S JUST A VAMPIRE! THE WEAKEST FORM OF HALF-BREED, NOT DEMON PURE. A VAMPIRE--
--THAT IS TWIN TO A SLAYER. THAT HAS HER PRESCIENCE, HER UNDERSTANDINGS ...
A VAMPIRE, NONETHELESS.
WITH POWER! POWER, YOU BRAINLESS LAKE OF FLESH, TO OPEN THE GATEWAY AND BRING THE HUMAN AND DEMON WORLDS CRASHING TOGETHER AGAIN. THAT MUST NOT BE.
NOT UNTIL WE ARE READY.
CAN THE GIRL ...
IT'S UNKNOWN. HIS STRENGTH IS HER WEAKNESS. IT'S TAKEN FROM HER.
AN INCOMPLETE VESSEL. SHOULD WE NOT SEND A CADRE OF DEMONS TO--
NO.
THAT PORTAL'S BEEN BREACHED TWICE. WE MUSTN'T RISK ...
...THE GIRL. SHE WILL HAVE TO DO ...

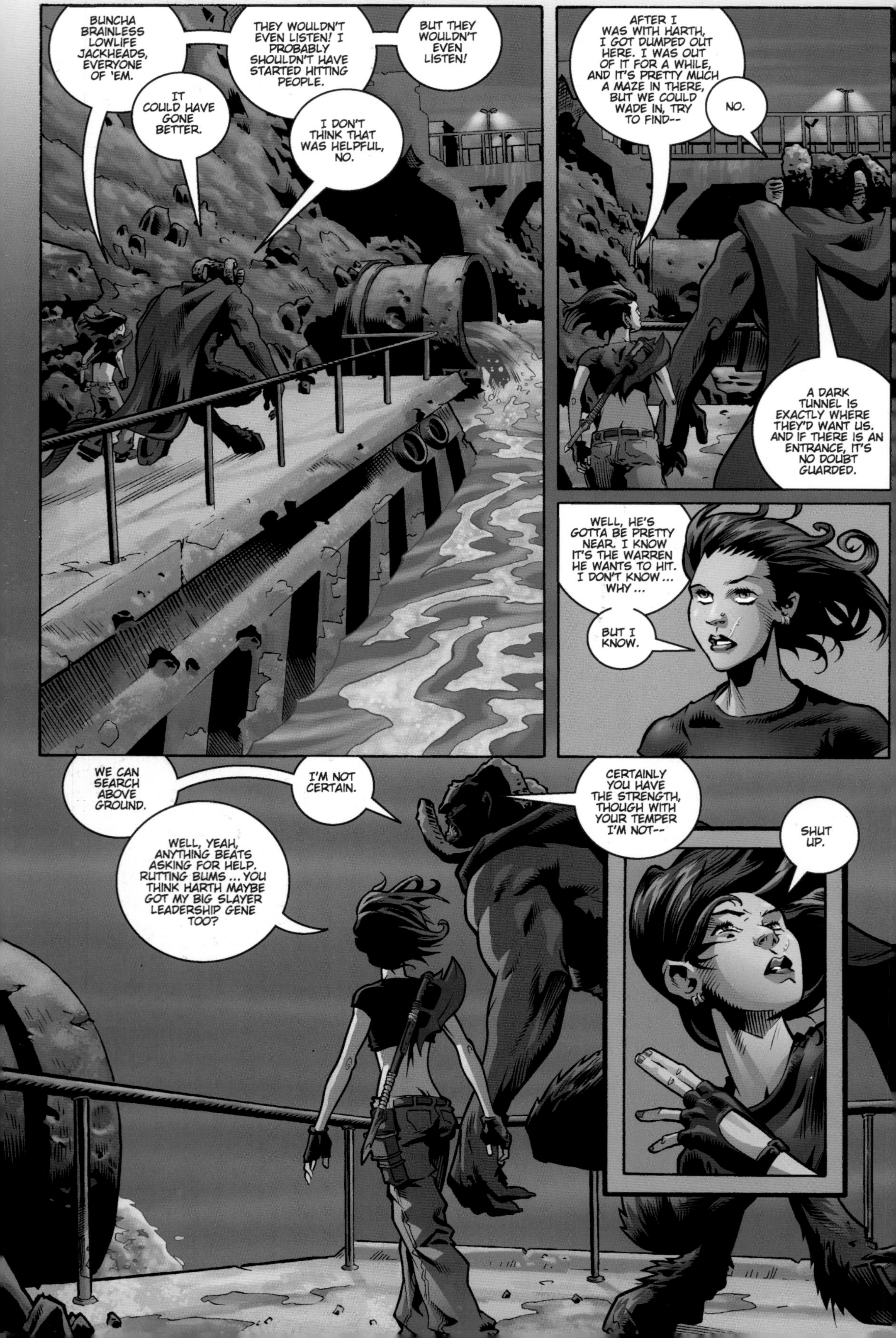
BUNCHA BRAINLESS LOWLIFE JACKHEADS, EVERYONE OF 'EM.
THEY WOULDN'T EVEN LISTEN! I PROBABLY SHOULDN'T HAVE STARTED HITTING PEOPLE.
BUT THEY WOULDN'T EVEN LISTEN!
IT COULD HAVE GONE BETTER.
I DON'T THINK THAT WAS HELPFUL, NO.
AFTER I WAS WITH HARTH, I GOT DUMPED OUT HERE. I WAS OUT OF IT FOR A WHILE, AND IT'S PRETTY MUCH A MAZE IN THERE, BUT WE COULD WADE IN, TRY TO FIND--
NO.
A DARK TUNNEL IS EXACTLY WHERE THEY'D WANT US. AND IF THERE IS AN ENTRANCE, IT'S NO DOUBT GUARDED.
WELL, HE'S GOTTA BE PRETTY NEAR. I KNOW IT'S THE WARREN HE WANTS TO HIT. I DON'T KNOW... WHY...
BUT I KNOW.
WE CAN SEARCH ABOVE GROUND.
I'M NOT CERTAIN.
WELL, YEAH, ANYTHING BEATS ASKING FOR HELP. RUTTING BUMS... YOU THINK HARTH MAYBE GOT MY BIG SLAYER LEADERSHIP GENE TOO?
CERTAINLY YOU HAVE THE STRENGTH, THOUGH WITH YOUR TEMPER I'M NOT--
SHUT UP.

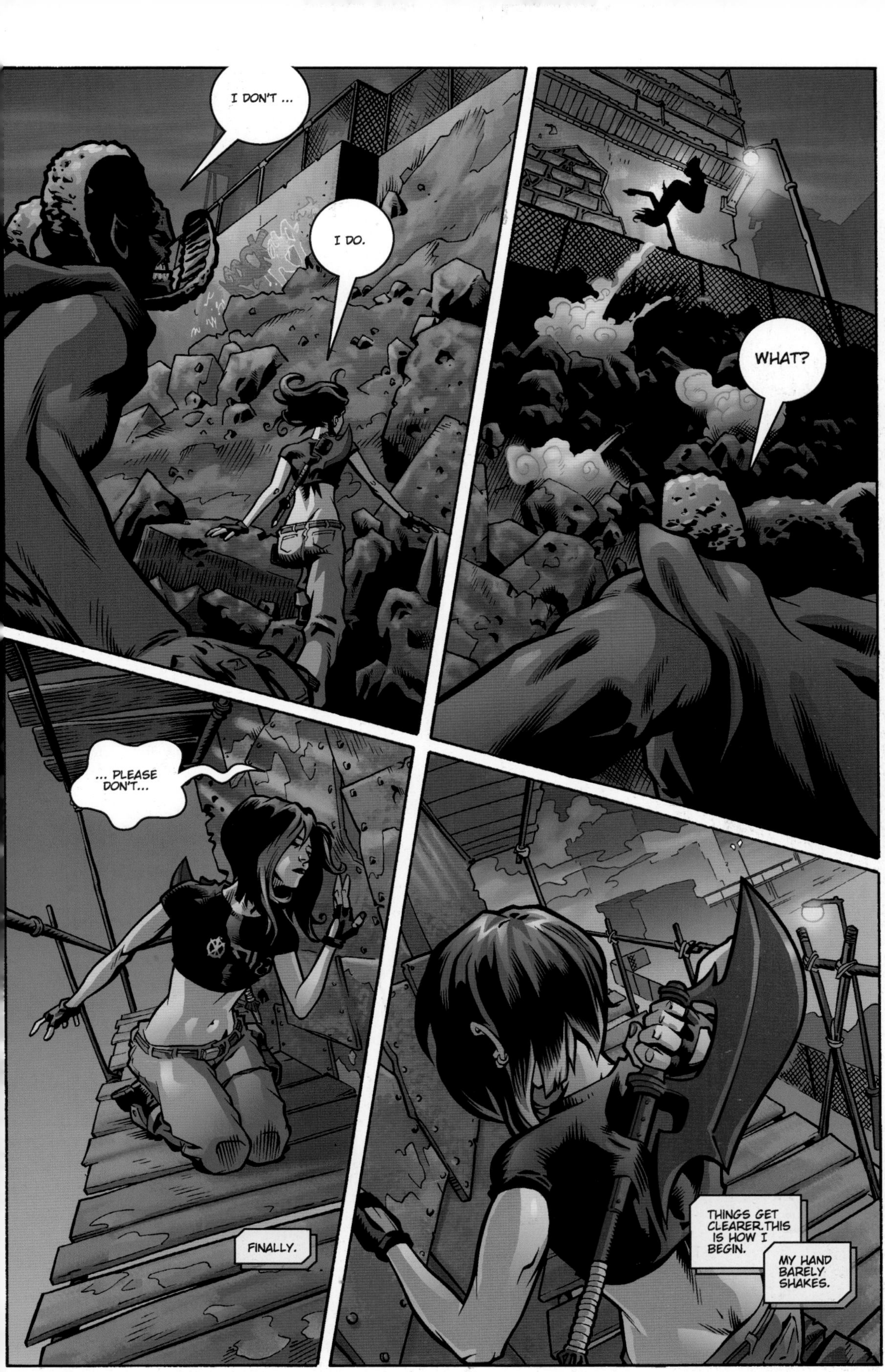
I DON'T ...
I DO.
WHAT?
... PLEASE DON'T...
FINALLY.
THINGS GET CLEARER. THIS IS HOW I BEGIN.
MY HAND BARELY SHAKES.

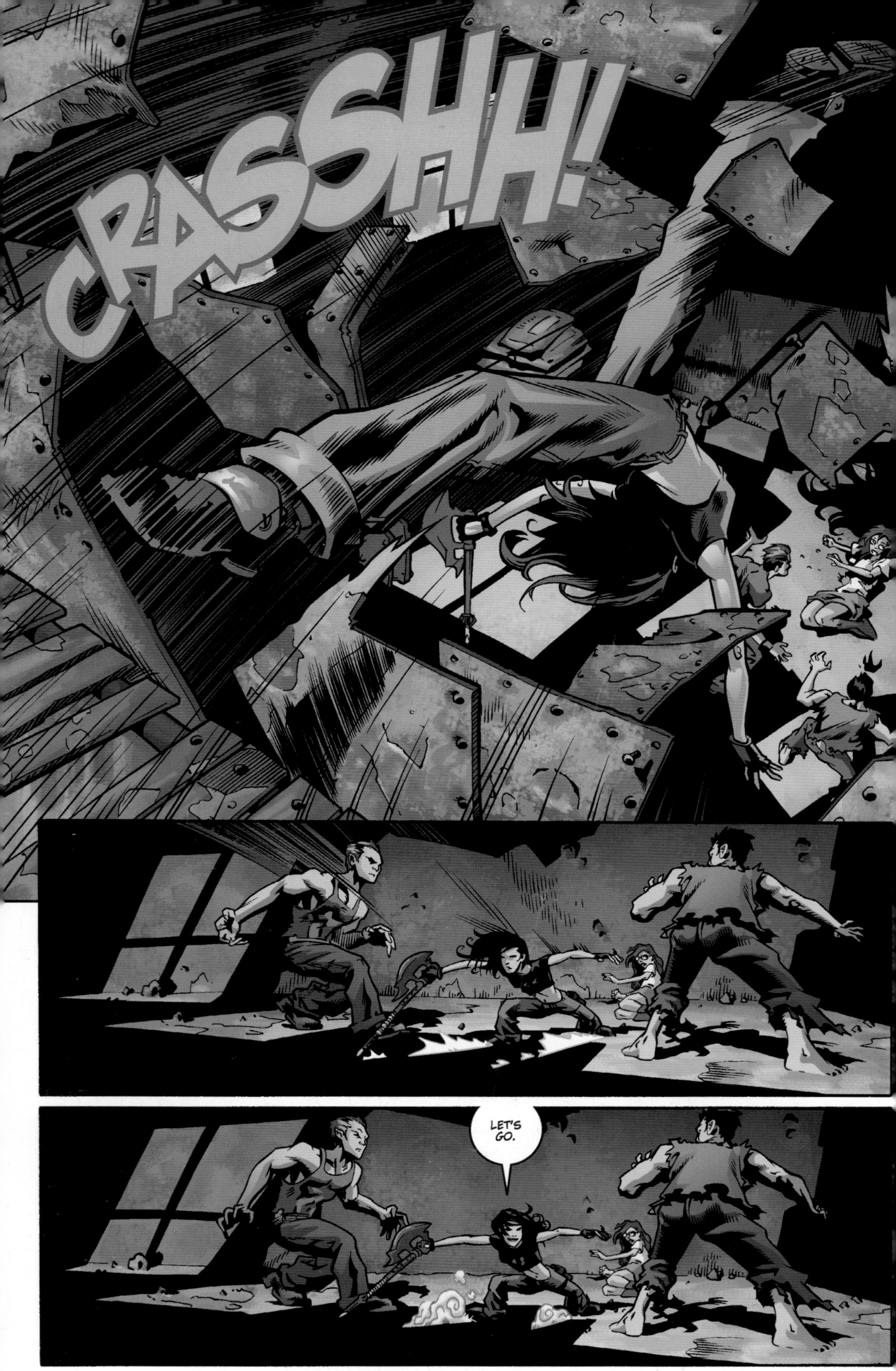
CRASSHH!
LET'S GO.

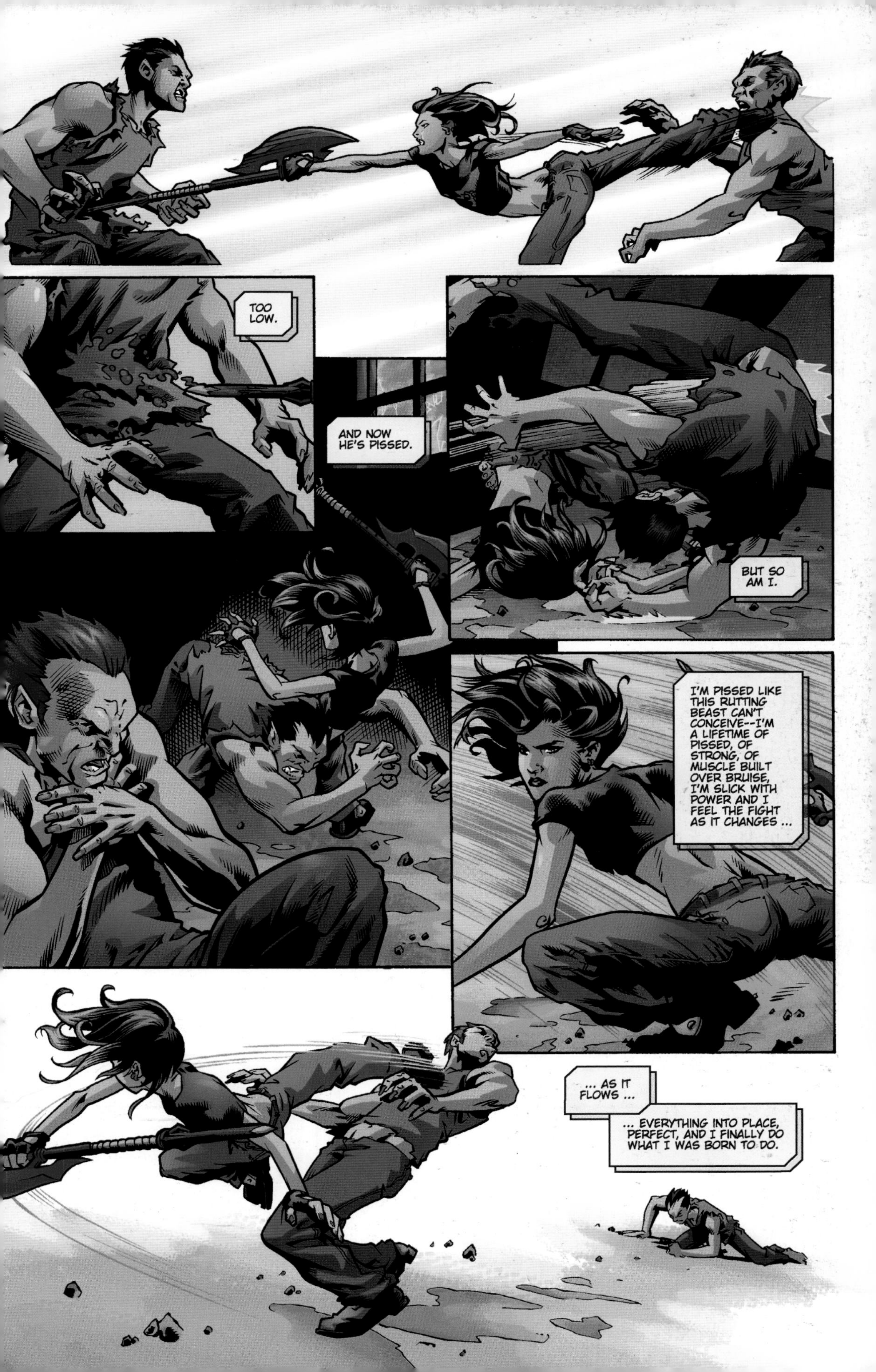
TOO LOW.
AND NOW HE'S PISSED.
BUT SO AM I.
I'M PISSED LIKE THIS RUTTING BEAST CAN'T CONCEIVE--I'M A LIFETIME OF PISSED, OF STRONG, OF MUSCLE BUILT OVER BRUISE, I'M SLICK WITH POWER AND I FEEL THE FIGHT AS IT CHANGES ...
... AS IT FLOWS ...
... EVERYTHING INTO PLACE, PERFECT, AND I FINALLY DO WHAT I WAS BORN TO DO.

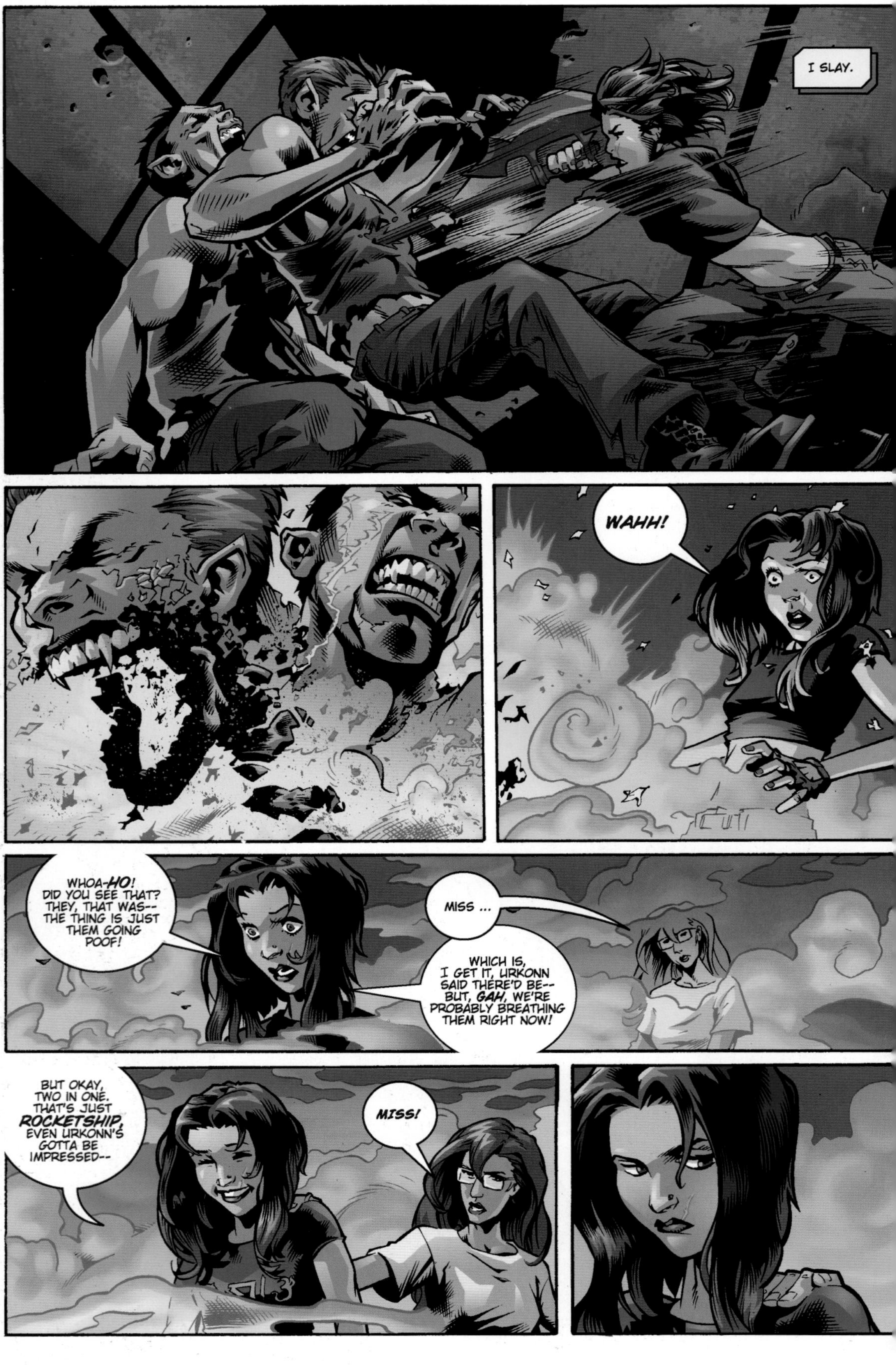
I SLAY.
WAHH!
WHOA-HO! DID YOU SEE THAT? THEY, THAT WAS-- THE THING IS JUST THEM GOING POOF!
MISS ...
WHICH IS, I GET IT, URKONN SAID THERE'D BE-- BUT, GAH, WE'RE PROBABLY BREATHING THEM RIGHT NOW!
BUT OKAY, TWO IN ONE. THAT'S JUST ROCKETSHIP, EVEN URKONN'S GOTTA BE IMPRESSED--
MISS!

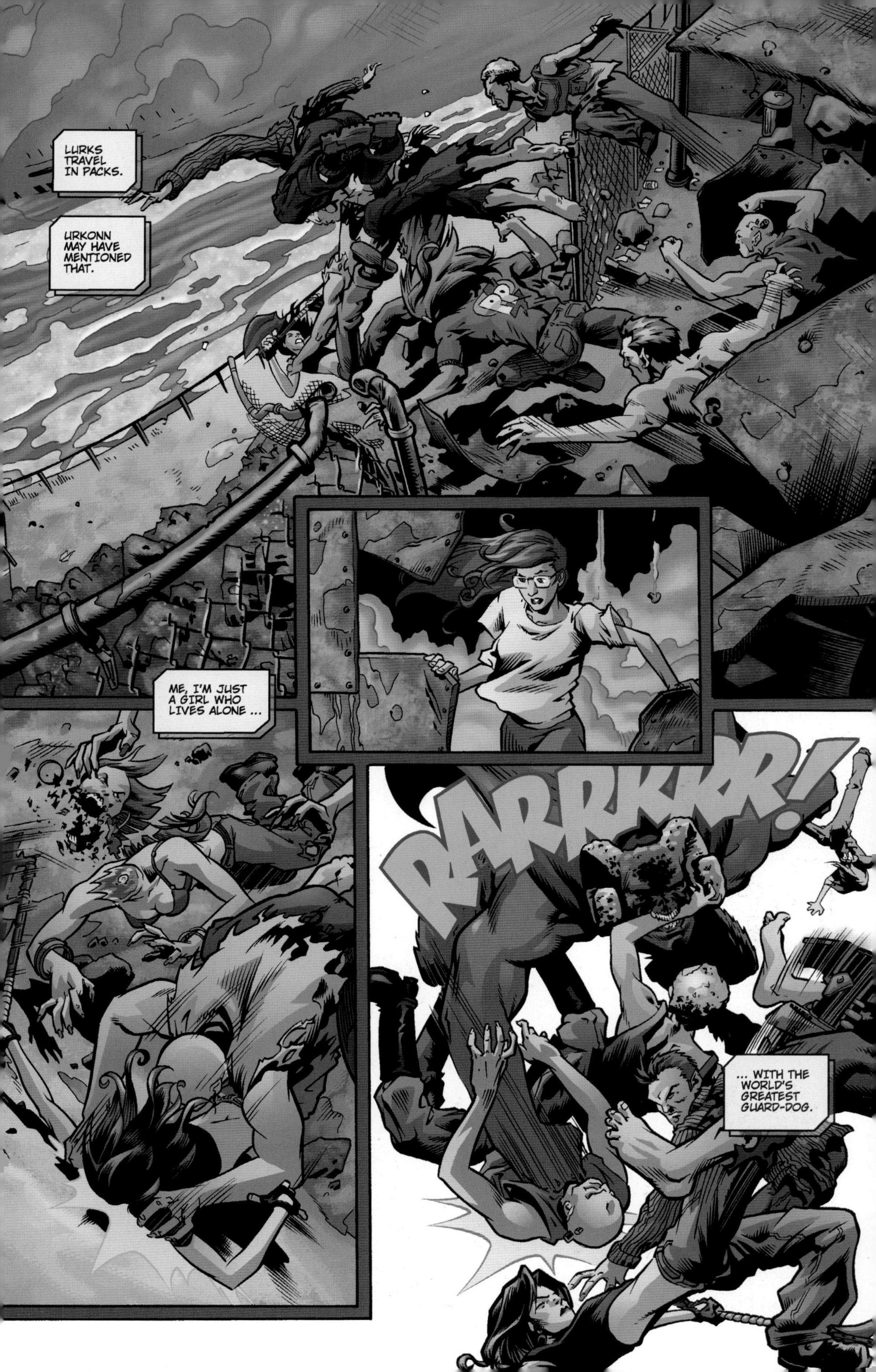
LURKS TRAVEL IN PACKS.
URKONN MAY HAVE MENTIONED THAT.
ME, I'M JUST A GIRL WHO LIVES ALONE ...
RARRKKOR!
... WITH THE WORLD'S GREATEST GUARD-DOG.

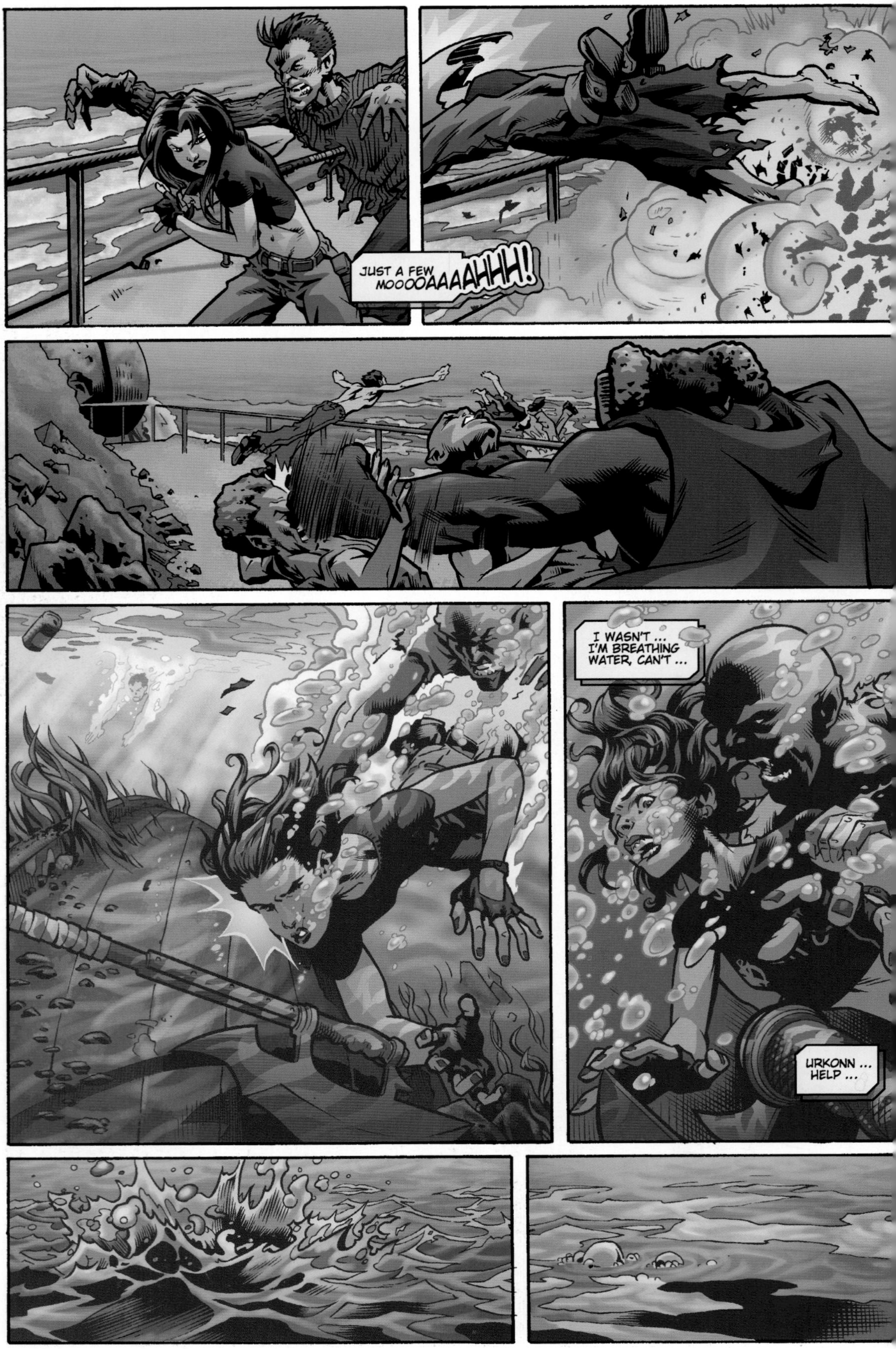
JUST A FEW MOOOOAAAAHHH!
I WASN'T ... I'M BREATHING WATER, CAN'T ...
URKONN ... HELP ...

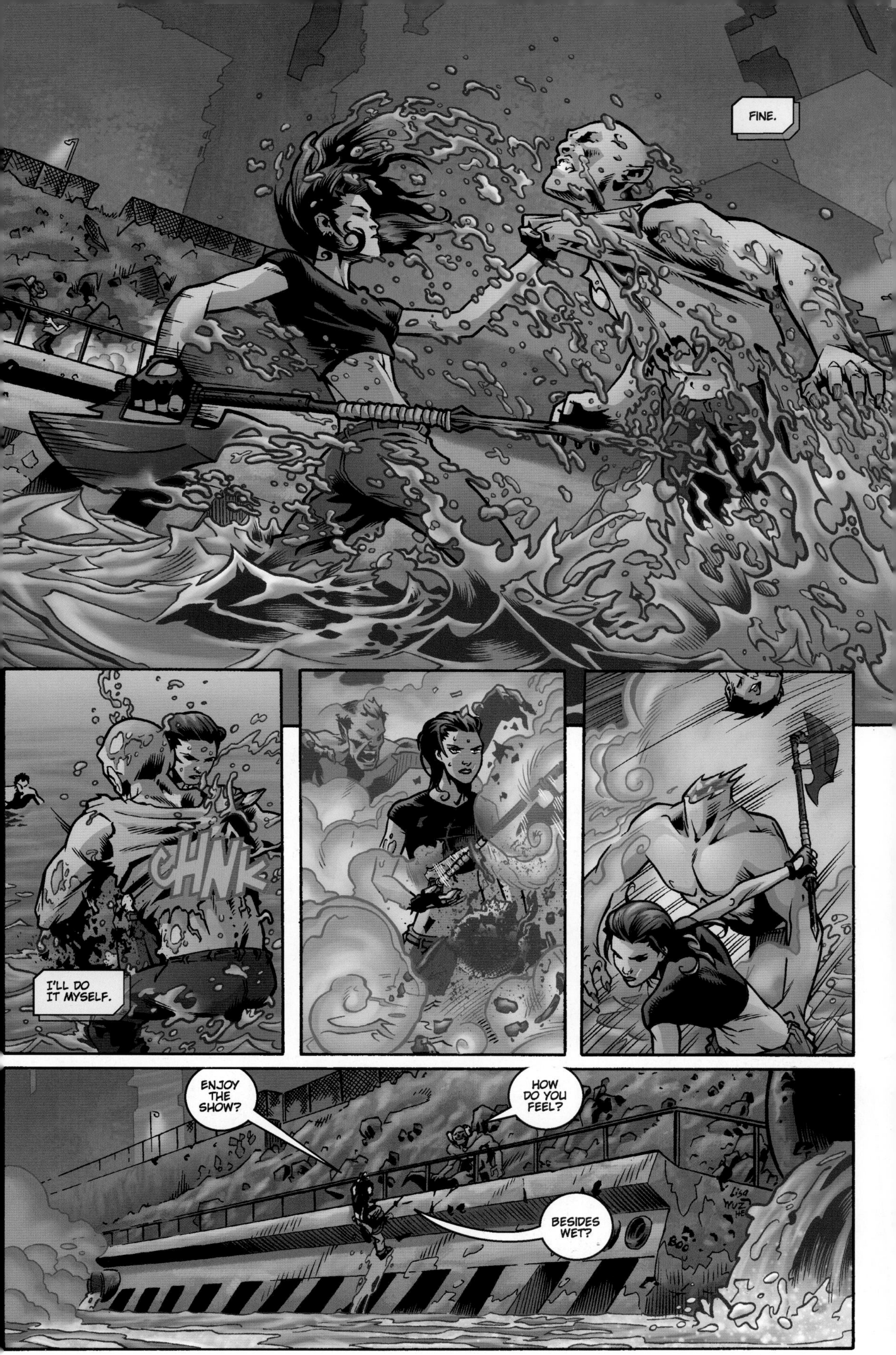
FINE.
CHNK
I'LL DO IT MYSELF.
ENJOY THE SHOW?
HOW DO YOU FEEL?
BESIDES WET?

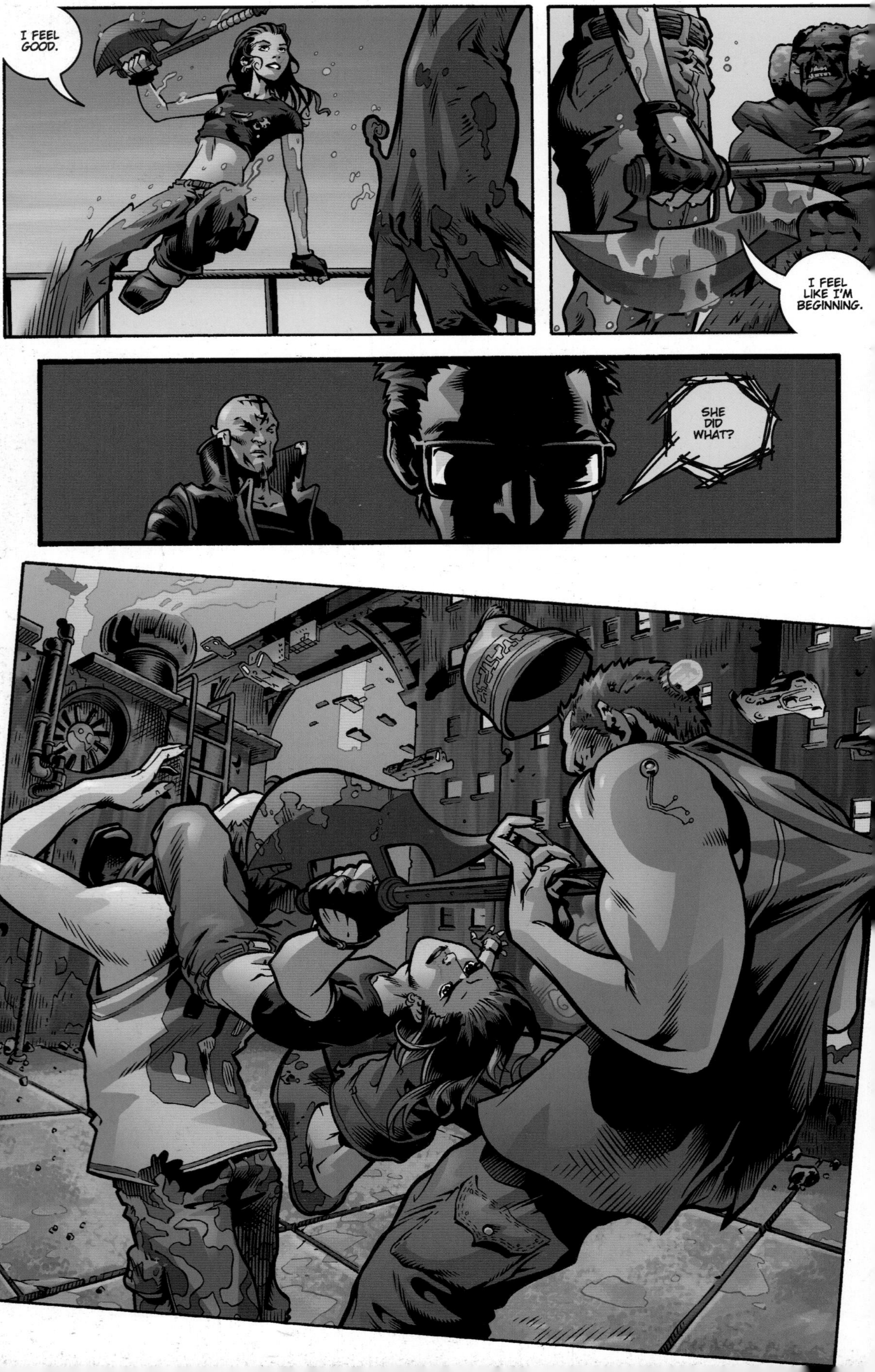
I FEEL GOOD.
I FEEL LIKE I'M BEGINNING.
SHE DID WHAT?

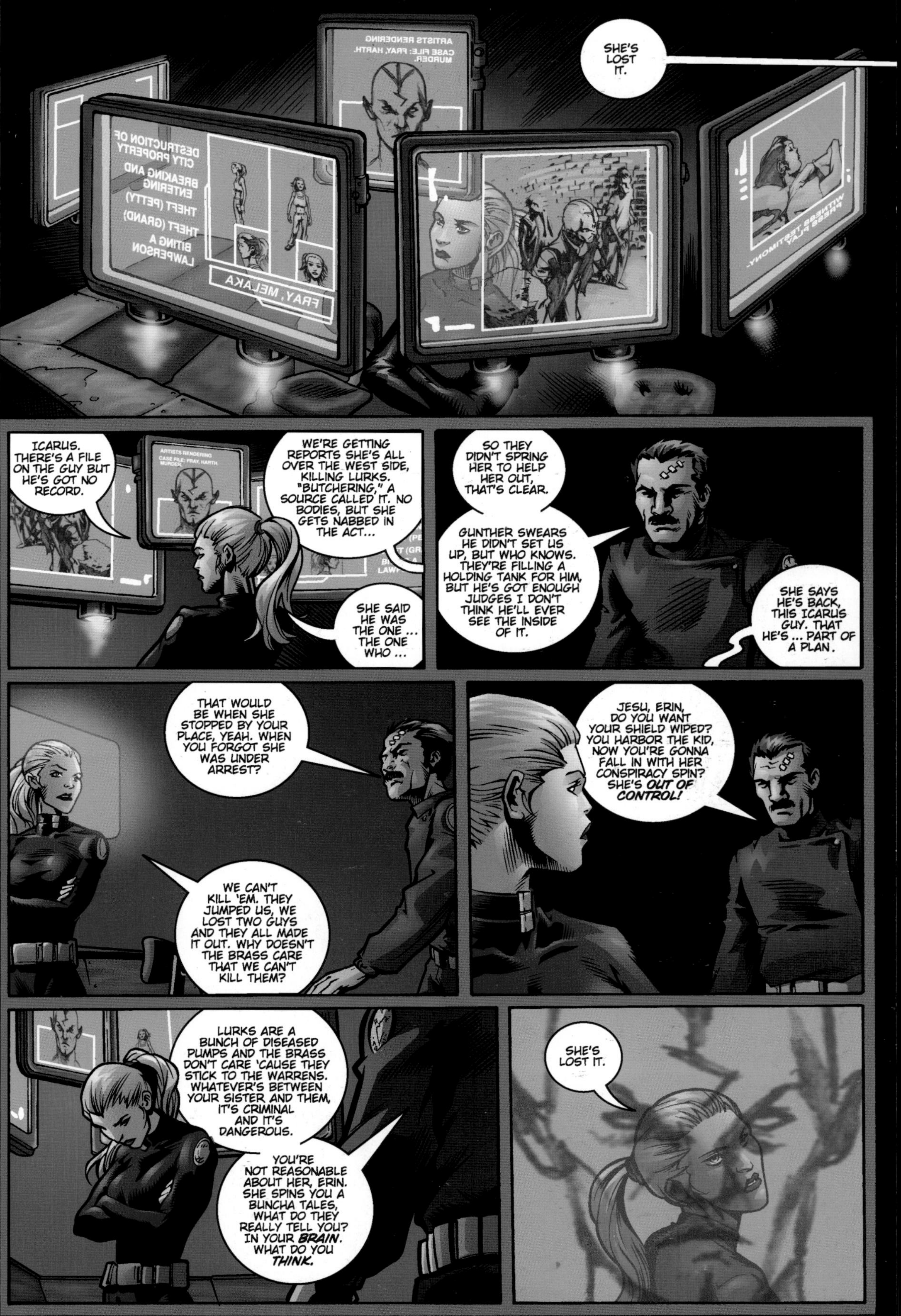
SHE'S LOST IT.
ARTISTS RENDERING
CASE FILE: FRAY, HARTH. MURDER.
DESTRUCTION OF CITY PROPERTY
BREAKING AND ENTERING
THEFT (PETTY)
THEFT (GRAND)
BITING A LAWPERSON
FRAY, MELAKA
WITNESS TESTIMONY. PRESS PLAY
ICARUS. THERE'S A FILE ON THE GUY BUT HE'S GOT NO RECORD.
WE'RE GETTING REPORTS SHE'S ALL OVER THE WEST SIDE, KILLING LURKS. "BUTCHERING," A SOURCE CALLED IT. NO BODIES, BUT SHE GETS NABBED IN THE ACT...
SHE SAID HE WAS THE ONE ... THE ONE WHO ...
SO THEY DIDN'T SPRING HER TO HELP HER OUT, THAT'S CLEAR.
GUNTHER SWEARS HE DIDN'T SET US UP, BUT WHO KNOWS. THEY'RE FILLING A HOLDING TANK FOR HIM, BUT HE'S GOT ENOUGH JUDGES I DON'T THINK HE'LL EVER SEE THE INSIDE OF IT.
SHE SAYS HE'S BACK, THIS ICARUS GUY. THAT HE'S ... PART OF A PLAN.
THAT WOULD BE WHEN SHE STOPPED BY YOUR PLACE, YEAH. WHEN YOU FORGOT SHE WAS UNDER ARREST?
WE CAN'T KILL 'EM. THEY JUMPED US, WE LOST TWO GUYS AND THEY ALL MADE IT OUT. WHY DOESN'T THE BRASS CARE THAT WE CAN'T KILL THEM?
JESU, ERIN, DO YOU WANT YOUR SHIELD WIPED? YOU HARBOR THE KID, NOW YOU'RE GONNA FALL IN WITH HER CONSPIRACY SPIN? SHE'S OUT OF CONTROL!
LURKS ARE A BUNCH OF DISEASED PUMPS AND THE BRASS DON'T CARE 'CAUSE THEY STICK TO THE WARRENS. WHATEVER'S BETWEEN YOUR SISTER AND THEM, IT'S CRIMINAL AND IT'S DANGEROUS.
YOU'RE NOT REASONABLE ABOUT HER, ERIN. SHE SPINS YOU A BUNCHA TALES, WHAT DO THEY REALLY TELL YOU? IN YOUR BRAIN. WHAT DO YOU THINK.
SHE'S LOST IT.

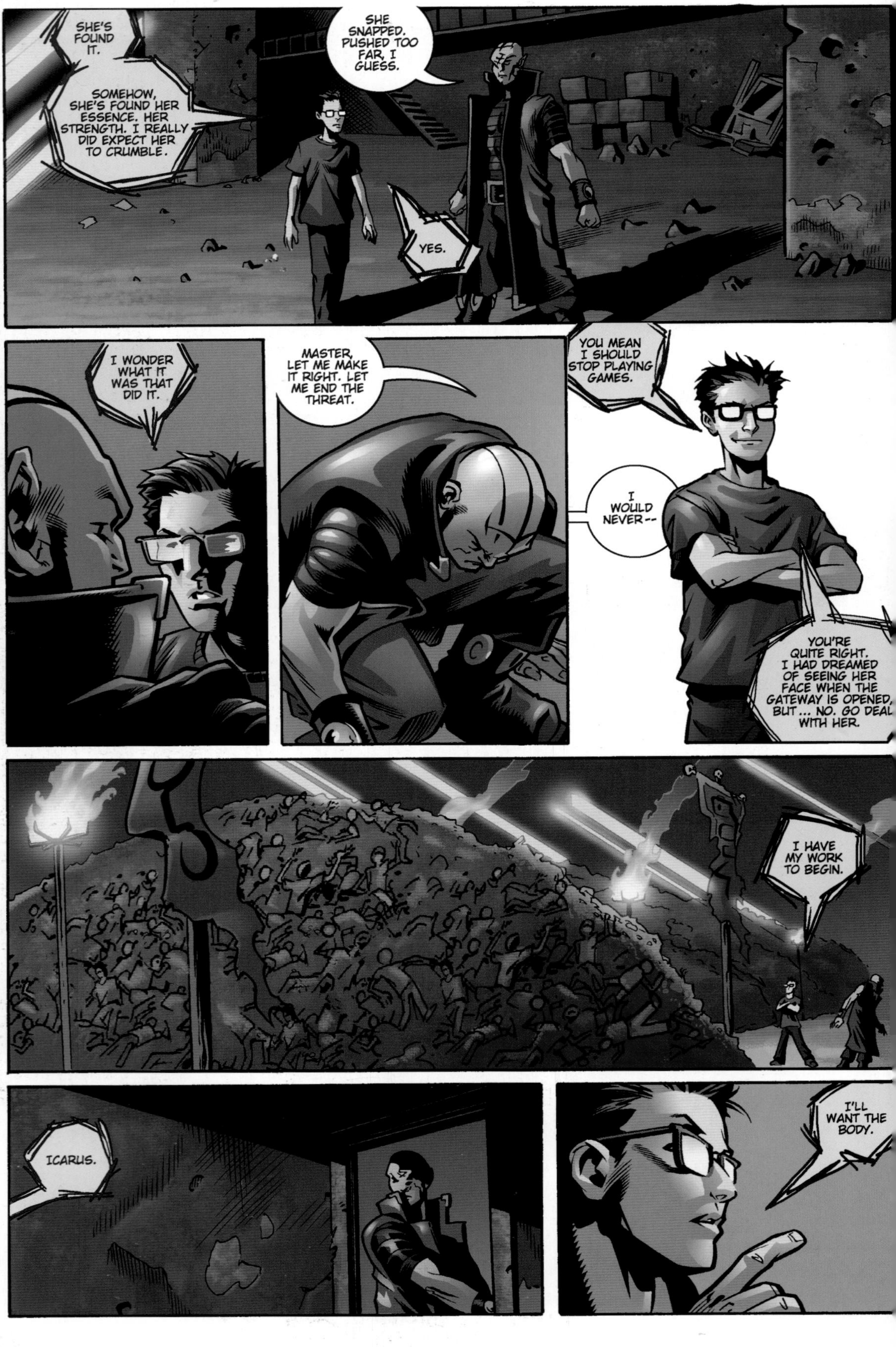
SHE'S FOUND IT.
SOMEHOW, SHE'S FOUND HER ESSENCE. HER STRENGTH. I REALLY DID EXPECT HER TO CRUMBLE.
SHE SNAPPED. PUSHED TOO FAR, I GUESS.
YES.
I WONDER WHAT IT WAS THAT DID IT.
MASTER, LET ME MAKE IT RIGHT. LET ME END THE THREAT.
YOU MEAN I SHOULD STOP PLAYING GAMES.
I WOULD NEVER--
YOU'RE QUITE RIGHT. I HAD DREAMED OF SEEING HER FACE WHEN THE GATEWAY IS OPENED, BUT... NO. GO DEAL WITH HER.
I HAVE MY WORK TO BEGIN.
ICARUS.
I'LL WANT THE BODY.

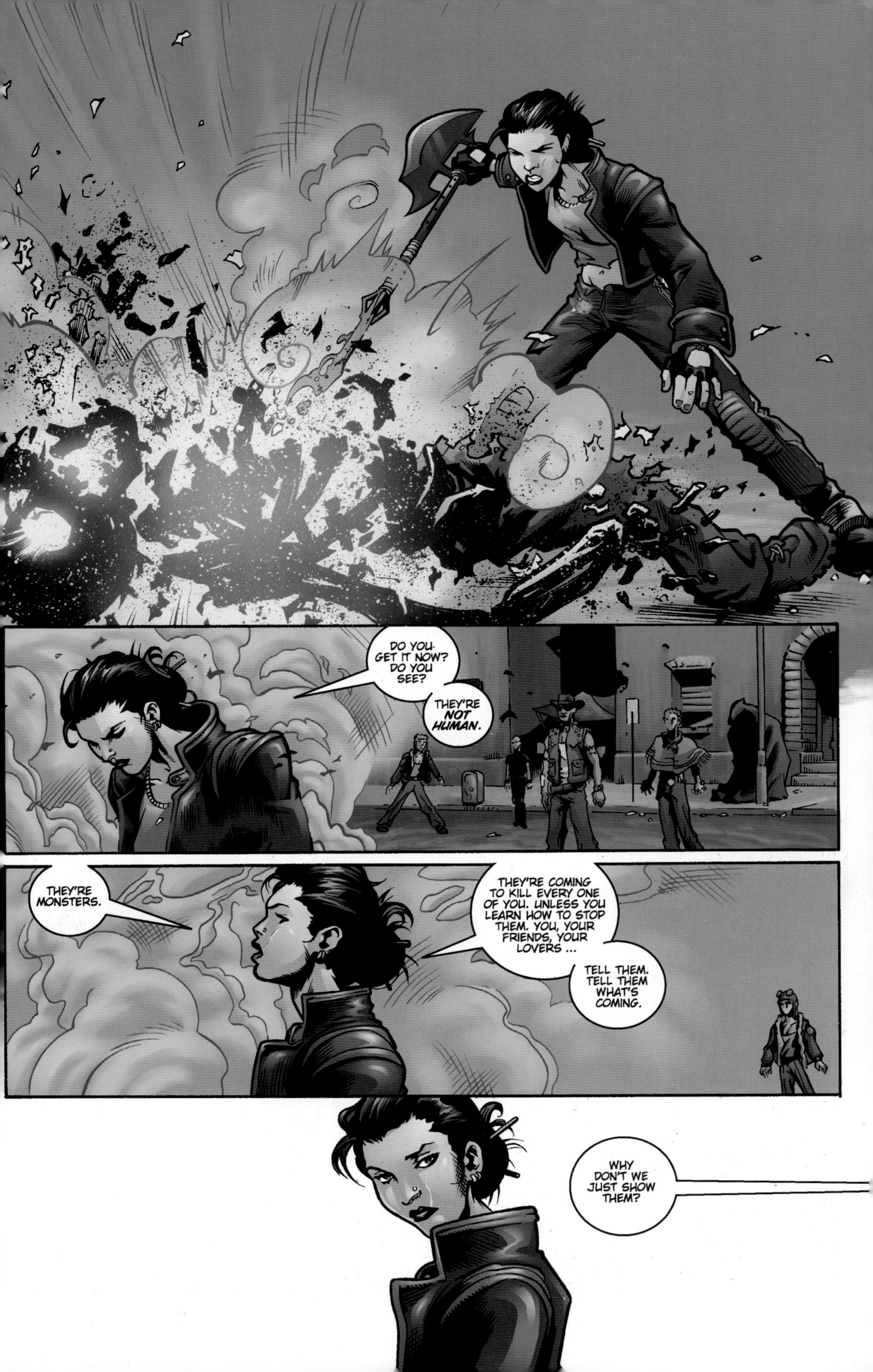
DO YOU GET IT NOW? DO YOU SEE?
THEY'RE *NOT HUMAN*.
THEY'RE MONSTERS.
THEY'RE COMING TO KILL EVERY ONE OF YOU. UNLESS YOU LEARN HOW TO STOP THEM. YOU, YOUR FRIENDS, YOUR LOVERS ...
TELL THEM. TELL THEM WHAT'S COMING.
WHY DON'T WE JUST SHOW THEM?

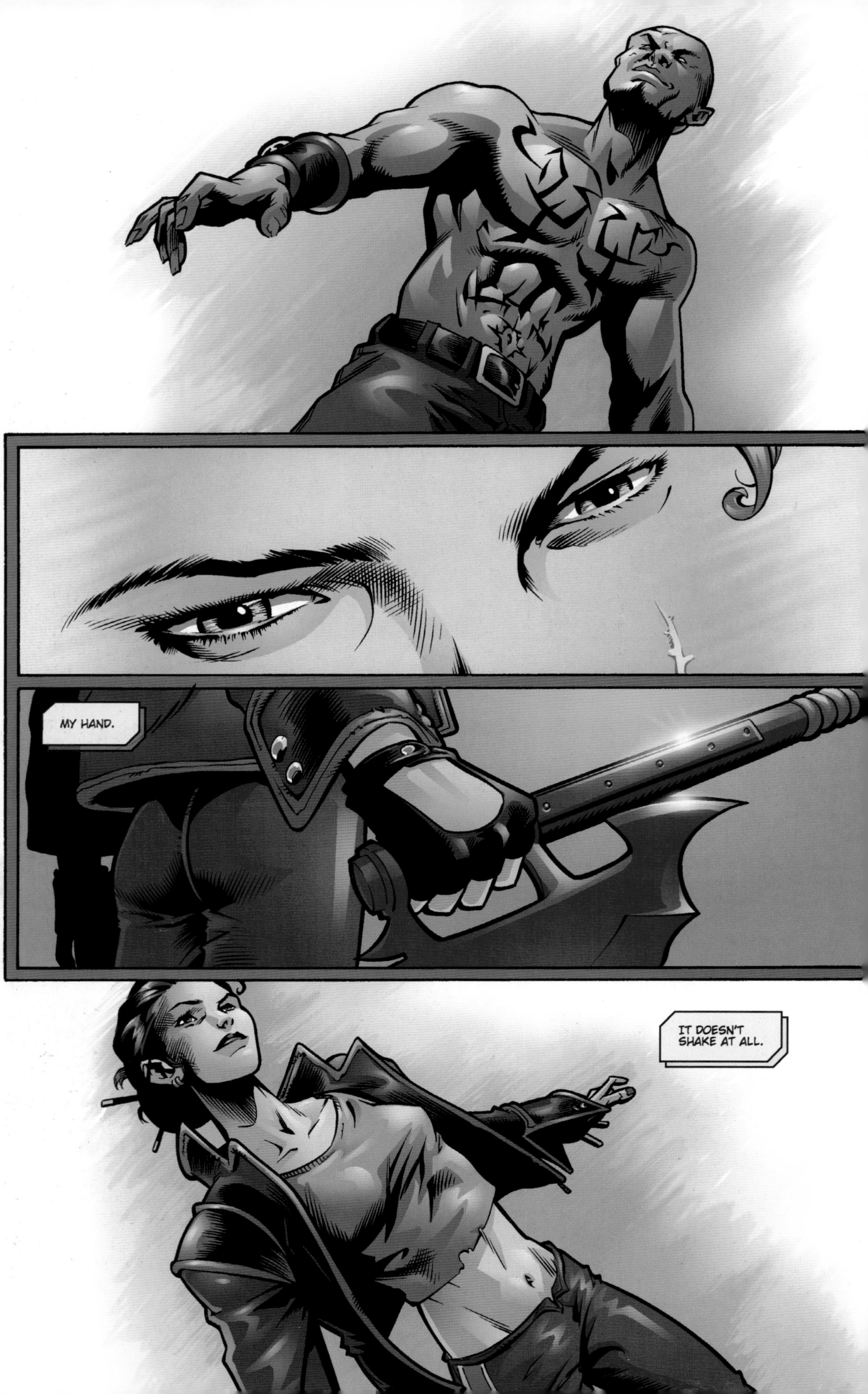
MY HAND.
IT DOESN'T SHAKE AT ALL.

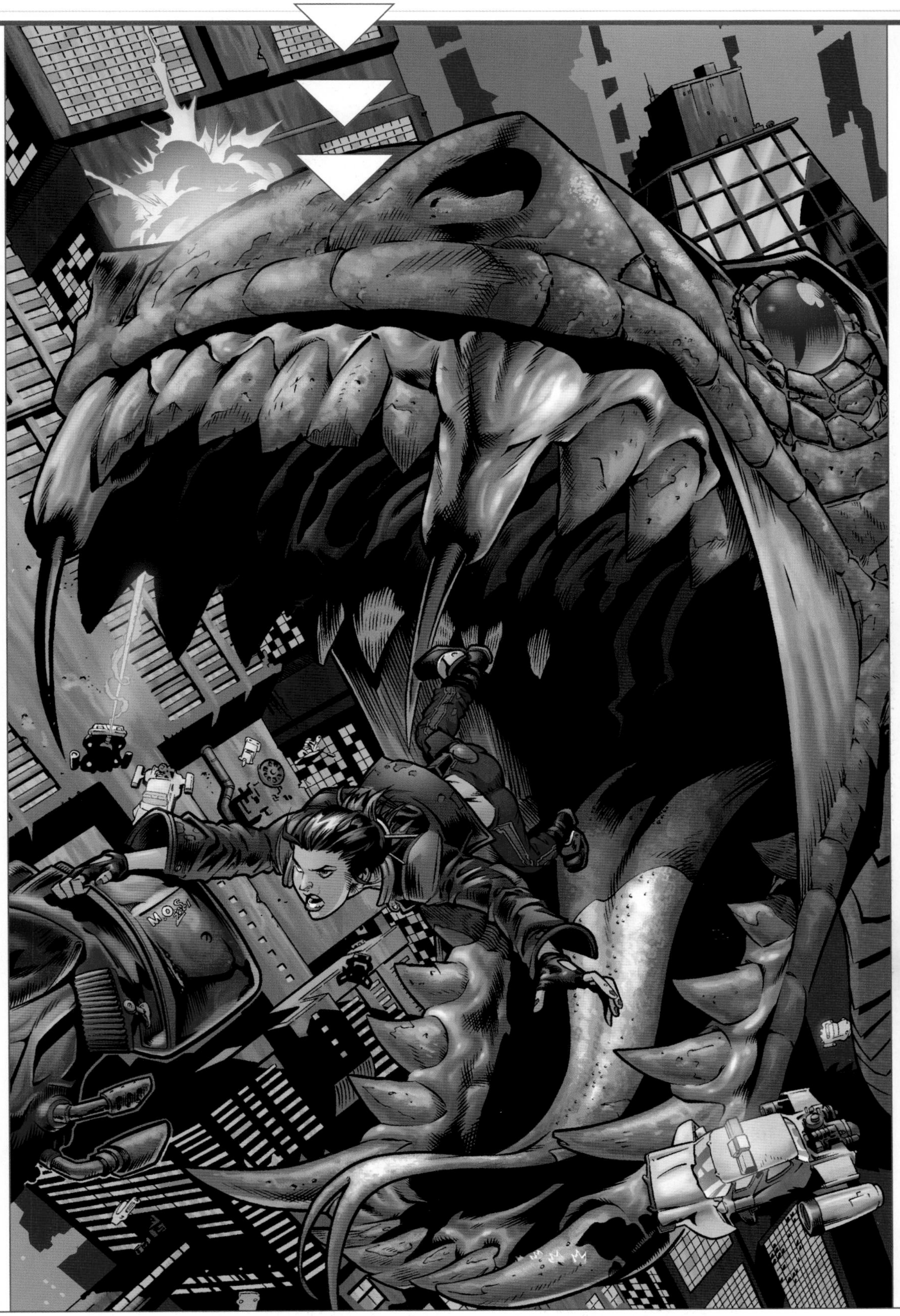
M.O.S

"Well, I'm fighting. Whatever it is.
Alone if I have to... but I'm fighting."

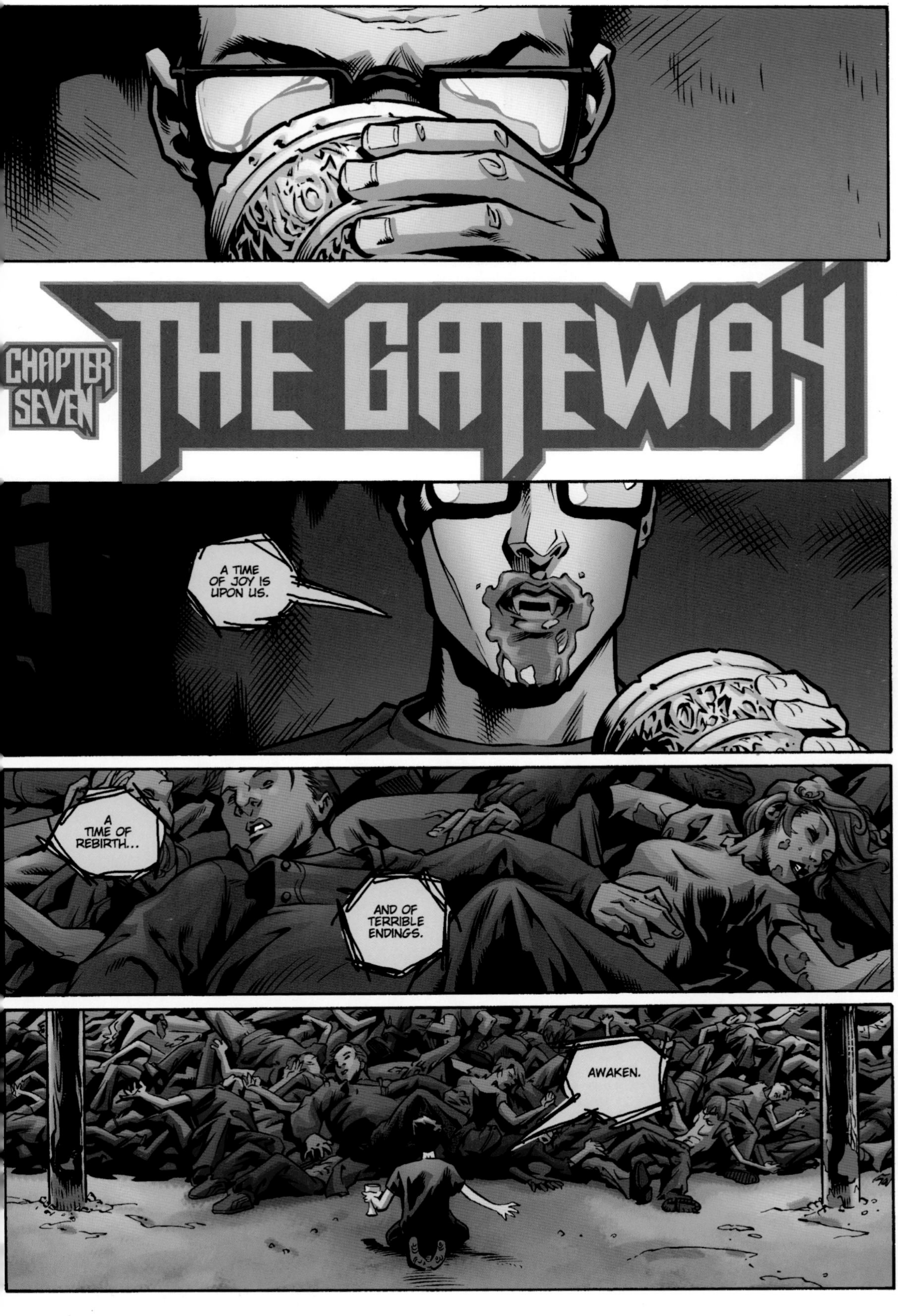
CHAPTER SEVEN
THE GATEWAY
A TIME OF JOY IS UPON US.
A TIME OF REBIRTH...
AND OF TERRIBLE ENDINGS.
AWAKEN.

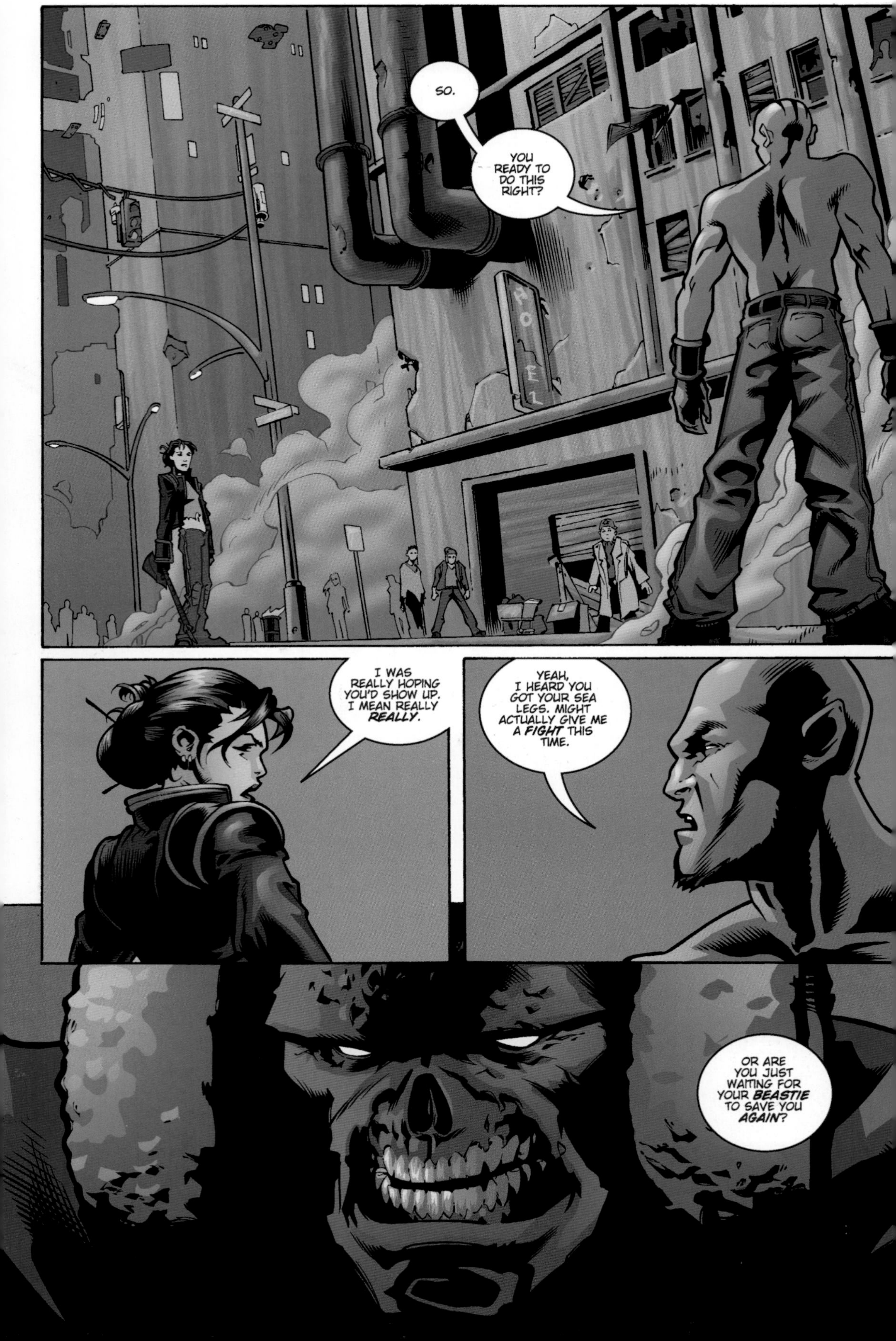

SO.
YOU READY TO DO THIS RIGHT?
I WAS REALLY HOPING YOU'D SHOW UP. I MEAN REALLY *REALLY*.
YEAH, I HEARD YOU GOT YOUR SEA LEGS. MIGHT ACTUALLY GIVE ME A *FIGHT* THIS TIME.
OR ARE YOU JUST WAITING FOR YOUR *BEASTIE* TO SAVE YOU *AGAIN*?

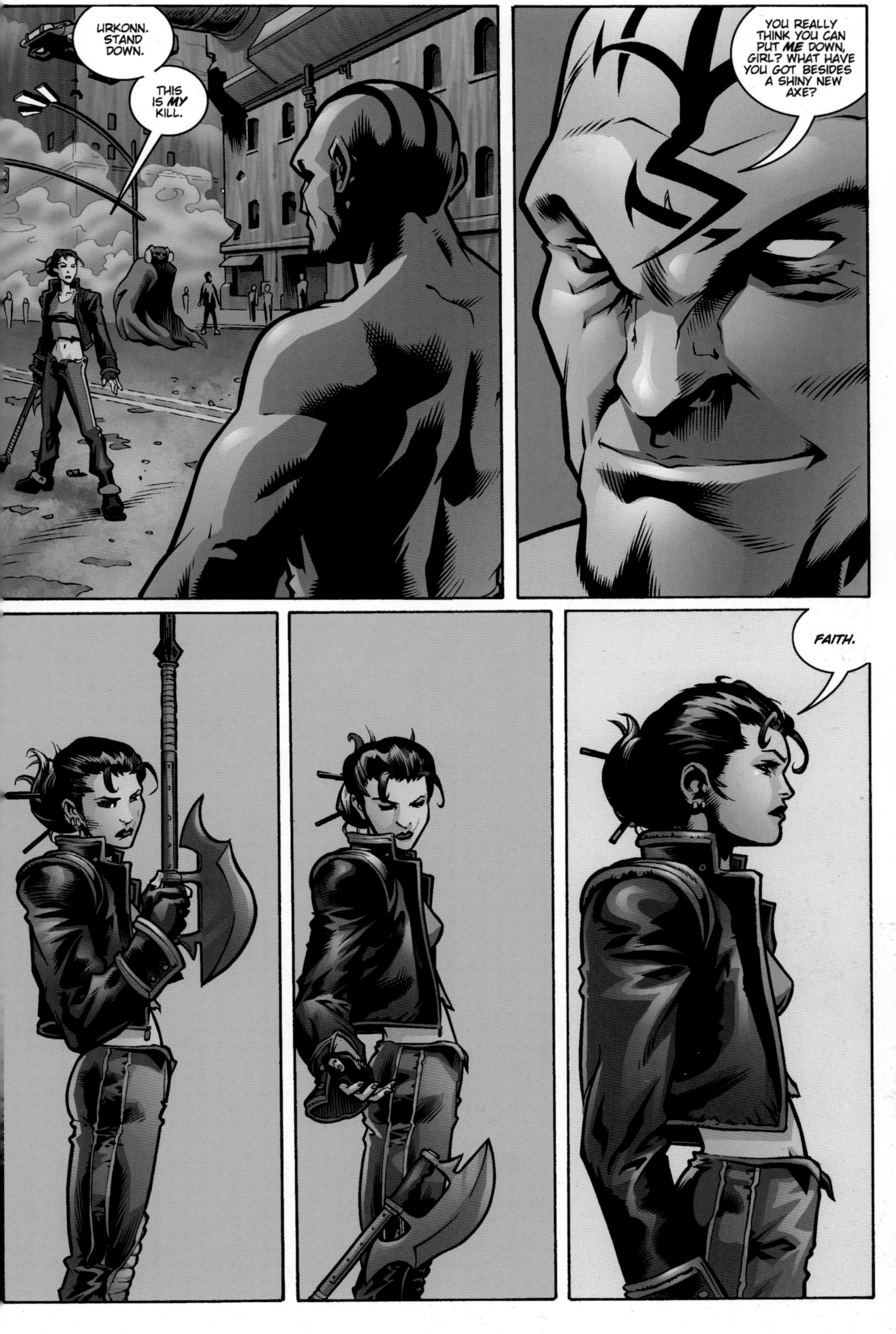
URKONN. STAND DOWN.
THIS IS MY KILL.
YOU REALLY THINK YOU CAN PUT ME DOWN, GIRL? WHAT HAVE YOU GOT BESIDES A SHINY NEW AXE?
FAITH.

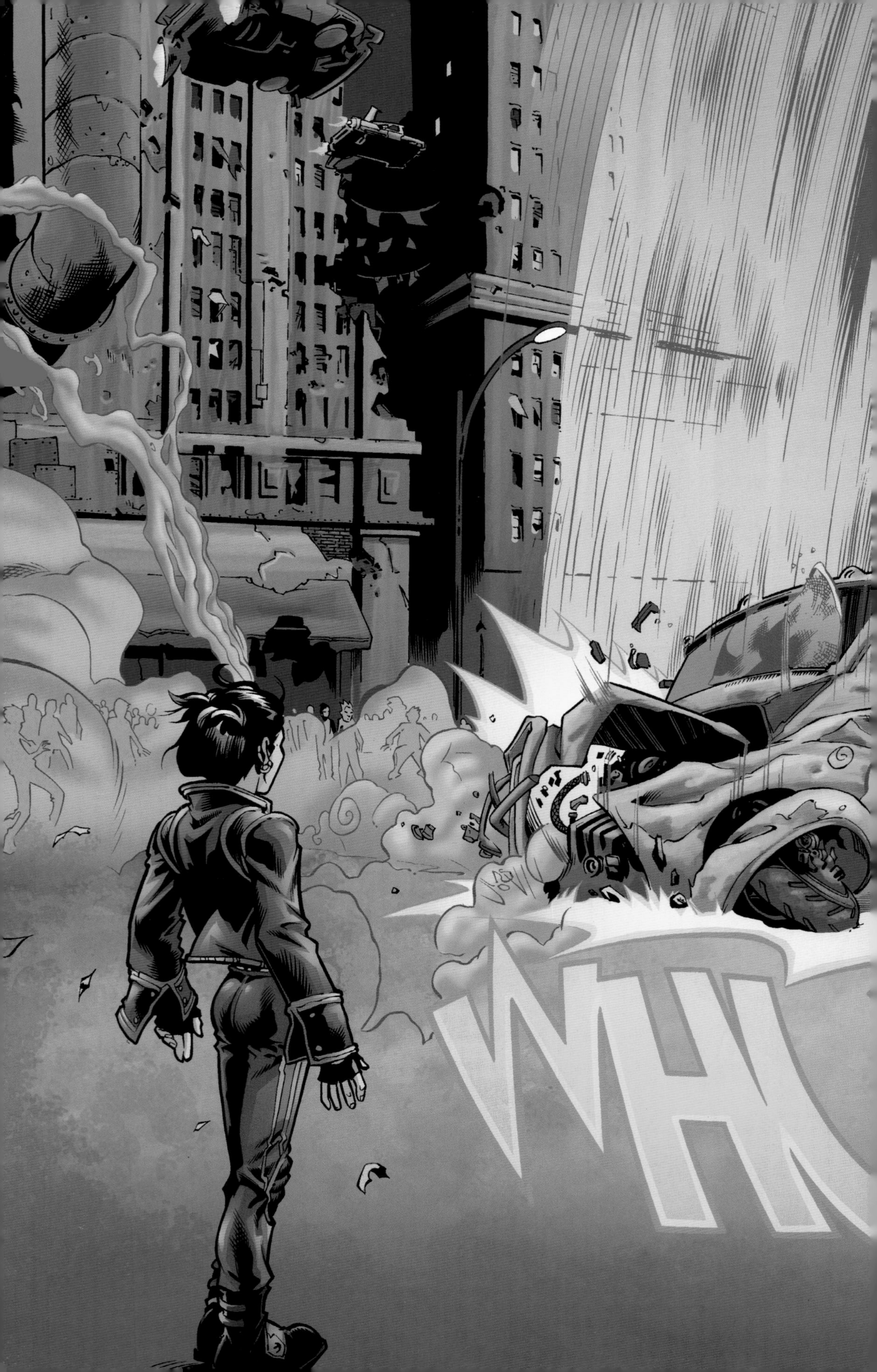
WH

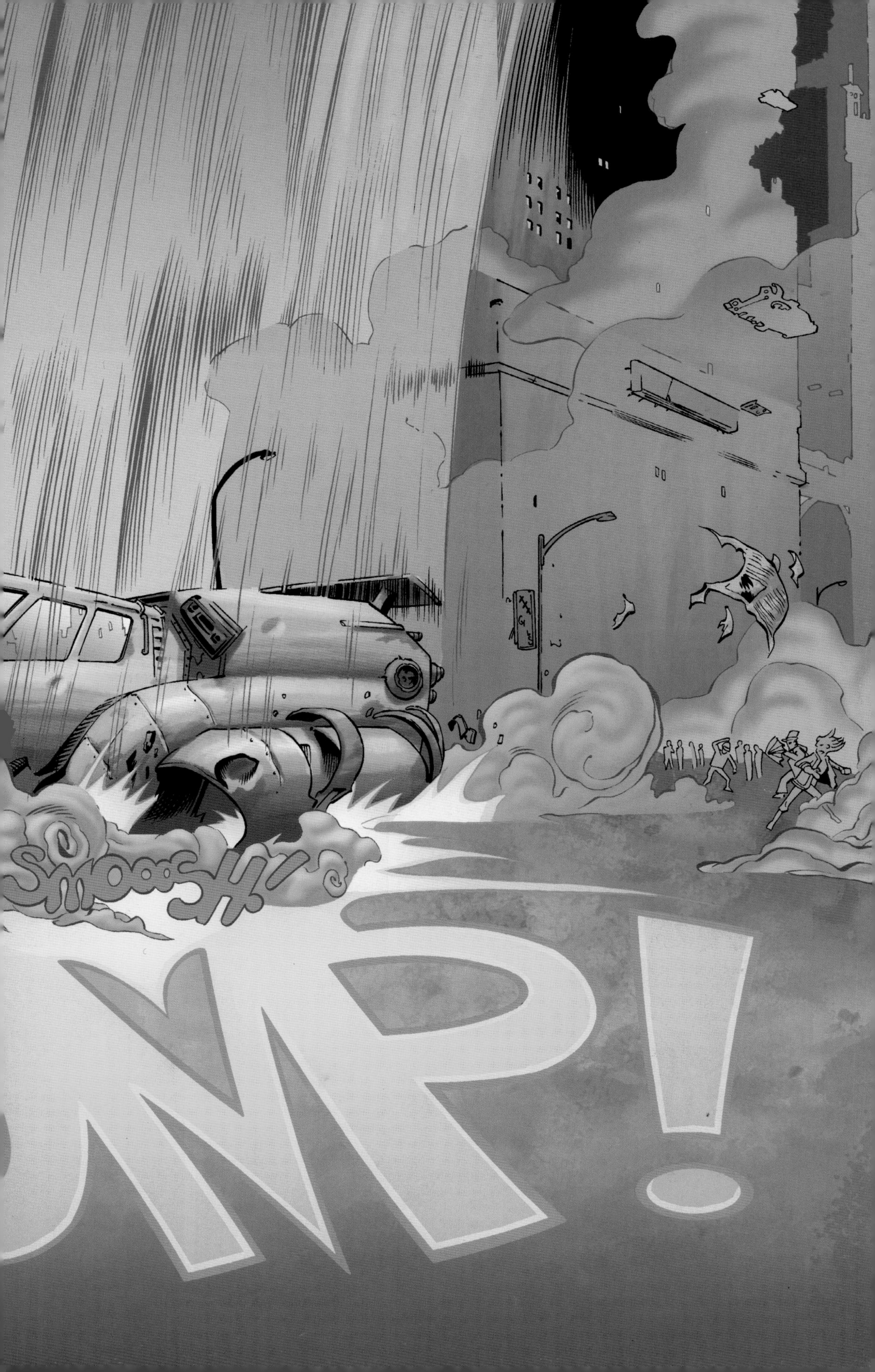
SMOOOSH!
MP!

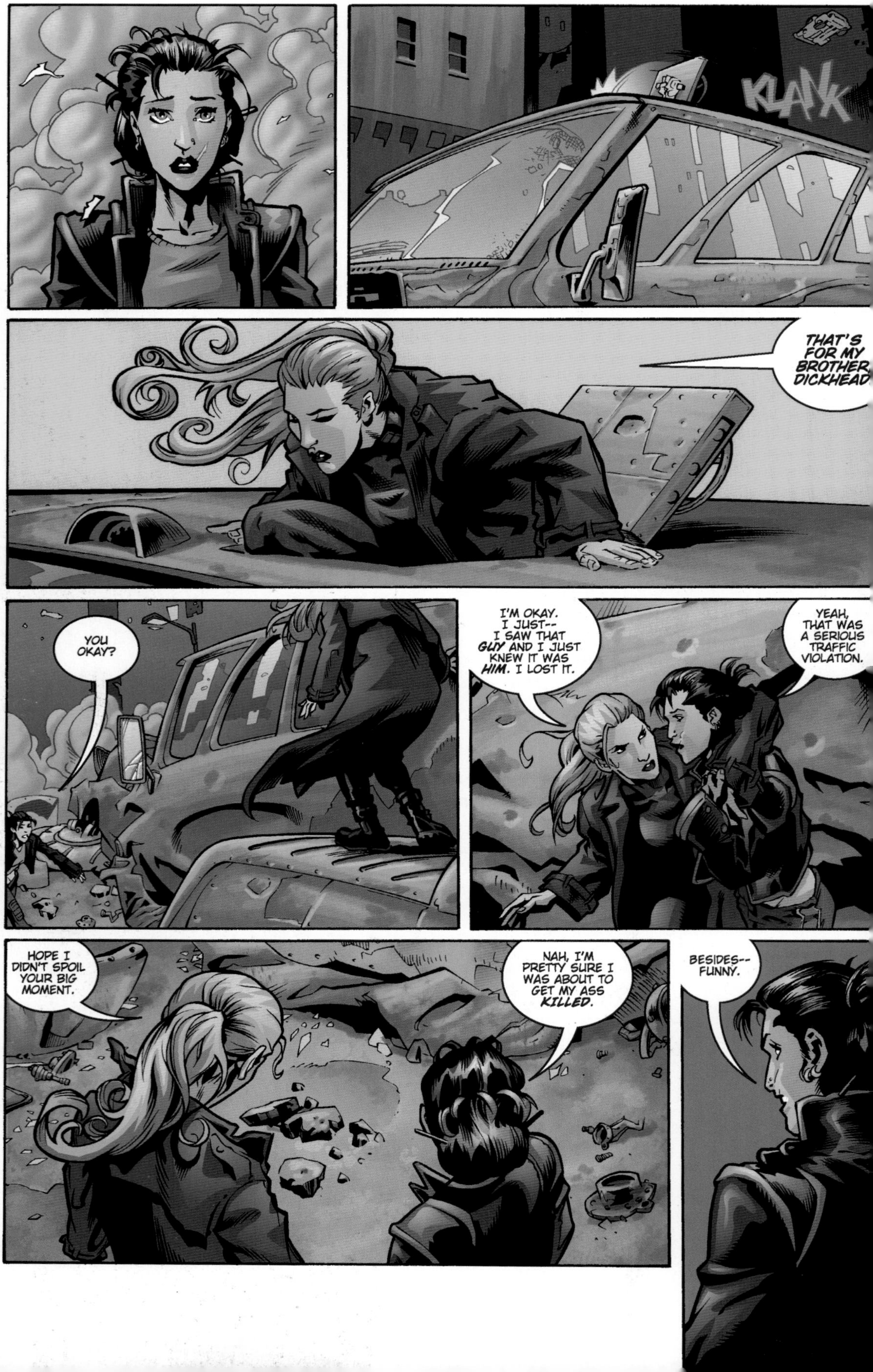
KLANK
THAT'S FOR MY BROTHER, DICKHEAD.
YOU OKAY?
I'M OKAY. I JUST-- I SAW THAT GUY AND I JUST KNEW IT WAS HIM. I LOST IT.
YEAH, THAT WAS A SERIOUS TRAFFIC VIOLATION.
HOPE I DIDN'T SPOIL YOUR BIG MOMENT.
NAH, I'M PRETTY SURE I WAS ABOUT TO GET MY ASS KILLED.
BESIDES-- FUNNY.

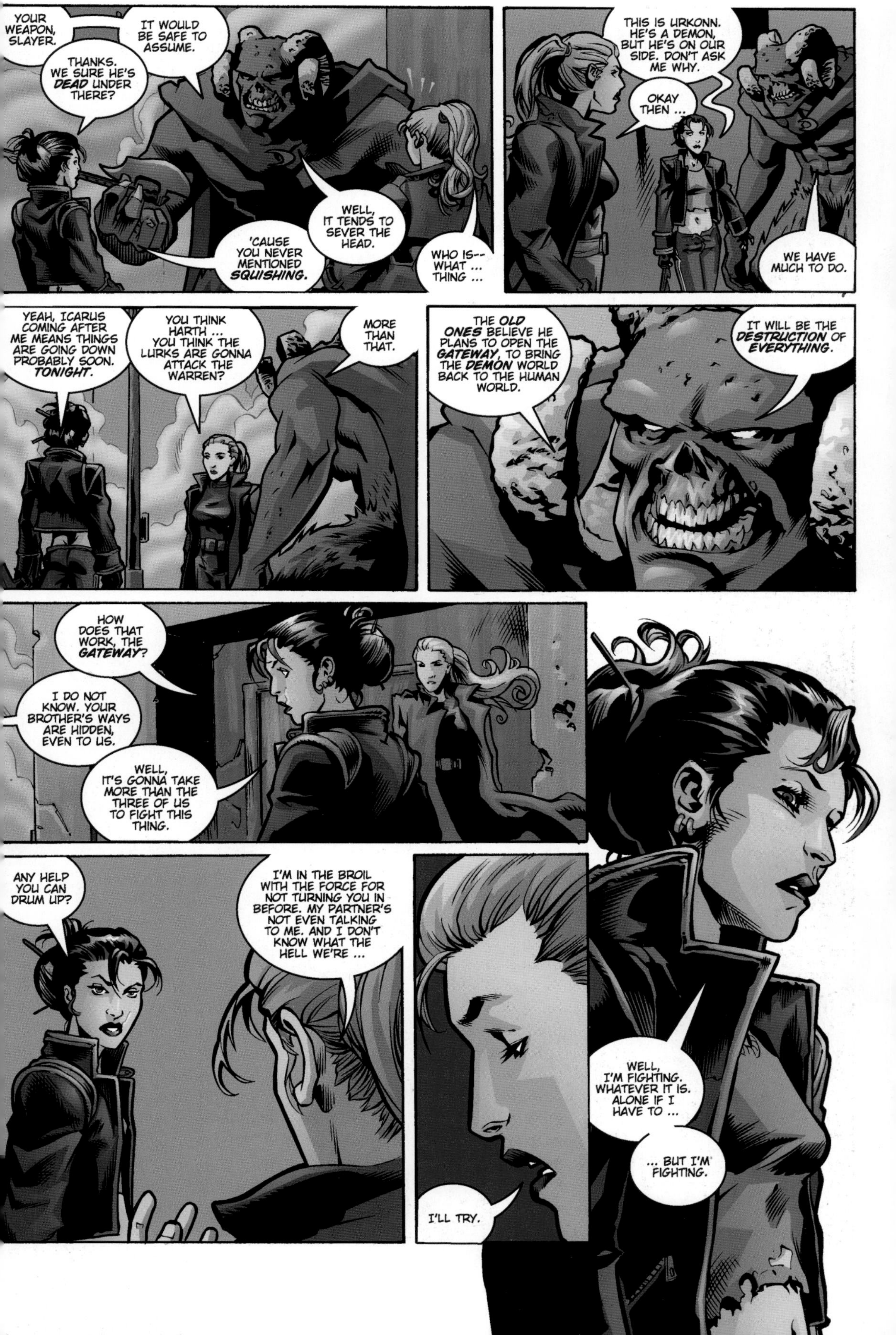

YOUR WEAPON, SLAYER.
THANKS. WE SURE HE'S DEAD UNDER THERE?
IT WOULD BE SAFE TO ASSUME.
'CAUSE YOU NEVER MENTIONED SQUISHING.
WELL, IT TENDS TO SEVER THE HEAD.
WHO IS-- WHAT ... THING ...
THIS IS URKONN. HE'S A DEMON, BUT HE'S ON OUR SIDE. DON'T ASK ME WHY.
OKAY THEN ...
WE HAVE MUCH TO DO.
YEAH, ICARUS COMING AFTER ME MEANS THINGS ARE GOING DOWN PROBABLY SOON. TONIGHT.
YOU THINK HARTH ... YOU THINK THE LURKS ARE GONNA ATTACK THE WARREN?
MORE THAN THAT.
THE OLD ONES BELIEVE HE PLANS TO OPEN THE GATEWAY, TO BRING THE DEMON WORLD BACK TO THE HUMAN WORLD.
IT WILL BE THE DESTRUCTION OF EVERYTHING.
HOW DOES THAT WORK, THE GATEWAY?
I DO NOT KNOW. YOUR BROTHER'S WAYS ARE HIDDEN, EVEN TO US.
WELL, IT'S GONNA TAKE MORE THAN THE THREE OF US TO FIGHT THIS THING.
ANY HELP YOU CAN DRUM UP?
I'M IN THE BROIL WITH THE FORCE FOR NOT TURNING YOU IN BEFORE. MY PARTNER'S NOT EVEN TALKING TO ME. AND I DON'T KNOW WHAT THE HELL WE'RE ...
I'LL TRY.
WELL, I'M FIGHTING. WHATEVER IT IS. ALONE IF I HAVE TO ...
... BUT I'M FIGHTING.

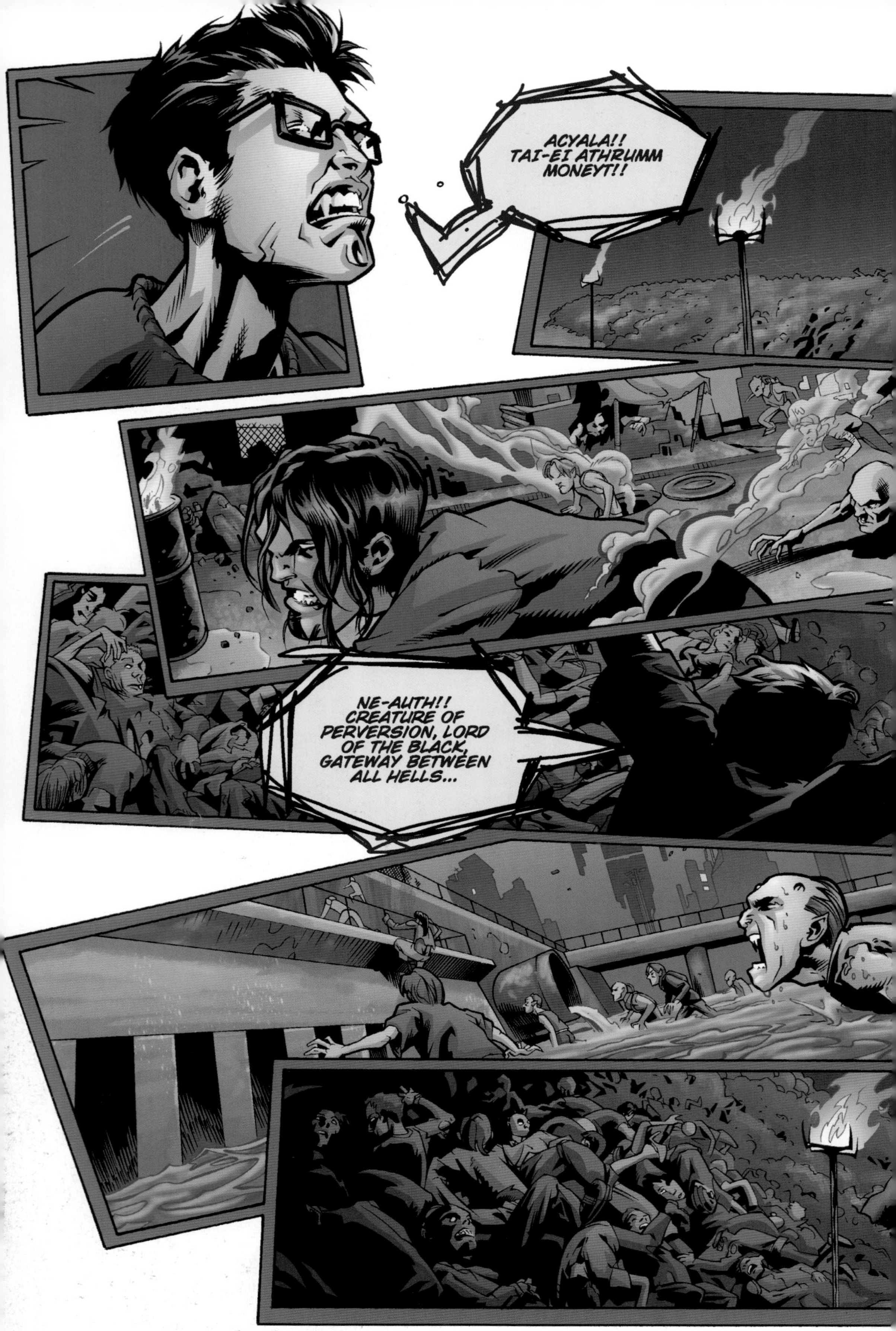
ACYALA!! TAI-EI ATHRUMM MONEYT!!
NE-AUTH!! CREATURE OF PERVERSION, LORD OF THE BLACK, GATEWAY BETWEEN ALL HELLS...

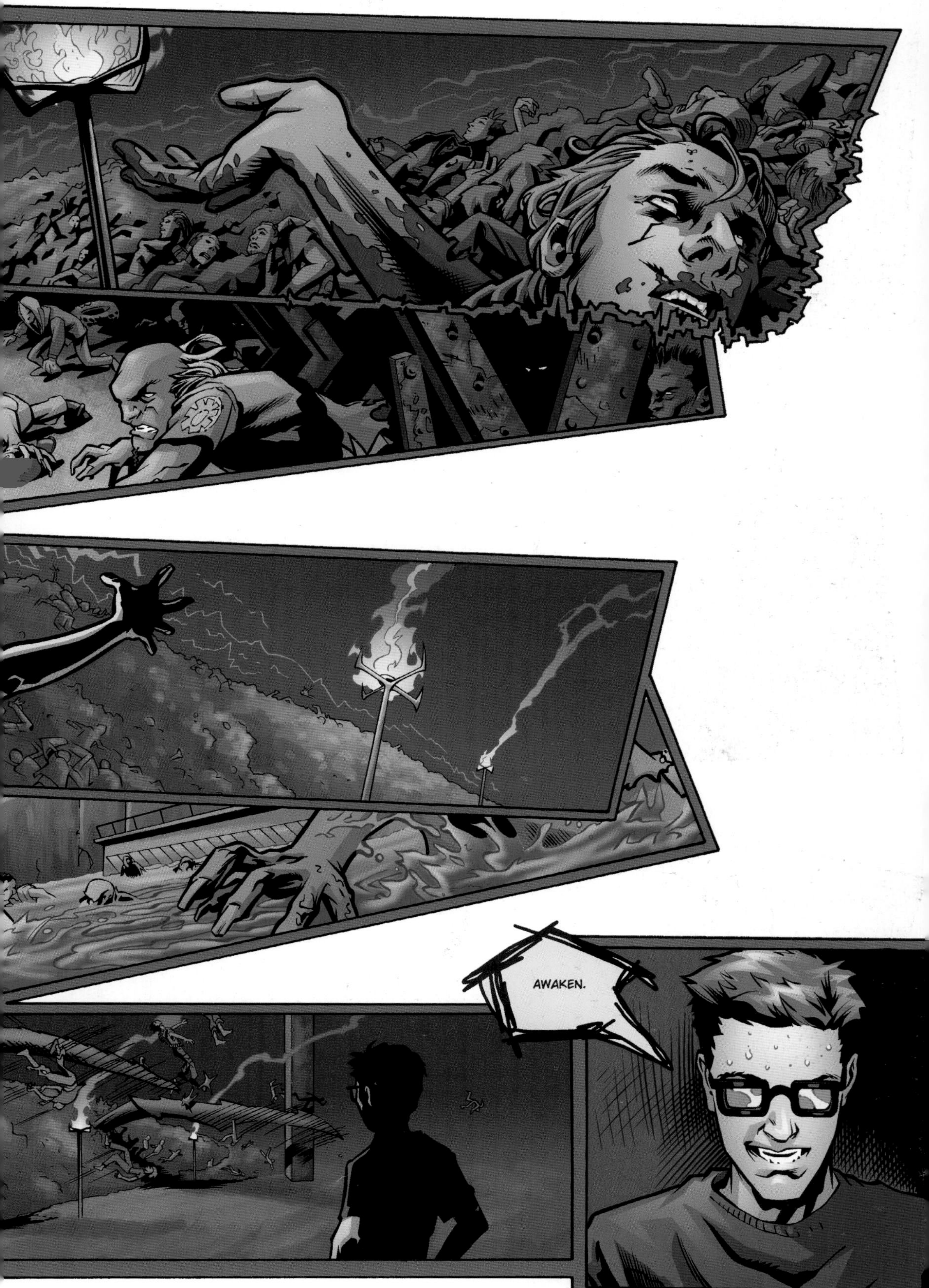
AWAKEN.

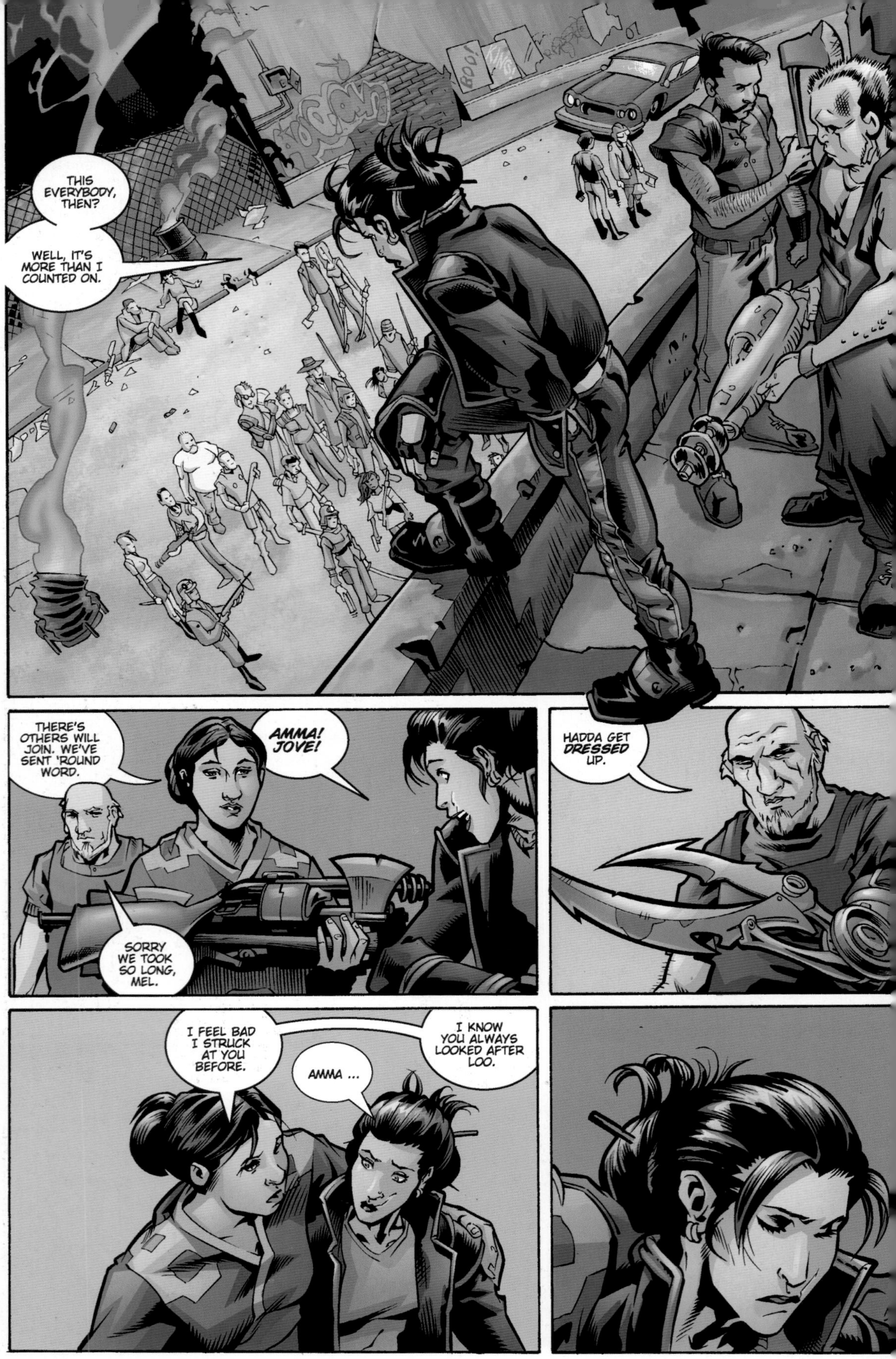
THIS EVERYBODY, THEN?
WELL, IT'S MORE THAN I COUNTED ON.
THERE'S OTHERS WILL JOIN. WE'VE SENT 'ROUND WORD.
AMMA! JOVE!
SORRY WE TOOK SO LONG, MEL.
HADDA GET DRESSED UP.
I FEEL BAD I STRUCK AT YOU BEFORE.
I KNOW YOU ALWAYS LOOKED AFTER LOO.
AMMA ...

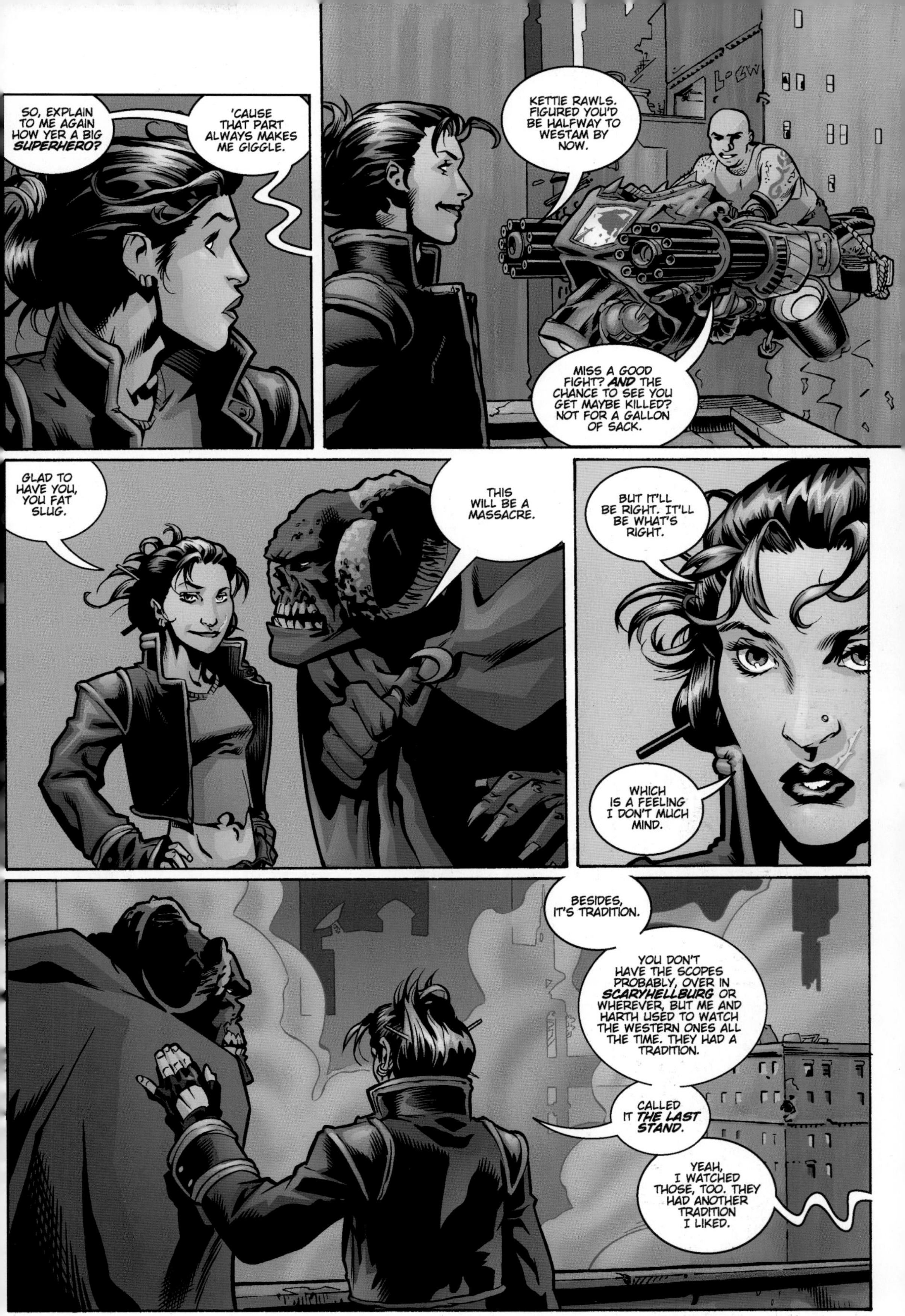
SO, EXPLAIN TO ME AGAIN HOW YER A BIG *SUPERHERO?*
'CAUSE THAT PART ALWAYS MAKES ME GIGGLE.
KETTIE RAWLS. FIGURED YOU'D BE HALFWAY TO WESTAM BY NOW.
MISS A GOOD FIGHT? *AND* THE CHANCE TO SEE YOU GET MAYBE KILLED? NOT FOR A GALLON OF SACK.
GLAD TO HAVE YOU, YOU FAT SLUG.
THIS WILL BE A MASSACRE.
BUT IT'LL BE RIGHT. IT'LL BE WHAT'S RIGHT.
WHICH IS A FEELING I DON'T MUCH MIND.
BESIDES, IT'S TRADITION.
YOU DON'T HAVE THE SCOPES PROBABLY, OVER IN *SCARYHELLBURG* OR WHEREVER, BUT ME AND HARTH USED TO WATCH THE WESTERN ONES ALL THE TIME. THEY HAD A TRADITION.
CALLED IT *THE LAST STAND.*
YEAH, I WATCHED THOSE, TOO. THEY HAD ANOTHER TRADITION I LIKED.

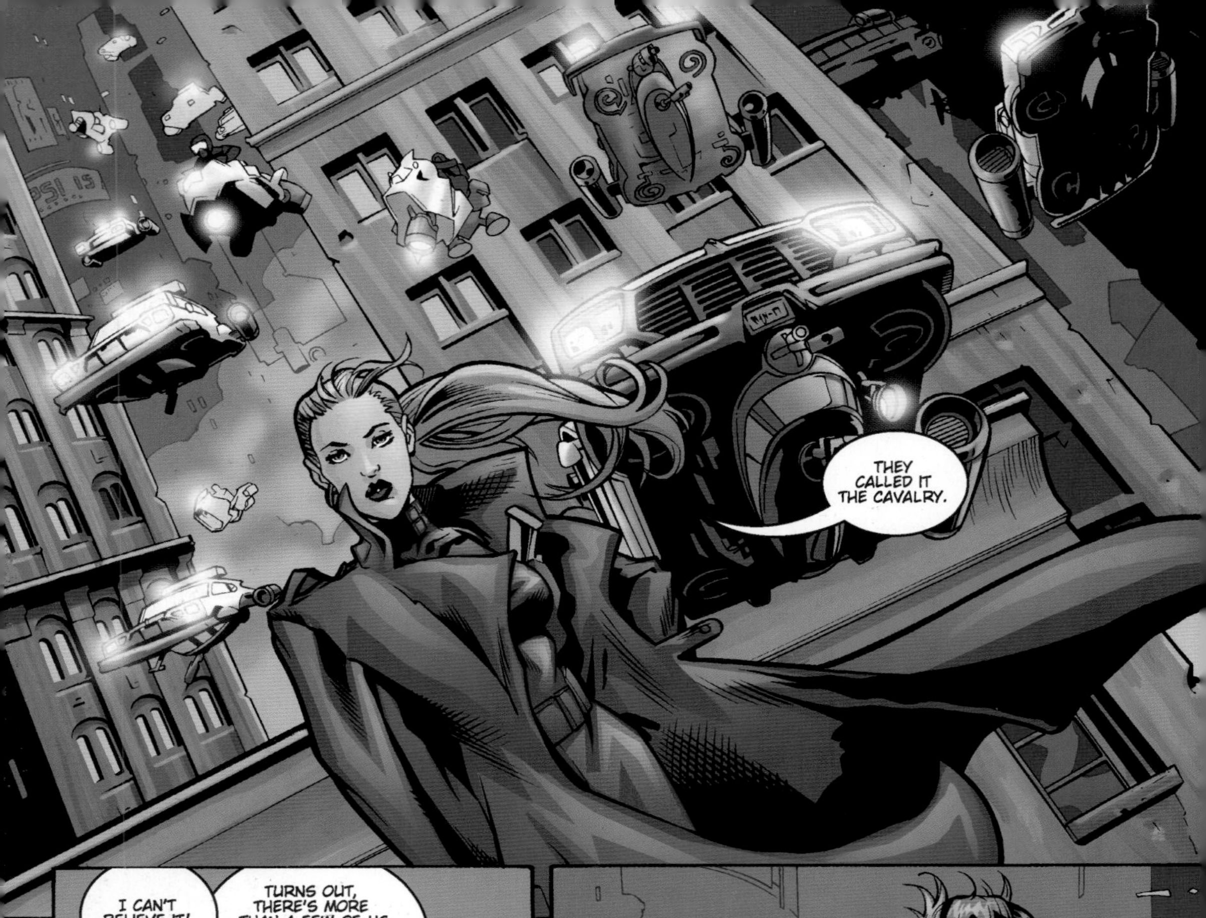
THEY CALLED IT THE CAVALRY.

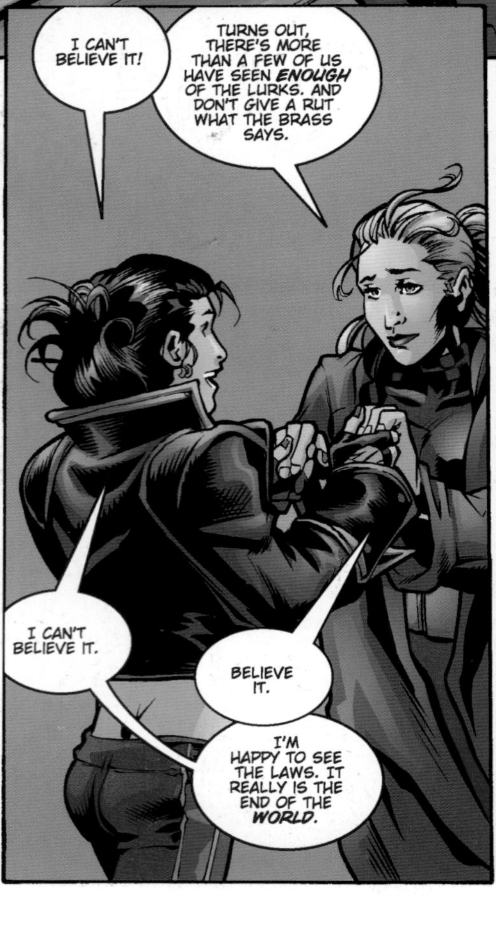
I CAN'T BELIEVE IT!
TURNS OUT, THERE'S MORE THAN A FEW OF US HAVE SEEN ENOUGH OF THE LURKS. AND DON'T GIVE A RUT WHAT THE BRASS SAYS.
I CAN'T BELIEVE IT.
BELIEVE IT.
I'M HAPPY TO SEE THE LAWS. IT REALLY IS THE END OF THE WORLD.

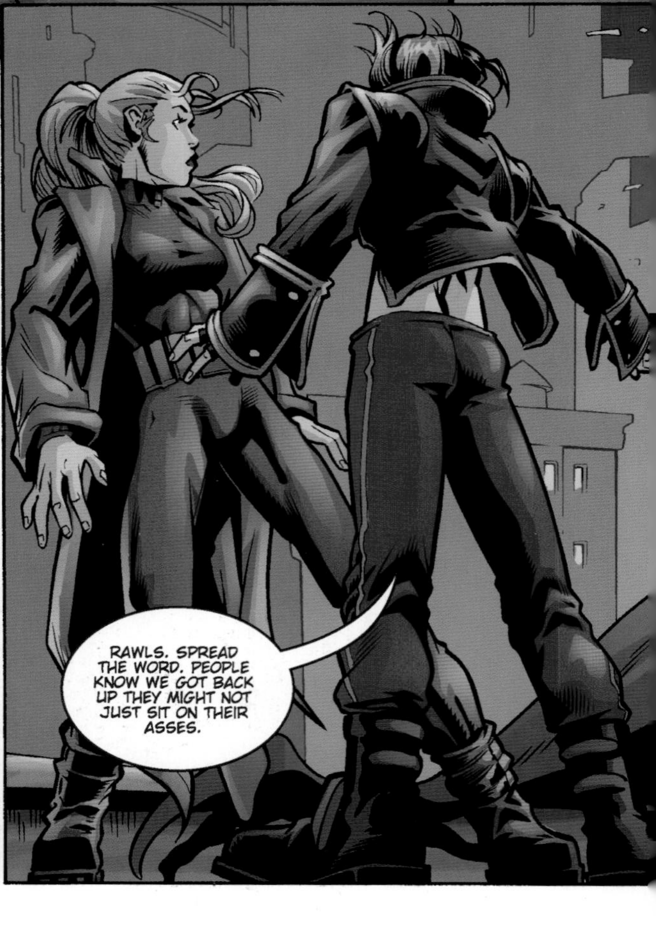
RAWLS. SPREAD THE WORD. PEOPLE KNOW WE GOT BACK UP THEY MIGHT NOT JUST SIT ON THEIR ASSES.

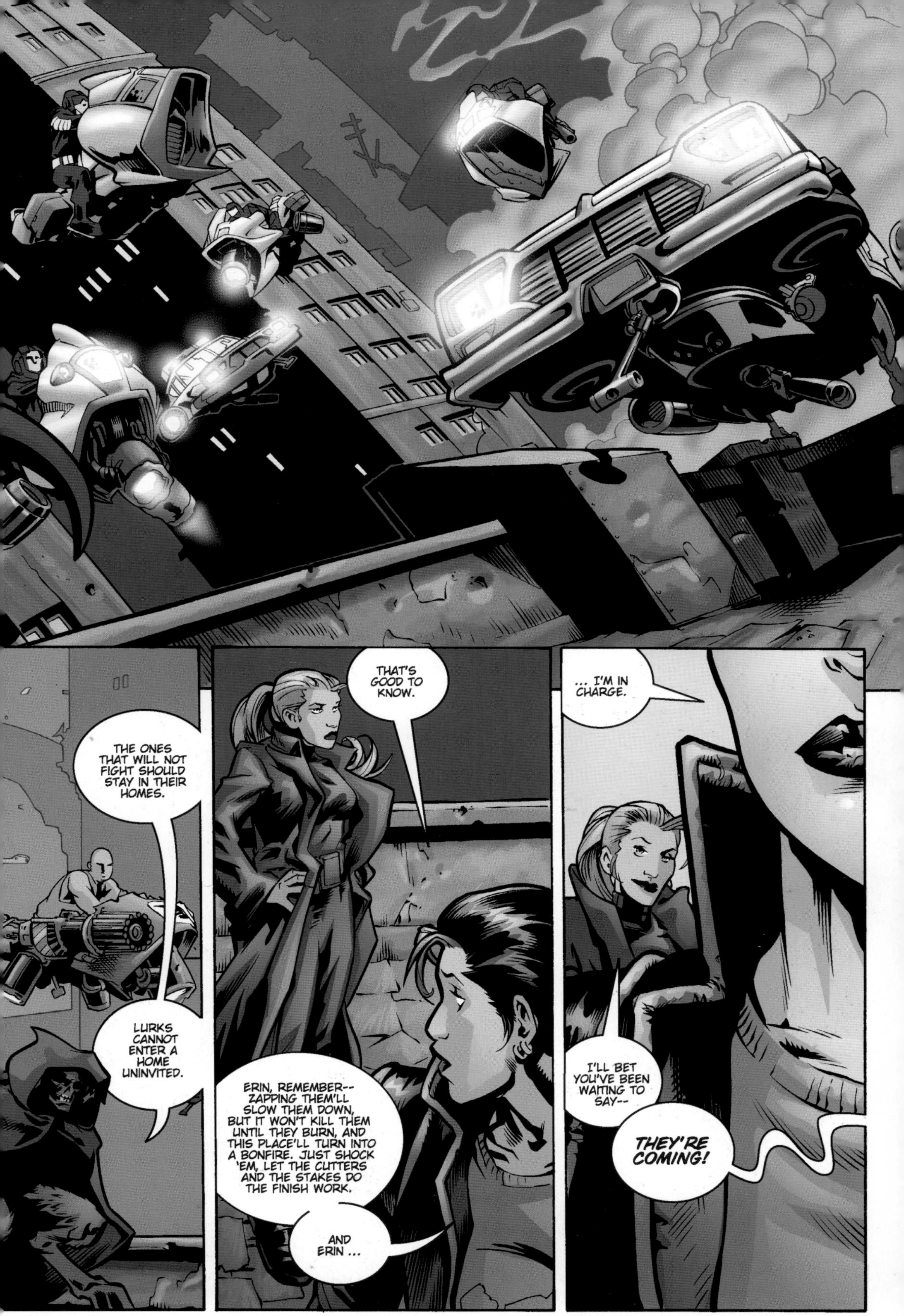
THE ONES THAT WILL NOT FIGHT SHOULD STAY IN THEIR HOMES.
LURKS CANNOT ENTER A HOME UNINVITED.
THAT'S GOOD TO KNOW.
ERIN, REMEMBER-- ZAPPING THEM'LL SLOW THEM DOWN, BUT IT WON'T KILL THEM UNTIL THEY BURN, AND THIS PLACE'LL TURN INTO A BONFIRE. JUST SHOCK 'EM, LET THE CUTTERS AND THE STAKES DO THE FINISH WORK.
AND ERIN ...
... I'M IN CHARGE.
I'LL BET YOU'VE BEEN WAITING TO SAY--
THEY'RE COMING!

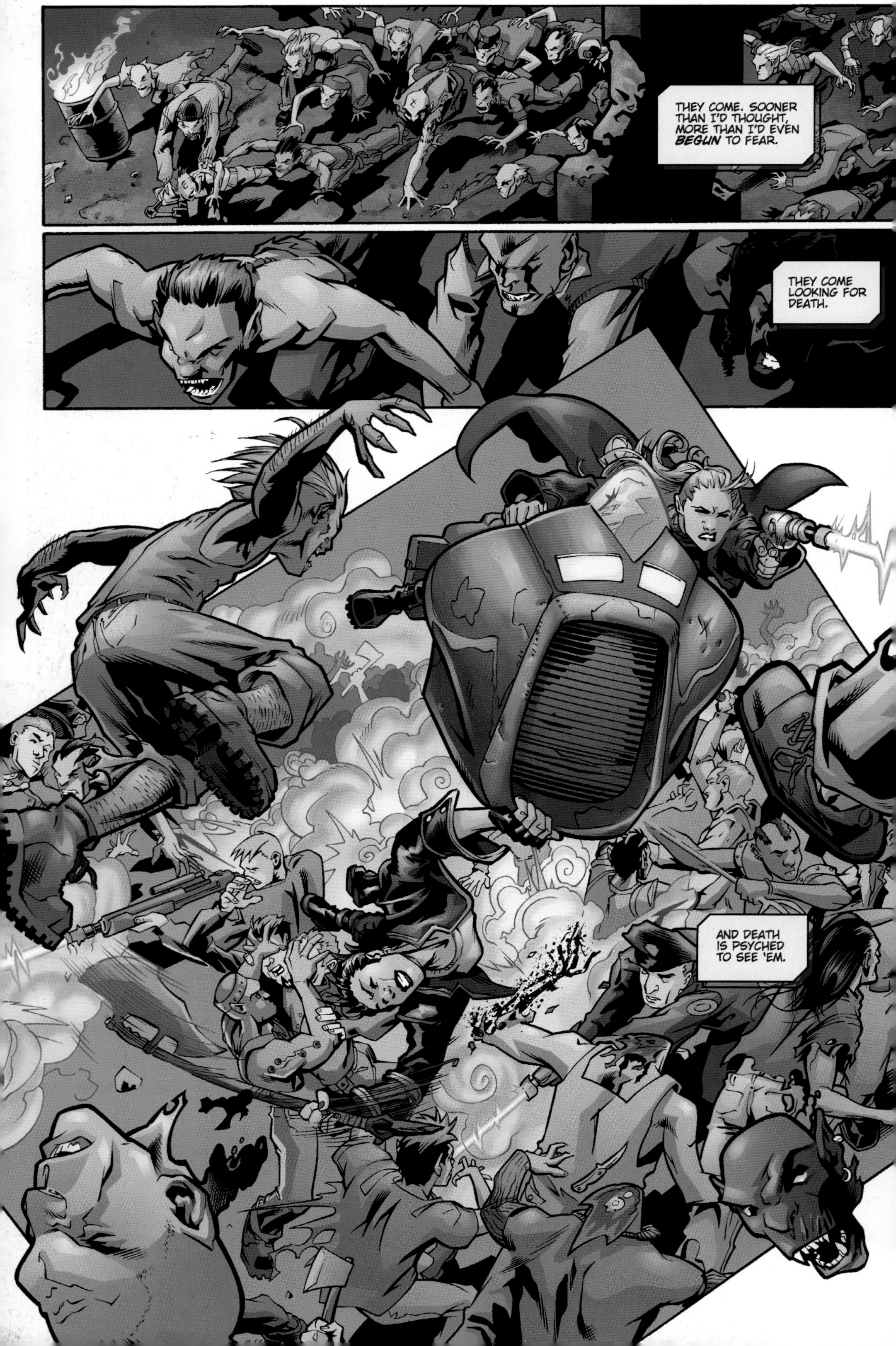
THEY COME. SOONER THAN I'D THOUGHT, MORE THAN I'D EVEN BEGUN TO FEAR.
THEY COME LOOKING FOR DEATH.
AND DEATH IS PSYCHED TO SEE 'EM.

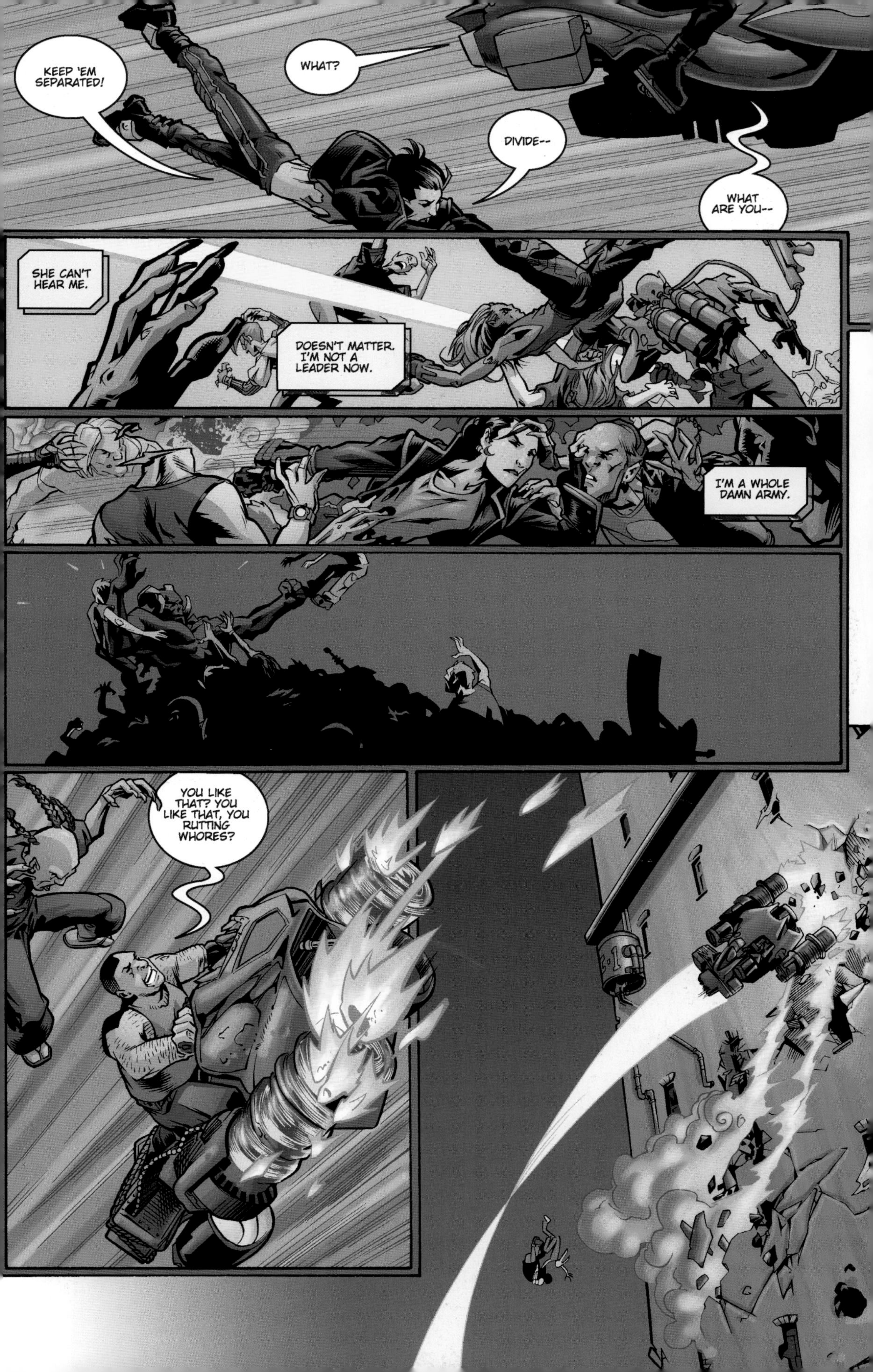
KEEP 'EM SEPARATED!
WHAT?
DIVIDE--
WHAT ARE YOU--
SHE CAN'T HEAR ME.
DOESN'T MATTER. I'M NOT A LEADER NOW.
I'M A WHOLE DAMN ARMY.
YOU LIKE THAT? YOU LIKE THAT, YOU RUTTING WHORES?

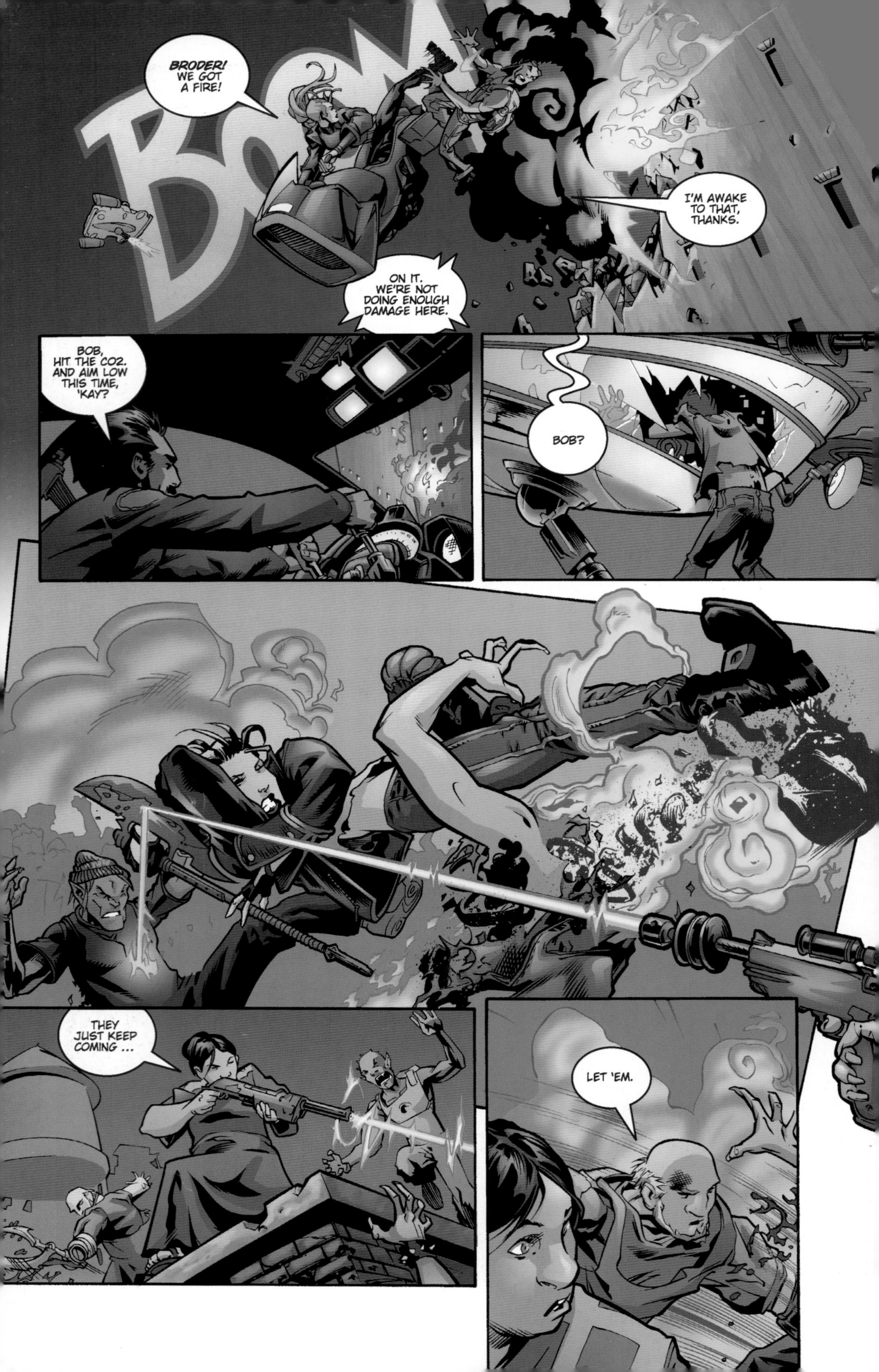
BOOM
BRODER! WE GOT A FIRE!
I'M AWAKE TO THAT, THANKS.
ON IT. WE'RE NOT DOING ENOUGH DAMAGE HERE.
BOB, HIT THE CO2. AND AIM LOW THIS TIME, 'KAY?
BOB?
THEY JUST KEEP COMING ...
LET 'EM.

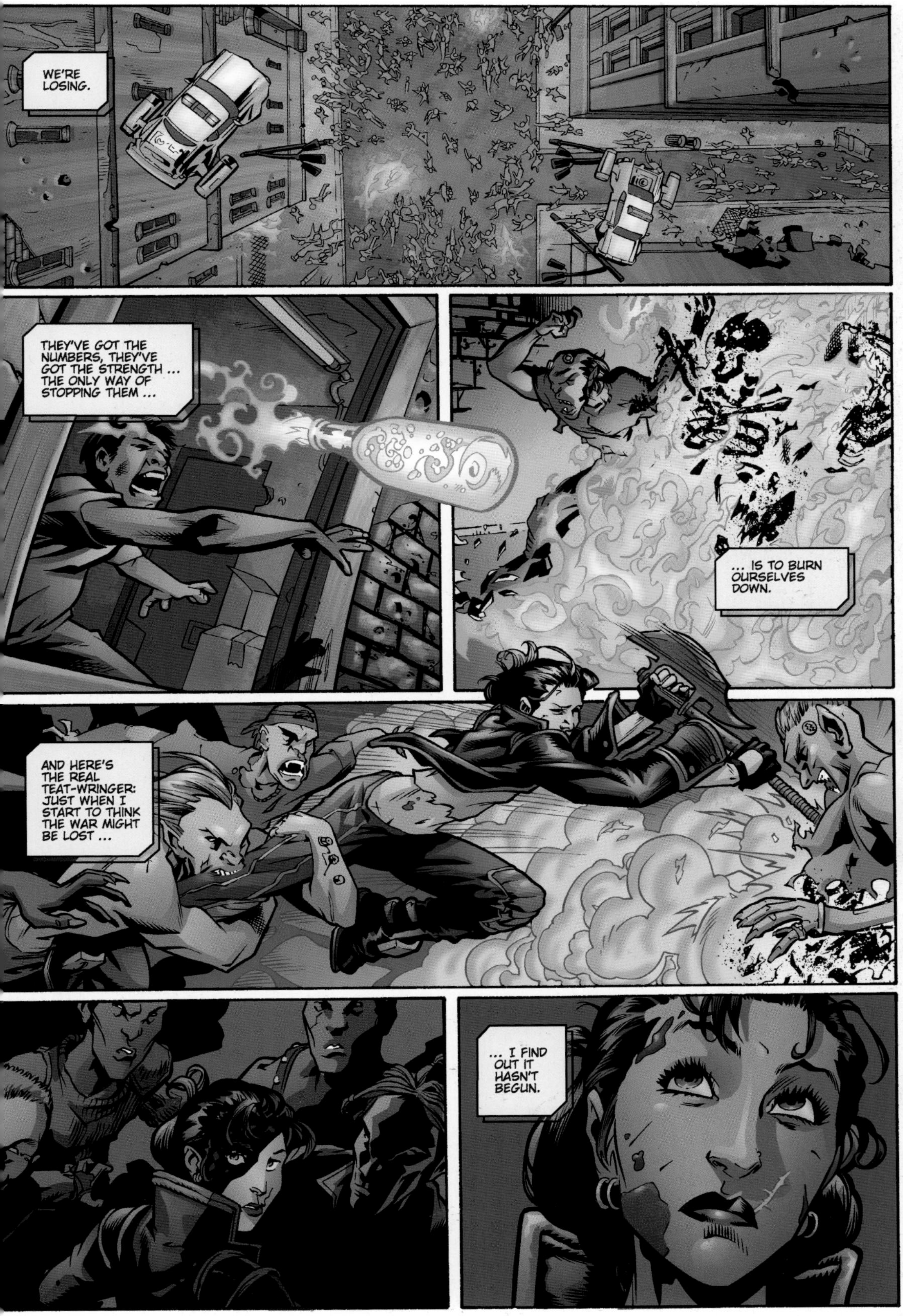
WE'RE LOSING.
THEY'VE GOT THE NUMBERS, THEY'VE GOT THE STRENGTH ... THE ONLY WAY OF STOPPING THEM ...
... IS TO BURN OURSELVES DOWN.
AND HERE'S THE REAL TEAT-WRINGER: JUST WHEN I START TO THINK THE WAR MIGHT BE LOST ...
... I FIND OUT IT HASN'T BEGUN.

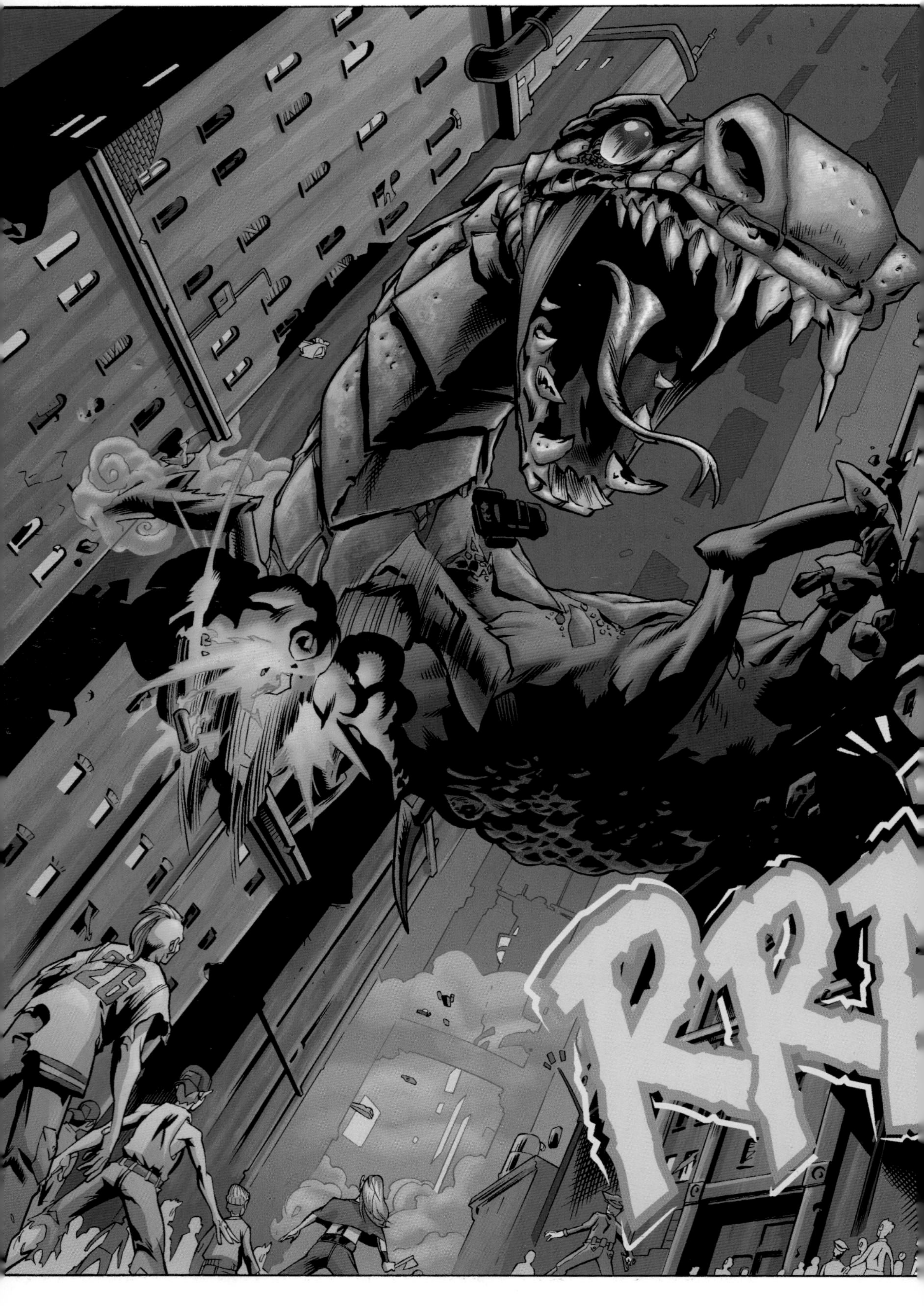
26
RR

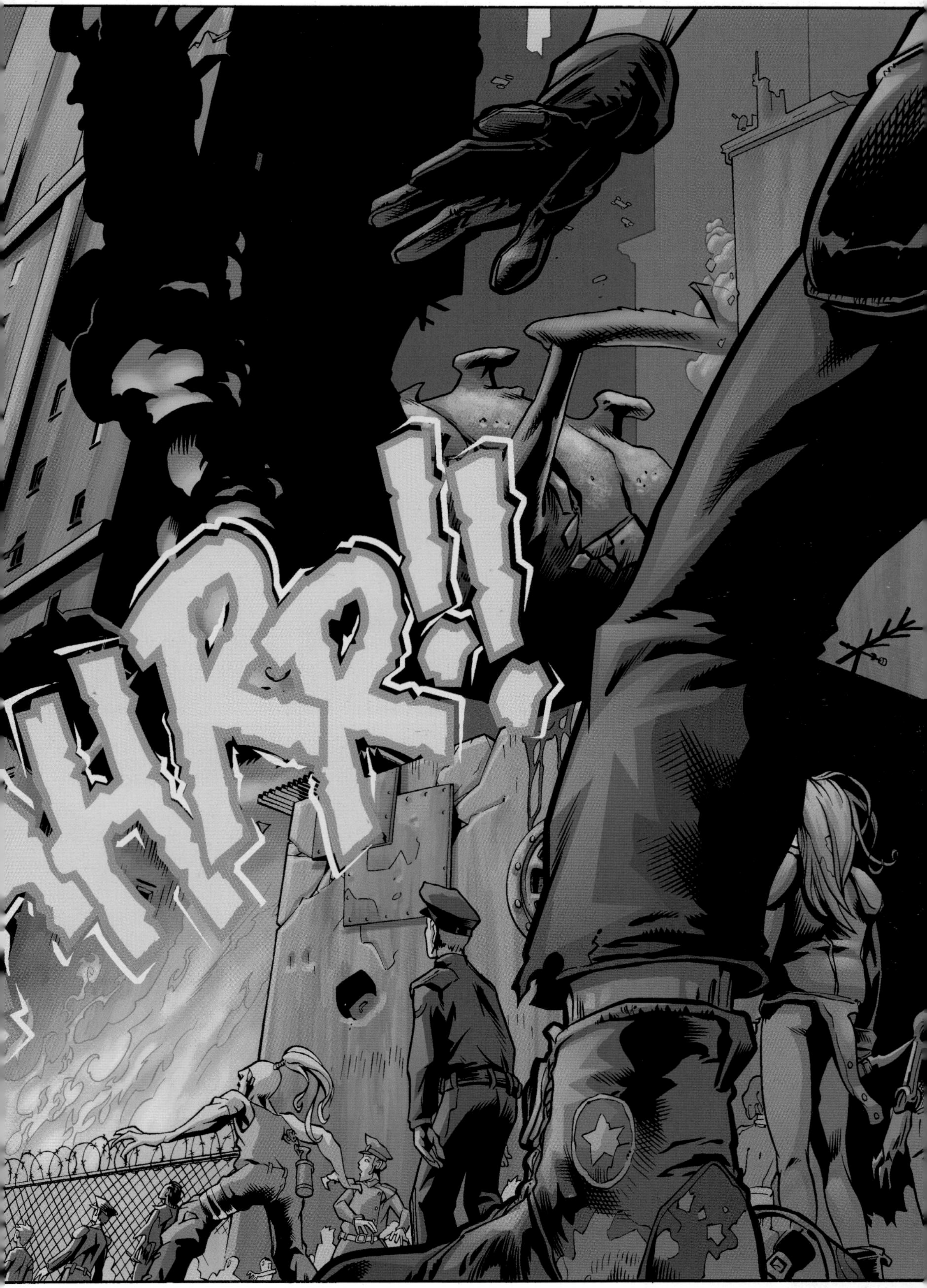
HRR!!

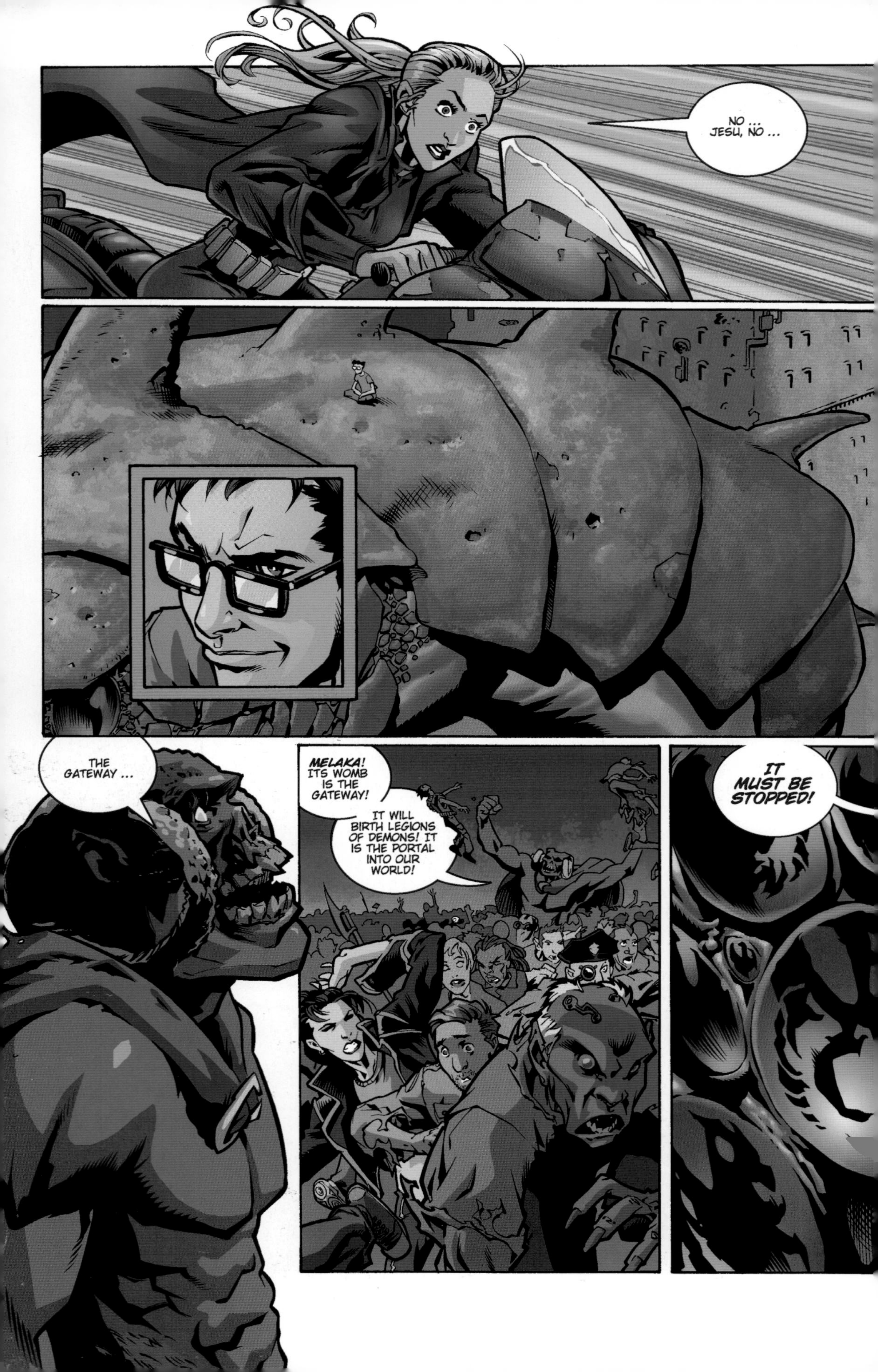
NO ... JESU, NO ...
THE GATEWAY ...
MELAKA! ITS WOMB IS THE GATEWAY!
IT WILL BIRTH LEGIONS OF DEMONS! IT IS THE PORTAL INTO OUR WORLD!
IT MUST BE STOPPED!

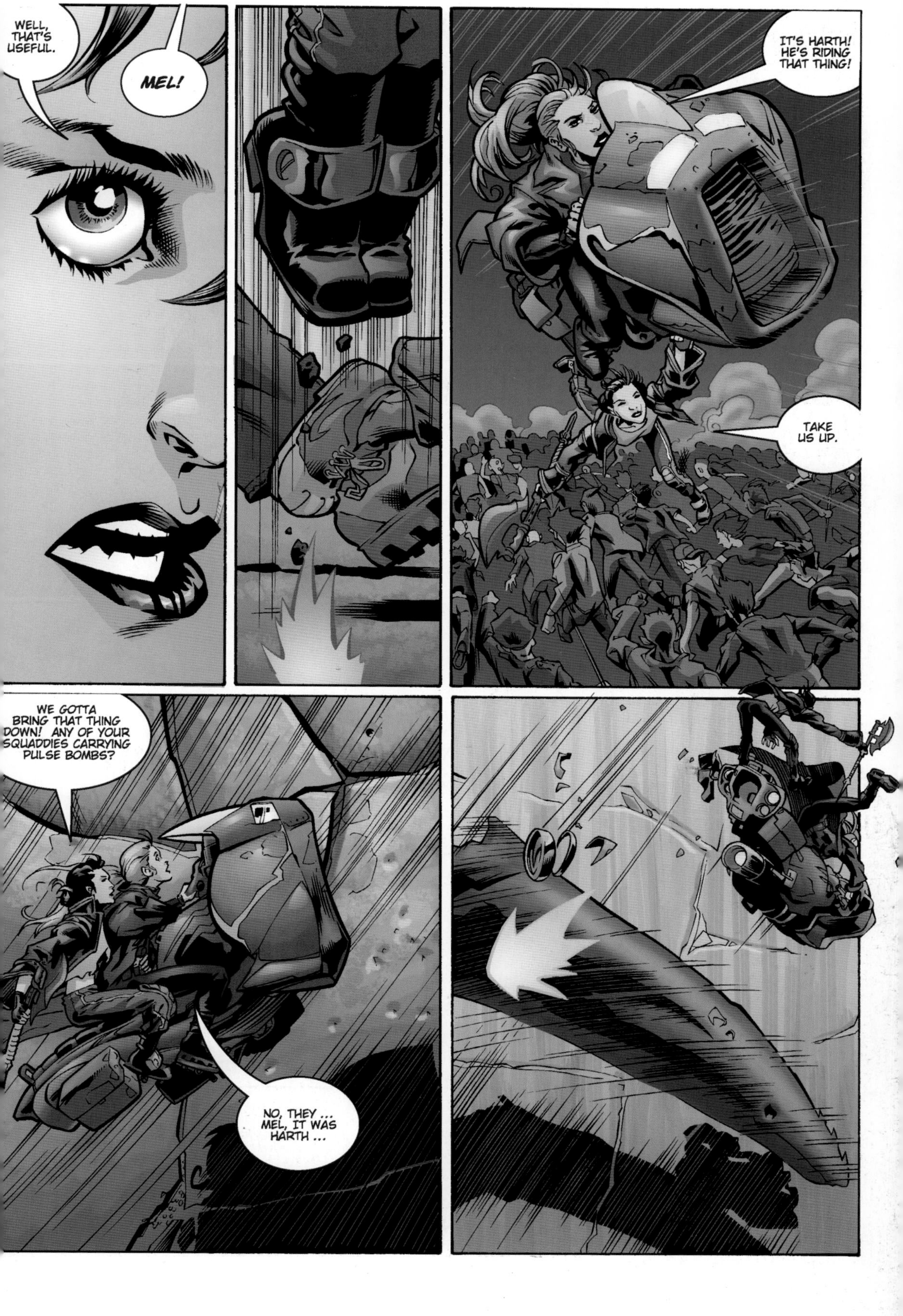
WELL, THAT'S USEFUL.
MEL!
IT'S HARTH! HE'S RIDING THAT THING!
TAKE US UP.
WE GOTTA BRING THAT THING DOWN! ANY OF YOUR SQUADDIES CARRYING PULSE BOMBS?
NO, THEY ... MEL, IT WAS HARTH ...

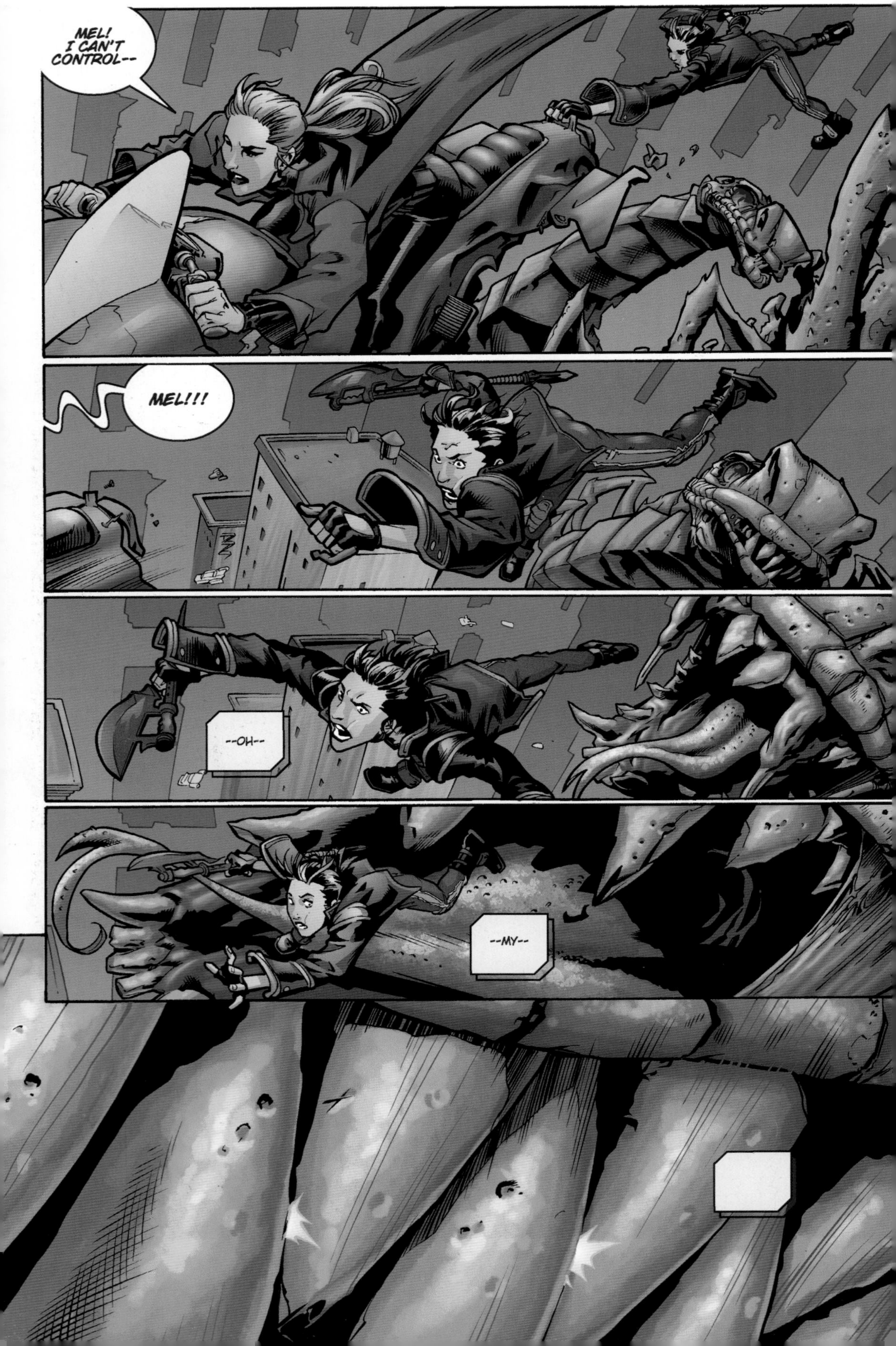
MEL! I CAN'T CONTROL--
MEL!!!
--OH--
--MY--

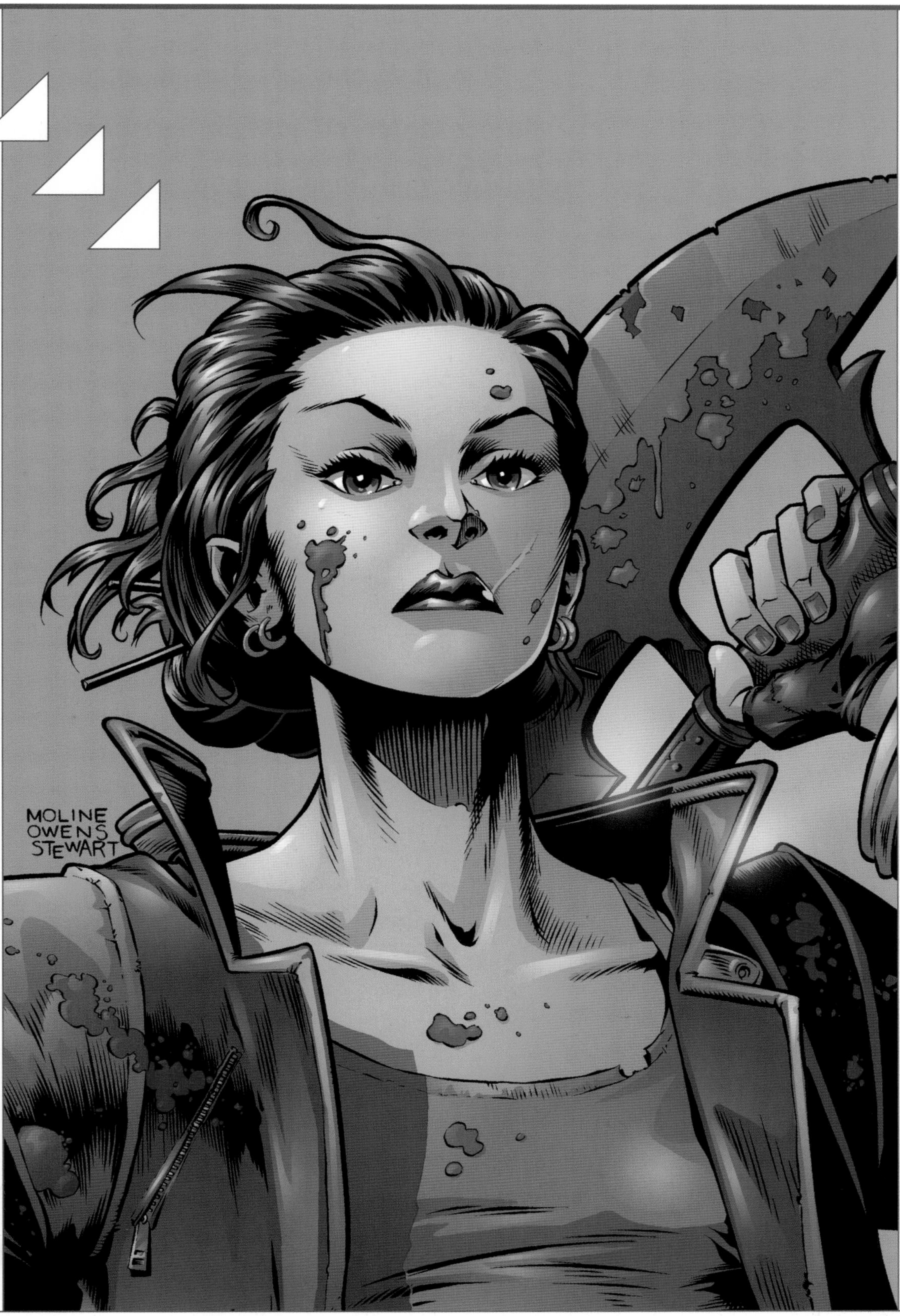
MOLINE
OWENS
STEWART

"I'm just one girl. No big hero, no protector of justice, not even a bona fide one-hundred-percent Slayer."

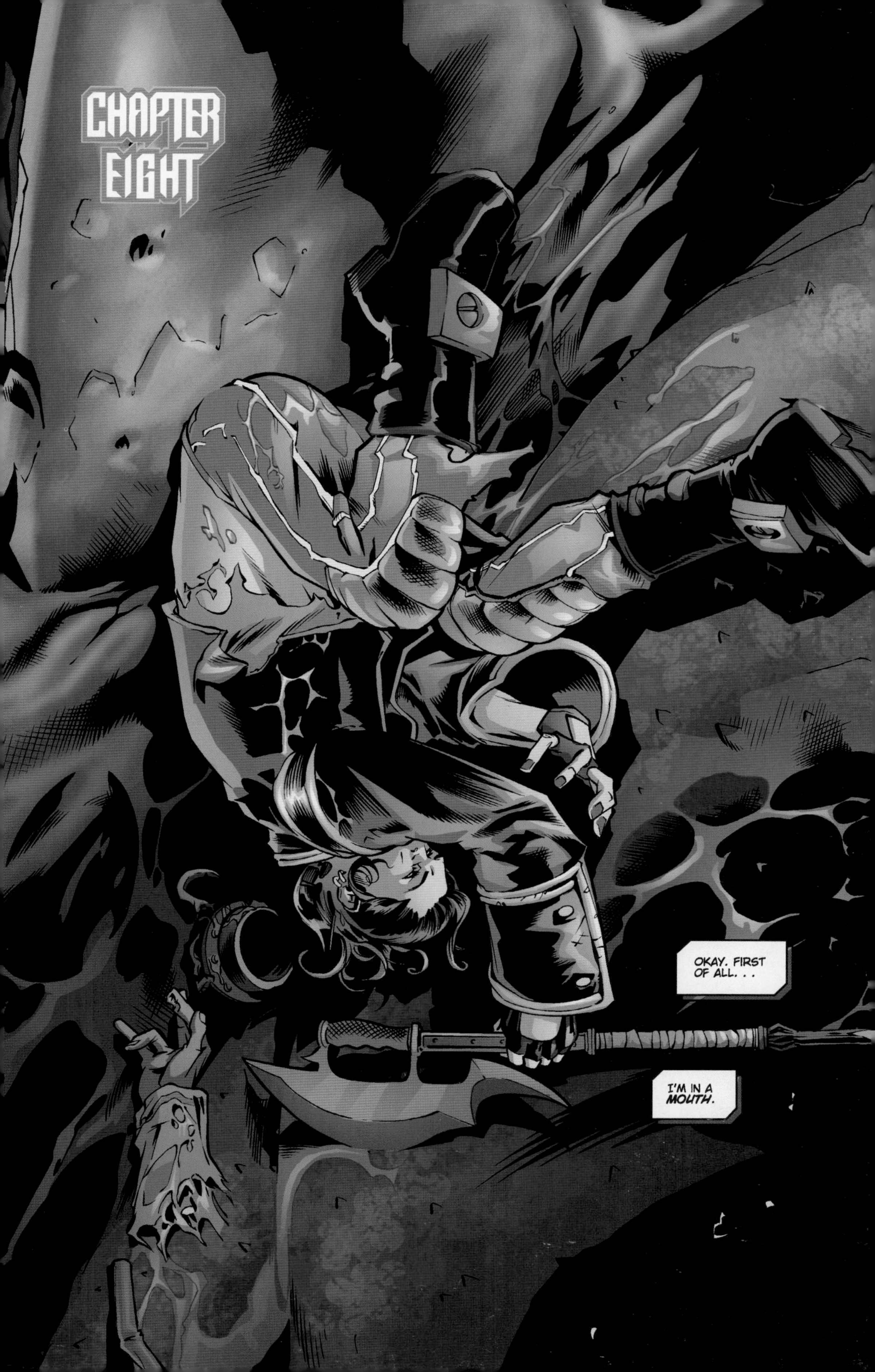
CHAPTER EIGHT
OKAY. FIRST OF ALL. . .
I'M IN A *MOUTH*.

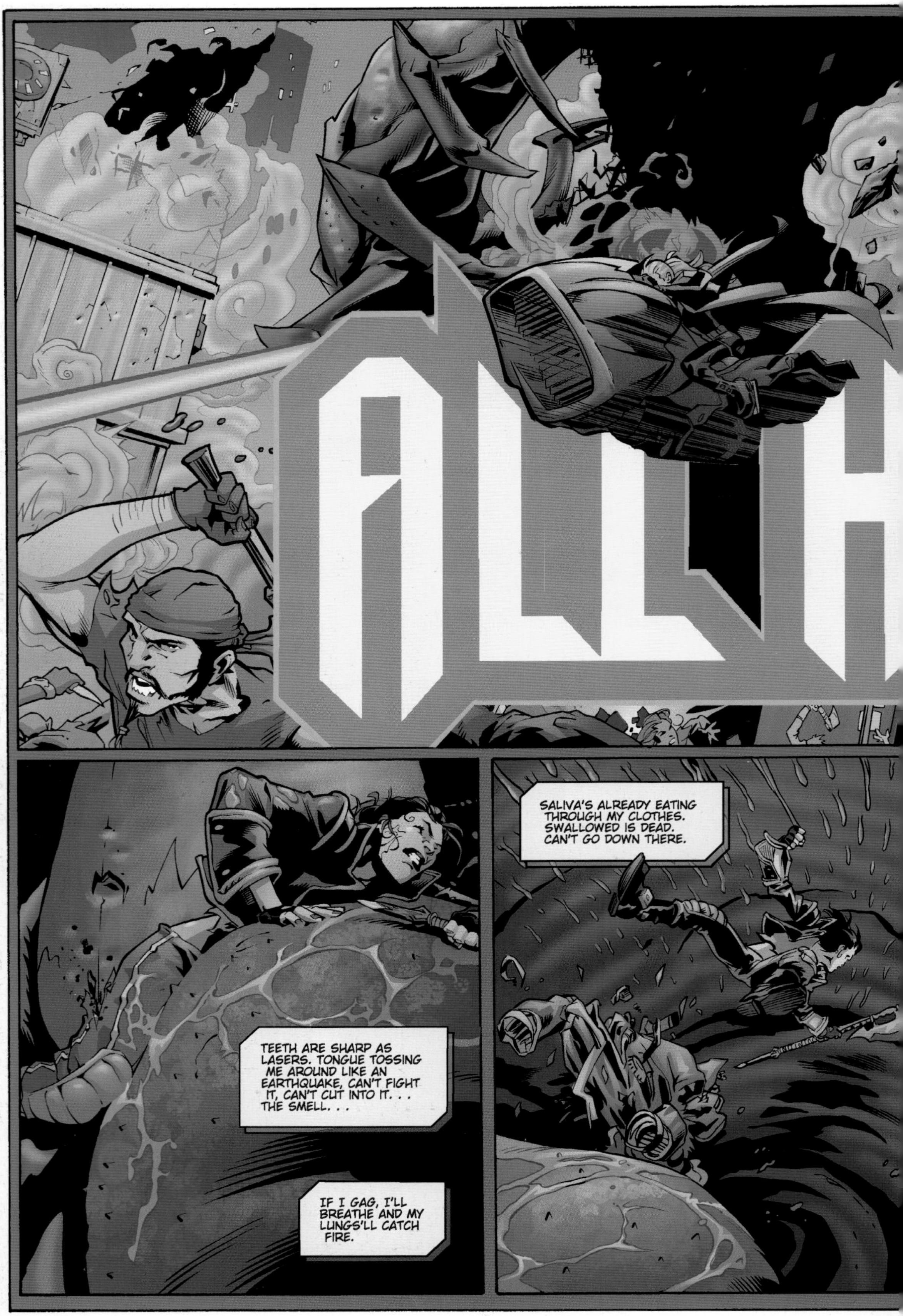
TEETH ARE SHARP AS LASERS. TONGUE TOSSING ME AROUND LIKE AN EARTHQUAKE, CAN'T FIGHT IT, CAN'T CUT INTO IT. . . THE SMELL. . .
IF I GAG, I'LL BREATHE AND MY LUNGS'LL CATCH FIRE.
SALIVA'S ALREADY EATING THROUGH MY CLOTHES. SWALLOWED IS DEAD. CAN'T GO DOWN THERE.

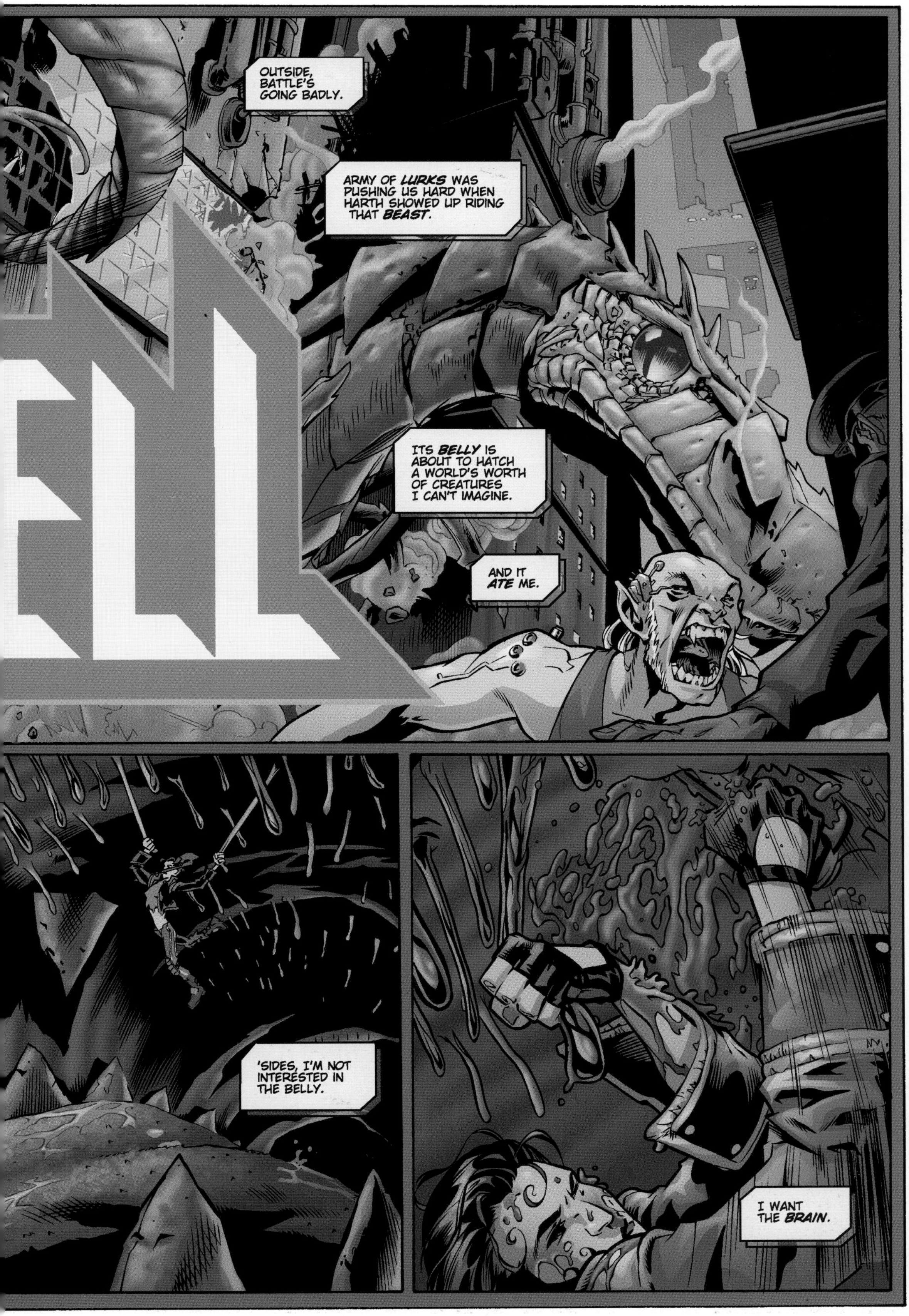
OUTSIDE, BATTLE'S GOING BADLY.
ARMY OF LURKS WAS PUSHING US HARD WHEN HARTH SHOWED UP RIDING THAT BEAST.
ITS BELLY IS ABOUT TO HATCH A WORLD'S WORTH OF CREATURES I CAN'T IMAGINE.
AND IT ATE ME.
'SIDES, I'M NOT INTERESTED IN THE BELLY.
I WANT THE BRAIN.

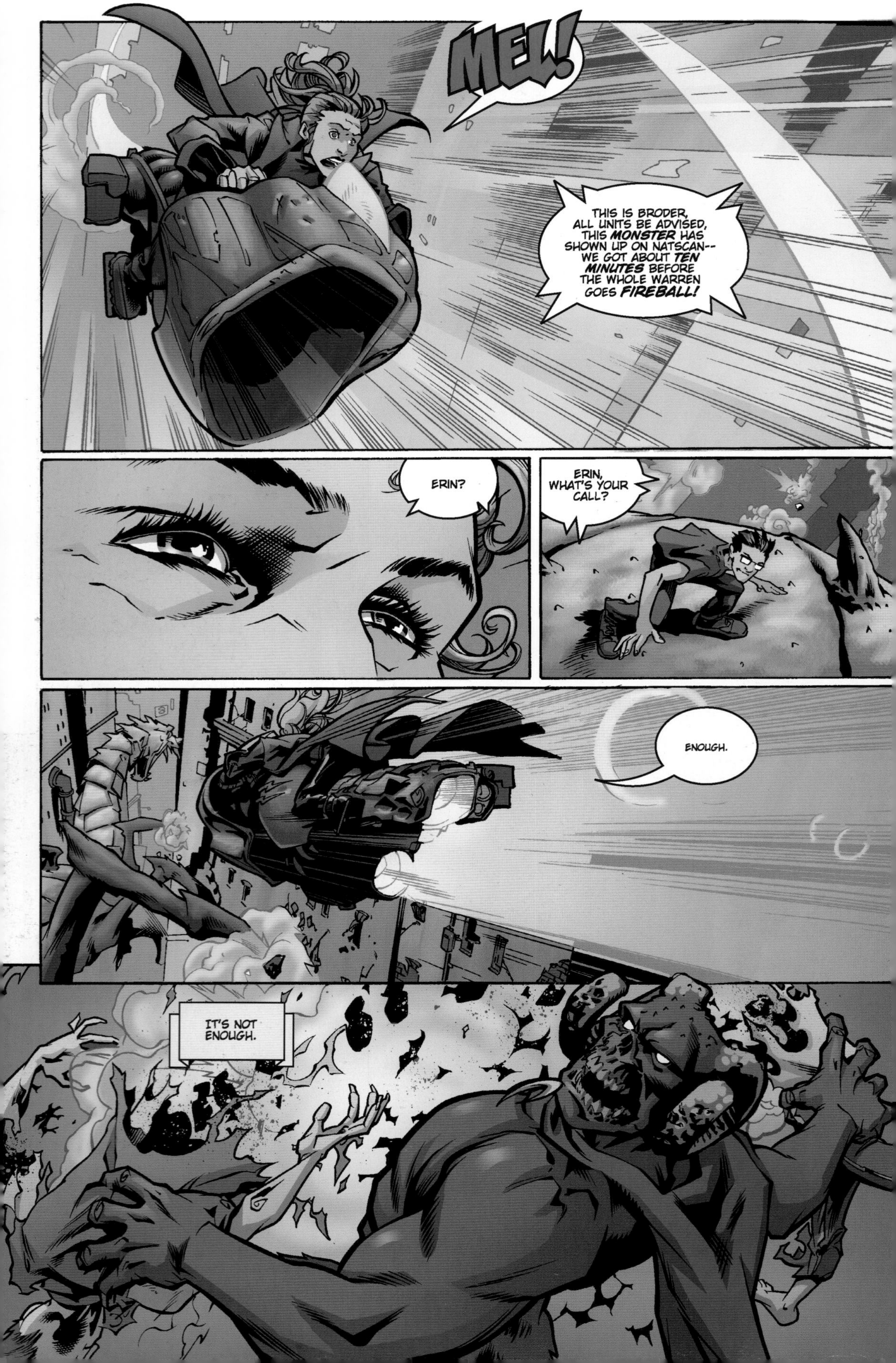
MEL!
THIS IS BRODER, ALL UNITS BE ADVISED, THIS MONSTER HAS SHOWN UP ON NATSCAN-- WE GOT ABOUT TEN MINUTES BEFORE THE WHOLE WARREN GOES FIREBALL!
ERIN?
ERIN, WHAT'S YOUR CALL?
ENOUGH.
IT'S NOT ENOUGH.

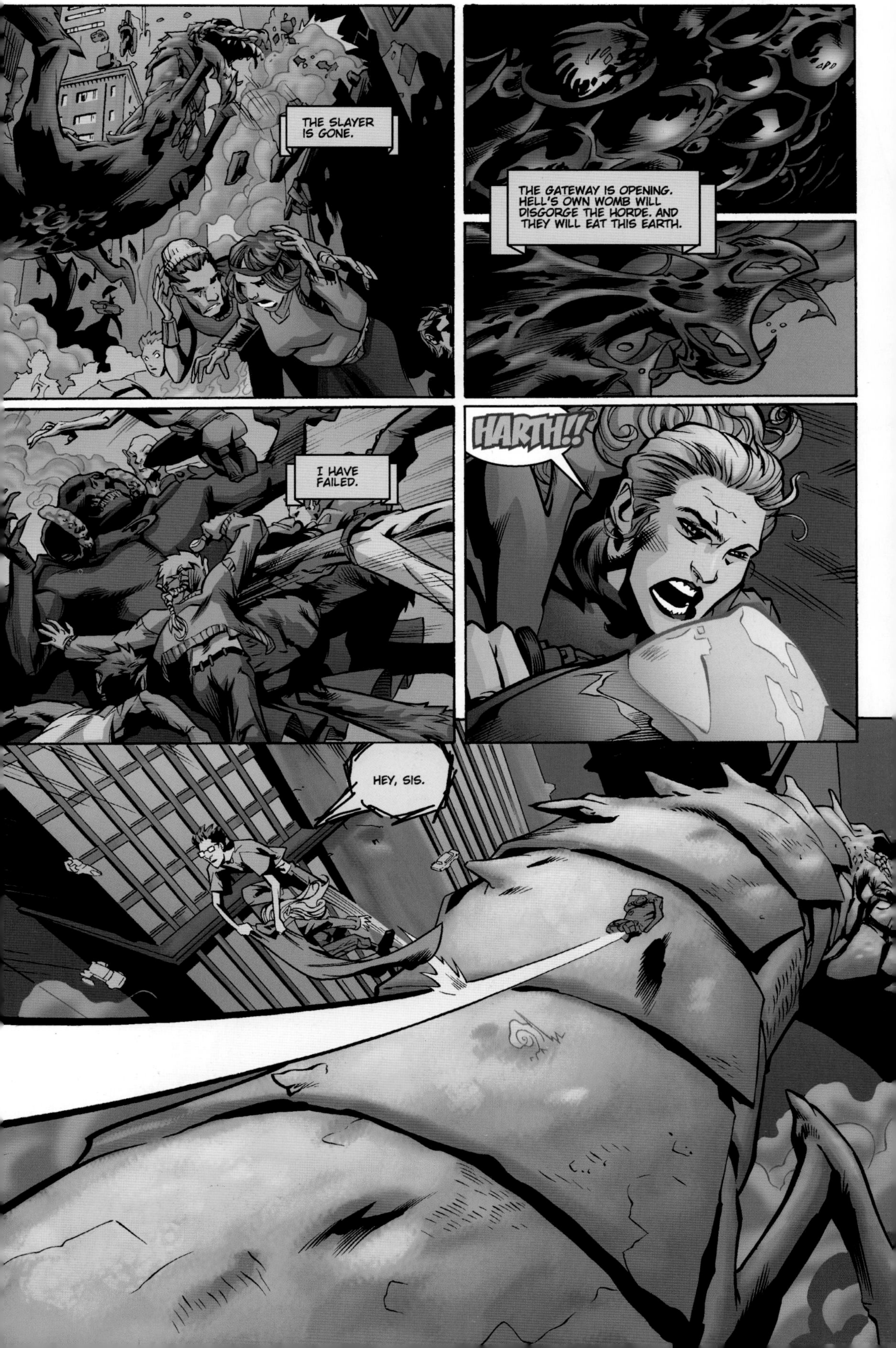
THE SLAYER IS GONE.
THE GATEWAY IS OPENING. HELL'S OWN WOMB WILL DISGORGE THE HORDE. AND THEY WILL EAT THIS EARTH.
I HAVE FAILED.
HARTH!!
HEY, SIS.

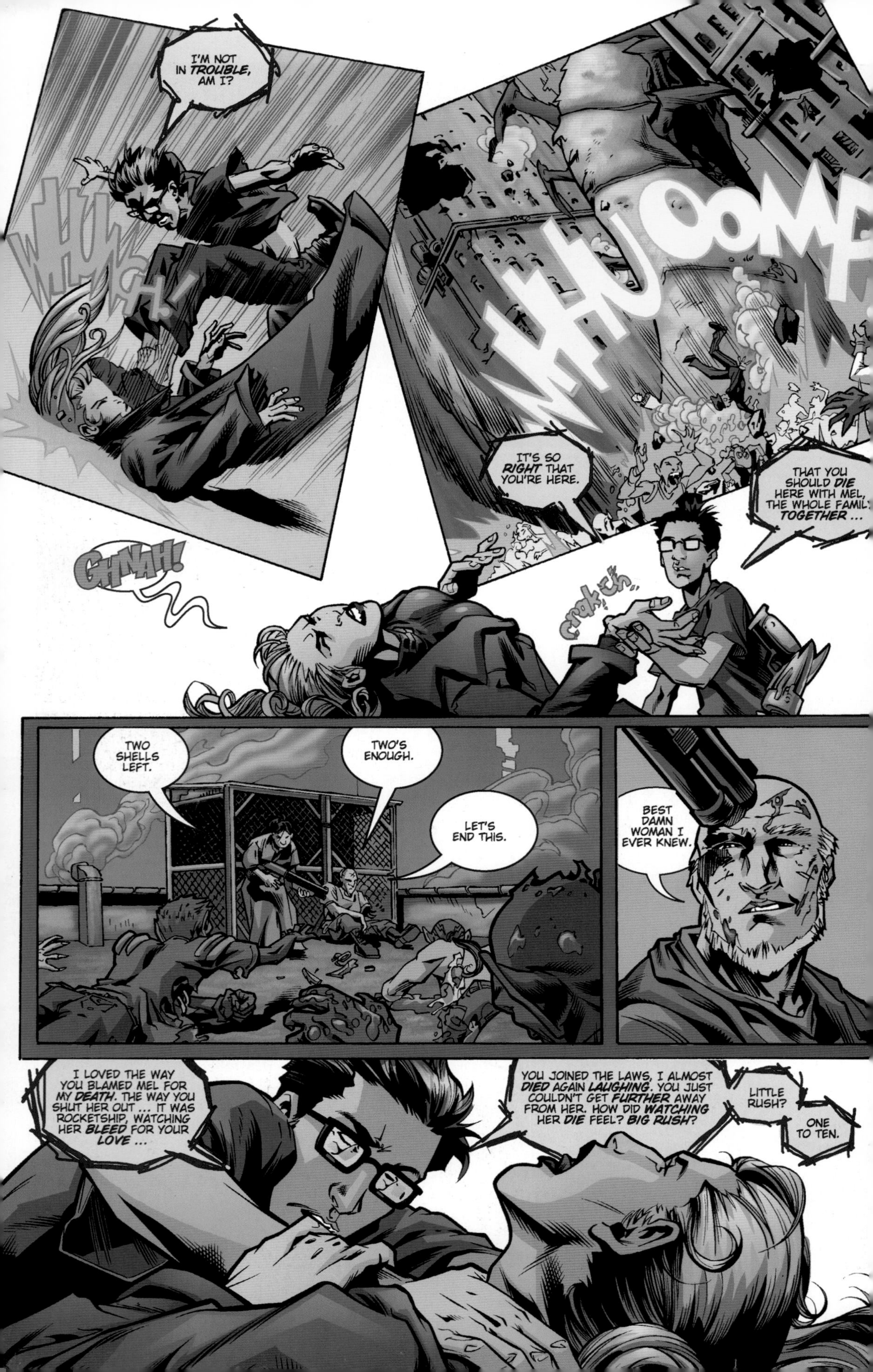

I'M NOT IN TROUBLE, AM I?
WHUMASH!
WHUOOMP!
IT'S SO RIGHT THAT YOU'RE HERE.
THAT YOU SHOULD DIE HERE WITH MEL, THE WHOLE FAMILY TOGETHER ...
GHNAH!
crak, ch
TWO SHELLS LEFT.
TWO'S ENOUGH.
LET'S END THIS.
BEST DAMN WOMAN I EVER KNEW.
I LOVED THE WAY YOU BLAMED MEL FOR MY DEATH. THE WAY YOU SHUT HER OUT ... IT WAS ROCKETSHIP, WATCHING HER BLEED FOR YOUR LOVE ...
YOU JOINED THE LAWS, I ALMOST DIED AGAIN LAUGHING. YOU JUST COULDN'T GET FURTHER AWAY FROM HER. HOW DID WATCHING HER DIE FEEL? BIG RUSH?
LITTLE RUSH?
ONE TO TEN.

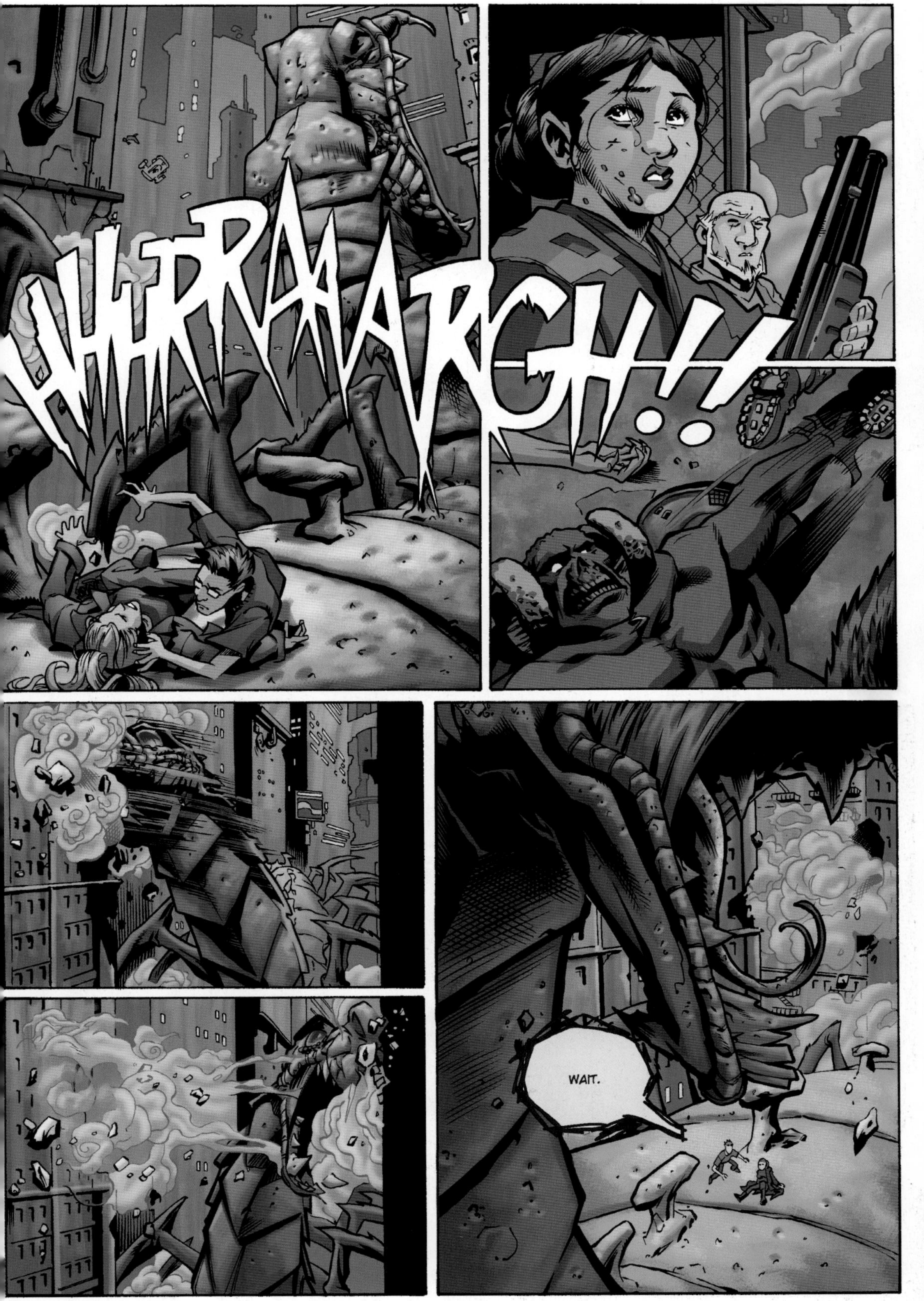
WHHRAAARGH!!
WAIT.

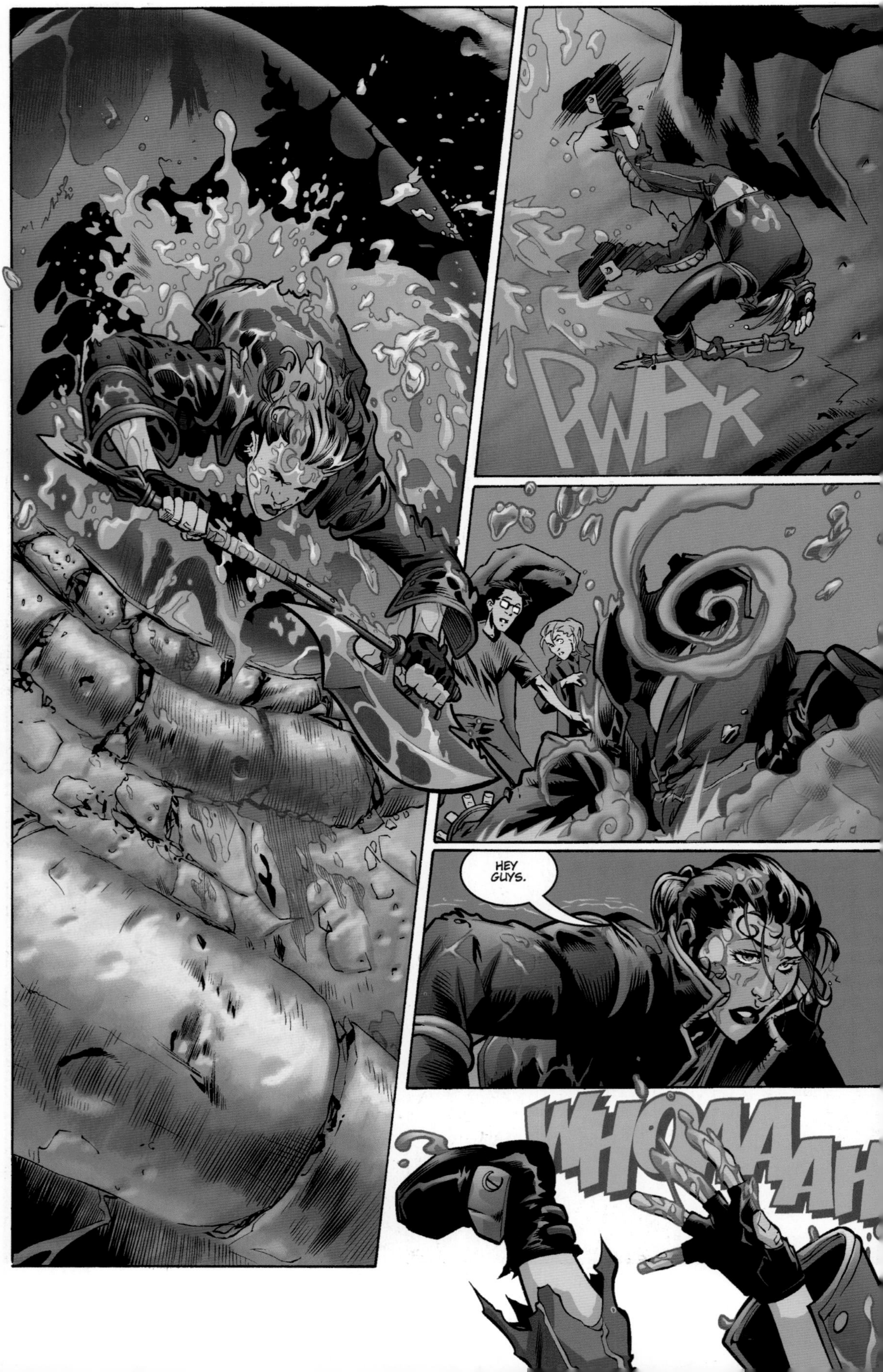

RWAK
HEY GUYS.
WHOAAAH

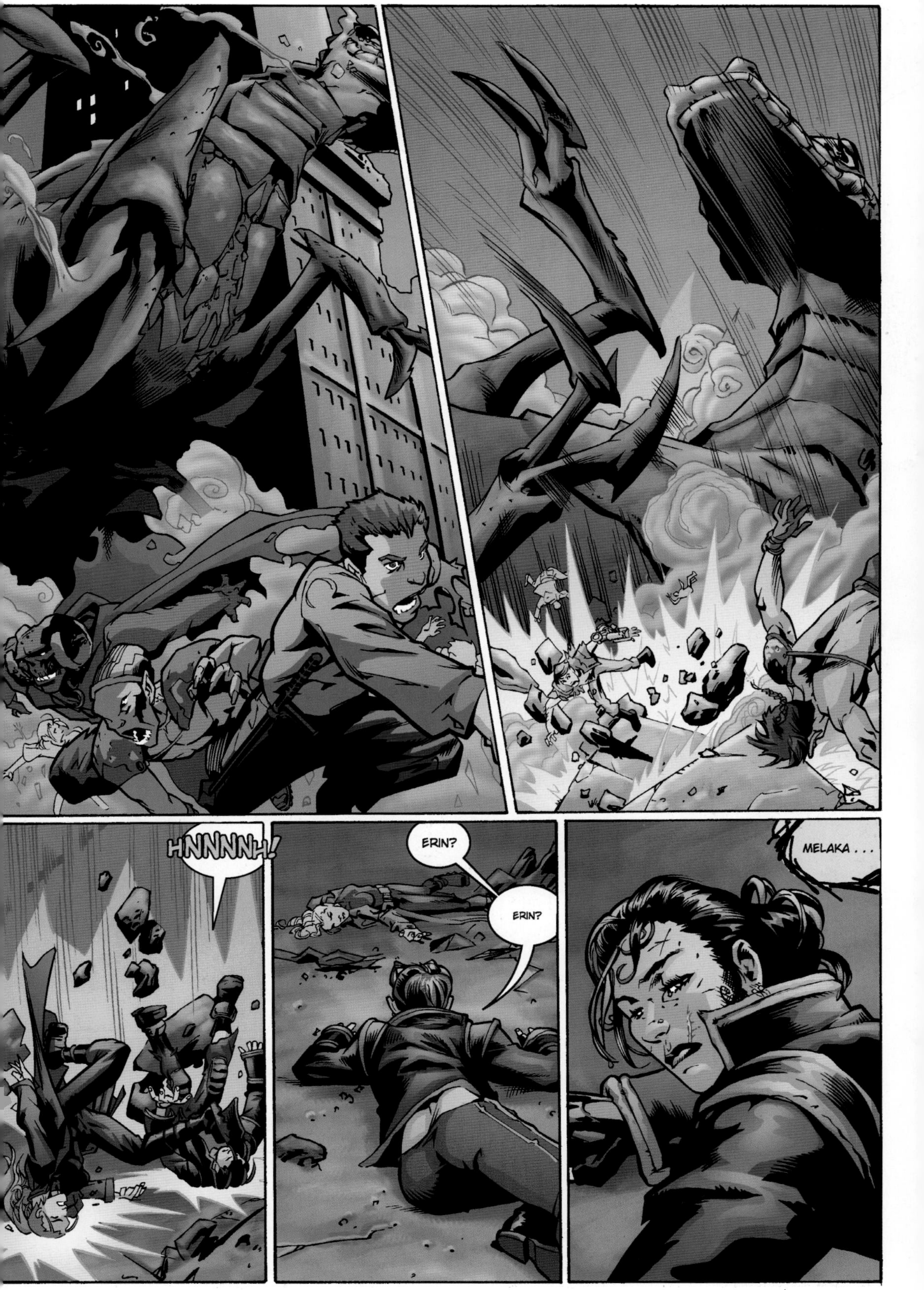
HNNNNH!
ERIN?
ERIN?
MELAKA . . .

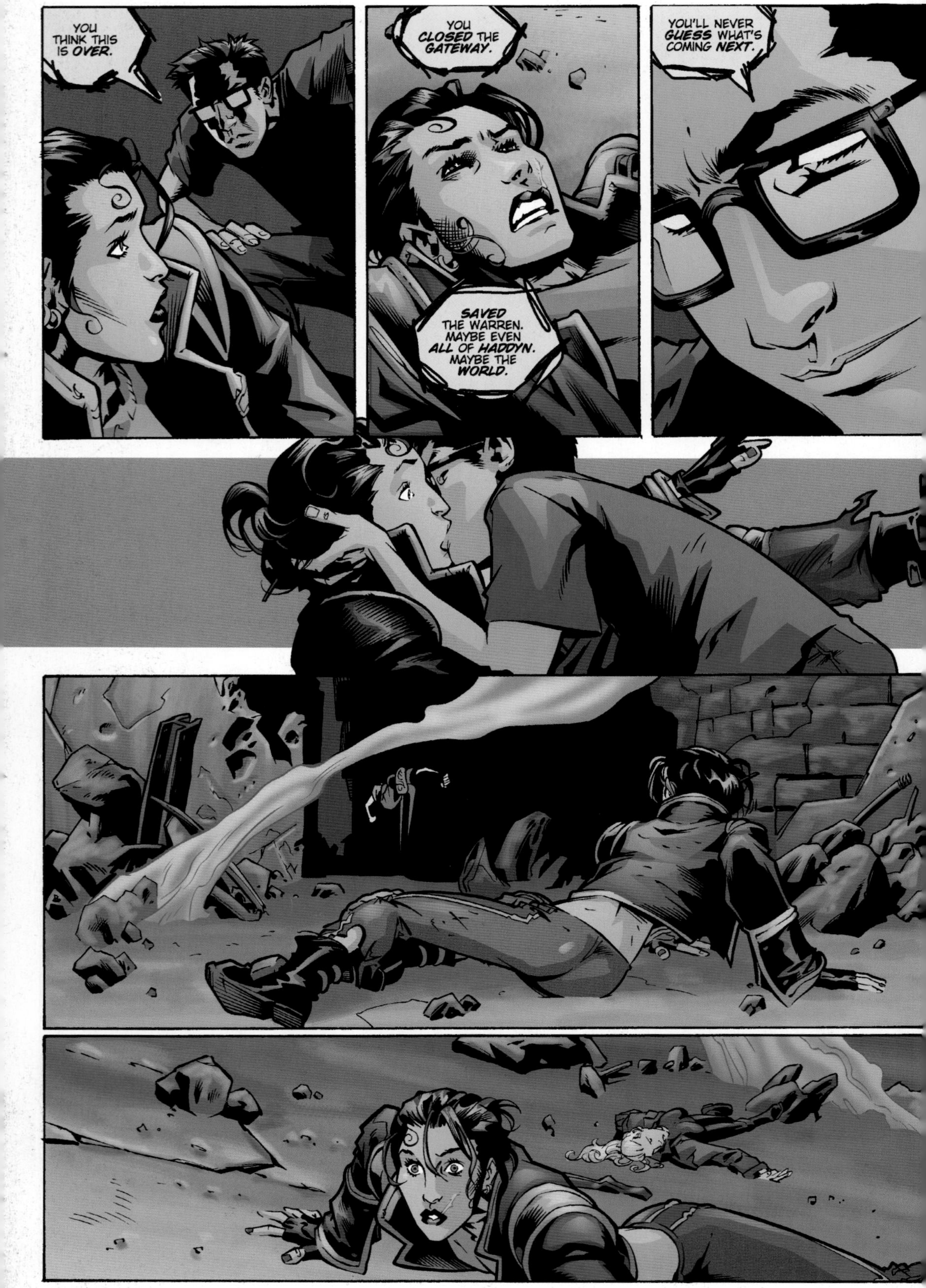
YOU THINK THIS IS OVER.
YOU CLOSED THE GATEWAY.
SAVED THE WARREN. MAYBE EVEN ALL OF HADDYN. MAYBE THE WORLD.
YOU'LL NEVER GUESS WHAT'S COMING NEXT.

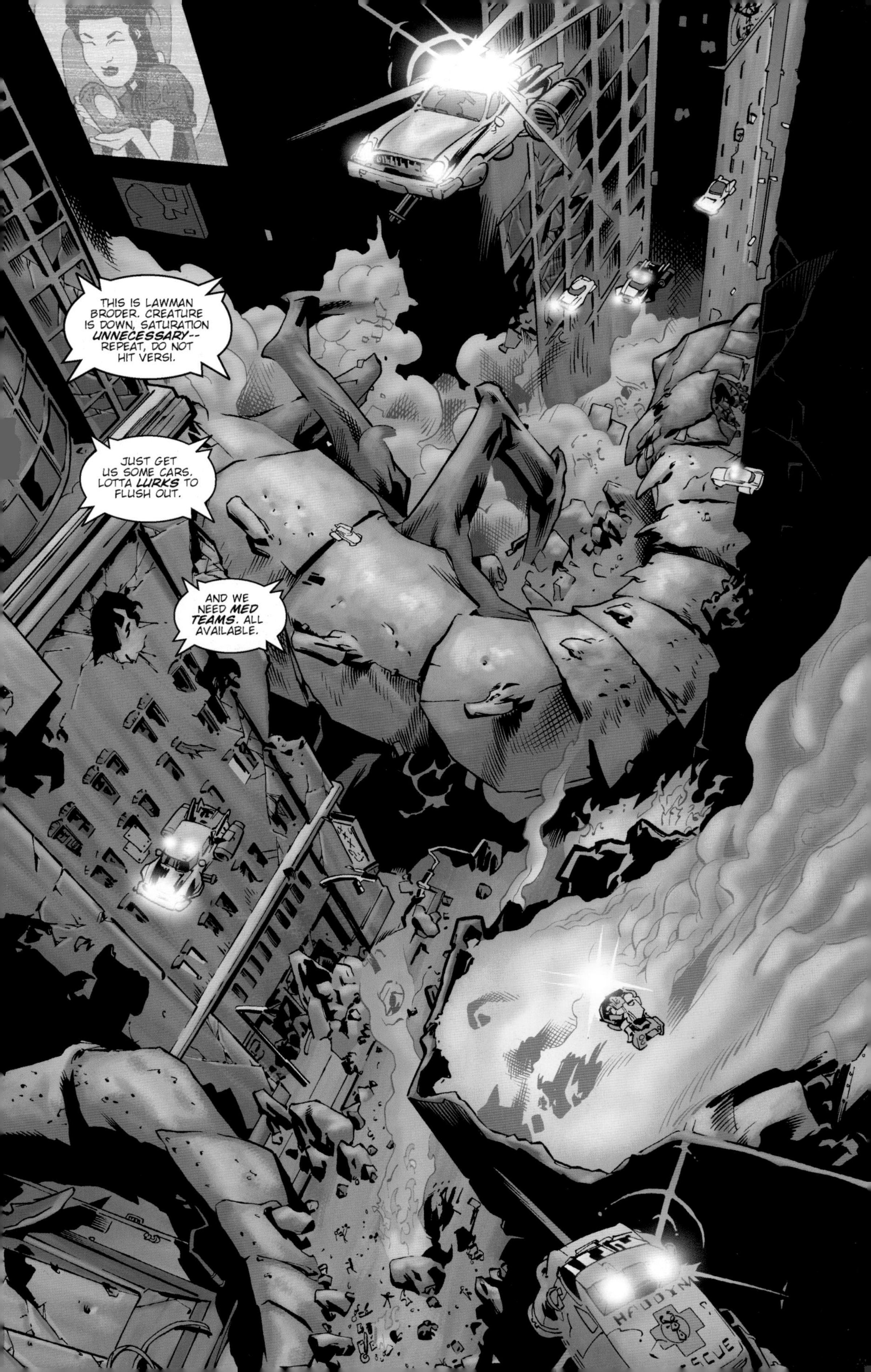

THIS IS LAWMAN BRODER. CREATURE IS DOWN, SATURATION UNNECESSARY-- REPEAT, DO NOT HIT VERSI.
JUST GET US SOME CARS. LOTTA LURKS TO FLUSH OUT.
AND WE NEED MED TEAMS. ALL AVAILABLE.

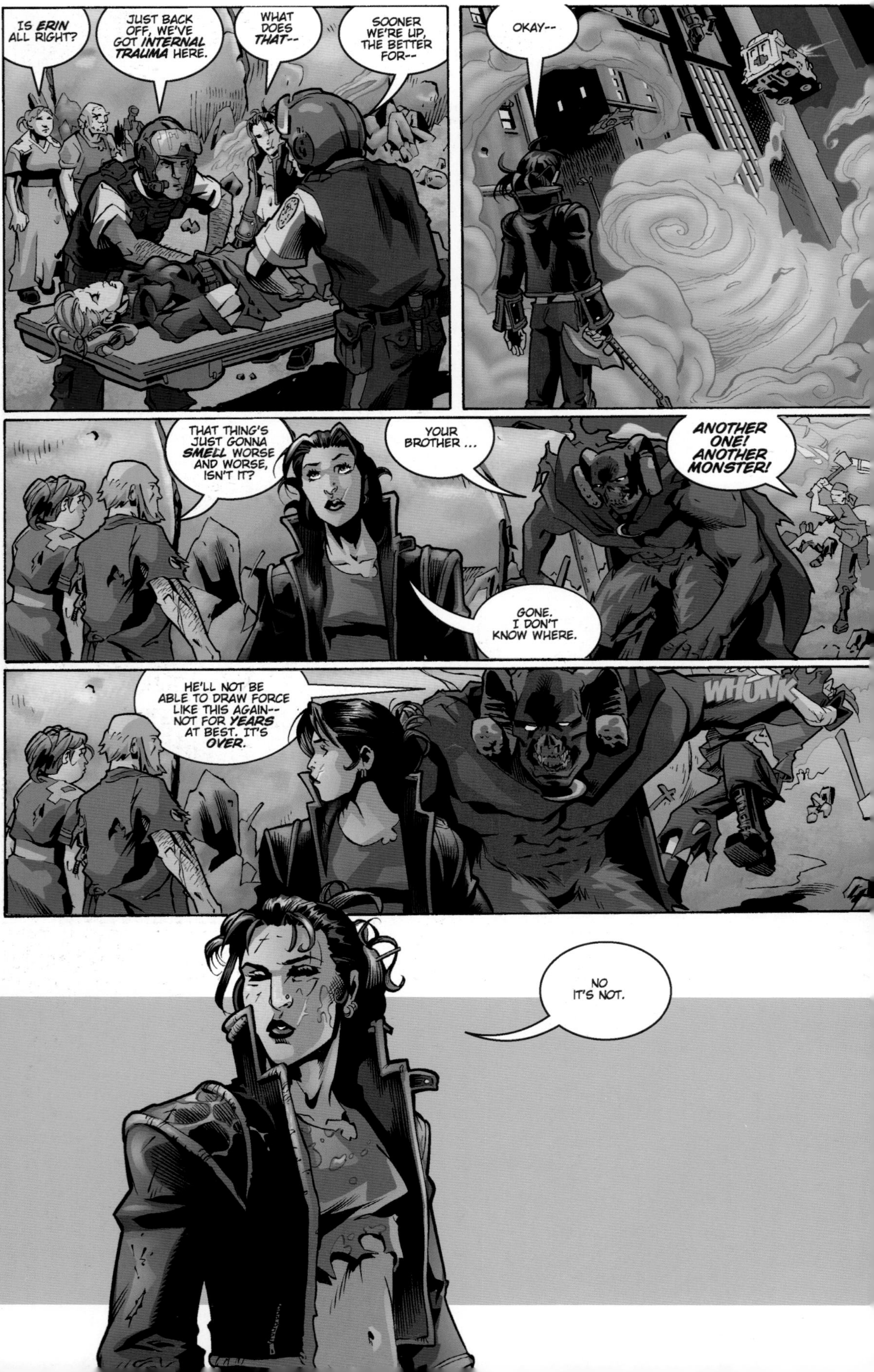
IS ERIN ALL RIGHT?
JUST BACK OFF, WE'VE GOT INTERNAL TRAUMA HERE.
WHAT DOES THAT--
SOONER WE'RE UP, THE BETTER FOR--
OKAY--
THAT THING'S JUST GONNA SMELL WORSE AND WORSE, ISN'T IT?
YOUR BROTHER ...
ANOTHER ONE! ANOTHER MONSTER!
GONE. I DON'T KNOW WHERE.
HE'LL NOT BE ABLE TO DRAW FORCE LIKE THIS AGAIN-- NOT FOR YEARS AT BEST. IT'S OVER.
WHUNK
NO IT'S NOT.

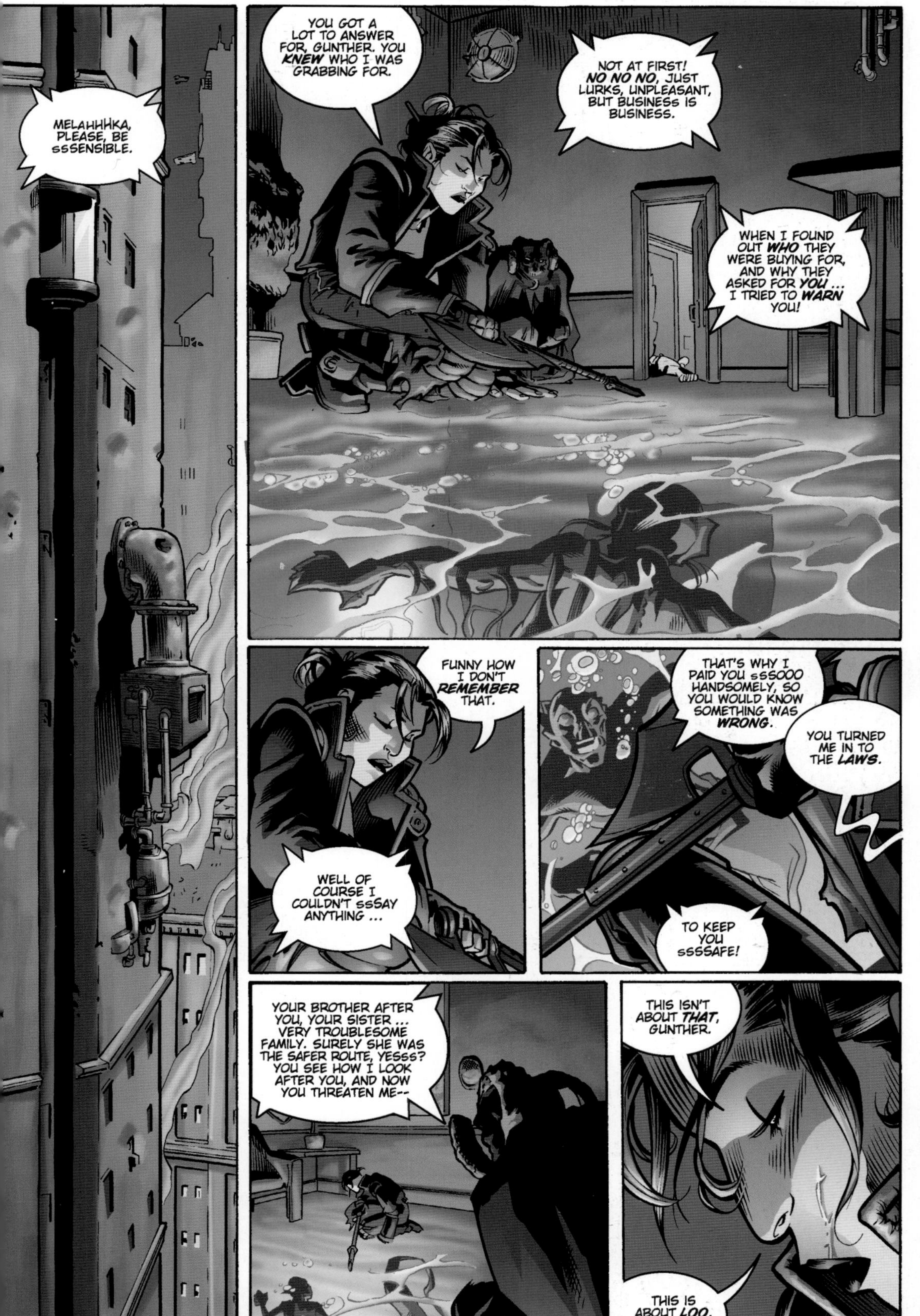
MELAHHHKA, PLEASE, BE sssENSIBLE.
YOU GOT A LOT TO ANSWER FOR, GUNTHER. YOU KNEW WHO I WAS GRABBING FOR.
NOT AT FIRST! NO NO NO, JUST LURKS, UNPLEASANT, BUT BUSINESS IS BUSINESS.
WHEN I FOUND OUT WHO THEY WERE BUYING FOR, AND WHY THEY ASKED FOR YOU ... I TRIED TO WARN YOU!
FUNNY HOW I DON'T REMEMBER THAT.
WELL OF COURSE I COULDN'T sssAY ANYTHING ...
THAT'S WHY I PAID YOU sssOOO HANDSOMELY, SO YOU WOULD KNOW SOMETHING WAS WRONG.
YOU TURNED ME IN TO THE LAWS.
TO KEEP YOU sssSAFE!
YOUR BROTHER AFTER YOU, YOUR SISTER ... VERY TROUBLESOME FAMILY. SURELY SHE WAS THE SAFER ROUTE, YESSS? YOU SEE HOW I LOOK AFTER YOU, AND NOW YOU THREATEN ME--
THIS ISN'T ABOUT THAT, GUNTHER.
THIS IS ABOUT LOO.

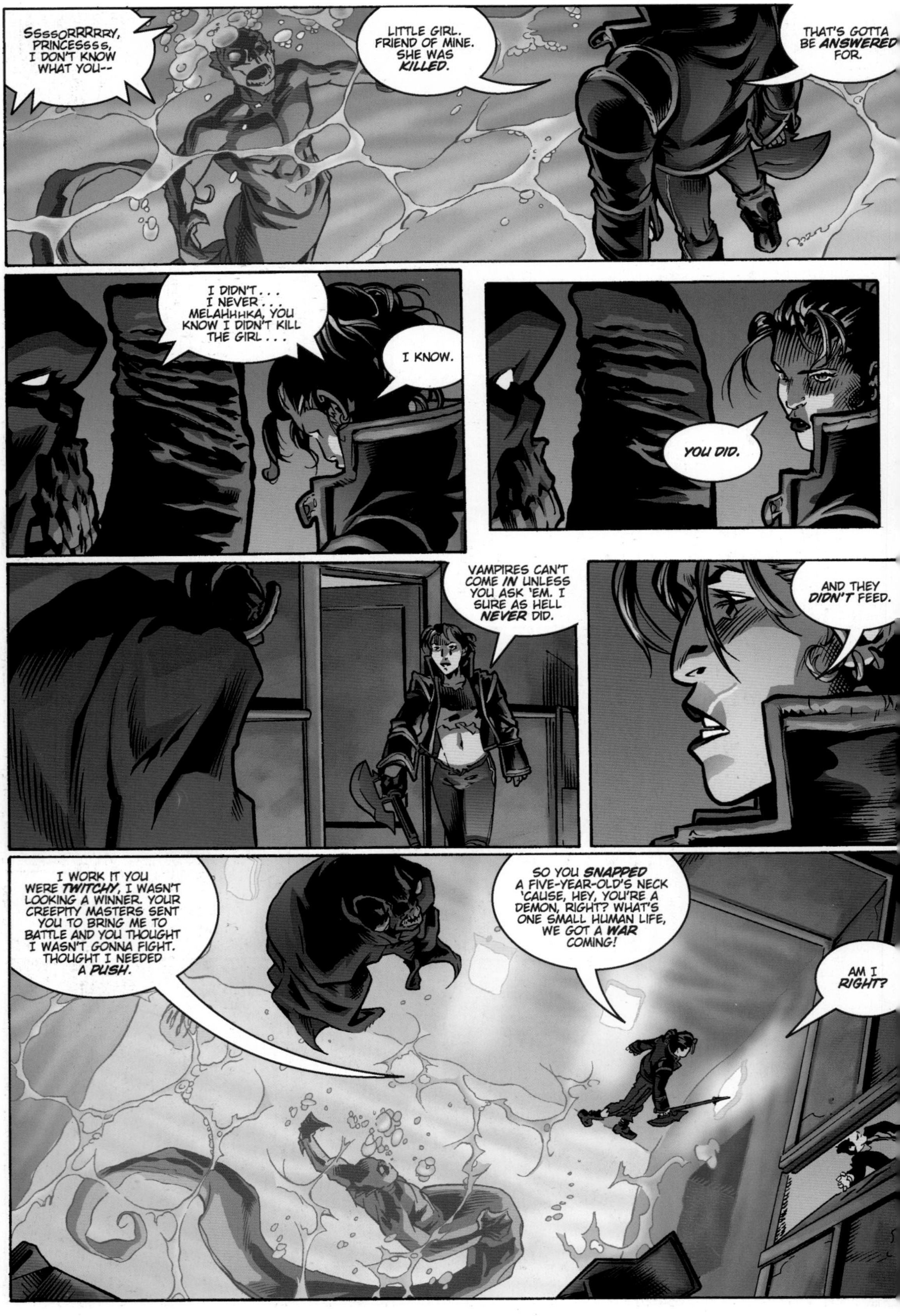
SsssoRRRRry, PRINCESSSS, I DON'T KNOW WHAT YOU--
LITTLE GIRL. FRIEND OF MINE. SHE WAS KILLED.
THAT'S GOTTA BE ANSWERED FOR.
I DIDN'T . . . I NEVER . . . MELAHHHKA, YOU KNOW I DIDN'T KILL THE GIRL . . .
I KNOW.
YOU DID.
VAMPIRES CAN'T COME IN UNLESS YOU ASK 'EM. I SURE AS HELL NEVER DID.
AND THEY DIDN'T FEED.
I WORK IT YOU WERE TWITCHY, I WASN'T LOOKING A WINNER. YOUR CREEPITY MASTERS SENT YOU TO BRING ME TO BATTLE AND YOU THOUGHT I WASN'T GONNA FIGHT. THOUGHT I NEEDED A PUSH.
SO YOU SNAPPED A FIVE-YEAR-OLD'S NECK 'CAUSE, HEY, YOU'RE A DEMON, RIGHT? WHAT'S ONE SMALL HUMAN LIFE, WE GOT A WAR COMING!
AM I RIGHT?

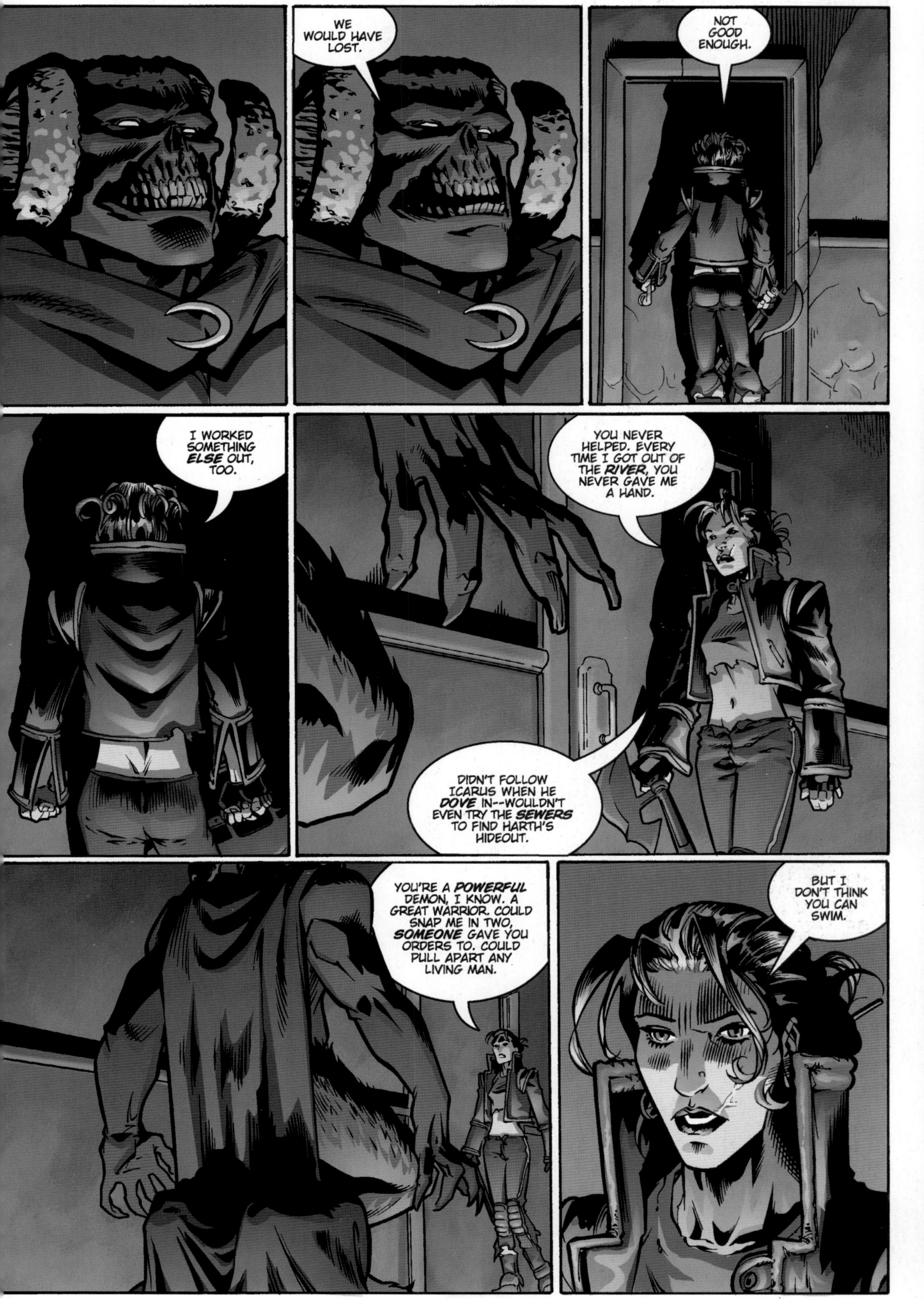
WE WOULD HAVE LOST.
NOT GOOD ENOUGH.
I WORKED SOMETHING ELSE OUT, TOO.
YOU NEVER HELPED. EVERY TIME I GOT OUT OF THE RIVER, YOU NEVER GAVE ME A HAND.
DIDN'T FOLLOW ICARUS WHEN HE DOVE IN--WOULDN'T EVEN TRY THE SEWERS TO FIND HARTH'S HIDEOUT.
YOU'RE A POWERFUL DEMON, I KNOW. A GREAT WARRIOR. COULD SNAP ME IN TWO, SOMEONE GAVE YOU ORDERS TO. COULD PULL APART ANY LIVING MAN.
BUT I DON'T THINK YOU CAN SWIM.

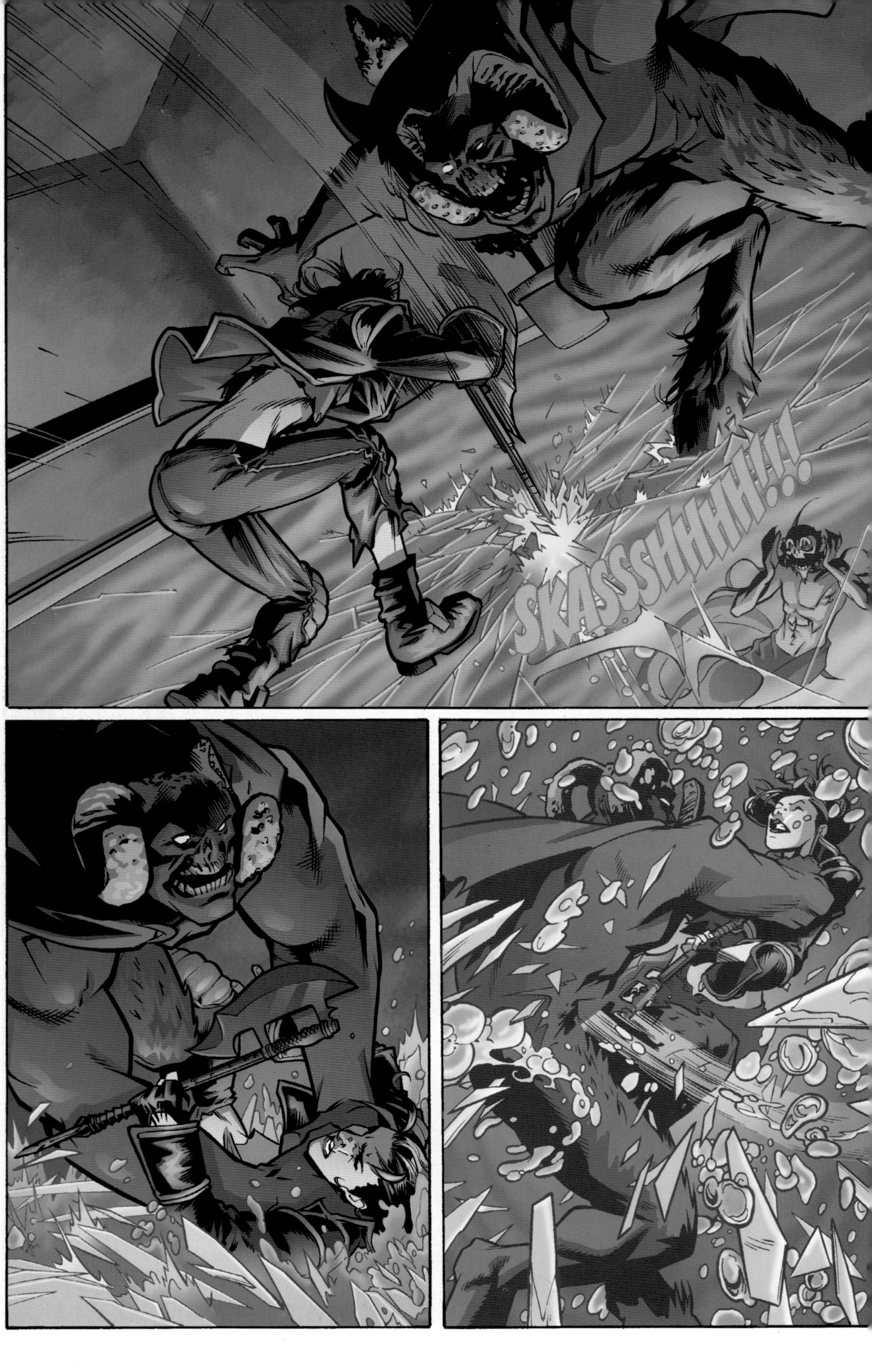
SKASSSHHHHH!!!

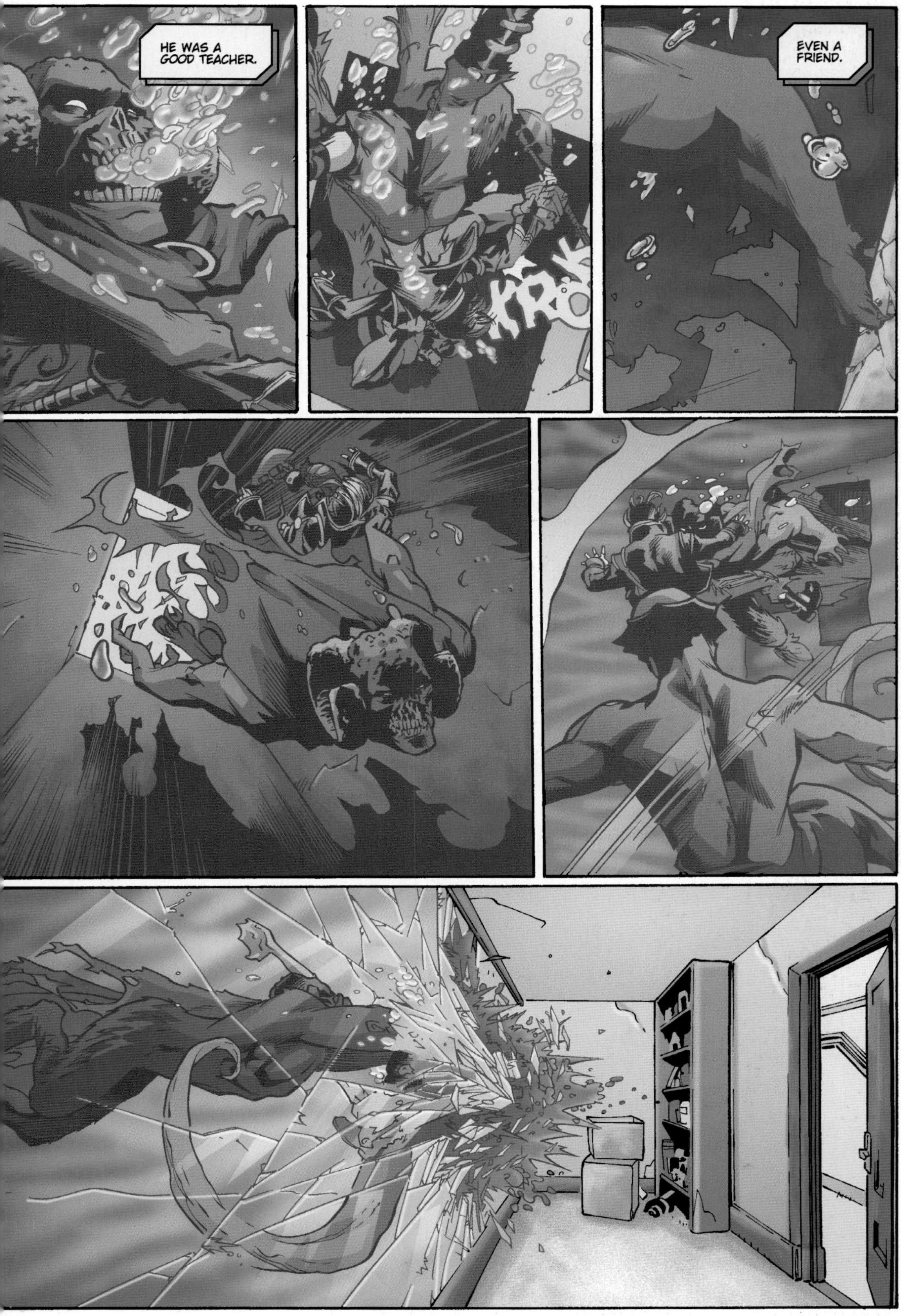
HE WAS A GOOD TEACHER.
KRA
EVEN A FRIEND.

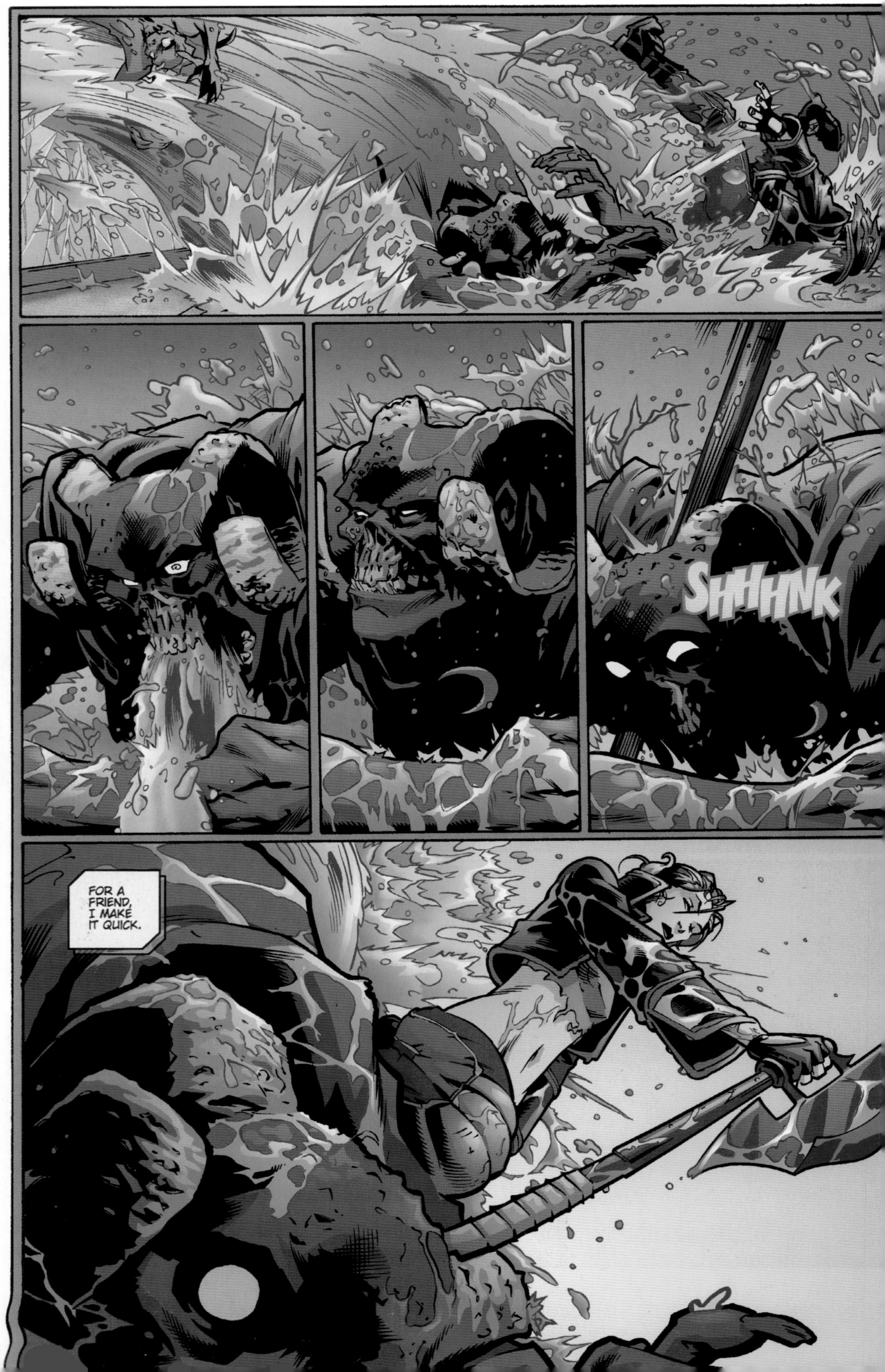
SHHHNK
FOR A FRIEND, I MAKE IT QUICK.

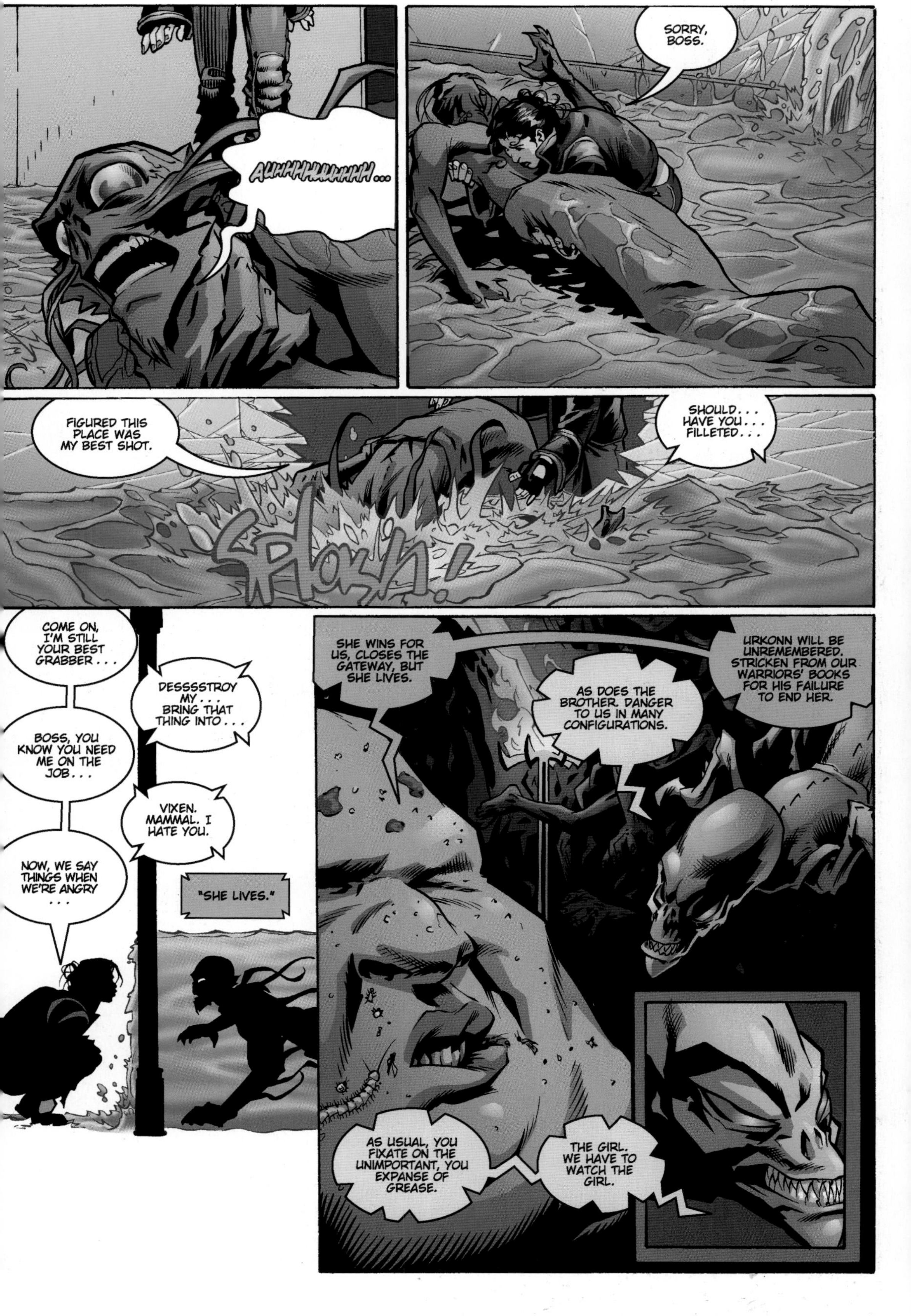
AUHHHHUUUHHH...
SORRY, BOSS.
FIGURED THIS PLACE WAS MY BEST SHOT.
SHOULD... HAVE YOU... FILLETED...
SPLOOSH!
COME ON, I'M STILL YOUR BEST GRABBER...
DESSSSTROY MY... BRING THAT THING INTO...
BOSS, YOU KNOW YOU NEED ME ON THE JOB...
VIXEN. MAMMAL. I HATE YOU.
NOW, WE SAY THINGS WHEN WE'RE ANGRY...
"SHE LIVES."
SHE WINS FOR US, CLOSES THE GATEWAY, BUT SHE LIVES.
AS DOES THE BROTHER. DANGER TO US IN MANY CONFIGURATIONS.
URKONN WILL BE UNREMEMBERED. STRICKEN FROM OUR WARRIORS' BOOKS FOR HIS FAILURE TO END HER.
AS USUAL, YOU FIXATE ON THE UNIMPORTANT, YOU EXPANSE OF GREASE.
THE GIRL. WE HAVE TO WATCH THE GIRL.

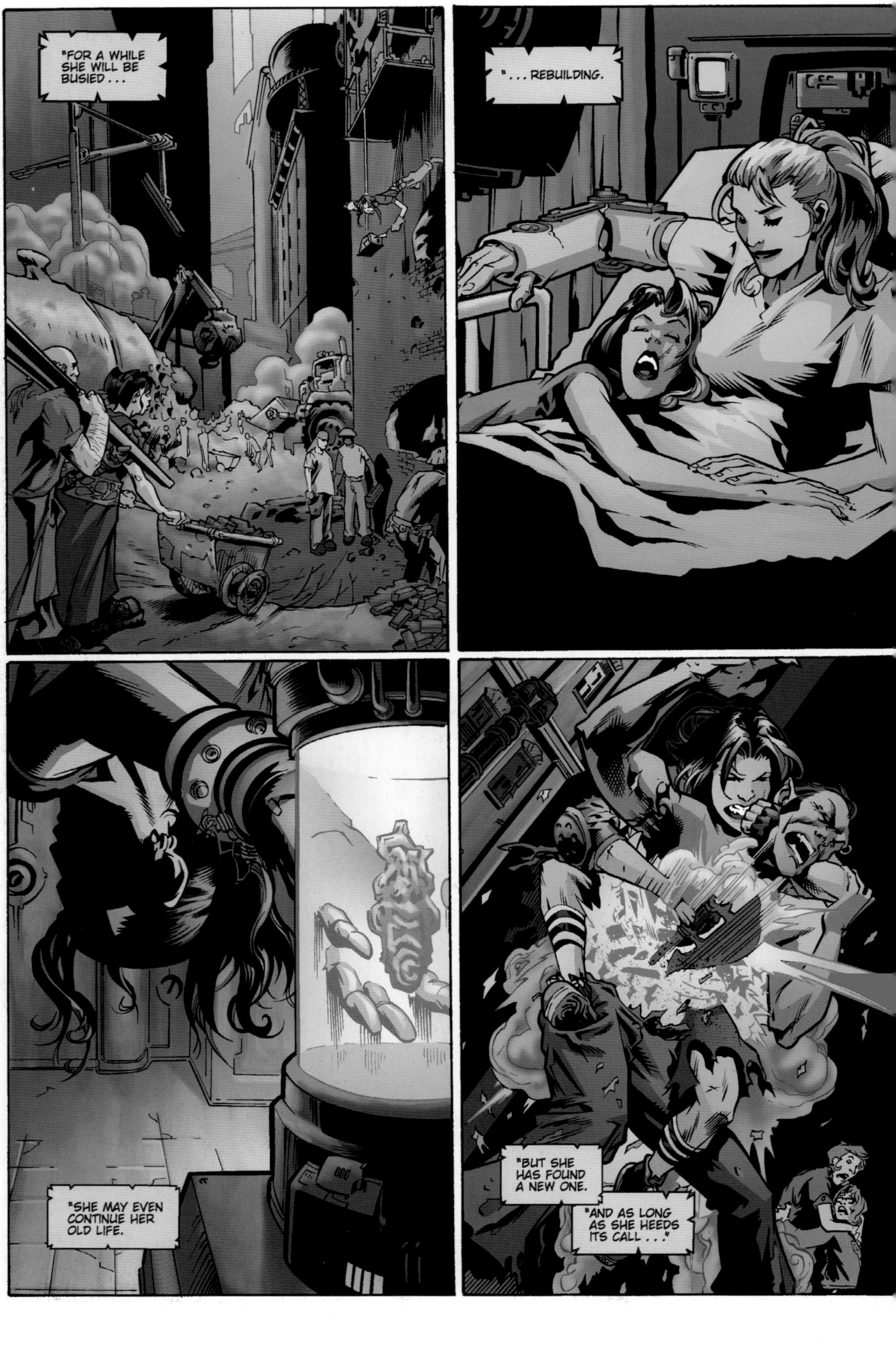
"FOR A WHILE SHE WILL BE BUSIED . . .
". . . REBUILDING.
"SHE MAY EVEN CONTINUE HER OLD LIFE.
"BUT SHE HAS FOUND A NEW ONE.
"AND AS LONG AS SHE HEEDS ITS CALL . . ."

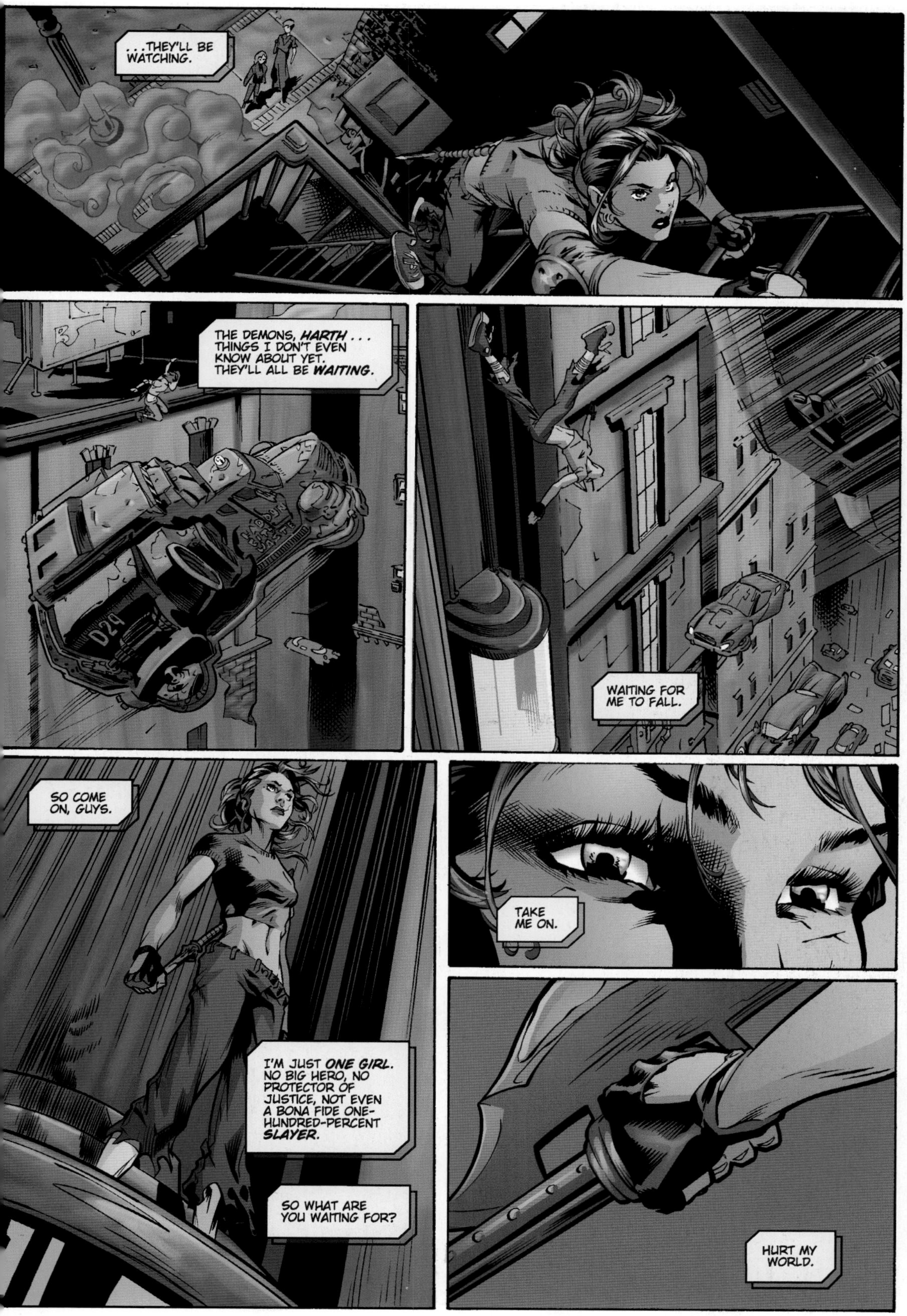
. . .THEY'LL BE WATCHING.
THE DEMONS, HARTH . . . THINGS I DON'T EVEN KNOW ABOUT YET. THEY'LL ALL BE WAITING.
WAITING FOR ME TO FALL.
SO COME ON, GUYS.
I'M JUST ONE GIRL. NO BIG HERO, NO PROTECTOR OF JUSTICE, NOT EVEN A BONA FIDE ONE-HUNDRED-PERCENT SLAYER.
SO WHAT ARE YOU WAITING FOR?
TAKE ME ON.
HURT MY WORLD.

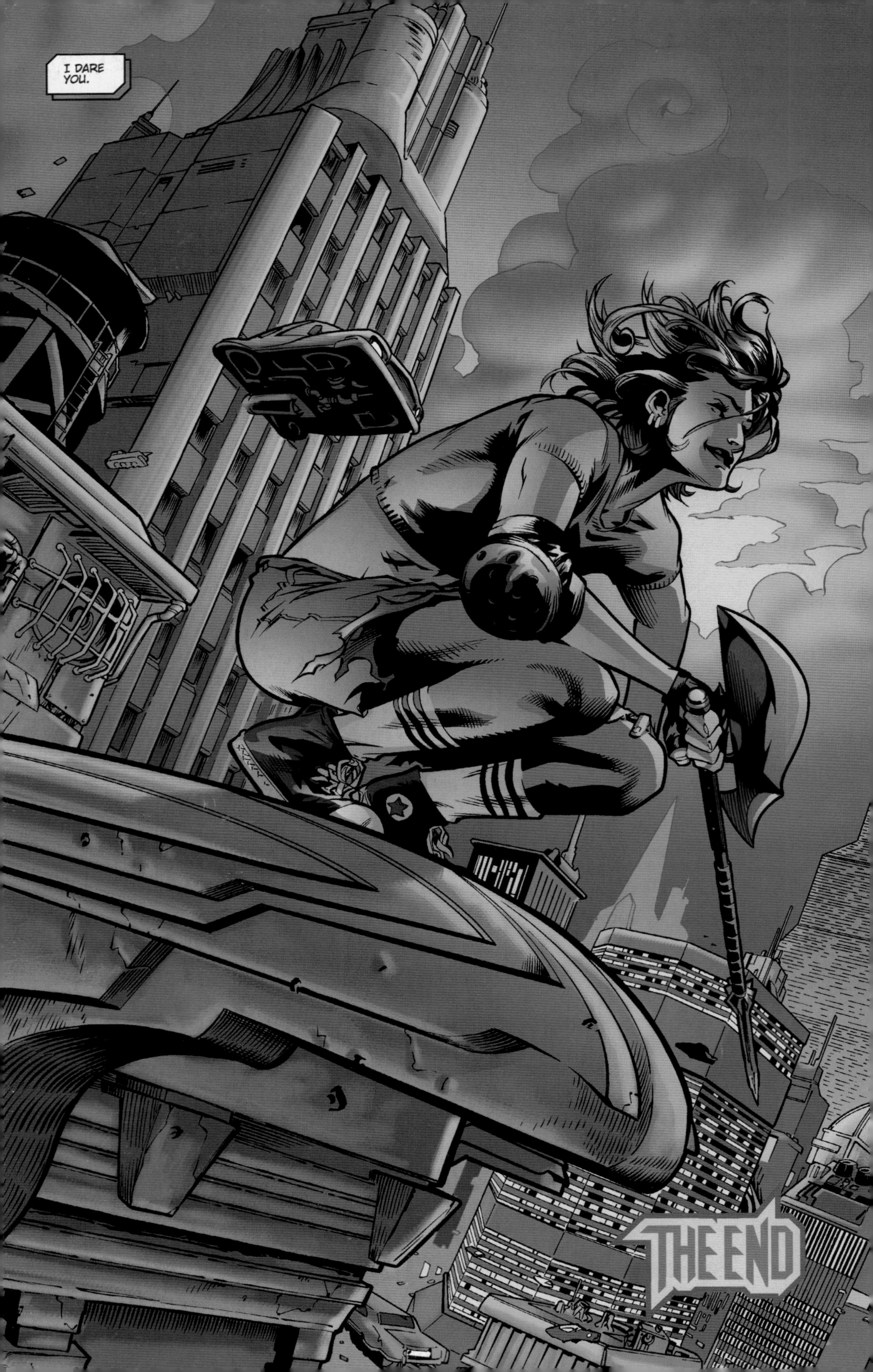
I DARE YOU.
THE END

FRAY™
Sketchbook

This section contains concepts and designs done by
Karl Moline for Melaka Fray and the world she lives in.

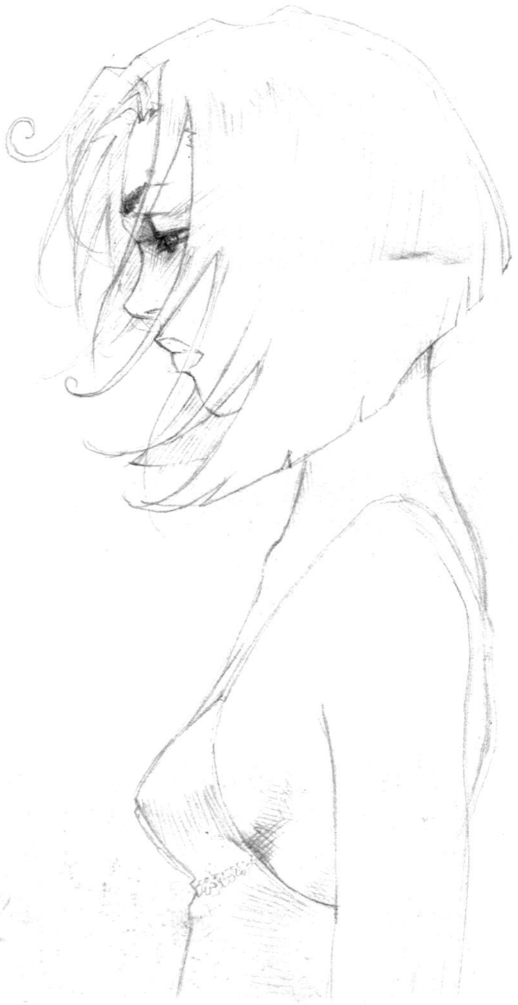

A premonition drawing of Fray. I had done this sketch prior to even getting contacted by Dark Horse. Joss made reference to Matilda from the film *The Professional* and I immediately thought of this drawing. Early designs were based loosely on this sketch.

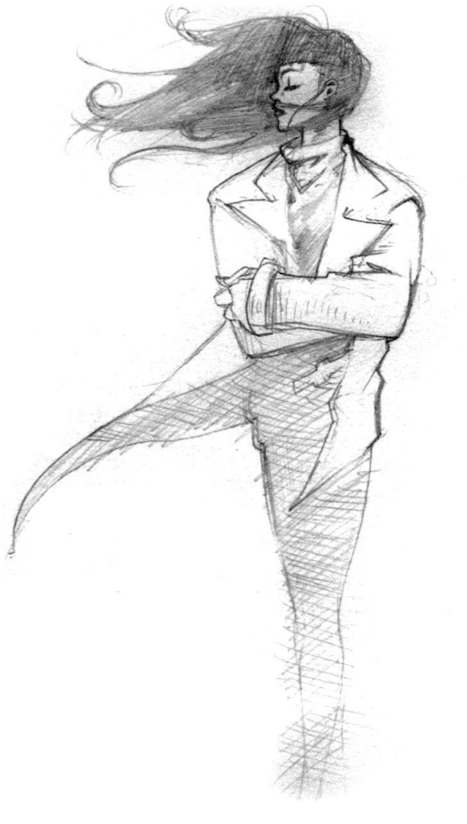

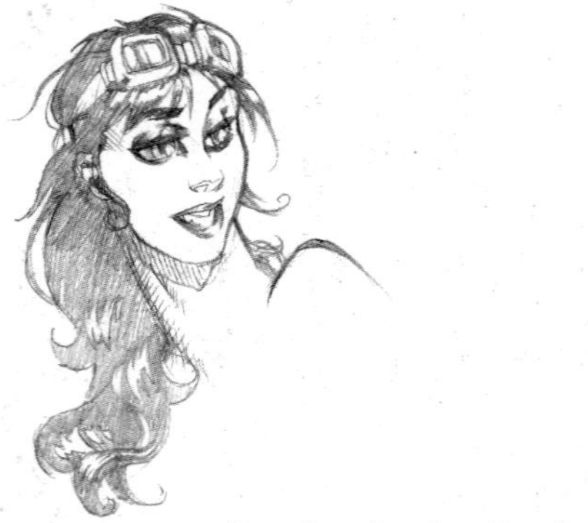
MOLINE

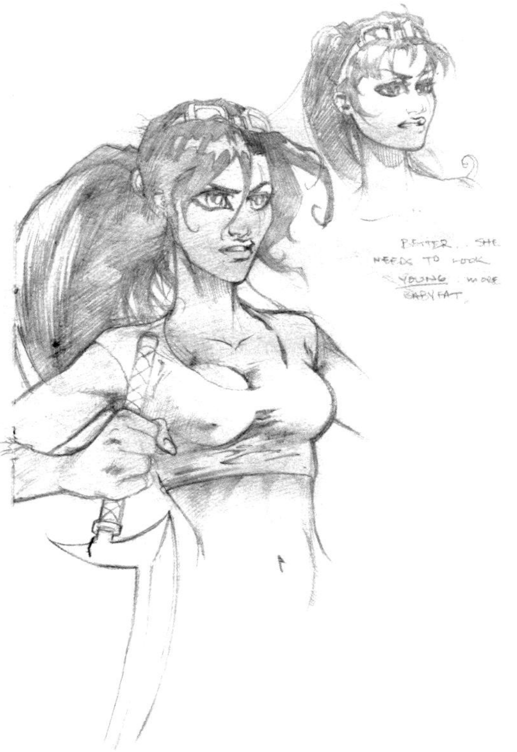
BETTER... SHE
NEEDS TO LOOK
YOUNG MORE
BABY FAT

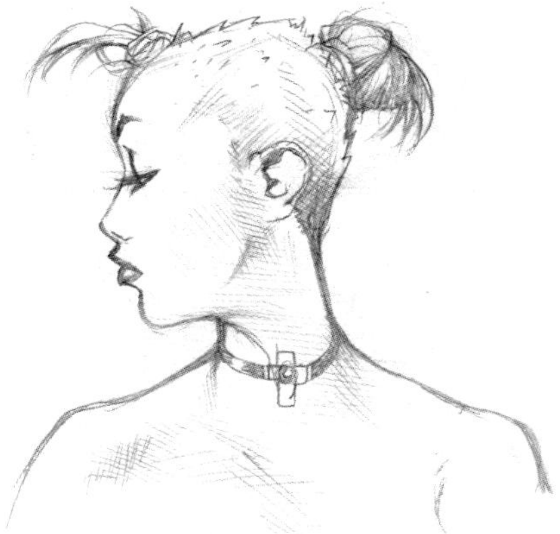

This is another character I was designing immediately prior to getting the job with Dark Horse. There were a lot of elements that made the shift to Fray (weapons and jacket elements mostly). The heroine, Victoria Paris...Tori for short...was a super-strong, fast-healing, intelligent monster slayer.

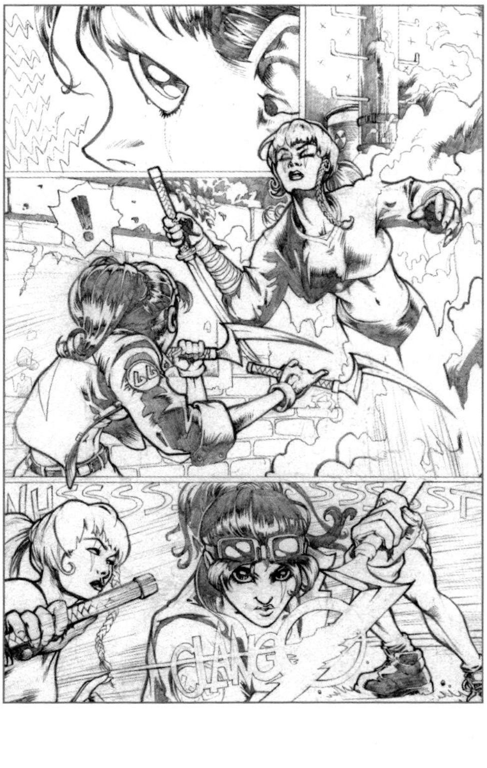
!
CLANG

Early (first) head shots of Fray. I was referencing proportions from Natalie Portman as Matilda.

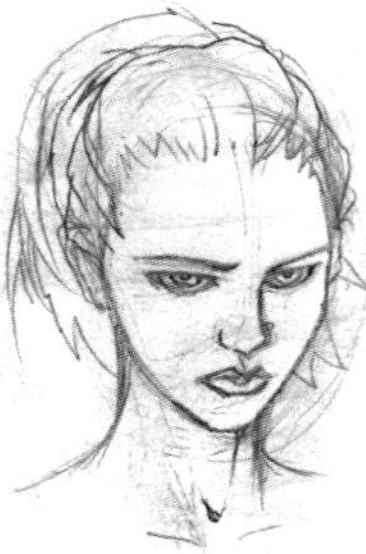

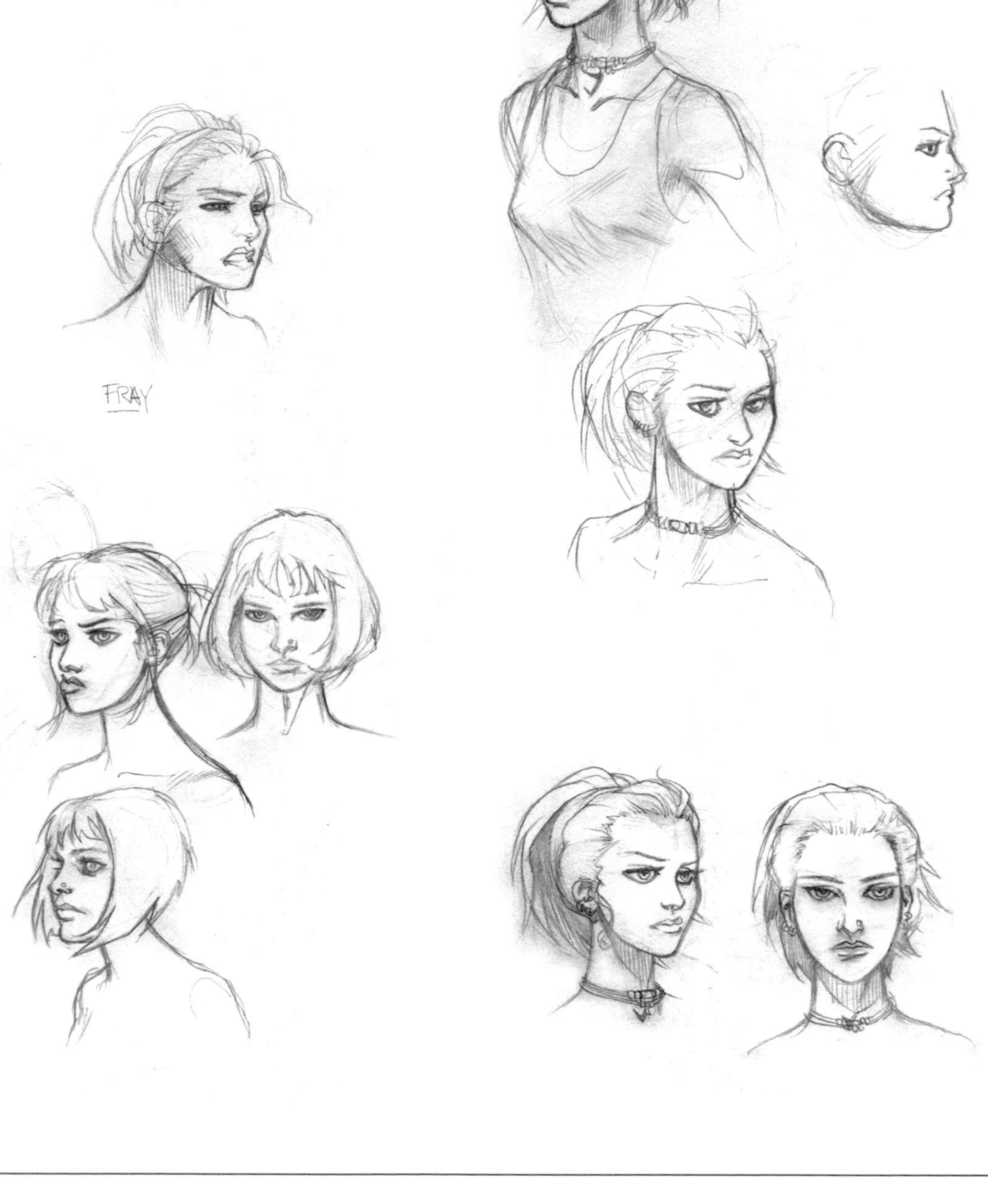
FRAY

Slayer vs. Slayer—a comparison study.

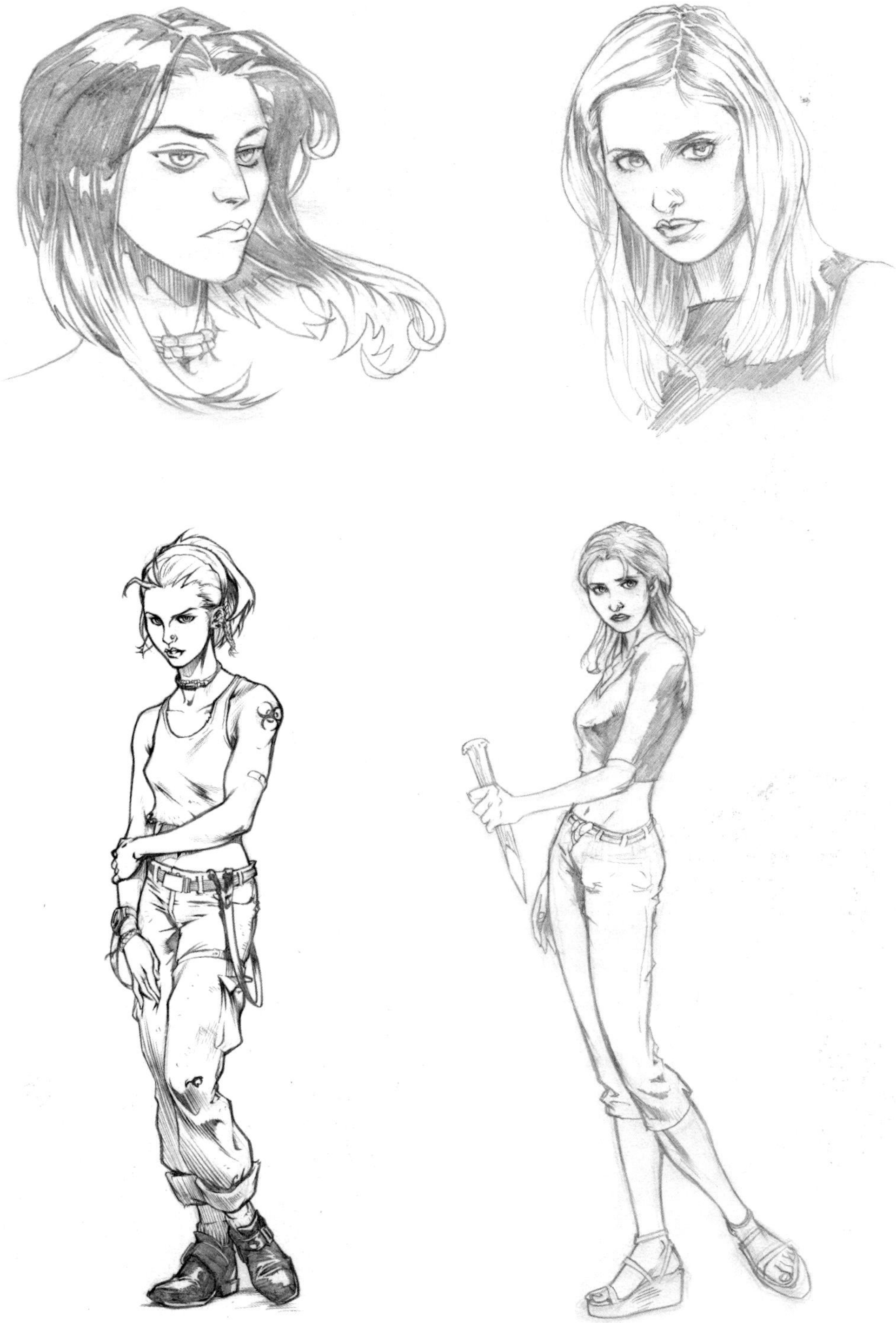

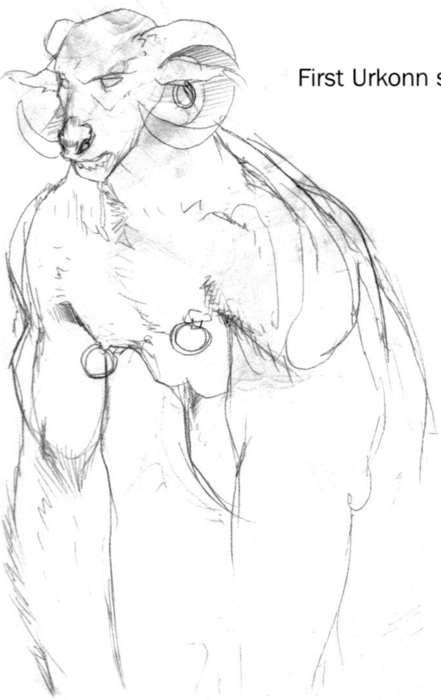

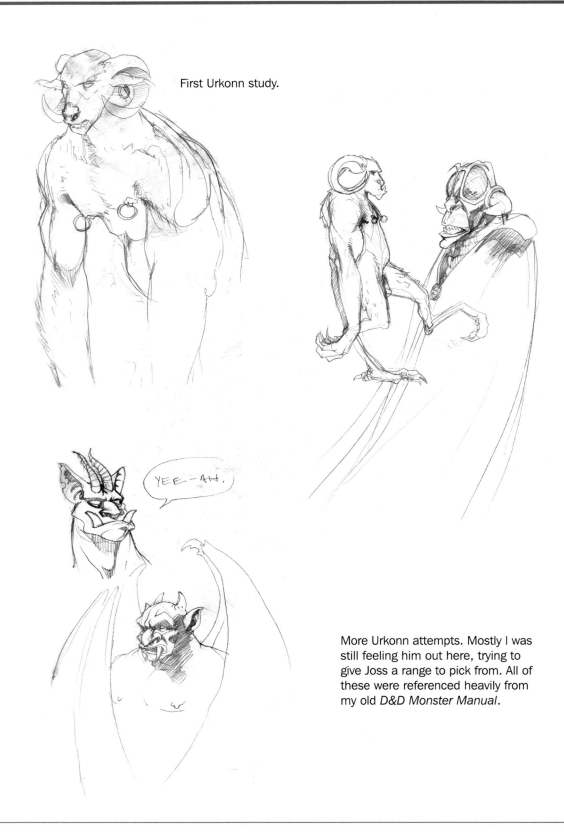

First Urkonn study.

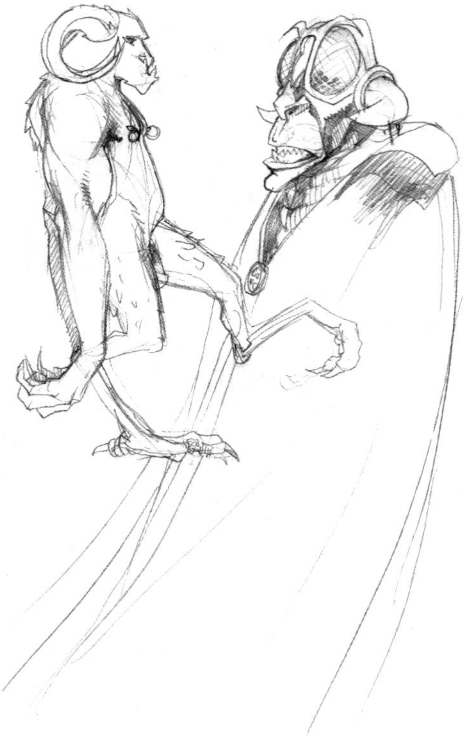

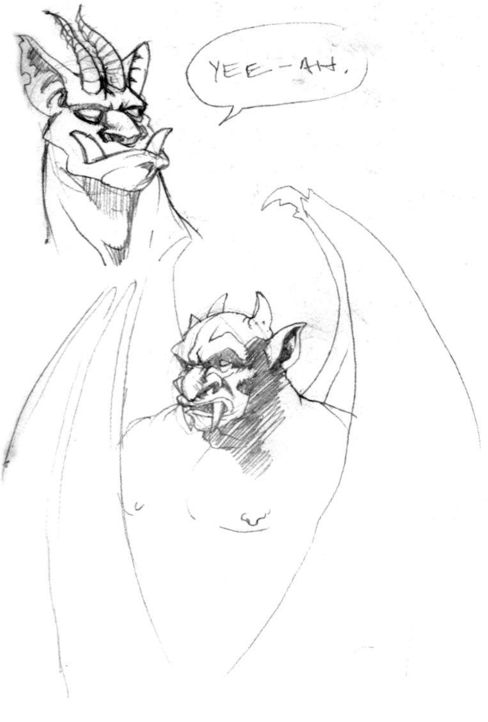
YEE-AH.

More Urkonn attempts. Mostly I was still feeling him out here, trying to give Joss a range to pick from. All of these were referenced heavily from my old *D&D Monster Manual*.

This was almost it, but the nose made him too wussy, so Joss had me rip the skin off his upper lip.

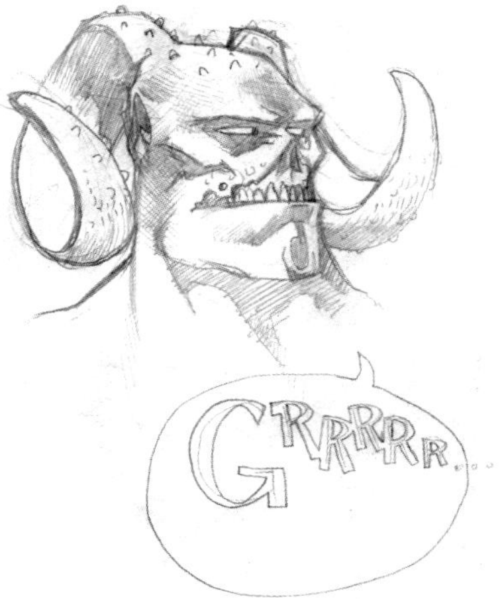
GRRRRRR...

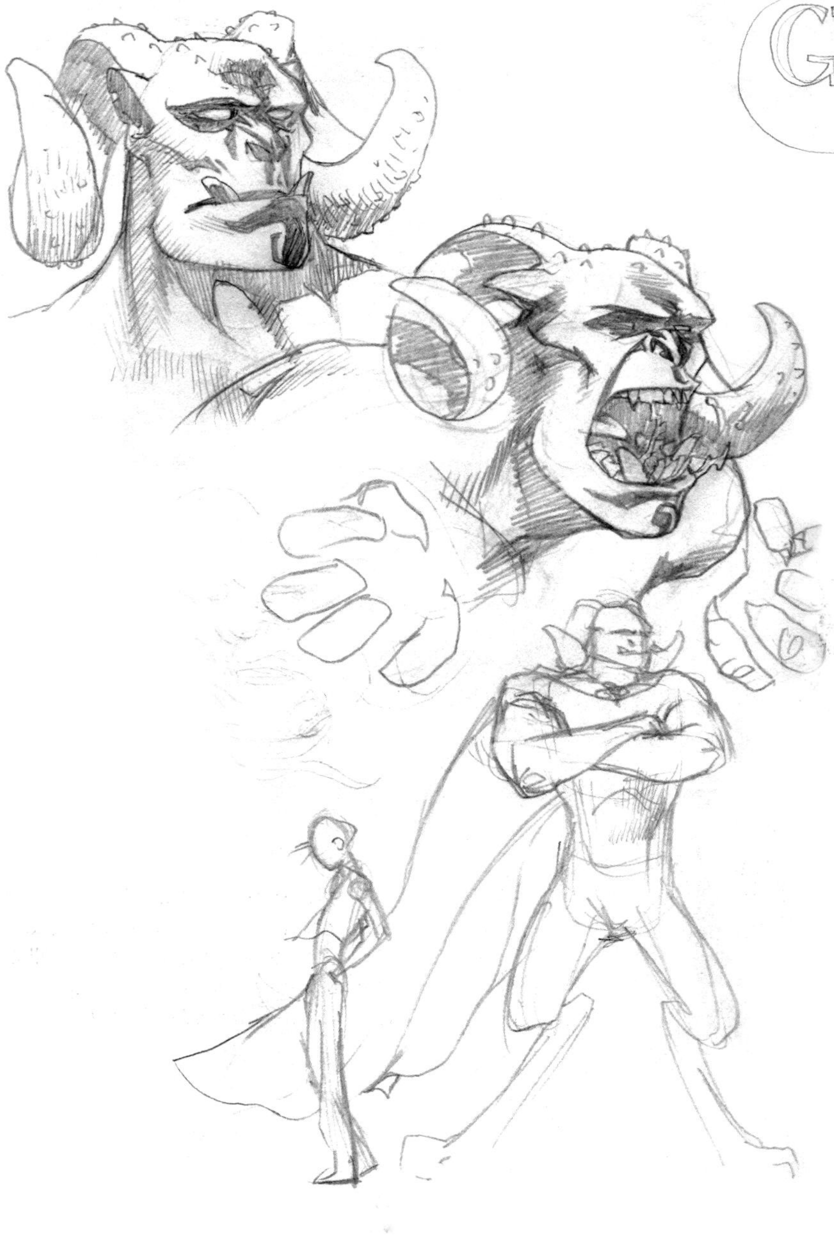

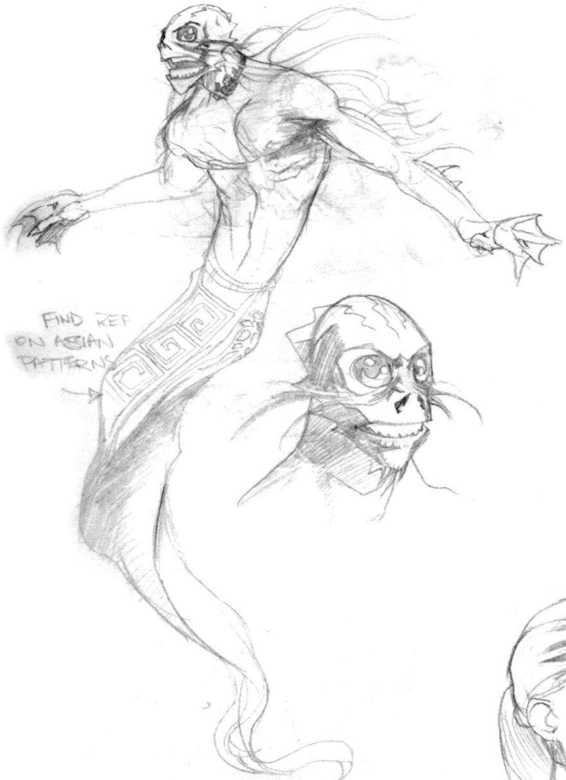
FIND REF ON ASIAN PATTERNS

First Erin study and first Gunther.
I was thinking of Sleestacks
from *Land of the Lost*.

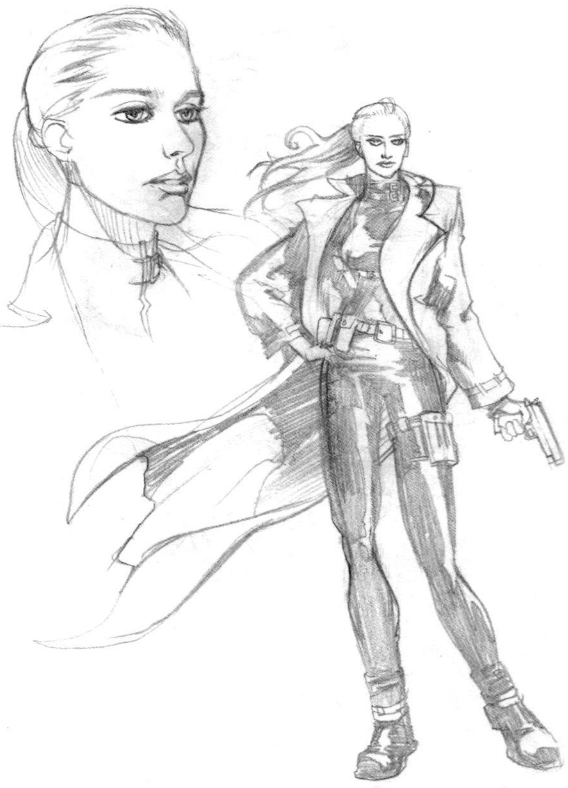

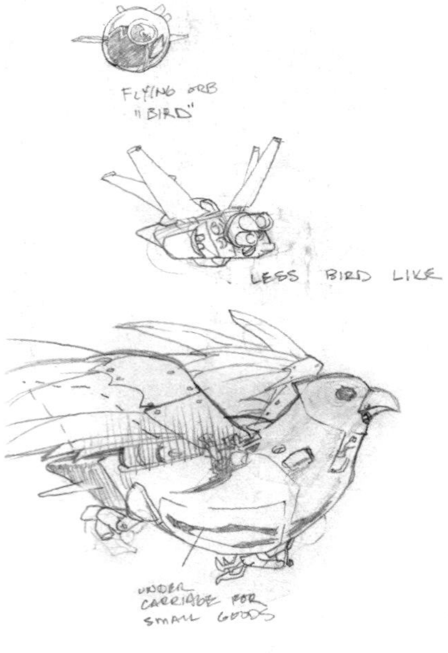
FLYING ORB
"BIRD"
LESS BIRD LIKE
UNDER CARRIAGE FOR SMALL GOODS

CALLY DON

Studies of Don, Cally,
and the Imp.

IMP
?

First Icarus designs.

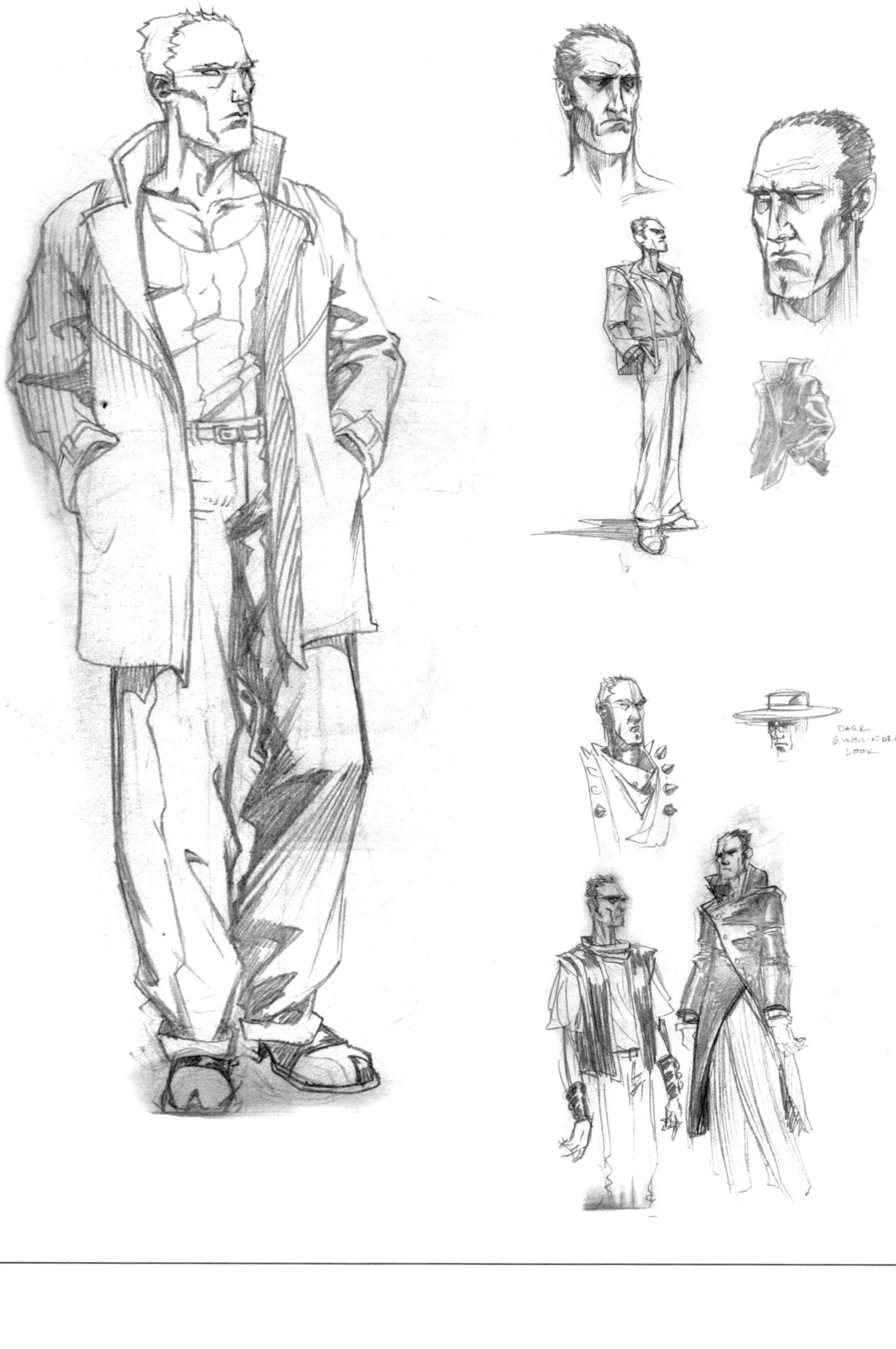
DARK GUNSLINGER LOOK

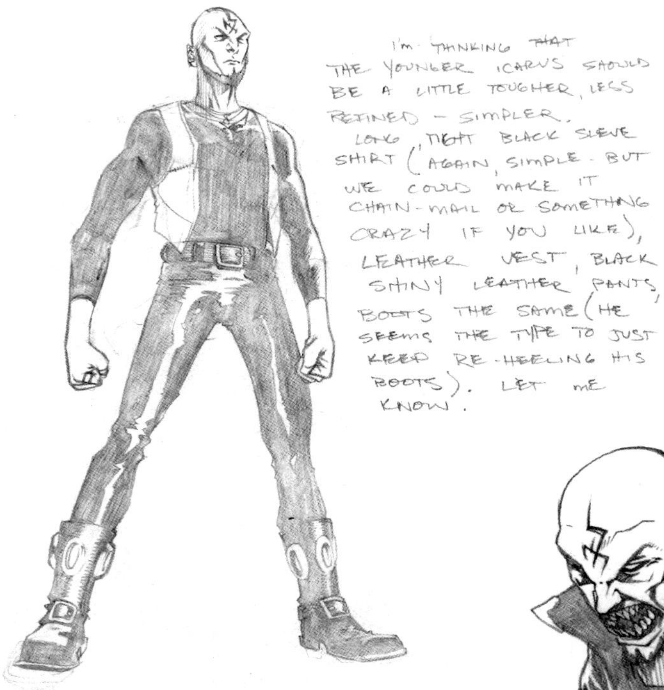
I'M THINKING THAT
THE YOUNGER ICARUS SHOULD
BE A LITTLE TOUGHER, LESS
REFINED - SIMPLER.
LONG, TIGHT BLACK SLEVE
SHIRT ('AGAIN, SIMPLE - BUT
WE COULD MAKE IT
CHAIN-MAIL OR SOMETHING
CRAZY IF YOU LIKE),
LEATHER VEST, BLACK
SHINY LEATHER PANTS,
BOOTS THE SAME (HE
SEEMS THE TYPE TO JUST
KEEP RE-HEELING HIS
BOOTS). LET ME
KNOW.

More Icarus sketches.

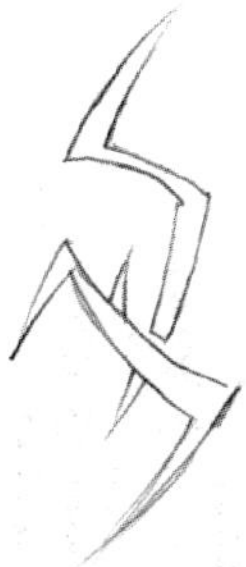

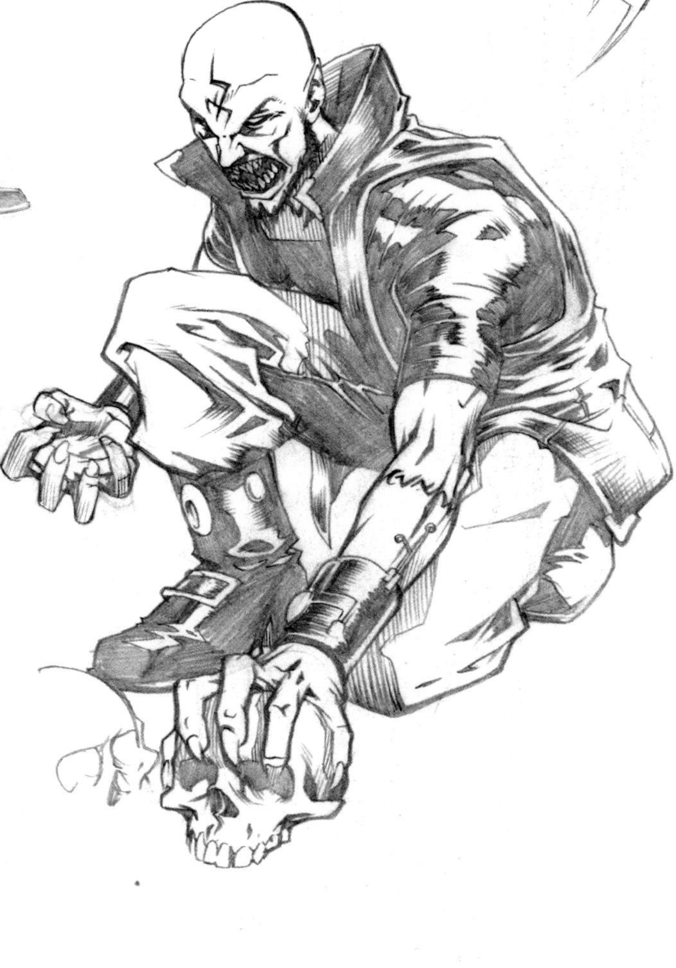

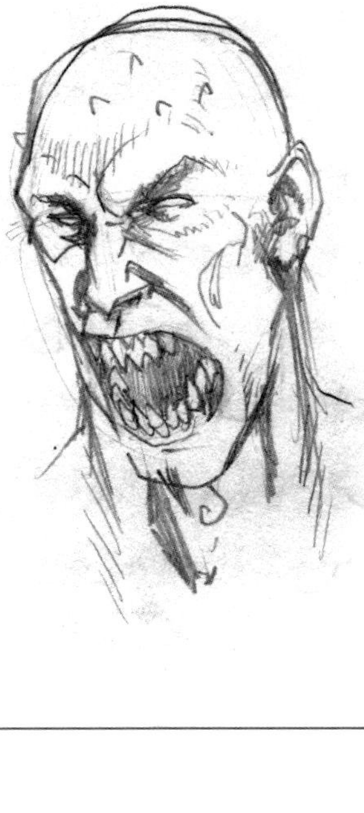

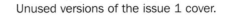

Unused versions of the issue 1 cover.

The piece to the right got me the job.
Inked by Andy and colored by Dave.
Also the first appearance of the
scythe. Below, my first take on Fray.

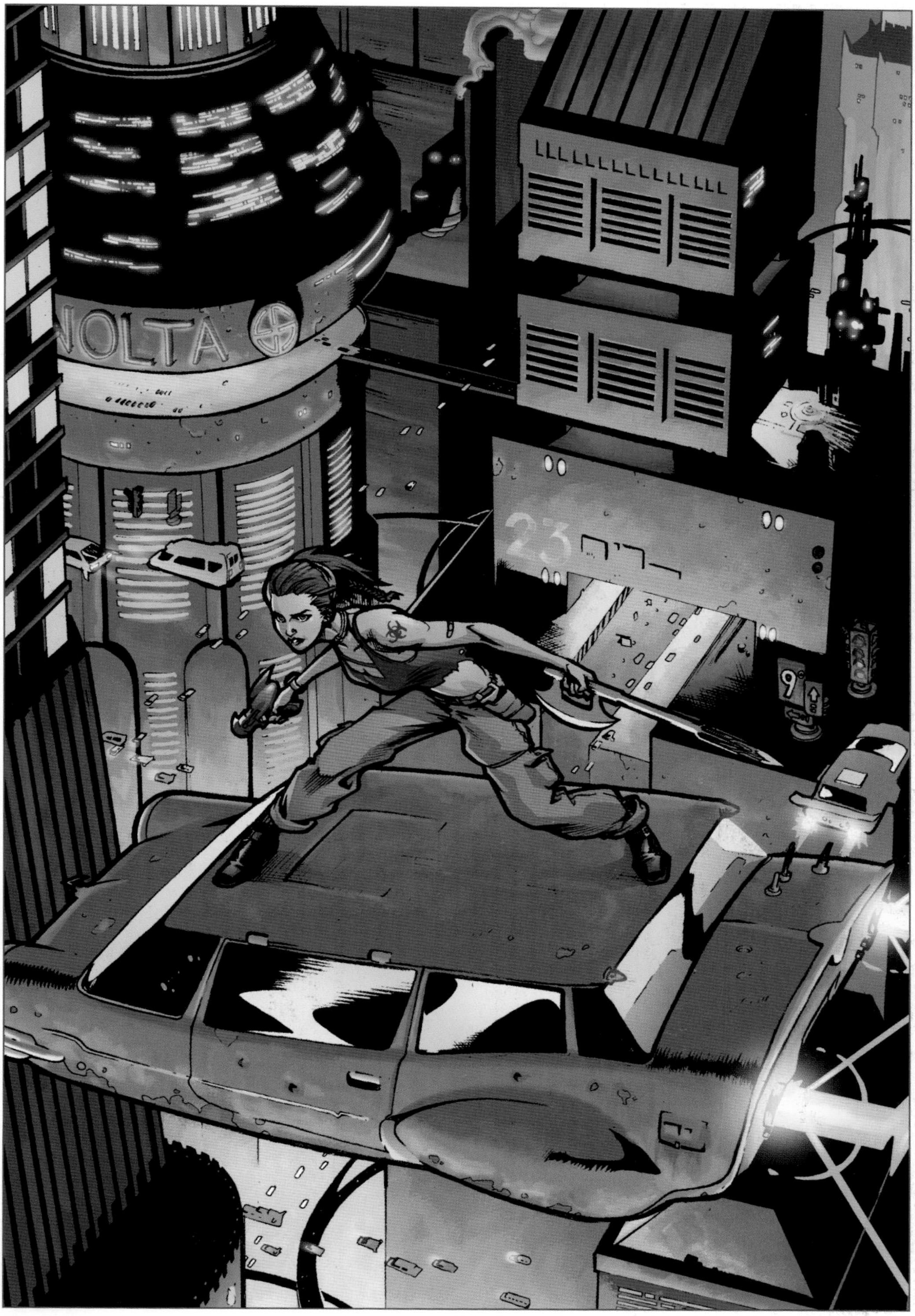
NOLTA
23
9

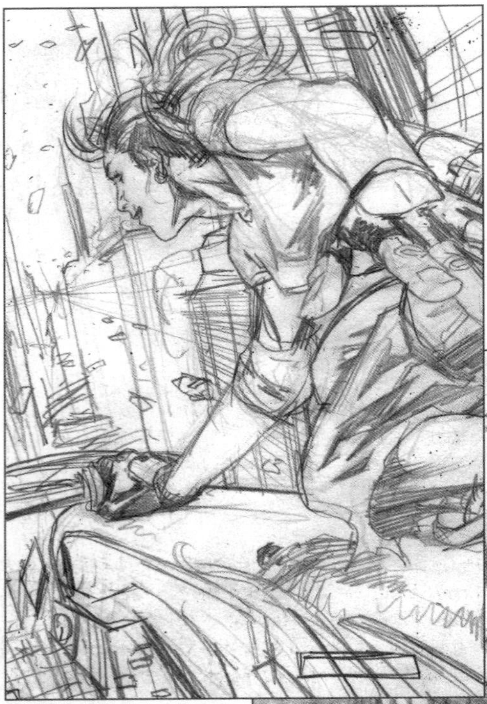

Sketches of the final page.

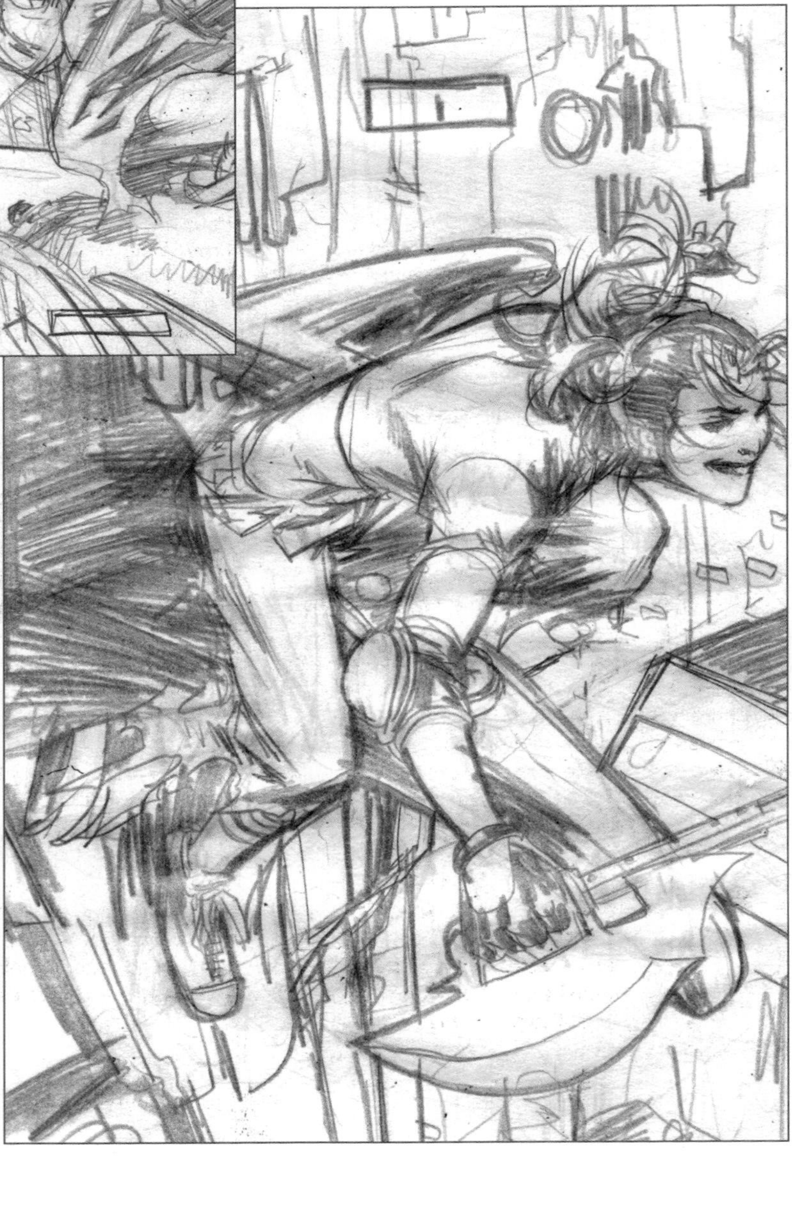

Creators

JOSS WHEDON lives in Los Angeles with his wife and son and some furniture. His television shows *Buffy the Vampire Slayer*, *Angel*, and *Firefly* have entertained hundreds of dozens of people around the world. This is his first comic book. (Sorry! Graphic Novel.) He plans to write some more.

KARL MOLINE attended the Maryland Institute, College of Art for two and half years before hitting the big time drawing comic books for the likes of Dark Horse. Before his run on *Fray*, Karl also contributed to *2099: World of Tomorrow* from Marvel Comics, *Vampirella Strikes* and *Ground Zero: Widow's Progeny*. He currently resides in sunny Dunedin, Florida, and is the regular penciller on CrossGen's *Route 666*.

ANDY OWENS broke into comics in the mid-nineties. In the past seven years he has worked for every major publisher, contributing to such titles as *Batman*, *Buffy the Vampire Slayer*, *X-Men*, and *Wolverine*. After living in southern California, he returned to his hometown of Spokane, Washington, where he still resides. Currently he is the regular inker on *Superman* and *Nightwing* for DC Comics, and is anxiously awaiting a possible sequel to *Fray*.

DAVE STEWART started his career at Dark Horse working as a design intern. Five years later he jumped into the life of a freelance colorist. Current and upcoming projects include: *Hellboy*, *Ultimate X-Men*, *Ultimate Six*, *Captain America*, *Conan*, *Trinity*, *Tom Strong*, *Superman*, *Batman*, and taking his wife on vacation (soon). No need to say, the man never sleeps.

MICHELLE MADSEN has a BFA from the Pacific Northwest College of Art. She worked as an in-house color separator at Dark Horse Comics before working freelance as a colorist and letterer. Michelle's current projects include *Lone*, *Kiss*, *Fused*, and colors and letters for assorted short stories and one-shots.

Also from Dark Horse

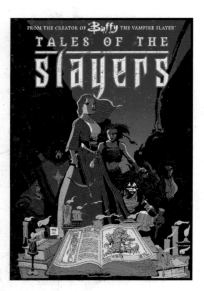

FROM THE CREATOR OF Buffy THE VAMPIRE SLAYER
TALES OF THE
slayers

Buffy the Vampire Slayer: Tales of the Slayers

Buffy is the latest in a long tradition of young women who've been trained to give their lives in the war against vampires. Now Joss Whedon and a select crew of writers from the *Buffy* TV series team up to present tales of the Slayers from centuries gone by, as well as a special story featuring Fray, by Whedon, Moline, and Owens. Joss also teams with comics superstars Leinil Francis Yu and Tim Sale for glimpses of Slayers gone by. Other contributors include Doug Petrie, Jane Espenson, Amber Benson, Rebecca Rand Kirshner, David Fury, P. Craig Russell, Gene Colan, and more.

SC, 96pg, FC, ISBN: 1-56971-605-6, $14.95

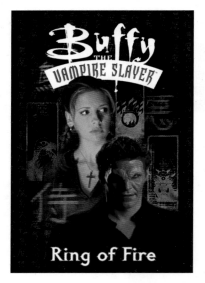

Buffy
THE
VAMPIRE SLAYER
Ring of Fire

Buffy the Vampire Slayer: Ring of Fire

Written by Doug Petrie, art by Ryan Sook, cover by David Stewart

From one of the writers of the television series and the most talked about artist on the comics series comes an intricate and explosive graphic novel. Set in Season Two of *Buffy the Vampire Slayer*, the story begins just after Angel killed Jenny Calendar. Giles is a wreck, and Buffy's not much better, knowing the man she loves is a homicidal maniac. But when the armor of a samurai demon is stolen, a battle is pitched to determine who will master the Ring of Fire.

SC, 80pg, FC, ISBN: 1-56971-482-7, $9.95

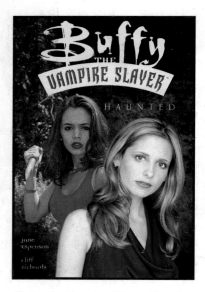

Buffy
THE
VAMPIRE SLAYER
HAUNTED
Jane Espenson
cliff richards

Buffy the Vampire Slayer: Haunted

Written by Jane Espenson, pencilled by Cliff Richards

A sinister presence stirs among the charred rubble of what used to be Sunnydale High. The ghost of Sunnydale's former Mayor has a bone to pick with Buffy. Now Buffy's left to face a body-snatching, blood-sucking poltergeist without knowing whose hand guides it, armed only with an enigmatic message from the comatose Faith: "You're already dead." Jane Espenson, long-time writer for the *Buffy* TV series, brings you the first appearance of Faith in comics, picking up directly from the Season Three finale!

SC, 96pg, FC, ISBN: 1-56971-737-0, $12.95

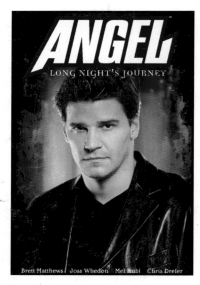

ANGEL
LONG NIGHT'S JOURNEY
Brett Matthews Joss Whedon Mel Rubi Chris Dreier

Angel: Long Night's Journey

Written by Joss Whedon & Brett Matthews, pencilled by Mel Rubi

Angel searches for a kidnapped child and stumbles upon a force of unspeakable evil and unimaginable power. Artist Mel Rubi takes us from the darkened mean streets of Los Angeles, to the dizzying heights of the city's skyscrapers, and face to face with some of the strangest, most grotesque, and most unsettlingly seductive creatures Angel has ever faced. Brett Matthews and *Angel* creator Joss Whedon have retooled and reinvented Angel, giving us a story that is much too big for the small screen.

SC, 104pg, FC, ISBN: 1-56971-752-4, $12.95